First there was

THE GREAT TOWNS OF THE WEST

"The most impressive of the new guides is *The Great Towns of the West.*"
The Denver Post

"Vacation planners will appreciate the wealth of revealing insights provided in a concise, well-organized format."
Booklist

"Vokac wrote his book for vacation planners and travelers, but even the armchair travelers will be intrigued."
Las Vegas Review-Journal

"Until now none of the big publishers has paid much attention to the cities outside the mainstream, many of which are worthwhile destinations. *The Great Towns of The West* does a fine job of covering towns that make travel off the interstate so fascinating."
Seattle Post-Intelligencer

"It is a beautifully done complete travel guide and one which should be in the library of anyone interested in exploring the West."
Santa Ynez Valley News, Solvang, CA

"One of the unique and useful features of Vokac's book is the listing of the best rooms in a town's lodging places."
The New Mexican, Santa Fe, N.M.

"I particularly like the opening sentences of each chapter, impressive in their brevity, charming in their approach."
San Francisco Examiner

"This is an excellent guide . . . one that you can use again and again."
The Province, Vancouver, B.C.

Now, there is also

THE GREAT TOWNS OF CALIFORNIA

Published in 1986, this is the most comprehensive guide yet to natural, civilized places throughout California that you can enjoy for vacations . . . or for the rest of your life.

THE GREAT TOWNS OF CALIFORNIA

A Guide To Special Places and Pleasures

David Vokac

San Diego, California

Library of Congress Cataloguing-in-Publication Data

Vokac, David, 1940 -
The great towns of California.

Includes index.
1. California—Description and travel—1981- —
Guide-books. I. Title.
F859.3.V65 1986 917.94'0453 86-1703
ISBN 0-930743-01-6

West Press
P.O. Box 99717
San Diego, Ca. 92109

First Printing, April 1986
Second Printing, September 1986

Preface

California has captured the imagination of people everywhere. No wonder. For sheer diversity and numbers of enticements, the Golden State is incomparable. Much has been written about the natural grandeur of renowned attractions like Yosemite and Redwood National Parks, and about big, vibrant cities like San Francisco and Los Angeles. However, detailed information about special places off the beaten path remains scarce.

My abiding interest in the West and a career in urban planning, most recently in California, eventually caused me to address the problem. In 1985, I wrote *The Great Towns of The West* to give all of the region's civilized, out-of-the-way towns in spectacular settings the careful attention they deserve. For the first time, all notable features were described in detail—and rated—for each of fifty exceptional places throughout the West. That work became the foundation for this guidebook, along with almost one year of thorough on-site research throughout California. No additional communities in California met the criteria first described in the premier guide. However, the originally-included sixteen California towns were found to be more desirable than ever.

The Great Towns of California is intended to serve as the most comprehensive guidebook ever published about these exciting places and their surroundings. Toward that goal, all leisure pursuits that adventurous individuals and couples might enjoy in each town were re-examined in even greater depth than before. As a result, the new guide is both a complete update and an expansion of the original. Hundreds of entries have been added, and rated. Some listings were downgraded to reflect their less impressive current status. A few others were dropped altogether.

As before, I personally evaluated each new feature anonymously, and independently of any payment or favor. Thus, every listing is rated and described on merit alone. I believe that this guide is as honest, accurate, and complete as possible.

For everyone who wonders what special places and pleasures lie beyond the cities of the Golden State, *The Great Towns of California* has the answers.

To Joan
whose inspiration and support made it possible

CALIFORNIA
REDWOOD NATIONAL PARK
LASSEN VOLCANIC NATIONAL PARK
Mendocino
Nevada City
Tahoe City
South Lake Tahoe
Calistoga
St Helena
Sonoma
Sonora
SAN FRANCISCO
SAN JOSE
YOSEMITE NATIONAL PARK
Pacific Grove
Monterey
Carmel
KINGS CANYON NATIONAL PARK
SEQUOIA NATIONAL PARK
Cambria
San Luis Obispo
Solvang
Ojai
LOS ANGELES
Palm Springs
SAN DIEGO
PACIFIC OCEAN
N
W
E
Scale in miles
0
100
One inch equals approx. 100 miles

Contents

Introduction

This is a unique guide to California's other desirable destinations—natural, civilized places beyond the famed national parks and booming cities. It was written to help you discover these sixteen remarkable out-of-the-way towns and their unforgettable surroundings, and enjoy them to the fullest.

A wealth of new information is presented in two ways that set this guidebook apart from the others. Attention is focused on leisure pursuits primarily of interest to adventurous individuals and couples. As a result, premium wineries and isolated hot springs receive as much attention as famous museums and amusement parks. Second, because the scope is limited to the best of California's remote towns and their surroundings, it was possible to identify, evaluate, and describe **all** of the special places and pleasures in each. Subjects normally included in guidebooks—attractions, restaurants, and lodgings—are presented in careful detail. In addition, several topics that are not usually addressed together in a single book—weather, shopping, nightlife, camping, and special events—are given the same thorough attention.

Following is a summary of the method used for the selection of the great towns; some general comments about each major subject category; and criteria used in obtaining information about location, the rating system, and prices.

Selection of California's Great Towns

There are more than 2,000 named settlements in California. Each of them was considered during the search for great towns throughout a vast 159,000-square-mile region that is the nation's third largest, and most populous, state. The term "great" is not used lightly in this book. As defined in Webster's, it can mean "much higher in some quality or degree; much above the ordinary . . . illustrious, superior, remarkable . . . highest in its class." A systematic process of elimination was used to find every town with these characteristics reflected in its size, location, natural and urban features. First, population was considered. Numerous studies have concluded that the most desirable population for an urban place is less than fifty thousand people. At the other extreme, villages with less than one thousand people are almost always too small to have all essential urban services and facilities. After eliminating cities and villages from further consideration, the 716 towns that are "the right size" were evaluated in terms of "independence." All towns less than ten miles from the nearest small city (with at least fifty thousand population) and farther (up to forty miles) from the largest metropolitan centers, were excluded. This was done because suburban communities are inevitably dominated by, and assume some of the characteristics of, the nearby city. The "natural setting" of each remaining town was then assessed. Mountains and the Pacific Ocean are the outstanding landforms and the ultimate attractions of California. All towns lacking impressive surroundings, i.e., more than a few miles from one or the other of these features, were omitted. Next, "environmental problems" like open-pit mining operations or smokestack industries near downtown caused additional communities to be rejected. Finally, to identify "destination towns"—places desired by visitors as well as residents—the quantity and quality of lodgings and amenities were evaluated. All towns that survived the entire process of elimination through this step were field-checked. A comprehensive survey was conducted in each. No additional towns beyond the sixteen first identified by using this selection process in *The Great Towns of The West* achieved superior scores.

Collectively, these sixteen are the most sought-after towns in the most exciting state in America. Individually, each offers unique enchantment that makes it a worthy destination for a weekend—or a lifetime.

Weather Profile

Weather plays a crucial role in recreation and leisure. Because of this, a great deal of care was taken in obtaining and presenting detailed weather information. The weather profiles for each town are intended to be the most complete in any guidebook.

Numeric data includes average high and low temperatures, rainfall, and snowfall for each month. The "Vokac Weather Rating"© (VWR) uses all of this (plus the frequency of precipitation) to measure the probability of "pleasant weather"—i.e., warm, dry conditions suitable for outdoor recreation by anyone dressed in light sportswear. The typical weather that can be expected each month is systematically rated from "0" to "10." A "0" signifies the most adverse weather with almost no chance that shirt-sleeves and shorts will be appropriate. Every increment of one on the VWR represents a 10% greater chance of pleasant weather. For example, a "5" is used where there is a 50% chance that any given day in the month will be pleasant. A "10" pinpoints "great" weather, with warm, dry days almost 100% assured. An easy-to-follow line graph is used to display each monthly VWR. Ratings of "7" or above indicate a high probability of desirable conditions for outdoor activity. Ratings of "6" or less suggest an increasing likelihood that the weather may restrict outdoor ventures and/or require special clothing. As an added convenience, each month on the graph has been subdivided into four segments, roughly corresponding to weeks. Readers interested in "fine-tuning" the VWR may find the smaller segments helpful. For example, if the ratings for October and November are "9" and "4," the position of the connecting line during the last week (segment) of October indicates a "7" rating. The implication is that weather during the last week in the month is normally still "good," but no longer as "fine" as it was earlier in the month. The data are also translated into concise narrative forecasts that describe what the weather will probably be like in each month, and in each season, of the year.

Attractions and Diversions

All notable attractions in each town are identified and described. Included are leisure-time destinations of special interest to adults—like wineries, nude beaches, and libraries—that are typically missing from conventional guidebooks. In addition, all kinds of diversions like bicycling, ballooning, horseback riding, and river running are described, and sources for equipment rentals and guides are named. As a convenience, favorite categories of attractions and diversions are always listed alphabetically under general headings such as "boat rentals," "golf," "warm water features," and "winter sports."

Shopping

Distinctive shops are among the most popular features of almost every great town. Yet, they are uniformly ignored in conventional guidebooks. In this book, all notable shops that emphasize locally produced gourmet foods or unusual items (especially those reflecting local artistry or craftsmanship) are described under "Food Specialties" and "Specialty Shops" for each town. The desirability of each downtown as a place to shop and browse is also discussed.

Nightlife

Life after dark is of particular interest to most adults. For each of California's great towns, the overall quality of places to go and things to do for an evening is summarized. Then, all first-rate live theaters, nightclubs, pubs, historic saloons, and other sources of nightlife are named. Each is described in terms of featured entertainment as well as furnishings and decor.

Restaurants

Both the quantity and quality of dining places are discussed, along with the predominant food style, for each town. All noteworthy restaurants are described in terms of food and atmosphere. (Service is not mentioned because it can vary so much over time—or even on a given evening.) Prices are summarized in categories from "low" to "extremely expensive" (see the discussion of "prices" later in this chapter). Meals served (B = Breakfast, L = Lunch, D = Dinner) are identified under the restaurant's name, along with days closed, if any. Specific hours of operation and special services (like approved credit cards) are not described, because they change frequently in most restaurants. Places that cater especially to families, fast-food shops, and most chain restaurants are generally excluded because of the adult orientation of this book and the emphasis on distinctive dining.

Lodging

A systematic effort was made to identify and describe all of the best and all of the bargain accommodations in each town. Most conventional motels and other sanitized lodgings clustered along highway strips and near freeway off-ramps are excluded. These places seldom reflect the charms of an area and are even less frequently bargains. Every town is summarized in terms of the number and quality of its lodgings, and the average percentage by which rates are reduced or increased apart from summer. Each uncommon lodging is portrayed in terms of amenities, both natural (like a lakeside location or an oceanfront beach) and man-made (i.e., outdoor pool, whirlpool, tennis courts, etc.). Also, wherever toll-free reservations are possible, the numbers are provided. Room decor and generally available room features are discussed. As a special added feature, hundreds of individual rooms with special views and/or furnishings are singled out. Thus, each exceptional room (starting with the best) is identified by number (or name), described, and priced. In addition, every effort was also made to include and depict all of each town's safe and clean bargain accommodations (priced at $30 per night or less per couple). The "regular room" price which completes each listing is the lowest price charged during prime time—on a summer weekend—for two people in a room with one bed.

Campgrounds

Two kinds of campgrounds are included: all places with a special natural setting (by a river or an oceanfronting beach, for example), and places with complete facilities (including hot showers) that are convenient to a great town. Natural and man-made attractions, as well as sanitary and individual site features, are consistently described. The base rate that ends each listing is the minimum price charged for two people occupying a tent site during prime time.

Location

It is hard to be lost for very long in any of the great towns because of their compact "human scale." To help the reader locate features without a map, every listing in this guide is addressed according to a street number and both mileage and direction from downtown. The term "downtown" covers all features within approximately one-quarter mile of the busiest, most intensely developed portion of the business district. Because this definition is used for each town, it is easy to compare numbers and kinds of features within and among downtowns, and to quickly estimate distances between any listings in each town. (Cambria has two downtowns. Distances and directions are given from the nearest of the two centers in this town.)

Ratings

All features listed in each town are rated. Three ratings are used. (1) A star preceding an entry denotes an especially notable example or source of a product or service. It is worth going out of the way for, if you are interested in that thing. (2) An entry is included, but not starred, if it is a good (but not exceptional) example or source of the product or service. (3) Places and activities that were not included were judged to be of only average or lower quality, readily available in many other places, or lacking in some important characteristic.

Evaluations of each feature were made anonymously, and independently of any payment or favor. As a result, each listing is rated on merit alone, and solely reflects the judgment of the author. A special effort was made to assure that ratings are comparable among all features and towns. For example, if a restaurant is starred, it is not merely one of the best available locally. It would be regarded as a place for a special dining experience in any city or town lucky enough to have it. Each individual feature was consistently evaluated both in terms of its overall quality and how well it succeeds in being what it purports to be. Thus, if a restaurant proclaims that it is a temple of haute cuisine, its rating was based both on the quality of the food and decor and on its success or failure to live up to a lofty aspiration. All rating information is somewhat perishable in any guidebook. After all, chefs move on, bed-and-breakfast inns change ownership, and shops discontinue certain merchandise over time. However, longer-than-normal staying power can be expected from the listings in this guide because they are the notable features in especially desirable areas.

Prices

Information is provided about the cost of all lodgings, campgrounds, and restaurants. Because prices change along with the economy and whims of management, there can be no assurance that specific prices quoted in the lodging and campgrounds sections will be in effect. However, the numbers will continue to illustrate comparable values, since price levels usually remain constant. For example, a "bargain" motel (with rooms costing $30 or less in 1986) can be expected to remain a relative bargain in later years—even though the price of a room increases—because other places in that area will typically increase their prices by about the same percentage as the bargain motel.

All quoted prices are projected for the summer ("high season") of 1986. They were obtained for every lodging listed in this book through field work and a systematic telephone survey conducted in the fall/winter of 1985. Each price is a per-night rate for two people in a room with one bed. Rates for one person are usually a few dollars less, and rates for two beds may be a few dollars more per night. Prices are for European plan accommodations (no meals) except as noted in the text for facilities that include one or more meals in their daily rates. The campground prices are the lowest forecast for 1986 per car with two persons for a site without electrical or other special hookups. It should be assumed for both lodgings and campgrounds that the use of on-premises facilities (like swimming pools, saunas, etc.) is included in the price of a room or campsite, unless fees or rental charges are noted in the description.

A basic price code was designed to provide a handy, accurate picture of the cost of an average meal in each restaurant. The same code is used for all listed restaurants. As a result, the cost of different kinds of fine dining can be compared within any great town, or contrasted with the cost of similar restaurants in any other great town. Five categories are used to define the cost per person for a "normal" dinner (soup or salad, average-priced entree, and beverage) not including wine, tip, or tax. The categories and related prices are:

Low :	less than $8
Moderate :	$8 - $14
Expensive :	$14 - $20
Very Expensive :	$20 - $30
Extremely Expensive :	more than $30

Some Final Comments

All information has been carefully checked, and is believed to be current and accurate. However, the author cannot be responsible for changes in name, address, phone number, prices, or quality of listed places and services since these are beyond his control. No malice is intended or implied by the judgments expressed, or by the omission of any facility or service, from this guide.

As with any guidebook, this one will be challenged about towns and features that were included, and those which were left out. A reader may disagree with the absence of a favorite town, or the fact that a place remembered fondly in one of the great towns has been excluded. Regardless, *The Great Towns of California* will achieve its purpose if it encourages you to go beyond the cities and famous landmarks to discover and experience the special pleasures of these enchanting places.

The author welcomes your comments and questions.

c/o West Press
P.O. Box 99717
San Diego, California 92109

Calistoga

Calistoga is the only town in the West that is esteemed for both wine and water. Surrounded by vineyards and wineries at the northern end of the renowned Napa Valley, it also hosts a remarkable cluster of small hot springs resorts and a bottling plant that ships the town's mineral water worldwide. The little valley is sheltered by the oak-covered foothills of towering Mt. St. Helena. An uncommon amount of good weather is enjoyed from late spring, which coincides with the release of new vintages, through early fall, when the harvest and crush attract the greatest influx of visitors. During this latter period, and on weekends throughout the year, lodgings are usually full to capacity. Throngs are increasing in response to growing interest in both premium wine and the sybaritic pleasures of hot springs resorts. Other unusual local attractions include a major glider port, a natural geyser, and a petrified forest. Nearby hills and the picturesque valley also offer fine bicycling and hiking opportunities. Still, the town's major preoccupation is with more relaxed diversions—like wine tasting, soaking in hot mineral water whirlpools, and taking ash baths.

Calistoga was founded in 1859 by Sam Brannan, California's first millionaire land developer who was also the publisher of San Francisco's first newspaper. Recognizing the potential of the area's warm springs, volcanic mud, and hot water geysers, he purchased a square mile near Mt. St. Helena and developed what was intended to become the "Saratoga of California," rivaling the famous New York resort. He, and others, also cultivated grapevines that are now part of vineyards producing premium wines recognized as some of the world's finest. For more than a century, Calistoga's economy was based on the health-related aspects of the natural hot springs and in growing, harvesting, and processing premium grapes. In recent years the complementary sybaritic relationship between fine wine and warm mineral springs spas has begun to attract visitors in pursuit of pleasure as well as cures.

Today, existing facilities are being updated, while new development remains determinedly low-keyed. Constriction of the valley to as little as one-half mile between steep foothills has focused growth around a compact and charming downtown. Recent skillful renovations have successfully restored a turn-of-the-century feeling to the classic main street. Almost all of the major hot springs spa and lodging facilities, plus the few good specialty shops, and a coterie of excellent restaurants and bars are located within easy walking distance of this appealing thoroughfare.

Elevation:

365 feet

Population (1980):

3,879

Population (1970):

1,882

Location:

74 mi. North
of San Francisco

Calistoga

WEATHER PROFILE

Vokac Weather Rating

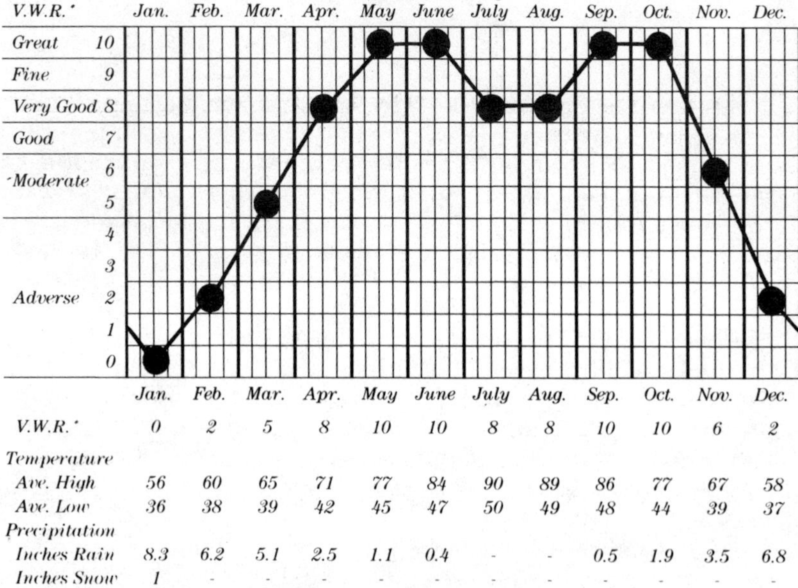

	Jan.	Feb.	Mar.	Apr.	May	June	July	Aug.	Sep.	Oct.	Nov.	Dec.
*V.W.R.**	0	2	5	8	10	10	8	8	10	10	6	2
Temperature												
Ave. High	56	60	65	71	77	84	90	89	86	77	67	58
Ave. Low	36	38	39	42	45	47	50	49	48	44	39	37
Precipitation												
Inches Rain	8.3	6.2	5.1	2.5	1.1	0.4	-	-	0.5	1.9	3.5	6.8
Inches Snow	1	-	-	-	-	-	-	-	-	-	-	-

**V.W.R. = Vokac Weather Rating: probability of mild (warm & dry) weather on any given day.*

Forecast

Month	*V.W.R.**		*Temperatures* *Daytime*	*Evening*	*Precipitation*
Jan.	0	Adverse	cool	chilly	frequent downpours
Feb.	2	Adverse	cool	chilly	frequent downpours
Mar.	5	Moderate	warm	cool	occasional downpours
Apr.	8	Very Good	warm	cool	infrequent downpours
May	10	Great	warm	cool	infrequent rainstorms
June	10	Great	hot	warm	negligible
July	8	Very Good	hot	warm	none
Aug.	8	Very Good	hot	warm	none
Sep.	10	Great	hot	warm	negligible
Oct.	10	Great	warm	cool	infrequent rainstorms
Nov.	6	Moderate	warm	cool	infrequent downpours
Dec.	2	Adverse	cool	chilly	frequent downpours

Summary

At the northern end of the Napa Valley, Calistoga's weather is moderated somewhat by marine air pouring through the gap in the Coast Range at the Golden Gate. As a result, there is almost no snow in **winter**. The season is usually cool and wet, with frequent heavy rainfalls contributing well over half of the year's normal precipitation. **Spring** is delightful. Emerald green hillsides accented by colorful patches of wildflowers are coupled with warm days, cool evenings, and fewer and lighter rainfalls as the season progresses. **Summer** days are hot and sunny, evenings are warm, and there is a virtual assurance that no precipitation will disrupt outdoor activities. **Fall** is perhaps the most desirable season. Warm sunny days, cool evenings, and infrequent rainfalls provide ample opportunities to get out and share in the celebration of the area's most renowned collaboration between man and nature—the bountiful grape harvest.

ATTRACTIONS & DIVERSIONS

★ ***Ballooning***

Once in a Lifetime Balloon Co.

P.O. Box 795 *942-6541*

The natural beauty of the wine country is unforgettably revealed in this company's early morning balloon flights. Afterward, they treat you to champagne and lunch.

★ ***Bicycling***

Hauschildt's

downtown at 1255 Lincoln Av. *942-4666*

Bicycle riding is very popular on scenic byways throughout the relatively flat Napa Valley. Individual or tandem bicycles can be rented here by the hour or day.

Flying

★ **Calistoga Soaring Center**

downtown at 1546 Lincoln Ave. *942-5592*

The unique thrill of soaring can be experienced behind a professional glider pilot on flights that originate and land near the middle of town. Because nearly ideal soaring conditions prevail much of the year in the upper Napa Valley, this is one of the West's major centers for the sport. In addition to rides, lessons and rentals can be arranged.

Golf

Mt. St. Helena Golf Course

.5 mi. N at 1434 Oak St. *742-9966*

A relatively level 9-hole course adjacent to the Fairgrounds offers scenic views of nearby Mt. St. Helena. It is open to the public with a practice range, club and cart rentals, and a snack shop.

★ **Old Faithful Geyser**

2.5 mi. N at 1299 Tubbs Lane *942-6463*

One of the few regularly erupting geysers in the world is appropriately located next to Calistoga. Super-heated water erupts to a height of sixty feet or more every forty minutes—approximately. The novel attraction is in a private park.

★ **Petrified Forest**

5 mi. W at 4100 Petrified Forest Rd. *942-6667*

This private park contains fossil redwood logs buried millions of years ago when ash covered a redwood forest uprooted by the concussion of the volcanic eruption of nearby Mt. St. Helena. The texture and fiber of redwoods up to 126 feet long and four feet in circumference are remarkably preserved.

Pioneer Park

downtown 1 blk. W on Lincoln Av. on Cedar St.

The tiny Napa River passes through this handsome little park. Several picnic tables under majestic shade trees overlook the stream.

Robert Louis Stevenson State Park
6 mi. N on CA 29
In addition to a scenic road through this undeveloped park, there is a five mile hiking trail to the top of Mt. St. Helena (4,343 feet elevation). From the top of the extinct volcano (the area's highest landmark) the Pacific Ocean, Bay Area, and Sierra Nevada are visible—on a clear day. A memorial one mile up the trail notes the cabin site where Robert Louis Stevenson honeymooned in 1880 and got his inspiration for "The Silverado Squatters."

★ **Russian River**
The gentle little Russian River offers more than fifty miles of slow-moving water, and a few easy riffles. Natural swimming holes backed by sunny, sandy beaches abound. Handsome, second-growth redwoods line the banks for miles. Swimming, fishing, sunbathing and floating are popular. From April thru October, rental canoes, all equipment, and transport between starting and ending points are provided by:

Trowbridge Recreation Inc.
24 mi. W via CA 29 at 20 Healdsburg Av. - Healdsburg *433-7247*

Sharpsteen Museum Complex
downtown at 1311 Washington St. *942-5911*
The museum features dioramas and exhibits prepared by one of Walt Disney's talented artists dedicated to Calistoga's offbeat history. Nearby are an authentically furnished 1860 cottage from Sam Brannan's original resort, and a peaceful little garden by the Napa River.

★ **Spring Lake Park**
14 mi. SW via Petrified Forest/Calistoga Rds. *539-8092*
At the far edge of the scenic hill country to the southwest of town, a large park has been developed around little Santa Rosa Creek Reservoir. It is a deservedly popular water recreation site in summer because of a big, picturesque swimming lagoon with a sandy beach. Rental rowboats, sailing, fishing, and bicycle and hiking paths are other attractions.

Warm Water Features

★ **Calistoga Spa**
downtown at 1006 Washington St. *942-6269*
Swimming in 83° mineral water in this private spa's new outdoor pool is open to the public year-round.

★ **Mineral Springs Spas**
downtown
Seven hotels and motels have an array of hot springs spa facilities apart from their accommodations to tempt the public. All are within walking distance of downtown. Guests can luxuriate in indoor and outdoor warm mineral water pools and hot mineral water whirlpools in a variety of genial settings. Steam baths, herbal and blanket wraps, and massage can also be reserved. The most unusual spa feature is the ash/mud bath, in which local volcanic ash is mixed with mud and hot mineral water to fill "mud relaxation tubs." Several places package all of the above features into a single sensationally sybaritic session lasting two hours.

★ **Pacheteau's Hot Springs Pool**
downtown at 1712 Lincoln Av. *942-5589*
The public is invited to swim in 90° mineral water in a big outdoor pool built decades ago against a luxuriously landscaped hillside. Closed Mon. and Nov. thru Mar.

Wineries
Calistoga is at the northern end of the world famous Napa Valley wine producing district. While the heart of the "wine country" is St. Helena, Calistoga is also surrounded by some of California's most outstanding vineyards and wineries. Several provide delightful tasting facilities for visitors.

★ **Chateau Montelena**
2.7 mi. N at 1429 Tubbs Lane *942-5105*
This renowned winery was established in 1880 in a castle-like building with imported facing stone and side walls built of native stone up to twelve feet thick. Oriental water gardens including pavilions, a junk, and islands connected by footbridges focus attention on a pretty little five acre lake. Tasting and sales 10-4 daily. Tours by appointment.

★ **Cuvaison**
3 mi. E at 4550 Silverado Trail *942-6266*
Established in 1970, this winery uses state-of-the-art equipment to concentrate on three premium wines. Idyllic vineyard views are a bonus of oak-shaded picnic grounds next to the winery. Tasting and sales 10-4 daily. Tours by appointment.

Hans Kornell Champagne Cellars
4.5 mi. SE via CA 29 at 1091 Larkmead Lane *963-2334*
Since 1958, this winery has been devoted to the production of traditional, bottle-fermented sparkling wines in the owner's native German style. Tours, tasting (one kind of sparkling wine), and sales 10:30-4:30 daily.

★ **Sterling Vineyards**
2 mi. SE at 1111 Dunaweal Lane *942-5151*
In 1973, a monastery-like winery with a resplendent white facade opened on a 400-foot knoll overlooking much of the Napa Valley. Worthwhile self-guided tours of the post-modern facility are reached by parking at the base and riding (for a fee) an aerial tram up the hill. Afterward, visitors can relax indoors or outdoors in one of the nation's most impressive settings for wine tasting. Sterling concentrates on four premium wines, and is one of the largest completely estate-bottled wineries in the country. Tasting, sales, and self-guided tours 10:30-4:30 daily (Apr. thru Oct.); Closed Mon.-Tues. (Nov. thru Mar.).

★ **Stonegate Winery**
1.8 mi. SE at 1183 Dunaweal Lane *942-6500*
Founded in 1971, this small winery is devoted to the production of four premium wines. A handsome tasting and retail sales room was recently completed. Tasting and sales 10:30-4:30 daily.

SHOPPING

Almost all of the retail businesses in Calistoga are clustered downtown. Remarkably, there are no outlying shopping centers. The highly strollable main street contains an intriguing mix of convenience and specialty shops, in addition to notable dining, drinking and lodging establishments.

Food Specialties

★ **All Seasons Cafe & Wine Shop**
downtown at 1400 Lincoln Av. *942-9111*
Beyond the gourmet deli is a wine cellar with one of the West's largest premium wine selections on display. Serious wine enthusiasts can partake of wine tastings by-the-glass or in-series-by-type of wine offered daily.

The Calistoga Wine Stop
downtown at 1458 Lincoln Av. *942-5556*
A good assortment of local and regional wines and related accessories are sold in a cheerful little shop in the Calistoga Depot complex.

★ **Continental Pastry and Coffee Shop**
downtown at 1353 Lincoln Av. *942-0279*
Some of the most outstanding pastries in the West are the specialty of this ingratiating little bakery. Ice cream is also served at the few tables by a picture window view of main street. Closed Mon. (also Tues. in winter).

Hauschildt's Ice Cream Parlor
downtown at 1255 Lincoln Av. *942-4666*
Many ice cream flavors and complete fountain service are features of this small shop with a deck by the tiny Napa River.

★ **Napa Valley Walnut Farms**
.5 mi. S at 414 CA 29 *942-4339*
Shelled walnuts from local trees are the specialty here. Sales continue from the beginning of harvest (mid-September) until sold out—usually around Easter.

Specialty Shops

Absolut Gallery
downtown at 1407 Lincoln Av. *942-9148*
Fine handcrafted works in wood, metals and other materials are featured in this new shop.

★ **Calistoga Bookstore**
downtown at 1343 Lincoln Av. *942-4123*
An excellent selection of titles for all ages is displayed, accompanied by mellow background music plus coffee or tea in a comfortable reading area. Poetry, discussion, and live music are occasionally offered in this big, appealing bookstore.

Calistoga Depot
downtown at 1458 Lincoln Av.
In 1868, this depot was completed as the terminus of the Napa Valley Railroad which served San Franciscans who came by steam ferry and train from Vallejo to enjoy the spa facilities. The tracks were removed beyond St. Helena about 1970. The depot was renovated in 1978 into a shopping complex specializing in arts and crafts and local wines.

Earthsongs
downtown at 1414 Lincoln Av. *942-0154*
An old drugstore has been converted into an inviting shop with an eclectic mixture of California-style arts and crafts, along with some nods to high-tech like the bionic chair.

NIGHTLIFE

In Calistoga, tranquility reigns each evening. A couple of distinctive lounges are worth a visit, however.

Lord Derby Arms
.7 mi. NE at 1923 Lake St. *942-9155*
Nearly a dozen tap beers and a variety of English-style foods like fish and chips and bangers and mash (same menu as Fox & Hound in St. Helena) are highlights in a multi-room roadside pub. A garden deck overlooks vineyards.

★ **Mount View Hotel**
downtown at 1457 Lincoln Av. *942-6877*
A pianist usually plays music for listening or dancing each evening. But, the stellar attraction is the sleek 1930s Art Deco lounge itself. Recent skillful renovation has fully restored the room into one of the valley's most romantic havens.

★ **Silverado Restaurant and Tavern**
downtown at 1374 Lincoln Av. *942-6725*
Comfortable Old Western decor is accented by a magnificent 1895 polished hardwood back bar. A number of premium wines are always available by the glass from a wine list that has been nationally acclaimed as one of the best in the country. Formal wine tastings are featured most Tuesdays. Quality tap beer hasn't been neglected either with Henry Weinhard's Private Reserve and Anchor Steam heading the list.

RESTAURANTS

Restaurants in Calistoga are very good, and almost all are concentrated on the main street. The best feature notable lists of the valley's wines to complement predominantly Continental or New California cuisine.

★ **All Seasons Cafe & Wine Shop**
downtown at 1400 Lincoln Av. *942-9111*
L-D. Sat. & Sun. brunch. *Moderate*
Gourmet smoked meats, barbecued ribs, pates, soups and salads, plus homemade pastries, desserts and ice creams are served in a cheerful

deli/cafe. Picnic foods to go are also featured along with an extraordinary assortment of regional wines.

★ **Bosko's of Calistoga**
downtown at 1403 Lincoln Av. *942-9088*
L-D. *Moderate*
Contemporary Italian specialties include a selection of well-made hot and cold pastas, salads and desserts, plus Napa Valley wines by the glass. Exposed brick walls, open rafters, twirling fans and sawdust on the floor have been incorporated into a casual and inviting deli/dining room. There is also takeout service.

★ **Calistoga Inn**
downtown at 1250 Lincoln Av. *942-4101*
L-D. No L on Mon.-Thurs. *Expensive*
A light touch with fine fresh ingredients results in some of California's best seafood and Continental specialties. Guests are surrounded by simple elegance in an attractively restored inn where polished hardwood floors and wainscoating contribute to a turn-of-the-century feeling.

★ **Cinnabar**
downtown at 1440 Lincoln Av. *942-6989*
B-L-D. *Moderate*
Light Continental cuisine is served in a handsomely remodeled Victorian-style bistro. Distinctive breakfast omelets are featured all day. Wines by the glass are poured at an alcove bar.

★ **Las Brasas**
downtown at 1350 Lincoln Av. *942-4056*
L-D. *Low*
The super-hot fire of an exhibition mesquite grill is used to prepare deliciously distinctive Mexican entrees featured in a stylish and lively dining room.

Mark West Lodge
12 mi. W at 2520 Mark West Springs Rd. *546-2592*
D only. Sun. brunch. Closed Mon. *Expensive*
Updated French dishes are served in a charming century-old landmark. The spacious dining room has been restored to casual elegance highlighted by an arresting full-sized nude sculpture. The grapevines next to the building may be the oldest in California.

★ **Mount View Hotel**
downtown at 1457 Lincoln Av. *942-6877*
L-D. B on Sat. & Sun. *Expensive*
Continental cuisine is skillfully prepared in nouvelle style, using the freshest available local produce. The meticulously renovated Art Deco dining room is a plush haven of nostalgic tranquility. During the summer, a mesquite wood barbecue is also offered several nights weekly in the delightful poolside patio.

★ **Silverado Restaurant**
downtown at 1374 Lincoln Av. *942-6725*
B-L-D. *Moderate*
Creative California cuisine highlighted by delicious homemade baked goods is served in comfortable country atmosphere where well-spaced tables are accented by fresh flowers and linen. One of the most extensive wine lists in the nation is available to guests in the dining room and in the handsome adjoining bar.

★ **Soo Yuan**
downtown at 1354 Lincoln Av. *942-9404*
L-D. *Low*
One of Calistoga's newest restaurants offers an extensive selection of fine Szechwan and Mandarin dishes in a casual little dining room.

LODGING

Because this is a hot springs mecca, most of the town's limited accommodations are oriented around a wide range of spa facilities. Most lodgings are surprisingly plain, and almost no rooms provide views of the scenic valley. Reservations should be made well in advance for visits in summer on weekends, or during fall grape-harvest time. There are no bargains. However, mid-week rates, and rates from late fall through early spring, are often at least 30% less than those shown.

★ **Calistoga Spa**
downtown at 1006 Washington St. *942-6269*
Guests may use the covered mineral whirlpool, the hot pool or the large cool mineral pool in the courtyard. New (fee) spa facilities include mud, whirlpool, or steambaths; blanket wraps; and massage. Rooms in the newer wings are spacious with wood-paneled interiors, open-beam ceilings, and comfortable furnishings. All have kitchenettes (no ovens) and cable color TV. (Nov. thru Feb. every fourth day is free.)
#17—end unit, windows on 3 sides, some privacy, mt. view, Q bed...$40
regular unit— Q bed...$40

Dr. Wilkinson's Hot Springs
downtown at 1507 Lincoln Av. *942-4102*
This nicely maintained modern motel has indoor and outdoor mineral pools free to guests. Kitchenettes are optional. Complete bath/health club facilities are available for a fee. Each unit has a phone and color TV.
deluxe room—refrigerator, K bed...$55
regular room— Q bed...$46

★ **Golden Haven Spa**
downtown at 1713 Lake St. *942-6793*
A contemporary motel in a quiet residential area has a naturally heated indoor pool, plus an outdoor redwood whirlpool with sundecks.

Complete (fee) bathhouse/health club facilities are also available. All well-furnished rooms have cable color TV with movies, and a refrigerator.

#27,#20—in-room raised whirlpool, K bed...$79
large room— K bed...$50
regular room—small, Q bed...$39

Hideaway Cottages
downtown at 1412 Fairway *942-4108*
A large outdoor mineral pool and whirlpool in a tranquil residential location are features of this newly restored old cottage colony. Kitchenettes are optional. Each unit has cable TV.

"El Paso"—1 BR, kitchen, Q bed...$42
regular room—small cottage, Q bed...$36

Larkmead Country Inn
4.5 mi. S at 1103 Larkmead Lane *942-5360*
One of the valley's most beguiling bed-and-breakfast inns is surrounded by vineyards. This gracious turn-of-the-century structure with an Italianate flavor is meticulously furnished with Persian rugs, antiques, and fine old paintings. Rooms have vineyard views and private baths. A Continental breakfast is included, as is a decanter of wine.

"Chablis"—corner, sitting porch with vineyard view, 2 T beds...$88
"Chenin Blanc"—spacious, corner room, love seat, D bed...$88
"Chardonnay"—small K bed...$84
regular room— D bed...$84

Le Spa Francais
.6 mi. NE at 1880 Lincoln Av. *942-4636*
A large outdoor pool, plus an indoor hot mineral water whirlpool and sauna, are features of this recently remodeled motel. A complete high-tech European spa facility (highlighting ash/mud baths) is available for a fee. Each room has a color TV.

deluxe room—Roman tiled tub, Q bed...$55
regular room— D bed...$39

★ **Mount View Hotel**
downtown at 1457 Lincoln Av. *942-6877*
A large outdoor pool and whirlpool occupy a garden courtyard highlighted by striking fountain sculptures behind this small landmark hotel. Carefully restored rooms and suites are each individually furnished in styles that reflect the hotel's Art Deco origins. Guests are served complimentary fresh croissants, orange juice, and coffee each morning in a pleasant downstairs room, and a bottle of Calistoga water is placed in each room.

#221—corner, nice view over pool, fine period furnishings, Q bed...$75
regular room— D or Q bed...$50

Nance's Hot Springs
downtown at 1614 Lincoln Av. *942-6211*
This homespun, vintage motel features a large enclosed hot mineral water whirlpool. Complete bathhouse facilities, including volcanic ash mud baths, are available for a fee. Each simply furnished unit has a phone, cable color TV and a kitchenette.
regular room— K bed...$40

Pacheteau's Calistoga Hot Springs
downtown at 1712 Lincoln Av. *942-5589*
Calistoga's historic cottage complex features the town's largest outdoor hot springs pool free to guests. It is on a luxuriantly landscaped slope. Complete bath/health facilities are available for a fee. Each small, simply furnished unit has a kitchen and a color TV.
regular room— 2 T or D bed...$40

★ **Roman Spa**
downtown at 1300 Washington St. *942-4441*
Luxuriant gardens surround motel buildings, an outdoor mineral pool and whirlpool, a building housing a Finnish sauna and hot indoor mineral whirlpool for guests, and complete (fee) bathhouse facilities. Each unit has a cable color TV. (Nov. thru Feb. every fourth day is free except weekends and holidays.)
#42,#46—new, end units, refr., lg. in-bathroom whirlpool tub with shower, Q bed...$78
regular room—newer motel unit, refr., Q bed...$45
regular room—older section, kitchenette, D bed...$38

CAMPGROUNDS

Campgrounds are scarce in the area. The best is a deservedly popular facility that is beautifully situated along a stream deep in a luxuriant forest of oak and pine.

★ **Bothe-Napa Valley State Park**
4.5 mi. S at 3601 CA 29 *942-4575*
A mixed evergreen forest along a picturesque little stream provides an ideal location for this state-operated campground. An outdoor pool and scenic hiking trails are other features. Flush toilets and hot showers are available. There are no hookups. Each of the well-spaced sites has a picnic table and a fire area. Many sites are tree-shaded, and several are by the creek. base rate...$6

Napa County Fairgrounds
.5 mi. N via Fairway at 1435 Oak St. *942-5111*
This county-operated facility is conveniently located near downtown. There is a fee for an adjoining 9-hole golf course. Flush toilets, hot showers, and hookups are available. Each closely spaced site has a picnic table. A few are tree-shaded. base rate...$7

SPECIAL EVENTS

Napa County Fair *fairgrounds* *July 4th Week*
All of the traditional features of an old-fashioned country fair and 4th of July celebration are present in this five-day event.

★ **Napa Valley Wine Crush** *Napa Valley* *Early Aug. - Early Nov.*
To learn all about the what, where, and when of the valley's wineries' harvest and crush, a 24-hour, toll-free hot line is available from August into November—call (800) 86-CRUSH.

OTHER INFORMATION

Area Code: *707*

Zip Code: *94515*

Calistoga Chamber of Commerce
downtown at 1458 Lincoln Av. *942-6333*

Cambria

Cambria is a whimsical village tucked into a pine forest by the sea. This southern gateway to the fabled Big Sur coast has become a refuge for artists and dreamers attracted by spectacular mountain-backed seascapes. A surprising number of museum-quality galleries and gourmet restaurants distinguish the two small downtown areas. Pine-covered hillsides and pastoral countryside are still unspoiled by either shopping centers or commercial strip development along the highway approaches to town. Cambria also benefits from a mild year-round climate. The tranquil beauty of the place is most apparent in spring, when wildflowers accent emerald landscapes, and crowds are usually light. During summer and fall, natural air conditioning provides ideal weather for exploring remote beaches and rugged coastal mountains. The ocean is too cold for swimming, but beachcombing, clamming, and fishing are popular and hiking, backpacking, and camping are enjoyed in the area. Excellent summer weather also attracts capacity crowds to nearby Hearst Castle, the area's most famous attraction.

Shortly after the Civil War, the first permanent settlement was established along Santa Rosa Creek by farmers and dairymen. They were lured by the year-round stream in a sheltered valley at the base of the Coast Range Mountains. By the 1880s, Cambria was an established dairying and mercury mining center. Soon, however, the town went into a long period of decline. The slump was finally reversed during the 1950s when major improvements began on California State Highway 1 and when Hearst Castle was opened to tourists as a state-operated facility.

Population has begun to increase dramatically again as the result of Cambria's recent emergence as both a low-keyed tourist destination and an arts and crafts center. Most of the town's businesses are clustered along the old main road in two charming districts. The original commercial center, "east village," has an idyllic sheltered location a mile inland from the ocean. Much recent development has also occurred in "west village" along Main Street nearer to the ocean. Numerous sophisticated galleries and specialty shops feature local arts and crafts in both centers. Romantic restaurants serving gourmet cuisine in quaint cottages or in ocean-view dinner houses are another of the village's attractions. Nightlife is scarce, but it is distinctive and diverse. In sharp contrast with most other California destinations, there are no big motel-chain or convention-oriented complexes. Instead, visitor facilities individually complement the serenity and natural beauty of this special place. Several luxurious small motels with ocean views are concentrated along Moonstone Beach Drive near west village.

Elevation:

60 feet

Population (1980):

3,061

Population (1970):

1,716

Location:

220 miles Northwest of Los Angeles

Cambria
WEATHER PROFILE
Vokac Weather Rating

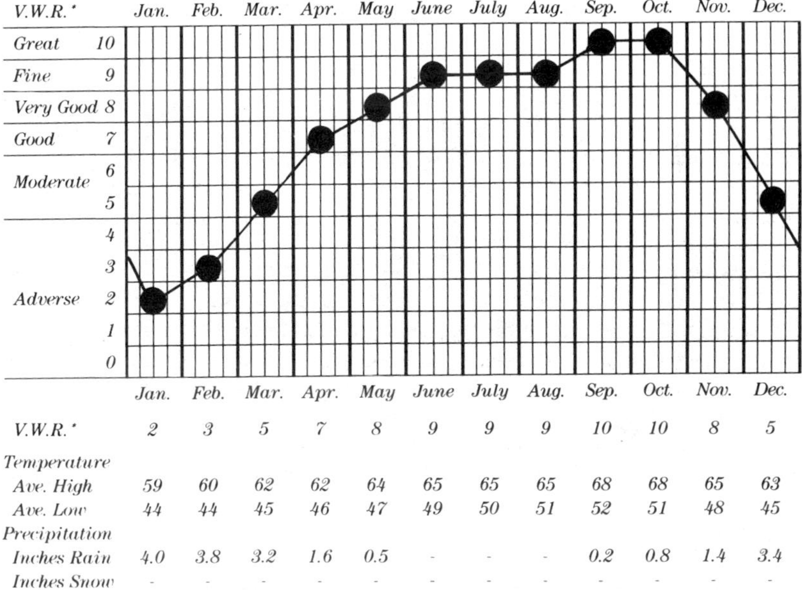

	Jan.	Feb.	Mar.	Apr.	May	June	July	Aug.	Sep.	Oct.	Nov.	Dec.
*V.W.R.**	2	3	5	7	8	9	9	9	10	10	8	5
Temperature												
Ave. High	59	60	62	62	64	65	65	65	68	68	65	63
Ave. Low	44	44	45	46	47	49	50	51	52	51	48	45
Precipitation												
Inches Rain	4.0	3.8	3.2	1.6	0.5	-	-	-	0.2	0.8	1.4	3.4
Inches Snow	-	-	-	-	-	-	-	-	-	-	-	-

**V.W.R. = Vokac Weather Rating: probability of mild (warm & dry) weather on any given day.*

Forecast

			Temperatures		
Month	*V.W.R.**		*Daytime*	*Evening*	*Precipitation*
Jan.	2	Adverse	cool	cool	frequent rainstorms.
Feb.	3	Adverse	cool	cool	occasional rainstorms
Mar.	5	Moderate	cool	cool	occasional rainstorms
Apr.	7	Good	cool	cool	infrequent rainstorms
May	8	Very Good	cool	cool	negligible
June	9	Fine	warm	cool	none
July	9	Fine	warm	cool	none
Aug.	9	Fine	warm	cool	none
Sep.	10	Great	warm	cool	negligible
Oct.	10	Great	warm	cool	infrequent rainstorms
Nov.	8	Very Good	warm	cool	infrequent rainstorms
Dec.	5	Moderate	cool	cool	occasional rainstorms

Summary

With a sheltered location by the ocean, Cambria has one of the mildest climates in the West. **Winter** is cool, with some fog but seldom a frost of any consequence. Occasional rainstorms that occur during this season contribute more than half of the average annual precipitation. Pleasant **spring** months offer uniformly cool days and evenings, with occasional fog and moderate-to-brisk winds, plus inconsequential rainfalls. **Summer** is consistently appealing, with brisk days, cool evenings, and no rainfall. In this classic naturally air conditioned seaside recreation area, the ocean unfortunately remains too cold for swimming. The most desirable season is **fall**, when the warmest and sunniest days of the year occur. Splendid weather usually prevails until the rainy season begins again in earnest after Thanksgiving.

ATTRACTIONS & DIVERSIONS

Bicycling

Cambria Pines Lodge

.5 mi. S of east village at 2905 Burton Dr. 927-4200

Bicycles can be rented by the hour or longer at the lodge to tour scenic coastal highways and byways.

★ **Big Sur Coast**

N for approximately 80 mi. on CA 1

The awesome combination of a mountain wilderness rising abruptly from an unspoiled sea inevitably delights those who visit the fabled Big Sur. A paved two-lane highway provides one of the West's most thrilling scenic drives and access to all of the features of this rugged coastline as it clings precariously to the western slopes of the Santa Lucia Mountains. Travelers should allow at least a full day to begin to appreciate the remote beaches and lush forested canyons, well-tended state parks, and unconventional galleries and restaurants that complement unforgettable scenery along the Big Sur coast.

★ **Cambrionia**

in west village on Main St.

A custom-built miniature Victorian mansion is uniquely perched atop Townes Antique Emporium. It is much-photographed for both its surprising location and intricate detailing.

Harmony

6 mi. SE on CA 1

This is a tiny old dairying community in the attractive rolling hill country inland from Cambria. The creamery buildings have been converted into a medley of shops, galleries, and restaurants amidst gardens and objects of art.

★ **Hearst Castle**

8 mi. NW on CA 1 - San Simeon 927-4621

"La Casa Grande" has a ridge-top position that gives it the appearance of a castle from the distant highway. The imposing 137-foot high cathedral-like main structure was William Randolph Hearst's private residence. It is now the focal point of the Hearst San Simeon State Historical Monument that also includes guest residences, terraced gardens, pools, sculpture, and unusual plants and animals. The extravagent collection of eclectic antiques and furnishings was accumulated during Hearst's lifetime of world travel. As the result, a tour of this unique estate is unforgettable. Visitors may only take conducted tours, of which there are four, each lasting about two hours. Reservations are often required during the summer.

Horseback Riding

Rancho San Simeon Stables

5 mi. NW off CA 1 927-8970

Rental horses are available for riding along scenic trails between the mountains and the sea.

★ ***Library***

in west village at 900 Main St. *927-4336*

The Cambria Public Library occupies a charming contemporary building. Skylights, sculptures, and padded seating in a greenhouse-styled window alcove all contribute to a bright and inviting interior. Closed Sun.-Mon.

Nitt Witt Ridge

just above west village

On a hillside a short walk above town is a whimsical bric-a-brac mansion. It was built incrementally since 1928 out of everything from bike parts to beer bottles by Art Beal, affectionately known as "Captain Nitt Witt." This classic example of folk art construction is listed in the National Register of Historic Landmarks. While it is a private residence that can only be viewed from the street, it is worth finding as another expression, along with Hearst's Castle, of what individuality is all about.

★ **San Simeon Beach State Park**

1.8 mi. NW at Moonstone Beach Dr./CA 1

Nearly two miles of shoreline with picturesque sandy beaches, blufftop trails, and ocean-view picnic sites have been set aside for the public in this inviting day use park.

★ **Shamel County Park**

.5 mi. W of west village on the coast

This day use facility has a parking area adjacent to Cambria's finest sandy beach, an outdoor swimming pool open in summer, and pleasant shady picnic sites.

Sportfishing

Virg's Sport Fishing

8 mi. NW off CA 1 at the pier - San Simeon *927-4676*

Full, half day, and twilight ocean fishing trips can be chartered here March thru October, or at the Morro Bay Embarcadero location year-round. Shore fishing is also popular off the rocky coast and sandy beaches near Cambria.

Warm Water Feature

Cambria Pines Lodge Pool

5 mi. S of east village at 2905 Burton Dr. *927-4200*

The public is invited to use (for a reasonable fee) the lodge's large indoor pool and whirlpool.

Winery

★ **Mastantuono Winery**

21 mi. E on CA 46 at Vineyard Dr. *238-0676*

An attractive roadside store gives visitors an opportunity to sample central California premium wines produced from grapes grown in the owner's nearby vineyards. Tasting and sales 10:30-6 daily (10-5 daily in winter).

SHOPPING

Cambria is in an early stage of becoming one of the major arts and crafts centers of the West. Several fine galleries and specialty shops already display quality works of local artisans. Almost all of the shops in the area are clustered in two tiny business districts—on Burton Drive (east village)—and about a mile west along Main Street (west village).

Food Specialties

★ **Linn's Fruit Bin**
5 mi. E on Santa Rosa Creek Rd. *927-8134*
Seasonal fresh fruits and vegetables are displayed and sold in this picturesque farmhouse shop along with homemade meat pies and country desserts, and a variety of fine fruit and berry preserves. Assorted gift packages will be mailed anywhere.

Oliver's Twist
in west village at 724 Main St. *927-8196*
Gourmet produce is the specialty, including excellent displays of local wines, local and international preserves, and more.

★ **The Upper Crust Bakery & Tea Room**
in east village at 2214 Main St. *927-8227*
Cinnamon rolls, donuts, croissants and other international pastry specialties and breads are all deliciously made from scratch in one of the West's great bakeries. A few tables and coffee are available. Closed Mon.

Specialty Shops

Cambria Book Co.
in west village at 784-C Main St. *927-3995*
An upstairs store has a small, well-organized selection of books, particularly paperbacks. Comfortable chairs are provided for browsers. Closed Mon.

Cambria News Center
in west village at 755 Main St. *927-4882*
Many metropolitan newspapers are displayed along with magazines and paperbacks.

Moonstones Gallery
in east village at 4070 Burton Dr. *927-3447*
Contemporary crafts by California artists plus regional food and wine products may be browsed while listening to classical music (tapes are also sold).

Quicksilver Gallery
in east village at 4070 Burton Dr. *927-8455*
Unique contemporary jewelry and metalwork are attractively displayed in the popular gallery's new location.

★ **Seekers**
in east village at 4090 Burton Dr. *927-4352*
This outstanding gallery features extraordinarily beautiful displays of museum-quality hand-blown glass, porcelain, ceramics, and wood carvings by local and other California artists.

★ **The Soldier Factory**
in west village at 789 Main St. *927-3804*
Fascinating toy soldiers, chess pieces, dragons, unicorns, and other whimsical creatures in a choice of polished or painted pewter are made and sold at this factory/showroom.

Spellbinders Gallery
in east village at 4070 Burton Dr. *927-3385*
Paintings and other wall hangings by local and regional artists are featured along with other quality objects of art in an inviting new gallery.

Thistle Books
in west village at 768 Main St. *927-5369*
Books are attractively displayed in this casual cultural salon where a piano is frequently in use.

NIGHTLIFE

Peace and quiet reign in Cambria, even in the evening. But, there are a few places with after-dark "action." Collectively, they offer a good range of casual entertainment and individualistic atmosphere.

Cambria Pines Lodge
.5 mi. S of east village at 2905 Burton Dr. *927-4200*
Dancing and entertainment are featured most nights in a large, comfortable lounge off the lobby of an atmospheric old wooden lodge. Live theater is also occasionally offered.

★ **Camozzi's Saloon**
in east village at 2262 Main St. *927-8941*
Games and occasional live music and entertainment have enticed residents and visitors into this appealingly funky old saloon for many years.

★ **Golden Lion Pub**
in west village at 774 Main St. *927-8842*
Live music and games are featured nightly amidst congenial English pub atmosphere. Dozens of imported and domestic beers are available, along with some traditional English dishes like steak-and-kidney pie, and pasties.

★ **Old Cayucos Tavern**
14 mi. SE on CA 1 at 130 N. Ocean Av. - Cayucos *995-3209*
Pool, darts, and shuffleboard are available anytime. A working fireplace and a couple of bigger-than-life pictures of cowgirls are part of the rustic decor. Legal gambling is an attraction in the back room, and live entertainment happens most nights in nearby Doc's Dance Hall.

★ **Pewter Plough Playhouse**
in west village at 824 Main St. *927-3877*
Live theater and art films are always worthwhile here, partly because of the whimsical charm of this stylish, intimate playhouse.

RESTAURANTS

A concentration of fine restaurants is one of Cambria's most compelling attractions. Creative gourmet cuisine is readily available, and atmosphere is remarkably varied—ranging from antique-filled old cottages to California-contemporary dining rooms with views of gardens, pine forests, or the ocean.

★ **Barbara's**
in east village at 2094 Main St. *927-4830*
B-L. Closed Sun. *Moderate*
The cinnamon rolls, muffins, and biscuits baked here are delicious, as are the distinctive omelets and other homemade dishes served in this pleasant little cafe.

★ **The Brambles**
in east village at 4005 Burton Dr. *927-4716*
D only. *Moderate*
An oakwood pit and oven are featured for preparing steaks, prime rib, and fresh seafoods. Homemade baked goods are another specialty of this long-time favorite. Tables set with full linen contribute to gracious dining amid antique decor in one of Cambria's original many-roomed 1890s clapboard cottages.

Cambria Pines Lodge
.5 mi. S of east village at 2905 Burton Dr. *927-4200*
B-L-D. *Moderate*
American fare is served in a refurbished rustic-wood lodge that is an enduring town landmark. Picture windows in the well-furnished dining room provide views of an adjacent sylvan garden and dining terrace.

Creekside Gardens
in east village at 2114 Main St. *927-8646*
B-L. Closed Mon. *Moderate*
An unusual range of homemade breakfast specialties is served in a cheerful little whitewashed cottage, or on a flower-strewn patio with a fine view of pine-covered hills.

The Flying Frog Restaurant
in east village at 4090 Burton Dr. *927-5656*
L-D. *Moderate*
Contemporary American fare and good adaptations of Mexican dishes are served in a cheerful new two-level restaurant with an inviting front bar.

The Golden Lion
in west village at 774 Main St. *927-8842*
L-D. *Low*
English specialties like Cornish pasties, sausage rolls, and steak-and-kidney pie complement classic pub atmosphere in a room with a large fireplace and live music nightly.

★ **Grey Fox Inn**
in east village at 4095 Burton Dr. *927-3305*
B-L-D. Sat. & Sun. brunch. *Moderate*
Contemporary American specialties are served in the graceful, intimate dining room of a charming old cottage, and on a beautiful vine-covered outdoor terrace when weather permits.

The Hamlet at Moonstone Gardens
2 mi. NW of west village on CA 1 *927-3535*
L-D. Closed most of Dec. *Expensive*
Conventionally Continental dishes are served in a casually antiqued dining room with a distant ocean view. Tables are also set in an exotic garden/nursery when weather permits. A good selection of premium wine-by-the-glass is available at the wine bar.

★ **Harlow's Dinner House**
.8 mi. S of east village at 2555 MacLeod Way *927-8619*
D only. *Moderate*
Skillfully prepared Continental specialties are enhanced by romantically elegant decor and backcountry views. The intimate dining room warmed by a raised fireplace is a new feature of Pickford House.

Harmony Valley Inn
6 mi. SE of east village on CA 1 - Harmony *927-5018*
D only. Sun. brunch. Closed Mon.-Wed. *Moderate*
American dishes are served amid antiques in several well-appointed dining rooms of a remodeled old creamery building.

Ian's
in east village at 2150 Center St. *927-8649*
D only. *Expensive*
New California dishes are served amidst post-Modern decor in this popular newer restaurant. Pastel colors soften the glass-topped tables, and artistically arranged prints and plants have been used to create beautifully tranquil dining rooms.

Moonraker
1.1 mi. NW of west village at 6550 Moonstone Beach Dr. *927-3859*
B-D. Closed Wed. in winter. *Expensive*
Seafoods New Orleans-style are a specialty in this oceanside restaurant. Because the casually elegant dining room has floor-to-ceiling windows on three sides, every guest has an expansive view of the Pacific.

★ **Picnique in the Pines**
in west village at 727 Main St. *927-8727*
B-L-D. Sun. brunch. Closed Mon. *Moderate*
International dinner specialties were recently added to the selection of delicious homemade croissants, scones, popovers, and pies, plus gourmet pates, crepes, and unusual salads, as compelling reasons to try this artistically decorated newer dining room. There are also a few tiny sidewalk tables, and meals will be packed for carryout picnics.

Rigdon Hall
in east village at 4022 Burton Dr. — *927-5125*
D only. — *Moderate*
This new restaurant offers a good selection of American dishes. Crisp linens and a choice of booths or tables enhance the capacious dining room.

The Sea Bear
in east village at 1602 Main St. — *927-4939*
B-L-D. — *Moderate*
Fresh seafood and quality steaks broiled over oak wood are the specialties. A gas fireplace warms one of the well-appointed, cozy dining rooms.

Sea Chest
.8 mi. NW of west village at 6216 Moonstone Beach Dr. — *927-4514*
D only. Closed Mon.-Tues. — *Moderate*
Shellfish and seafood are specialties of this popular, intimate restaurant with casual, nautical decor above Moonstone Beach. There is a fine ocean view from the Oyster Bar/dining room. The cozy main dining room has full linen, a picture window view of a flower field, and a much-used iron fireplace. Tables in the third room are set up for cards and board games as well as food and drinks.

The Way Station
14 mi. SE via CA 1 at 78 Ocean Av. - Cayucos — *995-1227*
L-D. B on Sat. & Sun. only. Closed Mon.-Tues. — *Moderate*
American specialties are served in a handsome Victorian setting or in a pleasant backyard garden. Many premium regional wines are offered by the glass in the adjoining bar.

LODGING

Accommodations reflect the serenity and natural beauty of this special place. Major motel chains with large facilities are thankfully absent. Reservations are often essential in summer, and on most Saturday nights. There are no bargains in summer. However, from fall through early spring, non-holiday rates are usually at least 20% lower than those shown.

★ **Cambria Pines Lodge**
.5 mi. S of east village at 2905 Burton Dr. — *927-4200*
The 1920s lodge and cabins above the village in a Monterey pine forest are being renovated. Recent additions include Cambria's best and largest heated pool and whirlpool, plus saunas, enclosed in a handsome glass-walled structure with a knotty-pine beamed ceiling. A forest-view restaurant and firelit lounge are also available. Each room has cable color TV.

#27,#26—spacious, wood-toned decor, pitched roof, raised fireplace, — K bed...$84
regular room—small cabin or lodge room, — D bed...$46

Cambria Village Motel
in east village at 2618 Main St. *927-4021*
This single-level motel is within easy walking distance of east village. Each of the renovated or newer rooms has a cable color TV.
#5—end, raised brick fireplace, full kitchen, Q bed...$46
regular room— Q bed...$42

★ **Fireside Inn - Best Western**
1.3 mi. NW at 6700 Moonstone Beach Dr. *927-8661*
This contemporary single-level motel is only fifty yards from Moonstone Beach and has a large outdoor pool and whirlpool. Each spacious, well-furnished room has a phone, cable color TV with movies, and a refrigerator.
#133,#131,#132—gas fireplace, in-bath whirlpool, ocean view across road, large, new, K bed...$95
#126,#128,#127—gas fireplace, in-bath whirlpool, ocean view across road, K bed...$85
#104,#101,#103,#102—gas fireplace, ocean view across road, K bed...$75
regular room— K bed...$55

The Hampton's Cabins
in east village at 2601 Main St. *927-4305*
Each of the small, older cabins in this complex has a tiny kitchen and cable color TV.
#1—spacious cabin, kitchen, Q bed...$35
regular room—small cabin, kitchen, D bed...$35
regular room—newer, upstairs in home, private bath, Q bed...$35

J. Patrick House
.5 mi. S of east village at 2990 Burton Dr. *927-3812*
An Early American-style bed-and-breakfast inn recently opened in a pair of large log cabins in the pines above town. Each individually decorated room has a wood-burning fireplace and a private bath. Fruit and homemade pastries are complimentary, as are wine and cheese by the fireplace each evening.
"Donegal" & Kerry"—pines view, raised fireplace, Q bed...$80
regular room— 2 T or Q bed...$80

★ **Moonstone Inn**
.7 mi. NW of west village at 5860 Moonstone Beach Dr. *927-4815*
A beautifully maintained small motel across the road from Moonstone Beach was skillfully converted into an English Tudor-style bed-and-breakfast country inn. A few rooms have ocean views and there are numerous nice touches: a wine and cheese hour in a glassed-in patio with a whirlpool and fireplace overlooking the ocean; Continental breakfast in bed; crystal ice buckets; and fresh flowers. Each room has cable color TV with movies, a phone, a refrigerator, and a gas fireplace.
#8—ocean view across road, K bed...$95
regular room— Q bed...$85

Pickford House

.8 mi. S of east village at 2555 MacLeod Way — *927-8619*

A newer bed-and-breakfast country inn on a hill south of town has captured some of the tranquility and craftsmanship of Cambria. Each unit is decorated in the style of the silent film era and each has a bath. A light breakfast in the morning is complimentary. Guests can join the public each evening by the fireplace in an inviting downstairs restaurant or bar.

"Pickford Room"—Victorian decor in pinks/blues, gas fireplace, fine mountain view, — K bed...$90
"Valentino Room"—sleek satin decor in maroon colors, gas fireplace, fine view, — 2 D beds...$90
regular room— — D bed...$65

★ **San Simeon Pines Resort**

1.7 mi. NW at 7200 Moonstone Beach Dr. — *927-4648*

This redwood ranch-style motel in a nicely landscaped pine forest has direct access to adjacent San Simeon Beach State Park and the ocean. A landscaped outdoor pool, beautiful par-3 (9-hole) golf course, and an outdoor games area are free to guests. Several rooms are in an unusual, deluxe, adults-only section. Each of the spacious, well-furnished rooms has color TV.

#76,#87—newer, pitched roof, brick fireplace (presto logs), windows on 3 sides, surf view, — K bed...$79
#62—newer, fine private view of surf, — K bed...$64
regular room— — Q bed...$49

CAMPGROUNDS

Campgrounds are scarce in the area. The best offers relatively primitive facilities in a choice location a short stroll from unspoiled ocean beaches.

★ **San Simeon State Beach**

3 mi. N of west village on CA 1 — *927-4509*

This large, state-owned campground occupies some gentle slopes an easy stroll from a long adjoining ocean beach. Beachcombing, fishing, and hiking are popular. Chemical pit toilets are provided. There are no showers or hookups. Each of the well-spaced grassy sites has a picnic table and a fire ring/grill. There are few trees, but some of the hilltop sites have fine ocean views. — base rate...$3

SPECIAL EVENT

Pinedorado *in west village* — *early September*

The year's biggest local celebration is three days of fun and games. Highlights include a parade, art show, melodrama, and barbecues.

OTHER INFORMATION

Area Code: *805*
Zip Code: *93428*

Cambria Chamber of Commerce

in west village at 767 Main St. - CA 1 — *927-3624*

Los Padres Natinal Forest - Pacific Valley Station

on CA 1 — *927-4211*

Carmel

Carmel is one of the world's loveliest collaborations between man and nature. On the southern side of the Monterey Peninsula, it is a unique seaside village of intense natural beauty above a slope of fine, white sand that extends into the surf of Carmel Bay. Homes and shops are carefully sited in a forest of pines and rare Monterey cypress. Gnarled branches of these picturesque trees frame views of the fabled Big Sur coastline. The mild climate is almost as remarkable as the setting. Snow and frost are rare, so lush vegetation and outdoor activities are enjoyed year-round. The verdant, flowery landscapes of spring and the warm days of summer and fall are especially appealing. During these seasons, capacity crowds enjoy strolling and shopping downtown and share a wealth of outdoor recreation. Beachcombing, sunbathing, bicycling, tennis, and some of the world's most famous golf courses are popular in town and nearby, along with sailing, surfing, and fishing off the scenic shore, and hiking, horseback riding, and camping in the majestic coastal wilderness to the south.

Father Junipero Serra built a mission on a site overlooking the mouth of the Carmel River in 1770. However, it wasn't until after the turn of this century that artists and writers began to build homes among the pines. They were attracted by the captivating location and the potential for a simple lifestyle. The sensitivity of these artists and dreamers fostered the charm that is still being nurtured.

Fairy tale cottages and fanciful houses and shops are one highly visible part of the legacy. Another part is the residents' continuing determination to retain the beauty and serenity of this place in spite of its overwhelming popularity. As a result of their efforts, the village still does **not** have: traffic lights, parking meters, neon signs, billboards, street lights outside the business district, buildings more than three stories high, or home mail delivery. It **does** have a compact downtown with an astonishing proliferation of fascinating places to stroll, shop, eat, drink, and sleep. Today, in an area smaller than one square mile, more than seventy distinctive galleries display everything from local to international arts and crafts at prices ranging from modest to mind-boggling. A wonderful assortment of uncommon specialty shops compete for the stroller's attention. The same area has the West's greatest concentration of gourmet restaurants featuring notable examples of most of the cuisines of the world. Here also, a profusion of architecturally unique buildings provide romantic lodgings. Carmel's artistic style has even favorably influenced recently-constructed nearby shopping centers, restaurants, and lodgings, which are among the most distinctive anywhere.

Elevation:

200 feet

Population (1980):

4,707

Population (1970):

4,525

Location:

132 miles Southeast of San Francisco

WEATHER PROFILE

Vokac Weather Rating

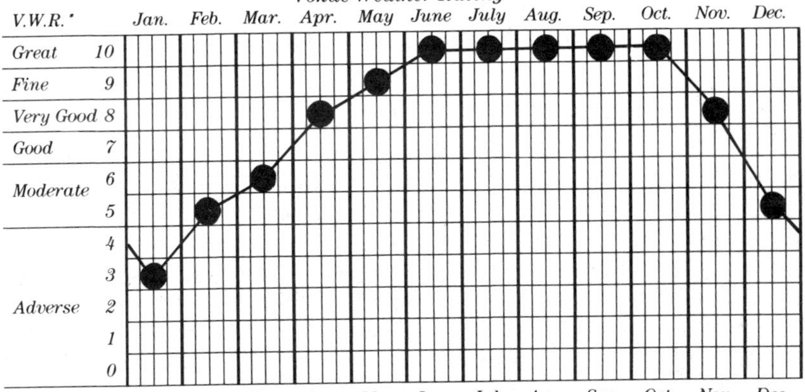

V.W.R.*	Jan.	Feb.	Mar.	Apr.	May	June	July	Aug.	Sep.	Oct.	Nov.	Dec.
Great 10												
Fine 9												
Very Good 8												
Good 7												
Moderate 6												
5												
4												
3												
Adverse 2												
1												
0												

	Jan.	Feb.	Mar.	Apr.	May	June	July	Aug.	Sep.	Oct.	Nov.	Dec.
*V.W.R.**	3	5	6	8	9	10	10	10	10	10	8	5
Temperature												
Ave. High	60	62	63	64	66	67	67	69	72	71	67	63
Ave. Low	41	42	44	45	47	49	51	52	52	50	46	43
Precipitation												
Inches Rain	4.5	3.1	2.5	1.5	0.5	0.2	-	-	0.3	0.5	1.8	3.2
Inches Snow	-	-	-	-	-	-	-	-	-	-	-	-

**V.W.R. = Vokac Weather Rating: probability of mild (warm & dry) weather on any given day.*

Forecast

Month	*V.W.R.**		*Temperatures* *Daytime*	*Evening*	*Precipitation*
Jan.	3	Adverse	cool	cool	frequent rainstorms
Feb.	5	Moderate	cool	cool	occasional rainstorms
Mar.	6	Moderate	cool	cool	occasional rainstorms
Apr.	8	Very Good	cool	cool	infrequent rainstorms
May	9	Fine	warm	cool	infrequent showers
June	10	Great	warm	cool	negligible
July	10	Great	warm	cool	none
Aug.	10	Great	warm	cool	none
Sep.	10	Great	warm	cool	negligible
Oct.	10	Great	warm	cool	infrequent rainstorms
Nov.	8	Very Good	warm	cool	infrequent rainstorms
Dec.	5	Moderate	cool	cool	occasional rainstorms

Summary

Spectacularly located by the sea on the southern curve of the Monterey Peninsula, Carmel has one of the West's most desirable climates. Pleasant weather for most outdoor activities is the rule, except during **winter**. Then, days and evenings are cool, but seldom include a frost of any consequence. Occasional heavy rainstorms during this season contribute well over half of the average annual precipitation. **Spring** marks the beginning of many months of mild weather for enjoying outdoor activities in light sportswear. The appeal of warm days, cool evenings, and diminishing showers is offset somewhat by sea breezes and coastal fog common during this season, however. **Summer** features uniformly warm days and cool nights, and almost no rainfall. Coastal fog is common in this naturally air conditioned seaside playground at this most popular time of year. The year's finest weather normally occurs in **fall**, with less fog and daytime temperatures early in the season that are normally the year's highest. Splendid conditions continue until around Thanksgiving, when the rainy season begins again in earnest.

ATTRACTIONS & DIVERSIONS

★ ***Bicycling***

Carmel Cycle Sport

4 mi. SE at 7150 Carmel Valley Rd. in Valley Hills Ctr. *624-5107*

One of the world's finest bicycle rides—the Seventeen Mile Drive—winds through Pebble Beach from Carmel. Even though it is primarily an auto route, bicyclists are allowed to use it (except after 11 a.m. on Sat. & Sun.) and are not required to pay the non-resident toll. This place rents bicycles by the hour and has information on local routes. Closed Sun.-Mon.

★ **Big Sur Coast**

S for approximately 80 mi. on CA 1

California Highway 1 is a narrow, paved two-lane road that winds and dips along the flanks of a mountain wilderness rising precipitously from an unspoiled shoreline. It is one of the world's most exhilarating scenic drives. Numerous hiking trails lead from roadside parking areas into groves of the southernmost coast redwoods and fern-shaded canyons, and to remote sandy beaches and coves. Well-located state parks along the route offer memorable camping and picnicking opportunities. Unique galleries, restaurants, and lodgings blend harmoniously into the unforgettable countryside.

★ **Carmel Beach Park**

.3 mi. W at the foot of Ocean Av.

Between the business district and the ocean at Carmel Bay is a town park featuring a pine-studded slope of fine, dazzlingly white sand. The picturesque beach backed by this splendid sand dune is a wonderful place for strolling, picnicking, and sunbathing. Ocean swimming is unpopular because of the undertow and cold water.

Carmel Mini-park

downtown on Dolores St. between Ocean & 7th Avs.

To get a better idea of how proud residents are of even the smallest public open space, stroll the meandering path and pause at a bench to consider the detailed landscaping in Carmel's tiniest park.

★ **Carmel Mission**

1 mi. S off CA 1 at 3080 Rio Rd. *624-3600*

Mission San Carlos Borromeo del Rio Carmelo is one of the most authentic links to early California history. Established on a site overlooking the mouth of the Carmel River in 1770 by Father Junipero Serra ("father of the California missions"), it was his residence and headquarters until his death in 1784. He is buried beneath the church floor in front of the altar. The carefully restored mission's museum has a notable collection of his memorabilia and other early relics.

★ **Carmel River State Beach**

1 mi. S on Scenic Rd.

A photogenic ocean beach composed of fine, sparkling white sand is an inviting attraction for beachcombers, picnickers, and sunbathers.

Swimming is regarded as unsafe because of currents, but most bathers would find the water too cold anyway.

Carmel Town Park

downtown at Ocean/Junipero Avs.

Manicured lawns with meandering paths and thoughtfully positioned benches, flower beds and flowering shrubs, plus noble shade trees, make this luxuriant little park a popular place to relax in the heart of town.

Golf

★ **Pebble Beach Golf Links**

2 mi. NW on Seventeen Mile Dr. *624-3811*

The home course of a renowned pro-am tournament is ranked as one of the ten best 18-hole championship golf courses in the nation. It is also one of the most picturesque anywhere. With reservations, it is open to the public with all facilities and rentals.

★ **Rancho Canada Golf Course**

2 mi. SE on Carmel Valley Rd. *624-0111*

Two scenic 18-hole championship golf courses are open to the public year-round with all facilities and rentals.

★ **Spyglass Hill Golf Course**

3 mi. NW on Stevenson Dr. *624-3811*

This Robert Trent Jones-designed championship 18-hole golf course in Pebble Beach is ranked among the nation's top forty. The spectacularly beautiful facility is open to the public with reservations. All facilities and rentals are available.

★ ***Horseback Riding***

Horses can be rented by the hour or longer for scenic rides in Pebble Beach or the Big Sur. For more information and reservations, contact:

Big Sur Trail Rides *667-2666*

Pebble Beach Equestrian Center *624-2756*

★ ***Library***

downtown at Ocean Av. & Lincoln St. *624-4629*

Behind a tiny garden park on the main street is the Harrison Memorial Library, an outstanding small public library. High arched windows on one side of a large main room allow sunlight to fill the vaulted space, and provide a charming view of colorful gardens. A great stone fireplace is used during winter, and upholstered chairs in the periodical reading area are very popular.

★ **Point Lobos State Reserve**

4 mi. S off CA 1 *624-4909*

Here is one of the most beautiful spots on the Pacific coast. The reserve includes six miles of rugged picturesque coastline. There are rocky headlands, Sea Lion Rocks, a natural grove of Monterey cypress, and Bird Island is just offshore. Unfortunately, poison oak is also naturally abundant, so hikers should be wary while using scenic shoreline trails. Whale watching is also popular from the headlands when the awesome animals pass by here close to shore on their annual 12,000 mile migration to Baja California each winter. Other attractions include a choice of shady or sunny picnic sites, tidepools teeming with marine life, secluded sandy beach coves, and shoreline fishing spots.

★ **Scenic Road**

S for approximately 2 mi. from foot of Ocean Av.

Whether walking, bicycling, or driving, this aptly named street delights everyone who uses it. Through green tunnels created by overhanging branches of majestic pines, past tiny rockbound coves and white sand beaches, unusual residences and colorful flower gardens, the route follows the shoreline to a panoramic viewpoint overlooking the mouth of Carmel River and the Big Sur beyond.

★ **Seventeen Mile Drive**

starts .5 mi. N via San Antonio Av.

One of the world's great scenic drives meanders through Pebble Beach and along the magnificent coastline between Carmel and Pacific Grove. It is a toll road except to bicyclists and residents. In addition to unforgettable seascapes, highlights include stately homes, legendary golf courses, and the Lodge at Pebble Beach. Gnarled trees clinging to rocky headlands at The Lone Cypress are among the West's most photographed landmarks.

Warm Water Feature

Blackthorne Spas

11 mi. SE off Carmel Valley Rd. at 4 Pilot Rd. *659-3241*

Several nicely landscaped hot tub enclosures, featuring open air privacy, redwood decks, hydrotherapy jets, soft music, and showers are rented by the hour every day until midnight.

Winery

★ **Chateau Julien**

6 mi. E at 8940 Carmel Valley Rd. *624-2600*

One of the central coast's newest wineries is concentrating on the production of several premium wines, primarily from grapes grown elsewhere in the central coast region. Impressive craftsmanship is apparent in the handsome new chateau-style winery building. Visitors may sample various wines daily. Tasting and sales 8-5 weekdays, noon-4 Sat. & Sun.

SHOPPING

The enormously popular downtown area of Carmel is unique. No other place has so many distinctive specialty shops, galleries, and restaurants in so little space with as little conventional commercialism. By banning tall or massive buildings, parking structures and meters, bright lights and billboards, emphasis has been successfully focused on artistic landscaping and personalized architectural details. As a result, an enchanting human scale has evolved that still somehow accommodates ever-increasing hordes of shoppers and strollers.

Food Specialties

Bagel Bakery
1.5 mi. SE at 173 Crossroads Blvd. *625-5180*
An assortment of New York-style bagels is served to take out, or in a small cafe with coffee, egg dishes, and other light fare.

★ **Carmel Bakery**
downtown on Ocean Av. near Lincoln St. *624-6265*
It's fun just to look at the whimsical creations made of edible bakery products, and to taste samples that are usually provided. But the real feature is a fine assortment of international pastries (like scones and croissants), breads, and cakes. They may be purchased to enjoy with coffee at one of the few tables, or to go.

Carmel Vintage Shoppe
downtown on Dolores St. between Ocean & 7th Avs. *624-3895*
Premium California wines are well-represented and attractively displayed in this shop. Many are discounted.

★ **The Carmel Wet Fish Market**
1.5 mi. SE at 100A Crossroads Blvd. *624-0931*
Picnickers will delight in the selection of smoked fish (especially salmon); jerky; and cooked shellfish with cocktail sauce to go. A superior selection of fresh fish is also displayed in the clean, bright showcases. Closed Sun.

★ **Carmel Wine & Cheese Co.**
1.5 mi. SE at 145 Crossroads Blvd. *624-2486*
A noteworthy selection of California wines is beautifully displayed, and selected wines can be sampled at the tasting bar. There are also many cheeses, pates, and other gourmet items like Lavash—an Armenian sandwich sold by the inch.

The Cheese Shop
downtown off Ocean Av. near Junipero Av. *625-2272*
A good selection of cheeses highlights the many gourmet foods and premium California wines featured in a downstairs shop in Carmel Plaza.

Fifth Avenue Deli
downtown on 5th Av. between San Carlos & Dolores Avs. *625-2688*
This tiny deli is jammed with an array of gourmet pates, luncheon meats, cheeses, wines, mustards, and other enticing provisions.

★ **La Patisserie Juliette**
1.5 mi. SE at 213 Crossroads Blvd. *625-9390*
Artistic renditions of authentic French pastries (like galettes) are made with all natural ingredients in a neat new carryout bakery. It's tucked away in a pedestrian cul-de-sac in Crossroads Center, but well worth finding.

★ **Linda's Cookie Basket**
1.5 mi. SE in The Barnyard *625-6175*
Buttermilk, banana nut, and raspberry are among the delicious and

unusual muffin flavors offered, along with similarly tasty cookies, in this small carryout shop. Samples are always available. Closed Mon.

★ **Mediterranean Market**
downtown at Ocean Av. & Mission St. *624-2022*
Tantalizing arrays of imported and domestic food delicacies provide a treat for all of the senses in one of Carmel's largest and most venerable sources of gourmet provisions. Highlights include first-rate cheeses, sausages, breads, and a good selection of wines.

Monterey Baking Co.
1.5 mi. SE at 107 Crossroads Blvd. *624-0929*
Croissants and other European pastries are featured along with sourdough and French breads here and at a downtown (on Ocean Av.) outlet of a burgeoning bakery chain.

★ **Mrs. M's Fudge**
downtown at 6th Av. & Mission St. *624-5331*
Fudges in all kinds of delicious flavors are made on the premises and displayed in a classic example of what a fudge factory should look like.

★ **Nielsen Brothers Market**
downtown at San Carlos St. & 7th Av. *624-6441*
Top quality produce and a full line of gourmet foods are showcased in downtown Carmel's largest epicurean haven. A fine selection of premium California wine is also showcased, and tastes of several are sold at the wine bar each day.

Sylvia's Danish Pastry Shop
1.5 mi. SE at 3650 The Barnyard *624-1198*
Good-looking Danish and French pastries are served in a casual little European-style tea room with coffee, or to go.

Specialty Shops

★ **The Barnyard**
1.5 mi. SE off CA 1 & Carmel Valley Rd. *624-8886*
Here is a premier example of the state of the art in recreational shopping. Profusions of flowers, music, and intriguing fountains and sculptures lend enchantment to a cluster of Western barn-style buildings housing more than sixty fine specialty shops, galleries, and restaurants.

★ **Books, Inc.**
downtown on Ocean Av. near Mission St. *625-2550*
One of the largest bookstores on the peninsula displays a full line of hard-covers and paperbacks in a bright, well-organized environment downstairs in Carmel Plaza.

★ **Carmel Art Association Gallery**
downtown on Dolores St. between 5th & 6th Avs. *624-6176*
One of Carmel's most esteemed art complexes is set apart by a beautifully landscaped garden setting. Eight galleries exhibit paintings, graphic art, and sculpture by association members, some of whom are renowned.

★ **Carmel Plaza**
downtown at Ocean Av. & Mission St.
A compact two-level complex in the heart of downtown offers a good assortment of specialty shops and restaurants built around a handsomely landscaped interior courtyard.

★ **Coast Gallery**
35 mi. S on CA 1 - Big Sur *667-2301*
The Big Sur's most outstanding gallery is the source of some extraordinary regional arts and crafts. The woodcrafted display cases are themselves museum-quality works of art. New Age music provides an appropriate backdrop for experiencing this one-of-a-kind circular landmark, and the adjoining sculpture garden and candle shop. Even the outdoor toilets are unique statements in neo-hot tub architecture and decor.

★ **Crossroads**
1.5 mi. SE off CA 1 & Rio Rd. *625-4106*
Carmel's newest major shopping complex is a colorful mosaic of contemporary California architecture and landscaping. A prominent Westminster chiming clock/bell tower is the centerpiece for what has become an array of more than one hundred distinctive specialty shops and restaurants.

★ **Highlands Gallery of Sculpture**
3 mi. S on CA 1 just after Fern Canyon Rd. *624-0535*
This captivating little gallery is devoted entirely to sculpture by more than a dozen well-known sculptors. Large pieces in wood, stone, and metal are displayed to maximum advantage in an adjacent oak-shaded garden.

How To Do Anything Bookstore
downtown at Ocean Av. & Monte Verde St. *624-5756*
This tiny, tucked-away shop lives up to its name with an impressive selection of literature to help you do-it-yourself, whether in the pursuit of work or leisure activities.

★ **Thunderbird Bookshop**
1.5 mi. SE at 3600 The Barnyard *624-1803*
One of the West's most remarkable bookstores has a large and excellent book selection. Shelves also line one wall in a comfortably furnished adjacent dining room, where patrons are free to eat, drink, browse, and read.

★ **Other galleries**
throughout downtown
Carmel is (as it has been for decades) home to a number of internationally renowned artisans. They are represented, along with many others, by about seventy galleries offering an awesome assortment of works in all media. Most are concentrated within two blocks of Ocean Avenue between Mission and Monte Verde Streets. A complete list and map is available from the Chamber of Commerce.

NIGHTLIFE

Carmel has a choice of intimate, romantic places to enjoy a quiet drink; spirited pubs with lively crowds; or dancing to live music nearby. Movies, live theater, and concerts also contribute to life after dark throughout the year.

★ **Forest Theater**
downtown at Mt. View Av. & Santa Rita St. *624-1531*
Carmel's oldest theater has been in existence for more than seventy years. It is still the setting for theater classics and occasional new plays on Thursday thru Sunday evenings. The natural outdoor locale has a special magic enhanced by two big outdoor firepits.

★ **Forge in the Forest**
downtown at 5th Av. & Junipero Av. *624-2233*
One of Carmel's most unusual watering holes has an ornate wooden bar and intriguing copper walls that gleam in the light of the room's fireplace. A tasty pub menu is served here and on an intimate fireplace-warmed patio.

★ **Highlands Inn**
4 mi. S on CA 1 *624-3801*
The resort's incomparable new cocktail lounge has a window-wall with an awe-inspiring seacoast panorama. A grand piano is beautifully played nightly by Jonathan Lee for patrons comfortably ensconced in glove-leather armchairs.

★ **Hog's Breath Inn**
downtown off San Carlos St. between 5th & 6th Avs. *625-1044*
In Clint Eastwood's famed dining and drinking establishment, the tiny bar smells seductively like a wine cellar. Drinks are also served with hors d'oeuvres in the flickering firelight of a romantic courtyard backed by an artistic wall-sized mural of a Carmel scene.

★ **It's Bud's Pub**
downtown off Lincoln St. between 5th & 6th Avs. *625-6765*
Tucked away in the Su Vecino Court is a deservedly-popular new Carmel-style pub. A gas fireplace and an old-fashioned popcorn wagon accent a handsome woodcrafted pub room outfitted with plush armchairs and a bar with padded/backed stools. Bud and Bass beers are on tap, along with a changing list of wines-by-the-glass. The pub grub in the next room is fine.

★ **The Lodge at Pebble Beach**
2 mi. NW off Seventeen Mile Dr. *624-3811*
In the plush Terrace Lounge, dancing to live music is featured on weekends.

Maxwell McFly's
downtown on Ocean Av. between San Carlos & Dolores Sts. *624-2515*
An attractive back bar, stained glass, and antique fans come together nicely in this popular watering hole.

The Other Place
1.5 mi. SE at 3770 The Barnyard — *625-0340*
Above Andre's, both the Other Place and Sundeck Garden Bar feature adult ice cream drinks and fresh fruit cocktails in a contemporary plants-and-wood setting. Furnishings include free-form redwood tables and benches and padded bar stools. Light meals are served all day, and the view of gardens and Big Sur mountains is special.

Sade's
downtown on Ocean Av. bet. Lincoln & Monte Verde Sts. — *624-9990*
The oldest bar in Carmel offers cozy atmosphere including a corner kiva-style fireplace and padded armchairs with an unusual outlook on the main street.

Studio Theatre Restaurant
downtown on Dolores St. between Ocean & 7th Avs. — *624-1661*
A choice of two entrees accompanies the live show featured Thursday thru Sunday evenings in the peninsula's only dinner theater.

Sunset Center Theater
downtown at San Carlos St. & 9th Av. — *624-3996*
Carmel's charming old cultural center includes a theater that features plays, films, concerts, and lectures at different times year-round.

RESTAURANTS

Fine dining, the most ephemeral of all artistic achievements, is an enduring passion in Carmel. Residents and visitors alike zealously seek out new "finds," and relish returning to old favorites among a mind-boggling array of urbane alternatives. The village probably has the most remarkable concentration of notable restaurants in the West.

Adobe Inn
downtown at Dolores St. & 8th Av. — *625-1750*
L-D. — *Moderate*
The specialty is prime rib cut to order. A salad bar, steak, and seafood are also offered. Comfortable decor is enhanced by intimate views of oak trees and cypress just beyond a window-wall. "Early Bird" dinners are very popular, as is Bully III, a cozy pub in the adjoining room featuring well-prepared short order items.

★ **Andre's**
1.5 mi. SE at 3770 The Barnyard — *625-0447*
L-D. — *Expensive*
Fresh fish and wild game are among Continental specialties served amidst luxuriant plants and elegant Old World stained glass, chandeliers, and hardwoods. One dining room features well-appointed enclosed booths, perfect for a romantic evening.

★ **Anton & Michel**
downtown on Mission St. between Ocean & 7th Avs. — *624-2406*
L-D. Sun. brunch. — *Expensive*
Gourmet cuisine carefully prepared by Swiss chefs is complemented by

a dignified Old World setting overlooking the Court of the Fountains. There is also a pleasant lounge with a fireplace.

Carmel Cafe
downtown at Mission St. & 6th Av. *624-1922*
B-L. *Moderate*
Country breakfasts, omelets, and other light fare, plus homemade desserts, are served in this small American-style cafe.

★ **Casanova**
downtown on 5th Av. between San Carlos & Mission Sts. *625-0501*
B-L-D. *Expensive*
Country-fresh French and Italian cuisine is served amidst casual elegance in several tiny rooms or on the enclosed garden patio. The homemade pasta, baked goods, and desserts are especially notable.

★ **Chez Daniele**
downtown off San Carlos St. near 7th Av. *625-1151*
B-L-D. *Moderate*
Hidden away in a courtyard is a place well worth finding for omelets, crepes, and specialty dishes like "The Cloud" which are outstanding. The tiny restaurant is thoroughly contemporary, with courtyard views and bunches of flowers for accents.

★ **Chez Felix**
downtown on Monte Verde St. between Ocean & 7th Avs. *624-4707*
D only. Closed Sun. *Expensive*
Traditional French cuisine is skillfully prepared from ingredients selected fresh each morning and served amidst intimate French Provincial decor in a long-established little restaurant.

Chutney's Gourmet Cafe
1.5 mi. SE at 230 Crossroads Blvd. *624-4785*
L-D. No D on Sun. *Moderate*
An emphasis on quality ingredients and freshness has gotten this new cafe off to a good start. Distinctive chutneys and desserts are made here to accompany a long list of innovative international specialties. The casually furnished dining area overlooks a partially open kitchen and cases full of good-looking deli items.

★ **Clam Box**
downtown on Mission St. between 5th & 6th Avs. *624-8597*
D only. Closed Mon. *Moderate*
The seafood served here is regarded as some of the best on the entire peninsula. Everything is carefully prepared and is as good as it looks and smells in this extremely popular little place.

Collage
downtown on 6th Av. between Mission & San Carlos Sts. *625-9990*
L-D. *Moderate*
In this new restaurant, the staff struggles with a too-ambitious range of international dishes, treated in the style of New American cuisine. The multilevel dining areas reflect the latest in casual high-tech 1980s decor.

★ **Creme Carmel**
downtown at San Carlos St. & 7th Av. *624-0444*
D only. Closed Sun. *Expensive*
On a short menu that changes frequently, the New California-style dishes are always fresh, innovative, and delicious, as are the unusual homemade desserts. Decor is refreshingly understated in the tucked-away little dining room of one of Carmel's finest young restaurants.

Crossroads Cafe
1.5 mi. SE at 211 Crossroads Blvd. *625-3165*
B-L. *Moderate*
Hearty all-American fare and comfortable, casual decor set the tone in this cheerful little coffee shop.

Em Le's Restaurant
downtown on Dolores St. near 5th Av. *625-6780*
B-L. *Moderate*
The nutty waffles served here are reason enough to stop in for breakfast. Homemade pies are the other specialty among conventional American fare. The cozy, plant-filled coffee shop is warmed by a corner brick fireplace in winter.

The Fabulous Toots Lagoon
downtown on Dolores St. between Ocean & 7th Avs. *625-1915*
B-L-D. *Moderate*
You might suspect that any place that toots its own horn by self-proclaiming that it is "fabulous" probably isn't. You'd be right. Unfortunately, breakfasts (which can be good) are only served in the humble front room. The classier back room is used exclusively for dinner, which can be disappointing.

Fish House on the Park
downtown at 6th & Junipero Avs. *625-1766*
D only. *Expensive*
Conventional seafood and some Continental dishes are served in Carmel's quietest and priciest fish house.

★ **Flaherty's**
downtown on 6th Av. between Dolores & San Carlos Sts. *624-0311*
L-D. *Expensive*
Skillfully prepared fresh seafood is the crowd-pleaser in a popular little restaurant where the lively, congested atmosphere resembles a modern Eastern-style seafood house.

★ **French Poodle**
downtown at Junipero & 5th Avs. *624-8643*
D only. Closed Sun. & Wed. *Expensive*
Classic French cuisine including homemade pastries is formally presented in an intimate, romantic setting. Jackets are required.

Friar Tuck's Restaurant
downtown at Dolores St. & 5th Av. *624-4274*
B-L. *Moderate*
Assorted omelets and waffles are breakfast offerings in a simply

furnished cafe presided over by an enigmatic replica of the friar himself.

From Scratch
1.5 mi. SE at 3626 The Barnyard *625-2448*
B-L. *Moderate*
Fresh, tasty dishes live up to the restaurant's name. The pleasant country-style dining room is enhanced by a large working fireplace. A landscaped dining patio adjoins.

★ **General Store**
downtown at 5th & Junipero Avs. *624-2233*
L-D. Sat. & Sun. brunch. *Moderate*
New California cuisine is served in an intimate dining room with closely spaced tables set with full linen and decorous furnishings. An artistically landscaped dining patio with a fireplace links the restaurant with a super lounge.

★ **Giuliano's**
downtown on Mission St. between 5th & 6th Avs. *625-5231*
L-D. No L on Sun. & Mon. *Expensive*
Northern Italian cuisine is treated seriously here. Mirrored walls, floral displays, and tables set with full linen backed by plush, closely spaced banquettes lend casual elegance to a pink-and-pretty little dining room.

★ **Glen Oaks**
26 mi. S on CA 1 - Big Sur *667-2623*
D only. Sun. brunch. Closed Mon. *Expensive*
Innovative Continental and American cuisine is skillfully prepared with a light touch, and served in a beautifully appointed firelit dining room in this acclaimed restaurant.

★ **The Gold Fork**
downtown on Ocean Av. between Dolores & Lincoln Sts. *624-2569*
D only. *Very Expensive*
Carmel's newest haven of haute cuisine has a wonderful way with Continental favorites. Fresh, quality ingredients are used to prepare classic dishes lightened up with an innovative yet disciplined approach to composition and sauces. In late 1985, a long-established restaurant was transformed into an elegant contemporary dining room that is a worthy showcase for a new culinary landmark.

★ **Highland's Inn**
4 mi. S on CA 1 *624-3801*
B-L-D. Sun. brunch. *Very Expensive*
Contemporary American dishes accompany what is arguably the world's finest seascape view from a public restaurant. The Pacific's Edge dining room is plush, comfortable, and big. Guests should request a window table when making reservations, especially for the celebrated Sunday brunch buffet. All of the new public rooms in this famous country motor inn are brilliant examples of the state of the art in contemporary architecture and decor.

★ **Hog's Breath Inn**
downtown off San Carlos St. between 5th & 6th Avs. *625-1044*
L-D. Sun. brunch. *Expensive*
Clint Eastwood's wood-and-stone one-of-a-kind restaurant offers good American food in intimate firelit dining rooms, or in an adjoining romantic courtyard warmed by fireplaces and heat lamps and overseen by a charming Carmel mural.

★ **It's Bud's Pub**
downtown off Lincoln St. between 5th & 6th Avs. *625-6765*
L-D. *Moderate*
English specialties like shepherd's pie, bangers and mash, and fish and chips highlight a full range of exceptional pub grub. The neo-Victorian poshness of the dining room, like the food and drink and the adjoining wood-toned pub, are unabashedly oriented to adult tastes.

★ **Jack London's Bar & Bistro**
downtown off San Carlos St. between 5th & 6th Avs. *624-2336*
L-D. *Moderate*
A popular rendezvous, this likably cluttered little bistro accompanies tap beers, wines by the glass, etc. with the most eclectic assortment of tasty dishes imaginable into the wee hours.

★ **Katy's Cottage**
downtown on Lincoln St. between Ocean & 7th Avs. *625-6260*
L only. *Expensive*
Deliciously updated Continental specialties are a perfect accompaniment to the charming Carmel cottage-style decor of this new restaurant.

★ **Katy's Place**
downtown on Mission St. between 5th & 6th Avs. *624-0199*
B-L-D. No D on Sat. & Sun. *Moderate*
This glorified coffee shop has a wonderful way with hearty American fare made from fresh local ingredients like Monterey Bay prawns and artichokes. Delicious omelets and other breakfast specialties are served all day.

★ **La Boheme**
downtown on Dolores St. near 7th Av. *624-7500*
D only. *Moderate*
One meal is served family-style nightly. The European country cooking involves careful preparation of the freshest available produce. Colorful, congested Old World atmosphere is a distinctive accompaniment to the delicious food.

★ **La Playa Hotel**
downtown at 8th Av. & Camino Real *624-6476*
B-L-D. Sun. brunch. *Expensive*
Continental cuisine with a disciplined light touch distinguishes the elegant new Spyglass Dining Room. Diners have an expansive picture window view of manicured grounds backed by Monterey pines and the ocean. A lovely dining terrace with the same view adjoins.

Le Bistro
downtown on San Carlos St. between Ocean & 7th Avs. *624-6545*
B-L-D. No D on Sun. *Low*
Light European specialties are emphasized, including egg crepe omelets and buttermilk waffles. A fireplace warms the casual wood-trimmed dining room in winter, and a tiny patio is popular on sunny days.

Le Coq d'Or
downtown on Mission St. between 4th & 5th Avs. *624-4613*
D only. Closed Sun. *Moderate*
A limited variety of French entrees and baked goods made on the premises are features of this casual, congested little restaurant.

★ **L'Escargot**
downtown on Mission St. between 4th & 5th Avs. *624-4914*
D only. Closed Sun. *Expensive*
Classic French gourmet cuisine is the highlight of a restaurant with a long-standing reputation for fashionable excellence. The dining room exudes the Gallic charm of a tastefully appointed French country cottage.

★ **The Lodge at Pebble Beach**
2 mi. NW via 17 Mile Dr. on Cypress Dr. *624-3811*
L-D. *Very Expensive*
The Cypress Room is the Lodge's original grand dining room, and formal elegance still accompanies an outstanding view of the famed golf course and Carmel Bay. Downstairs in the Club XIX, the atmosphere is casual for lunch, with terrace service available. In the evening, gourmet French dinners are presented in an opulent setting. Jackets are required for dinner.

★ **The Mandarin**
1.5 mi. SE at 133 Crossroads Blvd. *625-3367*
L-D. *Moderate*
China's regional cuisines are represented on a menu of more than one hundred dishes. Thanks to consistent, skilled preparation and quality ingredients, the young restaurant is off to a good start. The dining room is furnished with full linen table settings and minimal Oriental decorations.

★ **The Marquis**
downtown on San Carlos St. at 4th Av. *624-8068*
D only. Closed Sun. *Expensive*
Continental gourmet cuisine and homemade pastries are served in an elegant setting with some romantic touches like long white tapers in silver candle holders.

Mission Ranch Restaurant
1.5 mi. S at 26270 Dolores St. *624-3824*
D only. *Moderate*
Assorted simply-prepared American dishes are served in the long,

narrow dining room of a one-time dairy farm. Patrons have enjoyed food, drink, live entertainment, and views to Pt. Lobos from this complex for almost half a century.

★ **Nepenthe**
29 mi. S on CA 1 - Big Sur *667-2345*
L-D. *Moderate*
Simple American dishes are served in a restaurant that is so famous that the sophisticated traveler is likely to write it off as entirely for tourists. If they did, they'd miss one of the West's most inspiring settings. The handcrafted, wood-trimmed dining room/bar and adjoining terrace each has a free-standing fireplace and an unforgettable view of the Big Sur coast from a spectacular perch hundreds of feet above the water. Below, nearer the parking lot, the Cafe Amphora specializes in homemade desserts served on another view terrace. The Phoenix Shop in an adjoining building carries local arts and crafts, and an interesting assortment of books.

★ **Patisserie Boissiere**
downtown on Mission St. between Ocean & 7th Avs. *624-5008*
B-L-D. *Moderate*
An excellent selection of French baked goods is always displayed, and French specialties are served all day in this charming little restaurant with a fireplace, fresh flowers, and patio dining.

The Peppercorn
1.5 mi. SE in The Barnyard *625-1070*
B-L. *Moderate*
Breakfast omelets and an assortment of international specialties are served all day in a congested contemporary cafe with a fine picture window view of gardens in The Barnyard shopping complex. A high-tech kitchenware shop adjoins.

Pine Inn
downtown on Ocean Av. at Monte Verde St. *624-3851*
B-L-D. Sun. brunch. *Expensive*
Carmel's downtown landmark hotel offers American specialties in a large dining room furnished in posh Victorian decor or in an innovative contemporary courtyard covered by a spectacular glass dome. The inn also has a comfortable lounge.

Plaza Cafe
downtown on Ocean Av. bet. Junipero Av. & Mission St. *624-4433*
B-L-D. *Moderate*
Contemporary American and European dishes are given a light touch and complemented by Cloris' croissants. The attractively updated coffee shop with casual indoor and outdoor seating is accented by a large skylight.

★ **Quail Lodge**
4 mi. SE off Carmel Valley Rd. *624-1581*
D only. *Very Expensive*
Continental cuisine is served in the Covey, a newly refurbished showplace of contemporary elegance with beautifully appointed, well-spaced tables overlooking a lake and lush gardens of the renowned lodge. Jackets are required.

★ **Raffaello Carmel Restaurant**
downtown on Mission St. between Ocean & 7th Av. *624-1541*
D only. Closed Tues. *Expensive*
Acclaimed Northern Italian haute cuisine is the forte, along with notable homemade desserts. The fireplace-and-candlelight atmosphere is formally elegant, and jackets are required in one of Carmel's favorite and most prestigious restaurants.

River Inn
25 mi. S on CA 1 - Big Sur *667-2237*
B-L-D. D on Fri. & Sat. only in winter. *Moderate*
Hickory-smoked meats and homemade baked goods are featured on an all-American menu offered in a rustic-wood dining room with an enormous stone fireplace, an oversized chess set in the bar area, and a fine view of Big Sur Creek. Tables made out of solid pieces of polished redwood are adorned with local wildflowers. An inviting umbrella-shaded patio is used when weather permits.

★ **The Rio Grill**
1.5 mi. SE at 101 Crossroads Blvd. *625-5436*
L-D. *Moderate*
Exquisitely prepared New California cuisine attracts enthusiastic crowds to the paragon of Post-Modern dining. Changing specials highlight seasonally fresh ingredients in innovative ways. An abundance of crisp white linens and casually elegant table settings blend smoothly with pastel-colored walls accented by bold floral pictures. Premium wines can be purchased by the glass in the dining rooms and in the popular lounge.

★ **Robata Grill and Sake Bar**
1.5 mi. SE at 3658 The Barnyard *624-2643*
D only. *Moderate*
All kinds of modern Japanese dishes are prepared in a lively exhibition kitchen rimmed by a massive polished redwood counter that serves as a sushi bar. The costumed staff waits on diners in small rooms and alcoves comfortably furnished with padded booths and redwood tables. The adjoining firelit lounge and landscaped courtyard with a firepit are also popular.

Rocky Point
11 mi. S off CA 1 *624-2933*
L-D. *Very Expensive*
Oakwood-broiled steaks are the pricey specialty in a casual dining room

that, for a third of a century, has provided an expansive view of the Big Sur coast.

Royal Danish Bakery
downtown on San Carlos St. between 7th & 8th Avs. *624-3667*
B-L. *Moderate*
Light meals and Scandinavian pastry can be enjoyed in a little coffee shop or on a charming landscaped patio above the street.

St. Tropez
downtown on Junipero Av. between 5th & 6th Avs. *624-9018*
D only. Closed Tues. *Moderate*
Conventional French dishes and showy homemade desserts are served in congested little dining rooms.

★ **Sans Souci**
downtown on Lincoln St. between 5th & 6th Avs. *624-6220*
D only. Closed Wed. *Expensive*
Gourmet French cuisine is served amid comfortably elegant decor accented by a wood-burning fireplace, classical music, and well-spaced tables set with tall white candles and fresh flowers.

Shabu Shabu
downtown on Mission St. near Ocean Av. in Carmel Plaza *625-2828*
L-D. No L on Sun. *Expensive*
A limited selection of traditional Japanese dishes includes some prepared at the table. This small, simply furnished cellar restaurant is subdivided into semi-private booths with a choice of traditional or low padded seating.

Swiss Tavern Restaurant
downtown on Lincoln St. between 5th & 6th Avs. *624-5994*
D only. Closed Mon. *Moderate*
Traditional Swiss dishes are offered amidst European decor in a modest little upstairs dining room.

The Thunderbird
1.5 mi. SE at 3600 The Barnyard *624-1803*
L-D. No D on Mon. *Moderate*
A short list of tasty American dishes is served in a comfortably furnished dining room with a central fireplace; picture window views of an adjoining dining patio; gardens and mountains; and a wall of books to browse.

★ **Tuck Box Tea Room**
downtown on Dolores St. between Ocean & 7th Avs. *624-6365*
B-L-tea. Closed Mon.-Tues. *Moderate*
Everything served on the limited menu (scones, rhubarb in season, etc.) is fresh and homemade. The thatched cottage motif of this tiny English tea room is as picturesque as the food is good. There is almost always a waiting line, even when the quaint little courtyard is used.

★ **Ventana Inn**
28 mi. S off CA 1 - Big Sur *667-2331*
L-D. *Very Expensive*
Updated American dishes are served in a handsome contemporary dining room with a large wood-burning fireplace. The main attraction, however, is an expansive patio where meals and drinks are served, weather permitting, with an unforgettable view of the Big Sur coast.

Village Corner
downtown at Dolores St. & 6th Av. *624-3588*
B-L. *Moderate*
Greek specialties are featured in a casual coffee shop that is a locals' hangout. Patio dining is also available.

★ **Wagon Wheel**
4 mi. SE on Carmel Valley Rd. *624-8878*
B-L. *Moderate*
Generous portions, freshness, and quality are hallmarks in a rustic little Old West-style coffee shop that is one of the peninsula's most sought breakfast spots.

★ **Willow Tea Room**
1.5 mi. SE at 231 Crossroads Blvd. *625-6004*
L-tea. *Expensive*
The light meals and presentation teas are excellent, and the dining room is beautifully appointed. Even though meal schedules and serving areas are still in a state of flux, this new upstairs restaurant is well worth a visit.

Will's Fargo
12 mi. SE on Carmel Valley Rd. *659-2774*
D only. Closed Mon. *Expensive*
Steaks have been the specialty here for a quarter of a century. Customers must still troop into an exhibition butcher shop, specify their preference, and watch while the meat is cut before being seated in a large casual dining room overlooking a garden.

LODGING

The wonderful little inns of Carmel capture the romantic spirit for which the village is renowned. Most of these beguiling havens are within an easy stroll of both the heart of town and the beach. Even the larger motel-style accommodations are distinctively decorated, prettily landscaped, and oriented toward seascapes or town views. Rooms in town are all relatively expensive and inevitably full on weekends and throughout summer. Reservations at these times are appropriate. While there are no bargain rooms, off-season non-weekend rates are often reduced at least 20% below those shown.

★ **Adobe Inn**
downtown at Dolores St. & 8th Av. (Box 4115) *624-3933*
This newer contemporary motor inn features a small pool and sauna,

and has a covered garage, a restaurant, and lounge. Each spacious, lavishly furnished room has a wood-burning fireplace, a bar with refrigerator, cable color TV, phone, and private patio or deck nestled among oaks and pines. A complimentary Continental breakfast is offered.

#29,#30,#37—fine ocean views, K bed...$115
regular room— K bed...$110

Candle Light Inn
downtown on San Carlos St. bet. 4th & 5th Avs. (Box 1900) 624-6451
The grounds are nicely landscaped and there is a small pool in this attractive motel. Each newly redecorated room has a phone, cable color TV, and a refrigerator.

deluxe unit—fireplace, kitchen, K bed...$100
regular room— D or K bed...$77

Carmel River Inn
1.5 mi. SE on CA 1 (Box 221609; zip: 93922) 624-1575
The small Carmel River is adjacent to this modern motel, and there is an outdoor pool. Each room has a phone and cable color TV.

"riverside rooms"—2nd (top) floor, view deck above river, K bed...$44
regular room—cottage, Q bed...$38

Carmel Sands Lodge
downtown at San Carlos St. & 5th Av. (Box 951) 624-1255
This contemporary motel has an outdoor pool. All rooms have cable color TV and a phone.

#20—fireplace, balcony above street, some ocean view, K bed...$75
#21—fireplace, balcony above street, four-poster Q bed...$70
regular room— D bed...$48

★ **Carriage House Inn**
downtown on Junipero Av. bet. 7th & 8th Avs. (Box 101) 625-2585
Early American furnishings, handmade quilts, original oil paintings, brass beds, and bay windows are some of the embellishments in this newer, elegant little motor inn. All of the beautifully furnished rooms have wood-burning fireplaces, sunken tiled baths, refrigerators, cable color TV with movies, and phones. A complimentary Continental breakfast is brought to the room, along with the morning paper.

#8—corner, many large windows with pvt. oak view, K bed...$115
#3—unusually spacious, spectacularly furnished, K bed...$140
regular room—small, Q bed...$90

The Cobblestone Inn
downtown at Junipero & 8th Avs. (Box 3185) 625-5222
The courtyard in this newer bed-and-breakfast inn is nearly surrounded by more than two dozen rooms, each outfitted with a private bath, gas fireplace, cable color TV, and a phone. A complimentary Continental breakfast is offered in the dining room, along with appetizers and

beverages in the afternoon. For toll-free reservations, call: (800)222-4667.

deluxe room—spacious, wet bar/refrigerator, K bed...$130
regular room— Q bed...$100

Colonial Terrace Inn

.7 mi. SW on San Antonio Av. at 13th Av. (Box 1375) 624-2741

Located in a quiet residential area near the beach is a motel comprised of several older buildings on garden terraces. Each unit has a cable color TV and a phone.

#28—spacious, gas fireplace, some ocean view, Q bed...$95
#24A—small, corner gas fireplace, Q bed...$55
regular room— Q bed...$40

Cypress Inn

downtown at Lincoln St. & 7th Av. (Box Y) 624-3871

Built around a delightful courtyard, this large older inn exudes Mediterranean charm. All rooms have color TV and phones, and a complimentary Continental breakfast is offered.

"Tower"—tiny room, shared bath, 270° view over downtown, D bed...$32
#219—corner suite with big windows, pvt. tub/shower, K bed...$100
regular room—private bath, Q bed...$60

★ **The Dolphin Inn**

downtown at San Carlos St. & 4th Av. (Box 1900) 624-5356

A large outdoor pool is a major feature of this tastefully furnished motor inn. Each spacious room has a wood-burning fireplace, a phone, and cable color TV with movies. A complimentary Continental breakfast and the morning paper are delivered to your door.

#18—fine view, K bed...$93
regular room— 2 D or K bed...$78

Forest Lodge

downtown at Ocean Av. & Torres St. (Box 1316) 624-7023

A tiny motor lodge in a choice location features three units in three buildings. Each has a bath, phone, cable color TV, and refrigerator.

"Guest House"—spacious, big fireplace, view window/alcove, Q bed...$120
"Garret"—upstairs, windows on 3 sides, village/ocean view, 2 D beds...$90
regular room "Cottage"—1 BR, kitchenette, Q bed...$90

Green Lantern Inn

downtown at Casanova St. & 7th Av. (Box 1114) 624-4392

The beach is a short stroll from this older bed-and-breakfast cottage complex in a garden setting. Each well-maintained, attractively furnished room has a private bath and cable color TV.

"Magnolia"—large end unit, fireplace, pine view, K bed...$90
"Evergreen"—end unit, fireplace, ocean view, Q bed...$75
regular room— D bed...$55

★ **Highlands Inn**
4 mi. S on CA 1 (Box 1700) *624-3801*
One of the world's most magnificent coastal panoramas is the highlight of this large, wonderfully updated resort hotel high above the Big Sur coast. Public rooms in the main building—lobby, restaurant, lounge salon—are outstanding examples of opulent contemporary decor beautifully blended with an awesome setting. Landscaped grounds include a large outdoor pool, and three whirlpools with tranquil forest and ocean views. Each spacious, luxuriously furnished new unit has a phone and color TV with movies.
#219,#218,#209,#217,#216,#213,#212,#206,#202—fireplace, kit., lg. pvt. balc., raised in-bedroom whirlpool, floor/ceiling windows, awesome coastal view, (first 3 have) pitched roof, K bed...$225
regular room—in lodge, some have ocean view, K bed...$120

Hofsas House
downtown at San Carlos St. & 4th Av. (Box 1195) *624-2745*
Behind the alpine-chalet facade is a large, attractively furnished modern motel with a scenic outdoor pool, and a sauna. Each of the spacious rooms has cable color TV, a phone, and a refrigerator. For toll-free reservations, call (800)252-0211.
#37—fireplace, private balcony, K bed...$97
"fireplace unit"—fireplace, K bed...$97
regular room— Q bed...$66

★ **Horizon Inn**
downtown at Junipero & 3rd Avs. (Box 1693) *624-5327*
This is a small contemporary motel with colorful landscaping, an outdoor pool, and some fine panoramic views. All rooms have a phone, cable color TV, and a refrigerator. A complimentary Continental breakfast is brought to the room.
#19,#21—end, pvt. balc., gas fireplace, panoramic view to ocean, K bed...$125
#1—end, pvt. balc., gas fireplace, fine town view, K bed...$105
regular room— K bed...$85

★ **Jade Tree Inn**
downtown at Junipero & 6th Avs. (Box 3715) *624-1831*
On a rise above the village center, this large contemporary motel features panoramic views, and has an outdoor pool. Each room has cable color TV and a phone.
#58—gas fireplace, balc., panoramic view to ocean, K bed...$75
#55,#57,#59—gas fireplace, balc., fine view, K bed...$75
regular room— Q bed...$50

★ **La Playa Hotel**
downtown at Camino Real & 8th Av. (Box 900) *624-6476*
Carmel's most delightful in-town hideaway hotel is in a tranquil location convenient to both the beach and downtown. Completely remodeled in 1984, the large landmark is a showplace of luxurious dining and

drinking facilities. Dramatically landscaped grounds include an outdoor pool. Each beautifully furnished room has a phone, cable color TV, and a refrigerator. For toll-free reservations, call: (800)582-8900.

#441—full ocean view beyond lawn, K bed...$130
#170,#172—gas fireplace, near the pool, K bed...$140
regular room—some have town or ocean view, Q or K bed...$100

Lobos Lodge

downtown at Ocean Av. & Monte Verde St. (Box L1) 624-3874

Several buildings comprise this small motor inn on the main street a few blocks up from the beach. Each room has a gas fireplace, refrigerator, cable color TV, and a phone. A complimentary Continental breakfast and newspaper are served to your room.

#37—spacious, private walled balcony, K bed...$115
#18—private walled balcony, K bed...$90
regular room— K bed...$75

★ **The Lodge at Pebble Beach**

2 mi. NW on Cypress Dr. (Box 1128) - Pebble Beach 93953 624-3811

This large, world famous resort has an incomparable oceanfront location and a remarkable variety of amenities, including (for a fee) an 18-hole golf course, par-3 golf, thirteen tennis courts, and horseback riding. An outdoor pool, sauna, beach, and hiking trails are free to guests. There are also acclaimed restaurants. Each well-furnished room includes a wet bar and refrigerator, cable color TV, and a phone.

#197—spacious, superb ocean view from corner windows, Q bed...$250
"Portola Bldg."—overlooks 18th fairway and ocean view, fireplace, 2 Q beds...$230
regular room—new section, fireplace, 2 Q beds...$200

Monte Verde Inn

downtown on Monte Verde St. between Ocean & 7th Avs. 624-6046

A lovely old inn in the heart of the village has a garden patio and a variety of distinctive, recently upgraded rooms. Each has a private bath, and a color TV. A Continental breakfast is complimentary.

#2—top corner room, bright, pvt. ocean view, Q bed...$89
#4—spacious, fireplace, kit., pvt. balc., view of oaks/town, Q bed...$125
regular room— 2 T or D bed...$65

Ocean View Lodge

downtown at Junipero & 3rd Avs. (Box 3696) 624-7723

A small, nicely landscaped motel offers spacious units comfortably furnished in Early American decor. Each unit has a cable color TV and a phone.

#6—good ocean view, kitchen, living room with fireplace, Q bed...$102
#4—some ocean view, kitchen, living room with fireplace, K bed...$98
regular unit— Q bed...$68

★ **Pine Inn**
downtown on Ocean Av. at Monte Verde St. (Box 250) *624-3851*
Carmel's main street landmark is a handsome turn-of-the-century hotel. Elegant Victorian furnishings grace the lobby, public areas, and restaurants. A courtyard restaurant with a dramatic roll-back roof is especially notable. All of the tastefully decorated rooms have cable color TV, a phone, and bath.
#64—gas fireplace, refrigerator, K bed...$120
regular room— D bed...$60

★ **Quail Lodge**
4 mi. SE off Carmel Valley Rd. at 8205 Valley Greens Dr. *624-1581*
This renowned resort is a study in contemporary luxury. Deep in Carmel Valley, no expense was spared to create an ultimate leisure retreat. Manicured grounds provide a lovely setting for a picturesque (fee) 18-hole golf course, four (fee) tennis courts, three outdoor pools, a whirlpool, and rental bicycles. The main building houses an elegant, recently remodeled restaurant and lounge. Each expansive, sumptuously furnished room includes cable color TV and a phone. For toll-free reservations, call: (800)682-9303 in California, (800) 538-9516 elsewhere.
"balcony room" (there are 6)—gas fireplace, pvt. balcony, K bed...$195
regular "terrace" room— K bed...$165

★ **Sandpiper Inn**
1 mi. SW at 2408 Bayview Av. (zip: 93923) *624-6433*
Antiques and fresh flowers fill this small, beautifully maintained half-century-old bed-and-breakfast inn. In a quiet residential area just fifty yards from Carmel Bay, some rooms have fine ocean views. All rooms have private baths. A Continental breakfast in the morning and sherry in the evening are complimentary. Ten-speed bicycles can be rented by guests.
regular room—ocean view, Q or K bed...$105
regular room—garden view, fireplace, Q bed...$85

Svendsgaard's Inn
downtown at San Carlos St. & 4th Av. (Box 1900) *624-1511*
The beautifully oak-shaded grounds of this contemporary motel include an outdoor pool. Each of the nicely furnished rooms was recently upgraded, and has a cable color TV, phone, and refrigerator.
#4,#18—private, fireplace, K bed...$90
#10,#17,#37—fireplace, kitchenette, K bed...$90
regular room— Q bed...$65

Tally Ho
downtown at Monte Verde St. & 6th Av. (Box 3726) *624-2232*
Sunny gardens surround this tiny modern country inn. All units are individually furnished, have private baths, and cable color TV.

#5—fireplace, kitchenette, ocean view deck, phone, Q bed...$95
#10—big fireplace, kitchenette, pvt. view deck, phone, K bed...$145
regular room— Q bed...$85

★ **Tickle Pink Motor Inn**
4 mi. S on CA 1 at 155 Highlands Dr. (zip: 93923) *624-1244*
Spellbinding coastline views are the unforgettable attraction of this contemporary motel. All units have cable color TV, phone, and refrigerator. A complimentary Continental breakfast is offered.
#21,#20—top fl., spacious, fireplace, lg. balc., pvt. seascape view K bed...$139
#28—split level, fireplace, windows on 2 sides, pvt. seascape view, Q bed...$139
#14—1 BR, enormous suite, fireplace, deck, awesome view, K bed...$192
#15—as above, but no fireplace, K bed...$113
regular room—tree view, 2 T or K bed...$113

★ **Tradewinds**
downtown at Mission St. & 3rd Av. (Box 3403) *624-2776*
This delightfully contemporary motel features a large outdoor pool in a lush garden setting. All of the spacious rooms have cable color TV and a phone. A complimentary Continental breakfast is brought to the room.
#D,#19,#20—gas fireplace, wet bar, pvt. town view balc., K bed...$90
regular room— Q bed...$70

★ **Ventana Big Sur**
30 mi. S off CA 1 - Big Sur (zip: 93920) *667-2331*
One of the finest examples of Post-Modern architecture and decor in California blends into a hillside high above the awesome Big Sur coast. A very large outdoor pool, saunas, whirlpools, a dramatic restaurant and lounge, plus a sunny terrace with a fantastic coastal panorama all contribute to the motor inn's reputation as one of the West's most romantic adult hideaways. Each spacious, artistically appointed unit is of unfinished cedar, with a private tree-view terrace, color TV with movies, and phone. A complimentary Continental breakfast is brought to the room.
special unit—Franklin fireplace, wet bar, K bed...$185
regular room— Q bed...$145

The Village Inn
downtown at Ocean & Junipero Avs. (Box 5275) *624-3864*
This modern motel was recently remodeled. Each tastefully furnished room has cable color TV and a phone. A Continental breakfast is complimentary.

#19B—top, end, gas fireplace, kit., park/downtown views, K bed...$120
#32—end, windows on 2 sides, trees/main street views, K bed...$75
regular room— Q bed...$73

Wayfarer Inn
downtown at Mission St. & 4th Av. (Box 1896) *624-2711*

Each of the units in this charming inn/motel has color TV and a phone. Continental breakfast is complimentary.

#16—top, corner, fireplace, refr., some ocean view, Q bed...$85
#5—fireplace, kitchen, some view, T & Q bed...$95
regular room— Q bed...$55

Wayside Inn
downtown at Mission St. & 7th Av. (Box 1900) *624-5336*

A two-story motel was attractively upgraded recently. Each unit now includes a cable color TV with movies, phone, refrigerator, and a wood-burning fireplace. A complimentary Continental breakfast and newspaper are delivered to your door.

#23—kitchen, windows on 2 sides, K bed...$92
#18—kitchen, end unit, windows on 2 sides, K bed...$97
regular room— 2 Q or K bed...$77

CAMPGROUNDS

There are only a few campgrounds within many miles of the village. However, one of the West's finest is relatively close in the fabled Big Sur with complete facilities and a magnificent location by a small river deep in a redwood forest near the ocean.

★ **Andrew Molera**
24 mi. S on CA 1 - Big Sur *No Phone*

The state operates this uncommon little facility by the Big Sur River as a walk-in campground for tenters only. Trails lead to nearby remote and picturesque ocean beaches, and fishing and swimming in the river are popular. Pit toilets are available. There are no showers. Each site is well-spaced, and some are tree-shaded. base rate...$2

★ **Pfeiffer - Big Sur State Park**
27 mi. S on CA 1 - Big Sur *667-2315*

One of California's most acclaimed state-operated campgrounds is strung along a lovely little river in a luxuriant forest accented by majestic redwoods. Numerous well-maintained hiking trails provide easy access to surrounding mountains, a waterfall, and scenic unspoiled beaches along the fabled Big Sur coast. The river is popular for swimming and fishing. Flush toilets, hot showers, and hookups are available. Each well-spaced site in this big facility has a picnic table and a fire area. Most are tree-shaded and some are by the river. base rate...$6

Saddle Mountain Rec. Park
6 mi. SE via Carmel Valley & Schulte Rds. *624-1617*
This privately operated campground is located above the valley. There are hiking trails, a (fee) pool, and a recreation room. Flush toilets, hot showers, and hookups are available. Each site has a picnic table and fire area. A separate, oak-shaded area has been set aside for tenters.
base rate...$13

SPECIAL EVENT

★ **Carmel Bach Festival** *downtown at Sunset Center* *late July*
One of the West's most important musical events takes place primarily in Carmel's lovely cultural center. Three weeks of classical concerts and recitals are performed by some of the world's finest musicians before large and enthusiastic audiences.

OTHER INFORMATION

Area Code: *408*
Zip Code: *93921*
Carmel Business Association
downtown at San Carlos St. & 7th Av. *624-2522*
Tourist Information Center
downtown on Mission St. near Ocean Av. (Box 7430) *624-1711*
Los Padres National Forest - Carmel Office
1.5 mi. SE at CA 1/Carmel Valley Rd. *659-2612*

Mendocino

Mendocino is a lovely village with a thoroughly romantic appeal. It lies gently on an isolated grassy promontory overlooking a ruggedly beautiful coastline. Whitewashed redwood buildings exude authentic charm in their current roles as studios and galleries, specialty shops, gourmet restaurants, and quaint inns. Many of the buildings have withstood well over a century of rough winter storms sweeping across these unprotected headlands. Fortunately, the weather is predictably fine in summer, when days are inevitably brisk and occasionally foggy, and there is almost no rainfall. During this season, capacity crowds enjoy exploring the village, beachcombing secluded coves and headlands, hiking scenic coastal trails, or canoeing on the adjoining stream that spills out of a lush green forest of redwoods and firs. People seeking tranquility can find it here during other seasons when the crowds are gone. From fall through spring, a more leisurely pace and the warmth of much-used fireplaces offset normally cool, damp weather.

The town was settled in the 1850s by lumbermen from New England. They recognized the commercial potential for a sawmill on the headland above a deep water anchorage by a river with access to vast adjacent redwood forests. After nearly a century as a mill town, Mendocino began fading into oblivion after the last mill closed during the Depression. Its demise was averted by artists and others who were attracted by the natural beauty of the area, its isolation, and the low cost of housing. They were followed by a more affluent breed of urban escapist. Together these new residents carefully restored and preserved this authentic cluster of clapboard relics. In the 1970s the State of California gave a strong boost to the effort by acquiring the blufftop meadow that had been the millsite between downtown and Mendocino Bay. Both the meadow and neighboring Big River Beach will now remain in a natural state free from any development.

Today, Mendocino's legacy of Yankee-Victorian wood frame buildings flourishes along with picturesque water towers, picket fences, and boardwalks. An abundance of manicured gardens provides a colorful contrast to weathered whitewashed facades. Some of the carefully refurbished structures house unique specialty shops and galleries displaying fine locally-produced arts and crafts. Others have become romantic restaurants offering gourmet cuisine, or enchanting places to go for live entertainment or a quiet drink. Several of the most impressive old buildings are now bed-and-breakfast inns lavishly outfitted with local handicrafts and authentic period pieces.

Elevation:

60 feet

Population (1980):

1,008

Population (1970):

400

Location:

155 mi. Northwest of San Francisco

Mendocino

WEATHER PROFILE

Vokac Weather Rating

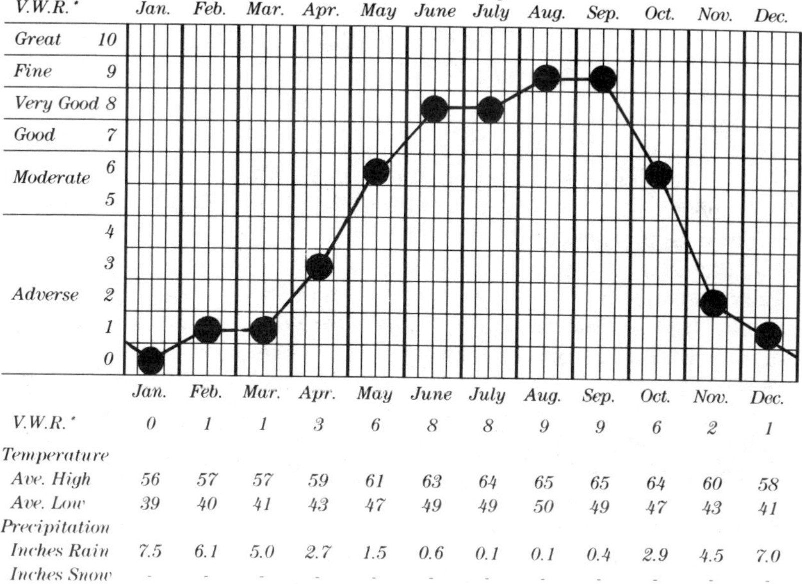

	Jan.	Feb.	Mar.	Apr.	May	June	July	Aug.	Sep.	Oct.	Nov.	Dec.
*V.W.R.**	0	1	1	3	6	8	8	9	9	6	2	1
Temperature												
Ave. High	56	57	57	59	61	63	64	65	65	64	60	58
Ave. Low	39	40	41	43	47	49	49	50	49	47	43	41
Precipitation												
Inches Rain	7.5	6.1	5.0	2.7	1.5	0.6	0.1	0.1	0.4	2.9	4.5	7.0
Inches Snow	-	-	-	-	-	-	-	-	-	-	-	-

**V.W.R. = Vokac Weather Rating: probability of mild (warm & dry) weather on any given day.*

Forecast

Month	*V.W.R.**		*Temperatures Daytime*	*Temperatures Evening*	*Precipitation*
Jan.	0	Adverse	cool	chilly	continual rainstorms
Feb.	1	Adverse	cool	chilly	continual rainstorms
Mar.	1	Adverse	cool	chilly	continual rainstorms
Apr.	3	Adverse	cool	cool	frequent showers
May	6	Moderate	cool	cool	occasional showers
June	8	Very Good	cool	cool	infrequent showers
July	8	Very Good	cool	cool	none
Aug.	9	Fine	warm	cool	none
Sep.	9	Fine	warm	cool	infrequent showers
Oct.	6	Moderate	cool	cool	occasional rainstorms
Nov.	2	Adverse	cool	cool	frequent rainstorms
Dec.	1	Adverse	cool	chilly	continual rainstorms

Summary

Sprinkled across an unprotected headland on the remote and rugged Northern California coastline, Mendocino is almost perpetually cool, and fog is common year-round. **Winter** days are normally cool and evenings are chilly. Because of the moderating infuence of the seaside location, there is seldom a frost of any consequence, and snowfalls are rare. Continual rainstorms during the winter months keep people indoors, however, and contribute more than half of the year's precipitation. **Spring** days and evenings are cool, but increasingly usable because of diminishing rainfall. **Summer** weather is normally fine. Occasional fog or brisk winds are balanced by an almost assured absence of rain, and the year's warmest days are suitable for comfortably exploring this hauntingly beautiful area. Unfortunately, the ocean is always too cold for swimming. **Fall** is uniformly cool, with increasingly frequent and heavier rainfalls as the season progresses.

ATTRACTIONS & DIVERSIONS

Bicycling

Mendocino Cyclery
downtown at 45040 Main St. *937-4744*
Bicycles can be rented here by the hour or longer to tour coastal highways and byways which make up in scenic quality whatever they lack in quantity or safety.

Boat Rentals

★ **Catch-a-canoe**
.7 mi. S off CA 1 at 44850 Comptche-Ukiah Rd. *937-0273*
Canoe rentals are available from April to October by the hour or day for trips up Big River. It's actually a gentle little river that flows through a narrow, undeveloped canyon where redwood and fir are interspersed with sandy beaches and swimming holes. Because the river is tidal for several miles, you can plan your trip to allow the flow of the tides to carry you up and back for an extraordinary experience.

★ **California Western Railroad**
11 mi. N at foot of Laurel St. - Fort Bragg *964-6371*
The "Skunk" line offers one of the West's most scenic train rides. From Fort Bragg on the coast, it twists through forty miles of rugged mountains highlighted by groves of redwoods along the Noyo River to Willits. More than thirty bridges, trestles, and tunnels are along the route—which is inaccessible by car. Diesel trains operate daily year-round. The round trip takes about seven hours. In addition, half-day tours can be reserved during the summer months when open observation cars are used.

Golf

Little River Inn Golf Course
3 mi. S at 7750 CA 1 *937-5667*
This challenging 9-hole course overlooking the ocean is open to the public. Facilities include a pro shop, driving range, putting greens, cart rentals, and a restaurant.

★ **Jug Handle State Reserve**
4.5 mi. N on CA 1 - Caspar
At Jug Handle Creek is a remarkable "ecological staircase" phenomenon. Five wave-cut terraces form a staircase with each step holding an ecosystem much older than the one below. On the partially submerged bottom terrace are tide pools with a wealth of marine life. A five-mile self-guided nature trail explores all five terraces.

Mendocino Coast Botanical Gardens
7.5 mi. N at 18220 CA 1 *964-4352*
More than two miles of self-guided hiking trails meander through seventeen acres of gardens owned by the Mendocino Coast Recreation

and Parks District. The ***Garden Cafe*** features light breakfasts or lunches indoors or on a deck by the gardens. Beyond, paths wind through natural woods and meadows interspersed with a profusion of rhododendrons, wild lilac, fuchsias, and other seasonal blooms. A fern canyon, rustic bridges, and picnic facilities are scattered along the way to a seaside cliff house.

★ **Mendocino Headlands State Park**
surrounding town on S, W, N sides *937-5397*
This park was created to protect the meadows, wave-carved bluffs, and natural bridges of the promontory that juts into the Pacific around town. Below the bluffs on the southeast side of town, the picturesque sandy beach at the mouth of Big River is also included. Scenic hiking trails, view overlooks, picnic sites, and restrooms are well-located. Heeser Drive is a paved scenic loop that follows the blufftop to an access for public fishing and to the beach on the west side of the promontory.

★ **Old Masonic Hall Sculpture**
downtown on Lansing St.
Don't miss the intriguing rooftop of this old building. The whimsical sculpture of Father Time braiding a maiden's hair captures both the artistic and romantic spirit of Mendocino in a century-old piece of whitewashed redwood.

★ **Russian Gulch State Park**
2 mi. N off CA 1 *937-0497*
One of the West's most outstanding coastal parks includes a picturesque sandy beach where a shallow creek empties into the ocean. Beyond, dramatic wave-sculpted headlands reveal coves, tide pools, and a partially collapsed blowhole to hikers and beachcombers. In the canyon near the mouth of the creek are about thirty shady campsites. A waterfall in a fern-edged grotto is the highlight of an easy 3.5-mile trail through dense forests along the creek.

★ ***Sportfishing***
9 mi. N on CA 1 - Noyo
Sportfishing is the major year-round attraction in Noyo. This tiny village lends a cluttered, unplanned sort of vitality to a sheltered site a few hundred yards inland from the mouth of the Noyo River. Nearby, coastal rocks and beaches, the jetty and wharves, and oceangoing party boats are all popular with fishermen, especially during the summer and fall salmon runs. Complete information on fishing charters and equipment rentals can be obtained at the Mendocino Coast Chamber of Commerce, or at:

Noyo Fishing Center *32450 N. Harbor Dr. - Noyo* *964-7609*
Sportsman's Dock *32100 N. Harbor Dr. - Noyo* *964-2619*

★ **Van Damme State Park**
2.5 mi. S off CA 1 *937-0851*
On scenic Little River, this splendid park has about eighty shady

campsites inland from the highway. Nearby is a sandy beach for sunbathing. The ocean is reasonably safe but inevitably cold for swimming. Sport diving (spear fishing, abalone diving, and underwater photography) and shore fishing are popular. Miles of hiking trails provide access to ocean views, a sword fern canyon, and an ancient pygmy forest of stunted conifers.

Warm Water Features

★ **Caspar Tubbs**
5 mi. N off CA 1 - Caspar *964-6668*
In a rustic natural setting on the grounds of the McCornack Center for the Healing Arts, hot tubs in enclosures open to the sky may be rented by the hour. Each private enclosure includes a whirlpool, sauna, sundeck, shower, and dressing room. Massage is also available by appointment.

★ **Sweetwater Gardens**
downtown at 955 Ukiah St. *937-4140*
Guests can rent a private room with a hot tub, sauna, and tiled bath; small private tubs; or a large communal hot tub by the hour in this serene and artistic facility adjoining a fine organic restaurant. Massage is also available by appointment. Upstairs above the communal hot tub is an overnight room with a double bed. Windows on all sides provide town and ocean views. A shower and toilet are downstairs.

Wineries

In the latest decade, vineyards and wineries have become as important as long-established apple orchards in the pretty little Anderson Valley inland from the Mendocino coast. Three small, family-owned wineries are now clustered along CA 128 near the tiny village of Philo.

★ **Edmeades Vineyards**
30 mi. SE on CA 128 *895-3232*
One of the area's earliest wineries dates from 1972. Visitors may sample the full range of premium wines in a rustic little hilltop tasting room. Tasting and sales 10-6 daily (11-5 daily Oct. thru May).

★ **Husch Vineyards**
29 mi. SE on CA 128 *895-3216*
This attractive little winery was founded in 1971. A wooden cabin has been made into a pleasant tasting room where all of the premium wines may be sampled. Tree-shaded picnic tables are nearby. Tasting and sales 10-6 daily.

★ **Navarro Vineyards**
30 mi. SE at 5601 CA 128 *895-3686*
The valley's youngest major winery was founded in 1975. A distinctive new woodcrafted building used for tasting the full line of premium wines also provides picture window views of the vineyards. An adjoining outdoor deck with umbrella-shaded picnic tables overlooks the lovely scene. Tasting and sales 10-5 daily.

SHOPPING

Mendocino has an enchanting little business district where strollers and shoppers are rewarded with intriguing buildings and nineteenth century architectural embellishments at every turn. Shops are clustered along one side of Main Street. Remarkably, the other side of this street is a broad, grassy meadow with unobstructed views extending to magnificent seascapes. The many galleries in town let visitors see how resident artists have translated such scenes into oils, watercolors, photography, and other media. Numerous specialty shops also reflect the deeply intertwined involvement of local merchants and artisans with the natural beauty of the captivating surroundings.

Food Specialties

★ **Brings Pastries**
downtown at 10540 Lansing St. *937-4188*
A delicious selection of European and American pastries and breads is served in a town-view coffee room, on an outdoor deck, or to go.

★ **The Cheese Shop**
downtown at 45050 Little Lake St. *937-0104*
In addition to a fine variety of imported and domestic cheeses, there are all kinds of gourmet food specialties like pates, baguettes, and homemade jellies and jams. Some items are displayed for tastes, too. Another section of the store has the area's best selection of premium California wines, especially Mendocino County labels.

★ **Chocolate Moosse**
downtown at 390 Kasten St. *937-4323*
Outstanding desserts like Blackout Cake are the specialty. However, the Blue Heron Inn's charming little Mendocino-style coffee shop is more than the sum of irresistible delicacies, knotty pine floors, whitewashed wainscoating, brick fireplace, pegged chairs, and handcrafted solid pine tables furnished with art-object sugar servers and fresh flowers.

★ **Lu's Bay Kitchen**
downtown at 460 Main St. *937-0243*
Mexican specialties made from fresh, quality ingredients are works of art in this tiny takeout stand in a garden. It's open every afternoon.

★ **Mendocino Bakery**
downtown at 10485 Lansing St. *937-0836*
Deliciously unrefined cinnamon rolls, scones, danishes, and other first class pastries, pizzas, and desserts are served to go or at tables set with fresh flowers overlooking the main street.

★ **Mendocino Ice Cream Co.**
downtown at 45090 Main St. *937-5884*
Homemade ice cream is the feature of a little ice cream parlor outfitted with polished wood booths and tables. The acclaimed Black Forest ice cream is especially rich.

★ **Mendocino Jams and Jellies**
downtown at 440 Main St. *937-0414*
Outstanding raspberry jam is a highlight among delicious jams, jellies, and chutneys made locally and sold in this attractive newer takeout shop. Tastes are offered.

Specialty Shops

★ **Book Loft**
downtown at 522 Main St. *937-0890*
This small shop upstairs above Alphonso's Mercantile emphasizes quality paperbacks. Sitting in the chair positioned to overlook a picture window view of the rugged coast while listening to classical music and browsing through books can be an unforgettable experience.

Gallery Bookshop
downtown at 319 Kasten St. *937-5796*
An excellent selection of hard-covers and paperbacks has been ingeniously packed into one small bookstore.

★ **Gallery Fair**
downtown at Kasten/Ukiah Sts. *937-5121*
Museum-quality wall hangings, sculpture, and unique art objects of wood by local and regional artists are beautifully displayed in this large two-level gallery.

★ **Highlight Gallery**
downtown at 45052 Main St. *937-3132*
Locally handcrafted furniture and decorative art objects are featured in one of Mendocino's newest major galleries. There is also a good selection of wall hangings.

★ **Mendocino Art Center**
downtown at 45200 Little Lake St. *937-5818*
The heart of the local art renaissance is a handsome little visual and performing arts complex. Visitors can watch painters, sculptors, potters, and other artisans at work in on-site studios. In addition, the public is invited to art fairs, wine tastings, afternoon concerts, plays, and other periodic events that take place here.

★ **Ruth Carlson Gallery**
downtown at CA 1 & Main St. *937-5154*
The works of local artists and craftspeople are attractively showcased in this large well-lighted gallery.

★ **The Sea Cottage**
downtown at 45120 Main St. *937-5758*
Premium wines of the region are served by the glass at a spectacular antique bar at the back of a room full of premium-quality antique furniture, crystal, and silver.

★ **Wind & Weather**
downtown at Albion/Kasten Sts. *937-0323*
In a tiny multilevel shop built into a wooden water tower, browsers are welcome to examine a remarkably extensive selection of old and new weather instruments and related paraphernalia sold here.

★ **Other Galleries**
downtown
Many fine galleries in addition to those listed here are concentrated within four blocks to the south and east of the Art Center. Excellent locally produced paintings, graphics, sculpture, ceramics, textiles, and jewelry are beautifully displayed.

NIGHTLIFE

A wide range of plays, concerts, and other productions are offered throughout the year, and gallery showings are a special feature on most weekend evenings. Several captivating lounges provide the right setting for a romantic interlude or a quiet drink. This is all in sharp contrast with the rowdy goings-on in a nearby roadhouse saloon where loud live music attracts drinkers, dancers, and people-watchers from miles around.

★ **Caspar Inn**
4.5 mi. N off CA 1 - Caspar *964-5565*
Live music and a big dance floor make this sprawling, funky old-time tavern the action spot in the area on weekends. It's a popular place to shoot pool, throw darts, and drink beer anytime.

★ **Heritage House**
5 mi. S on CA 1 *937-5885*
The genteel Apple Lounge near the resort's dining room offers plush sofas and armchairs in an intimate firelit room. Picture window views of verdant landscaping and rugged coastal headlands are inspiring.

★ **MacCallum House**
downtown at 45020 Albion St. *937-5763*
The Grey Whale Bar is a romantic little drawing room with plush sofas, a fireplace, and lush plants. Drinks and delicious appetizers are also served on an intimate enclosed porch. An atmospheric restaurant adjoins.

★ **Mendocino Hotel**
downtown at 45080 Main St. *937-0511*
The hotel's opulent Victorian-style lounge has all kinds of overstuffed furniture for comfortably relaxing over a quiet drink amidst polished hardwoods and stained glass decor. An adjoining enclosed garden salon is also beautifully decorated and furnished.

★ **Mendocino Performing Arts Company**
downtown at 45200 Little Lake St. *937-4477*
The Helen Schoeni Theatre is an intimate showplace where a variety of plays and concerts are performed throughout the year.

★ **Sea Gull Cellar Bar**
downtown at the corner of Lansing & Ukiah Sts. *937-5204*
Live entertainment is featured several nights a week in an upstairs bar that is a classic Mendocino-style gathering place. Comfortable armchairs overlook a wall of windows, spectacular raised-relief wood

murals, and several large, fanciful paintings. Drinks can also be enjoyed outdoors on a tiny redwood viewdeck.

RESTAURANTS

Some of the best restaurants in the West are located in and near town. In recent years, Mendocino has become a major source of New California cuisine, where seasonally fresh local ingredients are skillfully prepared in exciting new ways. Authentic Victorian surroundings and dramatic seascape views are also part of the allure of many fine local dining rooms.

★ **Albion River Inn Restaurant**

6.8 mi. S at 3790 N. CA 1 - Albion *937-4044*
D only. *Expensive*

This relative newcomer to the area is already established as one of the north coast's finest restaurants. Innovative fresh seafood dishes and other specialties are handled with a flair in the New California cuisine style. Fresh roses and ultra-modern candles adorn each table in a contemporary dining room warmed by a great brick fireplace. The picture window view of the outlet of Albion River and the ocean far below is awesome. Many local wines are available by the glass.

Brannon's Whale Watch Restaurant

downtown at 45040 Main St. *937-4197*
B-L-D. *Moderate*

A contemporary American menu is offered in a casual upstairs dining room with a fine ocean and town view, and a Franklin fireplace. Fresh flowers and raspberry jam pots decorate well-spaced tables. A sunny ocean view deck is also used when weather permits.

★ **Cafe Beaujolais**

downtown at 961 Ukiah St. *937-5614*
B-L-D. No D on Tues.-Thurs. & fall-winter. *Expensive*

Outstanding New California cuisine is served in a homey, woodcrafted dining room in a remodeled Victorian building. Fresh, locally grown produce is given a disciplined light touch for all meals. Breakfasts are especially renowned.

★ **Egghead Omelettes**

10 mi. N on CA 1 at 326 N. Main St. - Fort Bragg *964-5005*
B-L. *Moderate*

Toast from homemade bread, fine jam in pots, and real maple syrup provide evidence of the fact that breakfast is treated seriously here. Specialty omelets are served all day in a pleasant little dining room.

Heritage House

5 mi. S at 5200 N. CA 1 *937-5885*
B-D. Closed Dec.-Jan. *Expensive*

Meals are served to the public as well as guests in one of the West's most celebrated and historic inns. A window wall in the large, formally elegant dining room provides panoramic views of the spectacular coast.

★ **The Ledford House**
3.5 mi. S at 7051 N. CA 1 - Little River — *937-0282*
D only. Closed Sun. in winter. — *Very Expensive*
A short, interesting menu features California cuisine. Emphasis is on seasonally fresh, locally grown ingredients, and all baking is done on the premises. A rustic Civil War-era farmhouse overlooking a distant sea retains its historic charm with plush antique furnishings and a cozy fireplace.

★ **Little River Restaurant**
3 mi. S at 7750 N. CA 1 - Little River — *937-4945*
D only. Closed Mon.-Wed. — *Expensive*
Hidden away in the back of the Little River Post Office is a posh, tiny haven of New California cuisine. Nearly all of the prepared-to-order foods served during the two nightly seatings are homemade or homegrown.

Little River Inn
3 mi. S on CA 1 - Little River — *937-5942*
B-D. Closed last 3 weeks in Jan. — *Expensive*
Breads, soups, and desserts made in the inn's country kitchen enhance seafood and steak specialties. The spacious, beautifully furnished dining room is the focal point of a pre-Civil War mansion surrounded by gardens on a knoll overlooking the ocean.

★ **MacCallum House**
downtown at 45020 Albion St. — *937-5763*
D only. — *Very Expensive*
Well-regarded Continental cuisine is served in the romantic atmosphere of a stately Victorian mansion. An old cobblestone fireplace is the showpiece of the elegant, intimate dining room. Lunch on a porch with bay and ocean views is also very popular.

★ **Main Street Deli**
downtown at 45040 Main St. — *937-5031*
B-L-D. — *Moderate*
Several kinds of big, tasty croissants are a specialty of this deli/restaurant. Good light fare is served in a whitewashed, wood-trimmed dining room enhanced by ocean view tables and classical music.

★ **Mendocino Hotel**
downtown at 45080 Main St. — *937-0511*
B-L-D. — *Very Expensive*
New California cuisine is featured, and baked goods are made on the premises. The century-old hotel's large dining room is decorated in lavish Victorian style. An adjoining glassed-in section with a proliferation of plants is a delightful place for breakfast.

★ **New Boonville Restaurant**
38 mi. SE via CA 1 & CA 128 - Boonville — *895-3478*
L-D. Closed Wed. — *Expensive*
New California cuisine is enshrined here in flawless gourmet preparations of home-grown produce and meats. The dining room of an

old two-story hotel has been handsomely restored and updated with woodcrafted tables and benches, quality prints, and a lovely garden view. A handcrafted maplewood bar adjoins.

The Restaurant
10 mi. N at 418 N. Main St. - Fort Bragg *964-9800*
L-D. Closed Wed. *Moderate*
Distinctive contemporary dinners include an appetizer, soup and salad in this well-regarded restaurant. Unusual paintings and memorabilia personalize the dining rooms.

★ **Salmon Point Restaurant**
7.5 mi. S at 3000 N. CA 1 *937-0272*
D only. *Expensive*
Homemade sourdough bread arrives with a short interesting menu that ranges from venison stew to fresh local salmon in season, and features homemade ice cream. Well-separated tables are set with full linen, a candle and fresh flowers. Picture windows on three sides afford panoramic views of rocky coastal headlands. A solo guitarist contributes to the tranquility.

The Sea Gull
downtown at Lansing & Ukiah Sts. *937-5204*
B-L-D. *Moderate*
Fresh food is still prepared simply and well by the new owners of this local landmark. The interior is classic Mendocino. Handcrafted woods, fresh flowers, greenery, stained glass, and art objects abound.

★ **The Wellspring Restaurant**
downtown at 955 Ukiah St. *937-4567*
D only. Closed Tues. in winter. *Moderate*
Delicious homemade rolls and pastries complement fresh seafood and gourmet vegetarian specialties. Artistry and craftsmanship blend smoothly in a charming Mendocino-style dining room embellished with intriguing wall hangings extending to a lofty ceiling, an intimate balcony dining area, abundant greenery, and an occasional vocalist.

The Wharf
9 mi. N off CA 1 at 780 N. Harbor Dr. - Noyo *964-4283*
L-D. *Moderate*
Fresh seafood is conventionally prepared in this very large and popular fishhouse. A panoramic window view of the tiny fishing village and harbor is the real feature of the dining room and lounge.

LODGING

The creative spirit of Mendocino's artistic residents is evident in the many winsome accommodations available for visitors. Almost no conventional motels or large hotels despoil the setting. Instead, romantic little inns all along the coast reflect the area's Yankee Victorian heritage and magnificent surroundings in wonderfully personal ways. There are no bargains in summer in town. However, from fall through spring, non-weekend rates are often reduced at least 15% below those shown.

Albion River Inn
6.8 mi. S at 3790 N. CA 1 (Box 100) - Albion 95410 *937-4044*
On a high bluff overlooking the ocean at the mouth of Albion Harbor is a small rustic motel adjacent to an excellent view restaurant.
"Sea Cliff"—2 BR, kit. with ocean view, free-standing fireplace in BR, grand ocean view in LR, pvt. balc. over ocean, 2 Q beds...$90
ocean view room— Q bed...$70
regular room— Q bed...$55

★ **Big River Lodge**
1 mi. SE via CA 1 at 44850 Comptche-Ukiah Rd. *937-5025*
A two-story motel has been wonderfully transformed into a bed-and-breakfast inn. Most of the spacious rooms have fine ocean and town views across landscaped grounds. All units are decorated with local art and antiques, and have cable color TV, a phone, and a wood-burning fireplace. Bicycles are available free to guests. Canoes can be rented nearby to explore the unspoiled beauty of Big River. A Continental breakfast and a decanter of local wine are complimentary.
#22—expansive suite, fine shoreline views, K bed...$165
#24—excellent shoreline/town views, K bed...$120
#25,#23—fine ocean/town views, Q bed...$120
regular room—some ocean/town views, Q bed...$98

Coast Motel
8 mi. N at 18661 N. CA 1 - Fort Bragg 95437 *964-2852*
Several of the region's scarce **bargain** rooms and a swimming pool are features of this small motel. Each simply furnished room has cable TV with movies.
regular room— Q bed...$32
regular room— D bed...$28

★ **Glendeven**
2.4 mi. S at 8221 N. CA 1 - Little River 95456 *937-0083*
An elegant, beautifully furnished bed-and-breakfast inn occupies a large Victorian residence that has overlooked the headland meadows near the bay at Little River for well over a century. Recently, the artistic hosts added a second building of luxuriously furnished guest rooms to the lovely grounds. A complimentary breakfast is served in the morning in a charming garden-view sitting room, and wine is offered by the fire in the evening.
"Eastlin"—pvt. bath & entrance, parlor stove, bay view, rosewood Q bed...$80
"Garret"—top fl., pvt. bath, bay view, windows on 3 sides, Louis XV Q bed...$70
regular room—shared bath, D bed...$60

★ **Greenwood Pier Inn**
16.2 mi. S on CA 1 (Box 36) - Elk 95432 *877-9997*
A tiny cluster of enchanting cottages for adults is perched on a headland high above a wildly beautiful coastline of beaches, coves, and sea arches. Handcrafted furnishings and decor are used throughout. Each bedroom has a private bath and a wood-burning fireplace. A complimentary Continental breakfast is delivered to the room. The adjoining rustic cafe features California cuisine Friday through Sunday (closed Jan.-Feb.) with an emphasis on innovative preparations of fresh local produce and seafoods.

"Cliff House"—awesome private ocean view from bed and deck, metal fireplace, Q bed...$95
"Starfish"—fine ocean view, big brick fireplace, Q bed...$85
regular room—some ocean view, D bed...$65

★ **Harbor House**
16 mi. S on CA 1 (Box 369)- Elk 95432 *877-3203*
The blufftop setting of this classic country inn provides sensational views of the rugged coastline. Far below is a small private beach. The stately Edwardian main house is a marvel of hand-fitted virgin redwood from nearby Albion forests. Each luxuriously furnished room has a private bath and a fireplace or Franklin stove. Modified American plan rates include a gourmet breakfast and dinner in an elegant, intimate dining room.

"Harbor"—top fl., brick fireplace, pvt. coast view, windows on 3 sides, D & Q beds...$165
#1—cabin, Franklin stove, fine pvt. coast views, K bed...$140
#2—cabin, Franklin stove, fine pvt. coast views, 4-poster Q bed...$140
regular room—cabin, Q bed...$110

★ **Harbor Lite Lodge**
9 mi. N on CA 1 at 120 N. Harbor Dr. - Fort Bragg 95437 *964-0221*
The best views of Noyo Harbor and the tiny fishing village are enjoyed by guests in this contemporary motel on the bluff at the north end of the harbor bridge. There is a trail to the beach, and a sauna. Each spacious room has a phone and cable color TV.

#303—end, pvt. balc., fine harbor/village view, K bed...$58
#216,#214—pvt. balc., fine harbor/ocean view, 2 Q beds...$50
regular room— Q bed...$46

★ **Heritage House**
5 mi. S at 5200 N. CA 1 - Little River 95456 *937-5885*
The most celebrated inn along California's north coast is a luxurious and romantic complex of single-level buildings scattered over expansive landscaped grounds on a hillside above one of the most picturesque ocean coves anywhere. Each of the spacious rooms is decorated differently with furnishings that include many valuable antiques. Modified American plan rates include breakfast and dinner in the

opulent ocean-view dining room. Closed Dec. thru Jan.
"Sunset 2"—newer, awesome pvt. cove/ocean view, large tub, fireplace, K bed...$205
"Sunset 1"—newer, serene pvt. cove/ocean view, large tub, fireplace, K bed...$205
"Meadow 1"—fireplace, close to cove, awesome pvt. view, K bed...$195
"Vista 3"—end, wood-burning iron fireplace, grand pvt. views, 2 D beds...$215
"Romeo"—pvt. intimate cove view, fireplace, K bed...$205
"Juliet"—pvt. expansive cove view, fireplace, K bed...$205
"Same Time"—ocean/cove view, fireplace, K bed...$185
"Next Year"—ocean/cove view, fireplace, K bed...$205
"Vista 1"—brick fireplace, shared view deck, fine views, K bed...$195
regular room—some have ocean view, D bed...$115

Hill House Inn
.3 mi. N on Pallette Dr. (Box 625) *937-0554*
This handsome motel is a careful replication of a sprawling Victorian inn furnished in period decor. Each spacious, well-furnished room has a phone and cable color TV, and some have ocean views. A complimentary Continental breakfast is served to the room.
#201—corner, fine view across town to ocean, fireplace, K bed...$115
regular room—garden view, 2 D or K bed...$70

★ **Joshua Grindle Inn**
downtown at 44800 Little Lake St. (Box 647) *937-4143*
All of the rooms in this beautifully restored century-old home have private baths and carefully selected antique furnishings. Breakfast is included.
"Master"—fireplace, Q bed...$72
"Joshua Grindle", "Nautical"—views of town and ocean, Q bed...$66
regular room— Q bed...$59

Little River Inn
3 mi. S on CA 1 - Little River 95456 *937-5942*
The area's only 9-hole golf course is a feature of this long-established resort on extensive, well-landscaped grounds near the ocean, and there is a charming restaurant and lounge. Room decor varies from early California to contemporary, and many have ocean views.
#41—end, pvt. balc., great semi-pvt. view to ocean, K bed...$76
#17,#14—ends of single-level building, fireplace, K bed...$90
regular room—in the older main building, Q bed...$64

★ **MacCallum House**
downtown at 45020 Albion St. (Box 206) *937-0289*
One of Mendocino's earliest bed-and-breakfast inns occupies a century-

old mansion that may be the most photographed place in town. Outstanding antique and handcrafted furnishings are used throughout the main building and surrounding structures. Most bathrooms are shared. A complimentary Continental breakfast is served in the lovely firelit dining room.

#14 "Watertower"—split level, Franklin fireplace, pvt. bath, ocean view, Q bed...$85
#16 "Upper Barn Suite"—pvt. flowered deck, tiled shower, stone fireplace, ocean view, Q bed...$115
#19 "Barn Apartment"—big stone fireplace in BR, kit. with massive redwood counter tops, tiled tub with shower, Q bed...$95
#7 "Greenhouse"—Franklin fireplace, semi-pvt. bath, 2 D beds...$95
regular room—shared bath, D bed...$45

Mendocino Hotel
downtown at 45080 Main St. *937-0511*

Perhaps the most visible symbol of the town's Yankee heritage is this century-old three-story hotel. There is a kind of movie-set pizzazz to the completely rebuilt lobby, dining, and lounge areas that have been lavishly redecorated in Victorian style. Most of the guest rooms are small, individually decorated, and share bathrooms. A Continental breakfast is included, and served in the ***Garden Room***. For toll-free reservations, call: in California (800)352-6686; elsewhere (800)421-6662.

#224—private bath, private balcony, ocean view, canopy Q bed...$150
regular room—private bath, Q bed...$70
regular room—shared bath, D bed...$48

Mendocino Village Inn
downtown at 44860 Main St. (Box 626) *937-0246*

A century-old mansion, thoughtfully preserved and reoutfitted with some period furnishings, is now a bed-and-breakfast inn. A full complimentary breakfast is brought to the room.

#4—fireplace, corner, windows on 2 sides, private bath, color TV, 4-poster Q bed...$80
#8—fireplace, parlor, private bath, windows on 2 sides, color TV, Q bed...$80
#5—fireplace, corner window/hill views, shower, D bed...$60
"B"—attic, shared bath, view of hills, D bed...$45
regular room "A"—attic, shared bath, partial ocean view, D bed...$40

★ **1021 Main St.**
downtown at 1021 Main St. *937-5150*

Craftsmanship, creative furnishings, and views are beautifully combined in this uniquely furnished bed-and-breakfast inn. A sunken living room has the West's most remarkable fireplace—"Hot Lips." An outdoor hot tub affords guests a stunning ocean view, and a private path leads to a picturesque sandy beach. A full complimentary breakfast is served to the room, downstairs, or on a lovely ocean view deck.

"Zen House"—pvt. bath with sunken tub, antique fireplace, refr., pvt. deck with awesome ocean & river view, Q bed...$115
regular room—shared bath, ocean view, Q bed...$75

Sea Rock Bed & Breakfast Inn
.5 mi. N at 11101 N. Lansing St. (Box 286) *937-5517*
There is a good view of a beach and cove bordered by Mendocino Headlands from this small cottage colony. All of the comfortably furnished units have private baths and cable color TV. A Continental breakfast is included.

#12—Franklin fireplace, ocean view, Q bed...$70
regular room—some ocean view, Q bed...$59

★ **Whitegate Inn**
downtown at 499 Howard St. (Box 150) *937-4892*
A century-old residence has been converted into a handsome bed-and-breakfast inn. Each room is furnished with antiques and has a sitting area. Continental breakfast is complimentary, as is wine served in the early evening.

"Cypress Room"—large, Franklin fireplace, private bath, some ocean view, Q bed...$80
regular room "The Blue Room"—shared bath, T & Q beds...$60

CAMPGROUNDS

Several of the West's most outstanding campgrounds are near town. The two best are in luxuriant forests along creeks in little sheltered canyons an easy stroll from picturesque ocean beaches.

★ **Paul M. Dimmick Wayside**
19 mi. SE: 11 mi. S on CA 1 & 8 mi. E on CA 128 *No Phone*
The state operates this campground along a tranquil stretch of the gentle little Navarro River where it winds through a luxuriant second-growth redwood forest. Hiking is popular, as are swimming, canoeing, and fishing when conditions are right in the tiny river. Flush toilets, but no showers or hookups, are available. Each tree-shaded, well-spaced site has a picnic table and a fire area with a grill. base rate...$3

★ **Russian Gulch State Park**
2 mi. N on CA 1 (Box 440) *937-5804*
This state park facility has a splendid location by a small creek in a protected canyon just inland from a sandy ocean beach. Features include marked nature trails, a fern-lined path to a waterfall, an ocean cove, a blowhole, tidepools, and a pygmy forest. Surf fishing, sunbathing, scuba diving, beachcombing, and hiking are popular. Flush toilets and hot showers are available, but there are no hookups. Each tree-shaded, well-spaced site has a picnic table and a fire ring/grill. base rate...$6

★ **Van Damme State Park**
2.5 mi. S on CA 1 (Box 440) *937-5804*
Just inland from a magnificent sandy cove at the mouth of Little River, this superb state park facility is naturally landscaped with coastal redwoods shading rhododendrons and miles of lush green ferns lining both sides of Little River. Scuba diving, ocean fishing, sunbathing, and hiking are popular. There are flush toilets and hot showers, but no hookups. Each tree-shaded well-spaced site has a picnic table and grill.
base rate...$6

OTHER INFORMATION

Area Code: *707*

Zip Code: *95460*

Mendocino Coast Chamber of Commerce
9 mi. N on CA 1 at 332 N. Main St. - Fort Bragg *964-3153*

Monterey

Monterey is a magical medley of superlative history and geography. Located by Monterey Bay in what has been called one of the most beautiful natural amphitheaters in the world, this seaport has played a major role in the development of the West for more than two centuries. It is now a renowned destination with a superabundance of lovingly preserved historic landmarks and sophisticated contemporary amenities. An unusually temperate climate is the perfect complement to all of the urban pleasures. Snow and frost are rare, so lush vegetation and outdoor activities are enjoyed year-round. Emerald-green flower-strewn landscapes in spring, and warm, rainless weather in summer and fall are especially delightful. At these times, and on weekends throughout the year, Monterey hosts capacity crowds. Fishing, sailing, snorkeling, bicycling, tennis, golf, sunbathing, and beachcombing are all enjoyed. Probably the most popular activity, however, is exploring on foot. Beaches, wharfs, marinas, the cannery district, historic buildings, and major parks are among the pedestrian-oriented facilities that have been provided over the years along the entire waterfront and downtown.

In 1602, Sebastian Viscaino became the first white man to set foot in the area. He dubbed it Monterey after the count who was then viceroy of New Spain. It wasn't until 1770, however, that settlement began. In that year, Gaspar de Portola established the first of Spain's four California presidios and Father Junipero Serra dedicated the second mission in Alta California. (He relocated it to the present site near the Carmel River a year later.) Monterey was California's capital under Spain until 1822, when it became the Mexican regional capital. So it remained until 1846 when the United States annexed California. Many buildings dating from those momentous times remain downtown as tangible reminders of Monterey's importance in the early settlement of the West. After California became a state in 1850, the town became a whaling, fishing, and canning center. It wasn't until after World War II that its destiny as one of the West's most playful towns was fulfilled.

Today, Cannery Row and Fisherman's Wharf are ingenious transformations from an earlier hard-working era into vibrant and colorful leisure complexes. Nowhere is this more apparent than in the recently opened superstar of Cannery Row—the Monterey Bay Aquarium. From nearby, it looks like the sardine cannery it once was, while inside, the smell, noise, and toilers are gone, replaced by hordes of visitors intent on exploring some of the finest maritime exhibits anywhere. Downtown, carefully restored remnants of the past blend into an increasingly appealing melange of shops and galleries. Gourmet and view restaurants are numerous, and nightlife is as diverse and exuberant as anywhere in the West. Accommodations of all kinds are abundant. In fact, Monterey's two major man-made landmarks are strikingly contemporary high-rise hotels in the heart of downtown.

Elevation:

40 feet

Population (1980):

27,558

Population (1970):

26,302

Location:

130 miles Southeast of San Francisco

Monterey

WEATHER PROFILE

Vokac Weather Rating

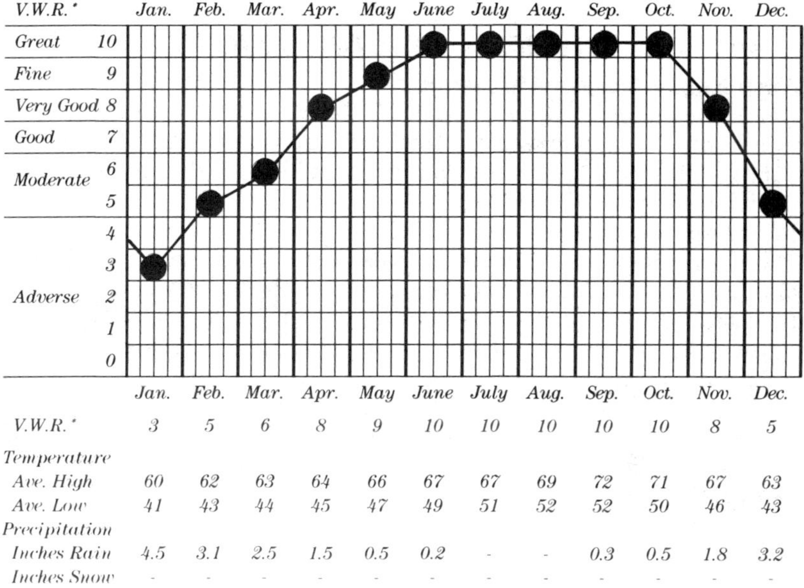

	Jan.	Feb.	Mar.	Apr.	May	June	July	Aug.	Sep.	Oct.	Nov.	Dec.
*V.W.R.**	3	5	6	8	9	10	10	10	10	10	8	5
Temperature												
Ave. High	60	62	63	64	66	67	67	69	72	71	67	63
Ave. Low	41	43	44	45	47	49	51	52	52	50	46	43
Precipitation												
Inches Rain	4.5	3.1	2.5	1.5	0.5	0.2	-	-	0.3	0.5	1.8	3.2
Inches Snow	-	-	-	-	-	-	-	-	-	-	-	-

**V.W.R. = Vokac Weather Rating: probability of mild (warm & dry) weather on any given day.*

Forecast

Month	*V.W.R.**		*Temperatures* *Daytime*	*Evening*	*Precipitation*
Jan.	3	Adverse	cool	cool	frequent rainstorms
Feb.	5	Moderate	cool	cool	occasional rainstorms
Mar.	6	Moderate	cool	cool	occasional rainstorms
Apr.	8	Very Good	cool	cool	infrequent rainstorms
May	9	Fine	warm	cool	infrequent showers
June	10	Great	warm	cool	negligible
July	10	Great	warm	cool	none
Aug.	10	Great	warm	cool	none
Sep.	10	Great	warm	cool	negligible
Oct.	10	Great	warm	cool	infrequent showers
Nov.	8	Very Good	warm	cool	infrequent rainstorms
Dec.	5	Moderate	cool	cool	occasional rainstorms

Summary

Monterey is located along Monterey Bay on the northeastern corner of the Monterey Peninsula which it shares with Pacific Grove and Carmel. With one of the West's most desirable climates, the area has nearly ideal weather year-round for comfortably enjoying outdoor recreation. Even in **winter**, there is no really bad weather. Days and evenings are cool, but usually frost-free. Occasional Pacific rainstorms during this season contribute well over half of the average annual precipitation. **Spring** marks the beginning of consistently mild weather for enjoying almost any outdoor activity. Warm days, cool evenings, and infrequent showers may be marred for some by sea breezes and coastal fogs that are also common during this season. **Summer** is splendid, with warm days and cool nights. There is almost no rainfall, but coastal fog is routine. **Fall** provides the year's best weather. The highest annual temperatures normally occur at this time, and fog is less frequent. Ideal conditions usually continue until after Thanksgiving when the rainy season begins again in earnest.

ATTRACTIONS & DIVERSIONS

Allen Knight Maritime Museum
downtown at 550 Calle Principal *375-2553*
The fishing and whaling era in Monterey is portrayed through a comprehensive collection of pictures, paintings, ship models, and maritime artifacts. Closed Mon.

★ ***Bicycling***
There are several exclusive bike paths and many scenic routes on the Monterey Peninsula. The most renowned is the Seventeen Mile Drive. Bicyclists can travel this private road free, but non-residents are not allowed to bike there after 11 a.m. on Sat. & Sun. Rentals and information are offered at:

Bay Bikes *1 mi. NW at 640 Wave St. in Cannery Row* *646-9090*
Freewheeling Cycles *downtown at 188 Webster St.* *373-3855*
Joselyn's Bicycles *1 mi. NW at 638 Lighthouse Av.* *649-8520*

Boat Rentals
Monterey Bay Yacht Center
downtown at Wharf #2 *375-2002*
Sailboats can be rented, and boating instruction is available here year-round.

★ **California's First Theater**
downtown at Pacific/Scott Sts. *375-4916*
Completed in 1847 as a boarding house and saloon, the building was loaned to some American soldiers who, for the first time in California, charged admission for their theatrical performances. Today, Victorian melodramas are performed here year-round.

★ **Cannery Row**
starts .5 mi. NW along Cannery Row
A few hulking cannery buildings and overpasses across Cannery Row still capture some of the flavor of the past. But, the canneries haven't been the same since sardines mysteriously vanished from Monterey Bay around 1950. The noise and the smell described in John Steinbeck's *Cannery Row* are gone—replaced by an imaginative assortment of shops and restaurants that have brought bright lights, the sound of music, and the smell of good food to ingeniously renovated old buildings and elaborate new structures. The Row's (and the peninsula's) star attraction is a superb aquarium that has sparked development of new hotels and other tourist-serving facilities on almost every vacant parcel in the area. For a quiet, authentic reminder of the earlier era, peer into the windows of the weathered clapboard building in the 800 block of Cannery Row that was Steinbeck's friend "Doc" Rickett's Pacific Biological Laboratory.

★ **Colton Hall**
downtown at 522 Pacific St. *375-9944*
This classic revival building of stone and adobe mortar was built as a town hall and school in 1848. It was the first American public building in California, and the state's first constitution was written here in 1849. The handsomely restored building is located in the civic center next to Friendly Plaza.

★ **The Custom House**
downtown near Fisherman's Wharf *649-2836*
This is the oldest government building in California. The northern portion of the carefully restored adobe dates from 1827. There are some interesting exhibits and a wall-enclosed garden.

★ **Fisherman's Wharf**
downtown at the N end of Olivier St.
The original commercial fishing activities that operated from this wharf have long since stopped. But the wharf is still here and the buildings have evolved into a colorful potpourri of shops, restaurants, and open-air fish markets for swarms of visitors drawn by the bracing nautical atmosphere. In addition to panoramic marine views, the wharf affords visitors close-up glimpses of the bay's most antic residents—harbor seals and sea otters. It is also the peninsula's major terminus for both sportfishing and sightseeing boats.

Golf

★ **Old Del Monte Golf Course**
1.5 mi. E at 1300 Sylvan Rd. *373-2436*
This beautifully landscaped, moderately hilly 18-hole golf course is open to the public year-round, and offers all necessary facilities and rentals.

Jack's Peak Regional Park
5 mi. SE via Fremont St. & Aquajito Rd.
Panoramic views of the peninsula are the feature of this large park covering the high forested hills south of town. A mile-long hiking trail provides a scenic loop to the top of the peak from the parking lot, which is also near picturesque sites for a picnic in the pines.

★ **Lake El Estero Park**
.3 mi. E on 3rd St.
This large landscaped park next to downtown has a small lake with boat rentals, walkways, and picnic areas. The most distinctive feature, however, is Dennis the Menace Playground where Hank Ketcham, creator of "Dennis the Menace," aided in the development of a variety of free-form "hands-on" pieces of play equipment. Narrow tunnels, balanced roundabouts, swinging bridges, giant slides, and other unusual devices attract children of all ages.

★ **Larkin House**
downtown at Calle Principal/Jefferson St. *649-2836*
Built in the 1830s with a combination of Spanish-colonial and New

England architectural features, this house became an architectural prototype widely copied in Monterey and throughout California. The carefully restored home of the first and only U.S. consul to Mexico in Monterey showcases outstanding antiques and furnishings. The interior can only be viewed on guided tours. Closed Tues.

★ ***Library***

downtown at 625 Pacific St. *646-3930*

The Monterey Public Library completed a major expansion and renovation in 1984. The large, modern library is now carpeted, and features a well-lighted reading area with upholstered chairs near picture windows.

★ **Monterey Bay Aquarium**

1.2 mi. NW at 886 Cannery Row *649-6466*

After seven years of planning and construction, the West Coast's largest aquarium opened in late 1984 in a completely remodeled cannery complex. Visitors are given a unique and exciting view of the native inhabitants of Monterey Bay—sea otters, octopuses, salmon, sharks, and several hundred other species of flora and fauna in a naturalistic setting. In addition to nearly one hundred close-up viewing tanks, and two giant tanks, the complex includes a restaurant, and an excellent book shop. Open 10-6 daily.

★ **Monterey State Historic Park**

downtown at 210 Olivier St. *649-2836*

The impressive history and architectural heritage of Monterey is carefully preserved on a seven acre site near Fisherman's Wharf, and in several downtown buildings.

★ ***Moped Rentals***

Motorized bicycles provide an exhilarating and relatively effortless way to tour the picturesque peninsula. Rentals can be arranged at these places by the hour or longer.

Monterey Moped Co. *1 mi. E at 1250 Del Monte Av.* *646-0505*
Olivercycle & Son *1.5 mi. E at 205 Ramona Av.* *373-2696*

"Path of History"

throughout downtown.

A faint red dashed line in the street is a long route route which goes by almost every old house in town. Each is marked with a plaque explaining its history and architecture.

Presidio of Monterey

.5 mi. N off Pacific St. *242-8414*

This is now the home of the U.S. Army Language School. A brochure and map are available for exploring ten historic sites on Presidio Hill. The Presidio Museum displays historical artifacts from the Indian, Spanish, Mexican, and American era.

Royal Presidio Chapel
.4 mi. SE on Church St.
The only one of California's four presidio chapels still standing has been in continuous use since 1795. Its Spanish-baroque facade is still intact.

★ ***Sportfishing***
downtown on Fisherman's Wharf
Several sportfishing boats leave daily year-round for deep sea fishing, and salmon fishing in season. Winter whale watching excursions and sightseeing cruises are also featured. The following operators, all located on Fisherman's Wharf, offer these services and all necessary equipment.

Chris' Fishing Trips *375-5951*
Monterey Sport Fishing Center *372-3501*
Randy's Fishing Trips *372-7440*
Sam's Fishing Fleet Inc. *372-0577*

★ **Stevenson House**
downtown at 530 Houston St. *649-2836*
Robert Louis Stevenson boarded at what was then the French Hotel in the fall in 1879. Many of his possessions are displayed in the adobe. The interior may only be seen on guided tours.

Wineries
Many good wineries have been developed within an hour's drive of Monterey in recent years. Complete information and maps can be obtained at the Chamber of Commerce or local bookstores. Two wineries have tasting facilities in town.

Bargetto Winery
1 mi. NW at 700-L Cannery Row *373-4053*
Founded in 1933, this winery is especially noted for fine natural fruit wines, as well as premium varietals. The winery is in Soquel, but this pleasant bayside facility has a good selection of wine-related items, and offers tastes and sales daily.

Monterey Peninsula Winery
5 mi. SE on CA 68 at 2999 Monterey/Salinas Hwy. *372-4949*
Founded in 1974, this winery strives with pure varietals in an old stone building with five-foot-thick limestone walls. Tasting, tours, and sales 10-dark daily.

SHOPPING

All three specialty shopping districts in Monterey—Cannery Row, Fisherman's Wharf, and downtown—are within a mile of each other. Collectively, these photogenic settings include a remarkable array of distinctive stores. Many are housed in artistically converted historic buildings. Monterey is one of the few towns where strolling and shopping are enjoyed as much in the evening as during the day.

Food Specialties

★ **Bagel Bakery**

.7 mi. NW at 210 Lighthouse Av. *649-1714*

Several different kinds of tasty bagels are produced four times daily. Since the freshest bagels are delicious, ask what just came out. This recently remodeled bakery, the best of a local chain, has a few self-service coffee tables adjoining the carryout line.

California Seasons

1 mi. NW at 501 Cannery Row *372-5868*

Monterey Jack cheese is the specialty. This and other cheeses can be purchased here, or shipped in gift boxes.

★ **Cannery Row Fudge Co.**

1 mi. NW at 700 Cannery Row *375-7763*

Fudge is made here daily on exhibition marble slabs. Samples are usually available in this bright new shop.

Carousel Candies

downtown at 241 Alvarado Mall *373-4129*

For a quarter of a century, this small shop has been making chocolates, fudges, brittles, and saltwater taffy in many styles on the premises. There is another outlet on Fisherman's Wharf, which also offers ice cream in waffle cones.

★ **Creme de la Creme**

.8 mi. NW at 360 McClellan Av. *373-3556*

Delicious pastries can be purchased to go, or to enjoy with coffee at a few attractively furnished tables. Everything made here is fresh, from scratch, and sensational. Closed Sun.-Mon.

★ **The Giant Artichoke**

16 mi. N on CA 1 - Castroville *633-3204*

The french-fried artichoke hearts served here are a tantalizing tribute to the "Artichoke Capital of the World." The large market/restaurant also has an outstanding display of seasonally available local and California produce, plus several sizes of marinated or water-packed artichoke hearts and other gourmet groceries.

Le Montmartre

downtown at 271 Bonifacio Pl. *646-1620*

Various French croissants are baked fresh daily, along with selected other French pastries, in this tiny takeout bakery.

★ **Monterey Wine Market**

1 mi. NW at 711 Cannery Row *375-6551*

This is an excellent place to learn more about local wines, since Monterey County wineries are showcased in several dozen wines offered for tasting daily. Light lunches are also served in this cheerful shop in a converted cannery.

★ **Oscar Hossenfellder's**
1 mi. NW at 640 Wave St. in Cannery Row *649-1899*
Fine homemade ice cream, and several different outstanding pies (including a truly towering lemon meringue pie), are specialties among light fare served to go, or in a unique dining area next to a full-sized, hard-working 1905 carousel in the cavernous interior of the ingeniously converted Edgewater Packing Company.

Viennese Bakery & Restaurant
downtown at 469 Alvarado St. *375-4789*
A large assortment of conventional pastries, coffee cakes, and desserts are available to go or as an accompaniment to meals served in an adjoining plain, popular coffee shop.

Specialty Shops

★ **Monterey Bay Aquarium Gift & Bookstore**
1.2 mi. NW at 886 Cannery Row *649-6466*
Books concerned with regional interests, nature, history, the sea, and related topics are unusually well displayed, along with appropriate souvenirs of a visit to Monterey and the Aquarium.

★ **Monterey Peninsula Museum of Art**
downtown at 559 Pacific St. *372-7591*
Permanent and changing displays of regional art are exhibited and sold, along with folk and Western art, and photography. Closed Mon.

NIGHTLIFE

The quality and diversity of nightlife is part of the great charm of this lively, romantic town. Lounges and nightclubs range from elegant bay view rooms to funky, cavernous dancehalls, while live music includes everything from easy-listening sounds to hard rock. There are also fine showplaces for live theater and movies. Most of the action is conveniently in or near Cannery Row and Fisherman's Wharf.

Boiler Room
1 mi. NW at 625 Cannery Row *373-1449*
Dancing to live rock music is the main event every night in a big lounge with two full bars on the third floor of Cannery Row Square overlooking Monterey Bay.

★ **California's First Theater**
downtown at Scott/Pacific Sts. *375-4916*
Here is the home of the oldest little theater group in existence still producing authentic melodramas of the Victorian era. For almost half a century, performances have been staged year-round in a historic little adobe where tables and chairs and bench seating furnish the right setting for this kind of entertainment.

Carrera's
downtown at 414 Alvarado St. *646-1415*
Dancing nightly to video music is a feature of this sleek new nightspot. Padded stools at the brass-topped bar are popular, and there are also

cushioned benches and tables and chairs.

★ **The Club**
downtown at Del Monte Av./Alvarado St. *646-9244*
Attractions range from live rock music through comedy to male burlesque at different times during the week. The big upstairs nightclub has three bars, one of the area's largest dance floors, and a bay view.

Cuckoo's Nest
downtown at 180 Franklin St. *373-4566*
Live music and dancing are featured nightly in this large contemporary lounge.

★ **Doc Rickett's**
1 mi. NW at 95 Prescott Av. in Cannery Row *649-4241*
Live country/western music and Monterey's biggest dance floor attract foot stompin' crowds every night to the big casual downstairs saloon.

★ **Doubletree Hotel at Fisherman's Wharf**
downtown at Alvarado St./Del Monte Av. *649-4511*
The Brasstree, a large and classy lounge atop the hotel, features a beautiful wharf and harbor view, plus live music for listening or dancing nightly. Closed Sun.

★ **Dream Theater**
1 mi. NW at Lighthouse/Prescott Avs. *372-1331*
This "contemporary movie palace" is surprisingly comfortable and accommodating. In addition to screening first-run films, the theater is outfitted with three types of seating—spacious contour, rockers, and love seats for couples.

★ **First National Fogbank Saloon**
1 mi. NW at 638 Wave St. in Cannery Row *373-5751*
Live jazz music happens most nights in a cozy and comfortable lounge that is a local favorite.

Flora's
1 mi. NW at Prescott Av./Wave St. in Cannery Row *375-1921*
Decorated in the Victorian rococo style of a bordello described in Steinbeck's *Cannery Row*, this flamboyant little lounge was remodeled in 1986.

Kalissa's
1.2 mi. NW at 851 Cannery Row *372-8512*
Impromptu live music is offered most nights along with a dozen coffees, plus beer, wine, and light meals. The tiny cabaret also features flamenco music and belly dancers at certain times each month.

★ **Mark Thomas' Outrigger**
1 mi. NW at 700 Cannery Row *372-8543*
Dancing to live music over the water at Cannery Row is offered most nights in the large main lounge. A dramatic fireplace-lit extension provides both unique bay views and a romantic setting for enjoying the exotic drinks featured here.

Monterey Sheraton
downtown at 350 Calle Principal — *649-4234*
The new Monterey Sheraton Hotel sports a spiffy ground floor lounge where live jazz happens nightly in the Monterey Bay Club.

The Rogue
downtown at Wharf #2 — *372-4586*
Casual live music for easy listening or dancing may be available, but you are assured of romantic harbor views from this comfortable, casual lounge built over the bay on the newer wharf.

Sly McFly's
1 mi. NW at 700 Cannery Row — *649-8050*
This hangout lost most of its antique cars in a recent remodeling, but greens and stained glass remain to give it some class. Pizza and munchies are available with drinks. The "ladies room" is still entered through the door of a 1930s sedan.

★ **Tuxedo's**
downtown at 100 Pacific St. — *373-1644*
Musical stylings played on a grand piano are a proper complement to the dark and formal elegance of this new epicurean salon, just as champagne is the beverage-of-choice to accompany the caviar, souffles, and gourmet appetizers served here. Elaborate floral displays, art objects, and plush furniture accent the glamorous surroundings.

★ **Wharf Theater**
downtown on Fisherman's Wharf — *372-2882*
Good live theater is featured most evenings year-round on the second floor of a skillfully converted old building near the end of the wharf.

RESTAURANTS

The town's rich heritage, its location near an abundance of choice fresh produce, and growing demand for memorable dining experiences have produced a bumper crop of illustrious restaurants in Monterey in recent years. Visitors have their choice of gourmet cuisines; views which range from intimate close-ups of the waterfront to panoramic overviews of the magnificent bay; and dining rooms in skillfully converted historic buildings as well as in lavishly decorated new structures.

The Cannery
1 mi. NW at 650 Cannery Row — *372-8881*
L-D. — *Expensive*
The ordinary seafood and Italian dishes and casual service contrast with the formal decor and bayfront view in this large and pricey new dining room.

Captain's Galley
1 mi. NW at 711 Cannery Row — *649-8676*
B-L-D. — *Moderate*
Omelets and seafood are given a short order treatment in a casual nautically themed restaurant on the second floor of a converted cannery. There is a partial view of Cannery Row and the bay.

The Cagtain's Gig
downtown on Fisherman's Wharf 373-5559
L-D. No L on Sun. *Low*
Simple seafoods like fish and chips and clam chowder are served to go, or at outdoor tables or in the upstairs loft. It's fast, fair, and funky, with a good bay view and Anchor Steam on tap.

Casa Maria
1 mi. NW at Cannery Row & Hoffman Av. 373-0611
L-D. *Moderate*
Standard Mexican fare and decor do not distinguish this chain-operated restaurant, but it does have a notable bayfront view. The adjoining cantina does a better job of framing the scenic backdrop.

Chart House
.8 mi. NW at 444 Cannery Row 372-3362
D only. Sun. brunch. *Expensive*
The conventional steaks, seafoods, and salad bar in this representative of a stylish restaurant chain don't equal the contemporary wood-toned dining room over the bay and the fine waterfront view.

★ **Clock Garden**
downtown at 565 Abrego St. 375-6100
L-D. *Moderate*
Monterey's most enduring theme restaurant is still a popular destination for casual Continental dining and homemade baked goods. An old adobe carriage house was ingeniously converted into a contemporary restaurant decorated with a colorful clock and bottle collection. A charming, walled garden patio with a fireplace and sculpture is used for alfresco dining.

Domenico's
downtown at 50 Fisherman's Wharf 372-3655
L-D. *Expensive*
Fresh fish and meats grilled on an open hearth over mesquite wood, plus homemade pasta and gelato, distinguish the most formal of the Wharf's many restaurants. Guests overlook the inner harbor from an elegant contemporary dining room with a European flair.

Doubletree Hotel at Fisherman's Wharf
downtown at Alvarado St./Del Monte Av. 649-4511
D only. *Expensive*
Peter B's on the Alley is the showplace among dining facilities of this newer landmark hotel. Contemporary American dishes are presented in a luxurious and tranquil dining room away from the hotel hubbub.

★ **The Fishery**
1.2 mi. S at 21 Soledad Dr. 373-6200
L-D. No L on Sat. Closed Sun.-Mon. *Expensive*
One of the peninsula's finest seafood restaurants features creative adaptations of Oriental styles of fresh fish preparation. Delicious entrees

are accompanied by a truly innovative salad bar. Full linen table settings, large aquariums, and hanging plants enhance the casual decor.

★ **Fresh Cream**
downtown at 100 Pacific St. *375-9798*
D only. Closed Mon.-Tues. *Expensive*
Extraordinary French cuisine awaits those who find this upstairs restaurant tucked away in the Heritage Harbor complex. A short list of entrees, which changes daily according to the freshest and finest ingredients available, is prepared with great finesse. The subdued elegance of the decor and intimate harbor views are perfect accompaniments.

Grandma's Kitchen
2.3 mi. E at 2310 Fremont St. *375-3033*
B-L-D. *Moderate*
Old-fashioned American dishes are treated simply and with respect in this friendly and funky alternative to mass-produced fast food chains.

★ **Hammerheads**
downtown at 414 Calle Principal *373-3116*
L-D. *Expensive*
Nearly a dozen kinds of duck dishes, steaks cooked over oak wood, and an enticing chocolate bar are among the specialties of this exciting source of New California cuisine. The luxurious post-modern decor is a far cry from the building's firehouse origin.

Kathy's on the Korner
downtown at 702 Cass St. *373-1712*
B-L. *Moderate*
Homemade foods, including delicious fruit muffins, are emphasized in this cheerful coffee shop.

Mark Thomas' Outrigger
1 mi. NW at 700 Cannery Row *372-8543*
L-D. *Expensive*
The Polynesian food and decor are all right, but the main attraction is the over-the-water location and dramatic bay views. A romantic little firelit lounge adjoins, and live entertainment and dancing are offered in the main lounge.

Mike's Seafood Restaurant
downtown at 25 Fisherman's Wharf *372-6153*
L-D. *Moderate*
This big relaxed restaurant sports one of the last of the old-fashioned, remarkably long menus that were once standard in seafood houses. For example, crab is prepared eight different ways. A fireplace and bay views enliven the dining room.

★ **Monterey Plaza Hotel**
.8 mi. NW at 400 Cannery Row *646-1700*
B-L-D. *Very Expensive*
Italian specialties are prepared with a disciplined light touch in Delfino's, the main dining room of the new hotel. The most formally

sophisticated restaurant on Monterey Bay shares a fine view of the water with a polished adjoining lounge.

Neil De Vaughn's
1 mi. NW at 654 Cannery Row — *372-2141*
D only. Closed Mon. — *Expensive*
A conventional menu of seafood and steak is treated with surprising indifference, considering the relative formality of this very large new restaurant on Monterey Bay.

Old Fisherman's Grotto
downtown at 39 Fisherman's Wharf — *375-4604*
L-D. — *Moderate*
Monterey clam chowder is the highlight of this long-established seafood house, along with Monterey Bay prawns. The large casual dining room has a bay view.

The Old House
downtown at 500 Hartnell St. — *373-3737*
D only. — *Expensive*
Continental cuisine is offered by the new owners (a touted Florida chain) in a recently remodeled historic building. Waiters and waitresses in black tuxedos contrast with the flowery decor of the spacious dining room.

Peacock Bar & Grill
.9 mi. NW at 611 Lighthouse Av. — *372-5565*
B-L-D. — *Moderate*
Traditional American dishes of all kinds are served, along with various homemade cheesecakes, into the wee hours. An old high-ceilinged store has been skillfully converted into a bright and brassy, plant-and-wood-trimmed new bistro. Multilevel dining areas are built around a handsome, handcrafted bar with comfortably padded stools.

★ **The Point**
downtown at 100 Pacific St. — *373-1644*
D only. Sun. brunch. — *Expensive*
A bonanza of dramatically displayed fresh pastas and exotic vegetables, and a high-tech frozen yogurt dessert island, hint that this exciting young restaurant may be the birthplace of a new generation of salad bars. Mesquite-broiled seafood and steaks are appropriate accompaniments. The expansive grey-and-purple-toned dining room that surrounds the raised salad and dessert island is a study in plush contemporary decor and careful detailing. Window walls on three sides give diners a close-up of Fisherman's Wharf and the bay.

Red Snapper Restaurant and Bar
downtown at 30 Fisherman's Wharf — *375-3113*
L-D. — *Moderate*
Fresh fish selections are posted on a blackboard in a comfortably furnished seafood house featuring a splendid view of the small boat basin. An adjoining bar shares the view.

The Rogue
downtown at Wharf #2 — *372-4586*
L-D. — *Expensive*
Fresh seafood and choice beef are accompanied by panoramic harbor views in a large, nautically themed bayside dining room. Formal service and linened table settings contrast with decor dominated by a fully outfitted fishing boat—complete with fish, crew, and sea gulls. A comfortable, raised bar shares the view.

Sancho Panza
downtown at 590 Calle Principal — *375-0095*
L-D. — *Low*
Mexican and early California-style dishes are served in a historic adobe and on a charming patio. A piano and harp are occasionally played in the main dining room, and fireplaces lend warmth both indoors and out.

Sandbar and Grill
downtown on Wharf #2 — *373-2818*
L-D. Sat. & Sun. brunch. — *Moderate*
Fresh seafoods highlight a contemporary American menu in this newer bar and grill with a boat's-eye view of the harbor and Fisherman's Wharf. Natural wood tones, plush blue seating, a classy island bar, and a piano accompaniment with dinner also contribute to the convivial atmosphere.

★ **Sardine Factory**
1 mi. NW at 701 Wave St. in Cannery Row — *373-3775*
D only. — *Very Expensive*
This large, celebrated restaurant serves gourmet Continental cuisine and their own pastries and ice cream in an elegant historic setting. The Captain's Room recalls the plush ambiance of the height of the Victorian era. The Conservatory Room is a striking glass-domed space with the feeling of an elegant garden. There is also a sophisticated lounge.

Serra's Landing
downtown at Pacific/Scott Sts. — *646-9744*
L-D. Sat. & Sun. brunch. — *Moderate*
Homestyle Southern Italian meals are offered in an attractive California mission-style restaurant or on a delightful outdoor patio overlooking Fisherman's Wharf and the bay.

Sheraton Monterey Hotel
downtown at 350 Calle Principal — *649-4234*
L-D. — *Expensive*
Ferrante's exhibition kitchen turns out innovative Italian dishes. But, they can't compete with the panoramic view of downtown, the Wharf, and bay from the floor-to-ceiling windows in the casual tenth floor restaurant of the new hotel.

Steinbeck Lobster Grotto
1 mi. NW at 720 Cannery Row *373-1884*
L-D. *Moderate*
The seafood menu is conventional, and the big casual dining room is family-oriented, but the restaurant is built over Monterey Bay. Patrons have a picture window view of the water. A glass-bottomed floor area gives diners at surrounding tables an unusual close-up view of breaking waves.

★ **Triples**
downtown at 220 Olivier St. *372-4744*
L-D. Closed Sun. *Very Expensive*
Continental and French cuisine is served in elegant dining rooms fashioned out of a carefully converted old cottage.

★ **Whaling Station Inn**
1 mi. NW at 763 Wave St. in Cannery Row *373-3778*
D only. *Very Expensive*
An oak pit broiler is used to prepare fresh fish and choice steaks in one of the peninsula's largest and most popular showcases of New California cuisine. Gourmet entrees are accompanied by the finest seasonal produce and the peninsula's first all-California wine list. Much polished wood, greenery, and stained glass complement the Victorian decor.

The Wharfside
downtown at 60 Fisherman's Wharf *375-3956*
L-D. *Moderate*
Contemporary seafood and a half dozen varieties of homemade ravioli are served in nicely-appointed dining rooms that occupy two levels in this large newer restaurant. The wharf and bay views from upstairs are excellent.

LODGING

Monterey has a remarkable diversity of accommodations. Visitors can select from luxurious resorts, convention or executive hotels, country-style inns, or an abundance of motels. Bargains are extremely scarce on weekends and during summer. On holiday and special event weekends, some places even raise their rates well above the summer rates shown. Prices are typically reduced at least 30% below those listed on non-weekends from late fall through spring, especially by many of the motels along Fremont Street starting about a mile southeast of downtown, and on Munras Avenue starting just south of downtown.

The Arbor Inn
.4 mi. S at 1058 Munras Av. *372-3381*
A whirlpool is a feature of this well-maintained motel. Each nicely furnished room has cable color TV and a phone. A free Continental breakfast is available.

#117—spacious, raised pressed-log fireplace, hill view, K bed...$84
regular room— Q bed...$64

Colton Inn - Travelodge
downtown at 707 Pacific St. *649-6500*
This modern motel has a convenient downtown location, and a sauna. Each nicely furnished room has cable color TV and a phone.
#309—top fl., pressed-log fireplace,
in-bath whirlpool, K bed...$73
#201—end, top fl., pressed-log fireplace,
shared creekside balc., K bed...$73
regular room— 2 Q or K bed...$73

Doubletree Hotel at Fisherman's Wharf
downtown at Alvarado St./Del Monte Av. *649-4511*
This convention-oriented landmark hotel between downtown and Fisherman's Wharf has a round outdoor pool, whirlpool, and (fee) tennis courts, and garage, plus a full range of conference halls, restaurant, lounges, and shopping facilities. Each well-furnished room has a phone and cable color TV with (fee) movies. For toll-free reservations, call: (800)528-0444.
6th floor—panoramic bay/town views, K bed...$140
regular room— 2 D or K bed...$110

El Castell Motel
2 mi. E at 2102 Fremont St. *372-8176*
A large indoor pool is the notable attraction of this well-maintained older motel. Each spacious room has a phone and cable color TV with movies.
regular room— K bed...$48

El Dorado Motel
.3 mi. S at 900 Munras Av. *373-2921*
This convenient, contemporary little motel is beautifully furnished. Each room has a phone and cable color TV with movies. A Continental breakfast is complimentary.
#14—end, top fl., pressed-log fireplace,
some bay view, Q bed...$73
regular room— Q or K bed...$63

Holiday Inn
2.5 mi. E at 2600 Sand Dunes Dr. *394-3321*
The Monterey Peninsula's first full-service beachfront hotel also has a large outdoor pool, and a sauna, plus a bay view-oriented restaurant and lounge. Bayside rooms offer floor-to-ceiling window views of Monterey across the water. Each spacious, well-furnished room has a phone and cable color TV with movies.
#470,#370,#270 (in Bldg. E)—pvt. balc., superb
bay view, K bed...$135
regular room— 2 D beds...$110

Hyatt Regency Monterey
1 mi. SE at 1 Old Golf Course Rd. *372-7171*
The peninsula's largest lodging facility is a well-landscaped

contemporary resort hotel. Twenty-one oak-shaded acres contain two outdoor swimming pools, whirlpools, parcours, and (for a fee) a beautiful 18-hole golf course and six tennis courts (two lighted). Elaborate convention, restaurant, lounge, entertainment, and some shopping facilities are also available. Each attractively furnished room has a phone and cable color TV with (fee) movies.

view room—some overlook golf course/hills, K bed...$155
regular room—some have open beam ceiling, overlook gardens, K bed...$125

★ **The Jabberwalk**
1 mi. NW at 598 Laine St. *372-4777*

A convent above Cannery Row has been charmingly transformed into an antique-filled bed-and-breakfast inn. There are many extras, like goose down pillows and comforters, fresh flowers, a complimentary breakfast, and evening hors d'oeuvres and aperitifs.

"Borogrove"—spacious, shower, windows on 3 sides, gas fireplace, superb bay view, K bed...$140
regular room—shared bath, Q bed...$75

Lone Oak Motel
2.1 mi. E at 2221 Fremont St. *372-4924*

This plain single-level motel has several unusually well-outfitted rooms. Each comfortably furnished room has cable color TV with movies and a phone.

#37,#36—spacious, gas fireplace, whirlpool in sep. room, in-bath steambath, refr., K bed...$90
#34—spacious, gas fireplace, refrigerator, K bed...$60
regular room— Q bed...$50

★ **The Mariposa**
.6 mi. S at 1386 Munras Av. *649-1414*

Opened in 1984, this elegant motor inn has an outdoor pool, whirlpool, and covered garage. But, the real feature is the guest rooms. Each is spacious, beautifully decorated with some ultra-modern flourishes, and has cable color TV and a phone.

#321,#223,"Spa Suites"—gas fireplace, in-room raised whirlpool, refrigerator, double shower, K bed...$130
regular room— Q bed...$72

Merritt House
downtown at 386 Pacific St. *646-9686*

A historic adobe and rose garden are the nucleus of a stylish motel. Each room has a gas fireplace, refrigerator, cable color TV, and phone, and is decorated with furnishings reminiscent of the Victorian era. A free Continental breakfast is served in the common room.

regular room— Q or K bed...$105

★ **Monterey Bay Inn**
.7 mi. NW at 242 Cannery Row *373-6242*
One of the peninsula's newest (1985) and finest motels is perched above the water of Monterey Bay. Amenities include two whirlpools (one has a fine bay view), health club, and a sauna. A wash-down area, lockers, and showers have been provided for scuba divers staying here and using the adjoining park. A complimentary Continental breakfast is served. Each spacious room is a study in exquisite contemporary appointments, and includes a remote-controlled cable color TV, bar/refrigerator, and a private balcony. For toll-free reservations, in California, call: (800)424-6242.
#411 thru #414—top floor, private super views of the bay, K bed...$145
#410 & #409—top floor, super views of the yacht harbor, K bed...$120
regular room—Cannery Row view, K bed...$95

Monterey Fireside Lodge
1 mi. E at 1131 10th St. *373-4172*
Raised gas-log fireplaces enhance each of the spacious, nicely furnished rooms in this contemporary motel, along with cable color TV, phones, and cooktop/refrigerator consoles. A hot tub is in the patio.
top floor room—vaulted ceiling, K bed...$80
regular room— Q bed...$70

Monterey Inn - Best Western
.3 mi. S at 825 Abrego St. *373-5345*
This handsome new motel has an outdoor pool and whirlpool, plus a covered garage. Each of the tastefully furnished rooms has cable color TV and a phone. A free Continental breakfast is offered in the lobby. For toll-free reservations, call: (800)528-1234.
#323—corner room on top (3rd) fl., windows on 2 sides, gas fireplace, pvt. balc. with town/bay view, K bed...$103
regular room— K bed...$73

★ **The Monterey Plaza**
.8 mi. NW at 400 Cannery Row *646-1700*
Late in 1985, Monterey's most sumptuous hotel opened on a choice bayfront location between Cannery Row and Fisherman's Wharf. By late 1986, a pool, health spa, and specialty shops will join the refined dining, drinking, and conference facilities that are already available along with valet parking in a security garage. Each spacious guest room is a study in genteel good taste, including his and her bathrobes and lotions, as well as a phone and color TV with movies. For toll-free reservations in California, call: (800)334-3999. Elsewhere, call: (800)631-1339.
#1301—corner, top floor, balcony over bay/Cannery Row, floor-to-ceiling windows, K bed...$200

#1302,#1202,#1102,#1002—corner, balcony over bay/Wharf, floor-to-ceiling windows, K bed...$200
#2427,#2327,#2227,#2127—corner, bay/Wharf views, floor-to-ceiling windows, K bed...$180
regular room—Cannery Row view, K bed...$140

★ **Monterey Sheraton Hotel**
downtown at Del Monte Av./Calle Principal *649-4234*
The peninsula's newest and tallest hotel opened in 1984. At a time when most towns are losing their landmark hotels, Monterey now has a second major downtown convention-oriented hotel. Amenities at the Sheraton include an outdoor pool, whirlpool, and saunas, plus a full range of convention, restaurant, and lounge facilities and (fee) security parking. Each spacious room has a phone and color TV. For toll-free reservations, call: (800)325-3535.
deluxe room—fine bay view, balcony, 2 D or K bed...$155
regular room—pool view, 2 D or K bed...$120

Motel 6
2 mi. E at 2124 Fremont St. *373-3500*
The **bargain** motel chain is represented by an extremely popular facility on motel row with an outdoor pool.
regular room—pay TV, D bed...$26

★ **Munras Lodge**
.3 mi. S at 1010 Munras Av. *646-9696*
This plush ultra-modern motel has a whirlpool and sauna. Each spacious, well-furnished unit has cable color TV and a phone.
"Honeymoon Suite"—whirlpool in room, his/her bathrooms, gas fireplace, K bed...$125
#31—top fl., corner, wet bar, pvt. balc., harbor/palm view, gas fireplace, K bed...$85
#37—corner, top floor, private view, gas fireplace, K bed...$80
regular room— K bed...$65

★ **Old Monterey Inn**
.6 mi. SW at 500 Martin St. *375-8284*
A historic mansion built in 1920 has been converted into a gracious bed-and-breakfast inn in a lovely park-like setting. All rooms have private baths, and there are many charming extras—oversized beds, goose-down comforters, complimentary breakfast, and evening wine and cheese.
"Library"—lg. windows on 3 sides, stone fireplace, pvt. tub/shower, K bed...$145
"Rookery"—cozy, fireplace, skylight, pvt. shower, pvt. view, Q bed...$130
regular room "Heatherwood"— K bed...$110

Park Crest Motel - Best Western
.4 mi. S at 1100 Munras Av. *372-4576*
Attractive landscaping and excellent furnishings give distinction to this

small contemporary motel with an outdoor pool. Each room has cable color TV and a phone.

#41—end, top floor, Monterey pines view, K bed...$79
#34—end, top floor, magnolia/park/ocean view, K bed...$79
regular room— K bed...$72

The Pelican Inn
.5 mi. S at Munras Av./Cass St. *375-2679*

An outdoor pool is a feature of this small, recently upgraded motel. Each of the cozy, nicely furnished rooms has a phone and color TV.

#109,#103,#204—raised fireplace, refrigerator, Q bed...$70
regular room— Q bed...$60

Rancho Monterey Motel
.5 mi. S at 1200 Munras Av. *372-5821*

This small single-level motel has nicely landscaped grounds and an outdoor pool with a slide. Each room has cable color TV and a phone.

regular room— Q or K bed...$55

★ **The Spindrift Inn - Best Western**
1 mi. NW at 652 Cannery Row *646-8900*

The first bayfront lodging in the midst of Cannery Row opened in late 1984. It is a motor inn of quiet elegance offering complimentary valet parking, Continental breakfast in the morning, and wine and cheese in the afternoon. Each of the large, beautifully appointed rooms has a wood-burning fireplace, refrigerator, two phones, and remote-controlled cable color TV, plus down feather beds and down pillows. For toll-free reservations in California, call: (800)841-1879.

#407,#307—fine bay view, window alcove seats, Q or K bed...$189
regular room—overlooks Cannery Row, Q or K bed...$139

The Victorian Inn - Best Western
.8 mi. NW at 487 Foam St. in Cannery Row *373-8000*

This impressive motel opened a block from the bay in the Cannery Row area in 1985. There is a whirlpool in the patio, and underground parking. Each of the compact rooms is furnished with good reproductions, and has a wood-burning fireplace, a window seat or balcony, a remote-controlled color TV, and two telephones. Continental breakfast and afternoon wine and cheese are complimentary. For toll-free reservations in California, call: (800)223-4141.

#307,#308,#309—partial bay view from private balcony, Q bed...$119
regular room— Q bed...$99

★ **West Wind Lodge**
.4 mi. S at 1046 Munras Av. *373-1337*

An attractive enclosed pool is the center of interest, and there is also a sauna in this stylish newer motel. Each spacious, well-furnished room has a phone and cable color TV with movies.

"executive unit" (several)—gas fireplace, kitchen, K bed...$100
regular room— Q bed...$65

CAMPGROUNDS

Surprisingly, there are only two campgrounds near town.

Laguna Seca Recreation Area
7 mi. SE via CA 68 at 1025 Monterey Rd. *422-6138*
This large, county-operated campground near a small reservoir has boat rentals, and features boating and fishing. Flush toilets, hot showers, and hookups are available. Each of the sites has a picnic table, fire ring and grill. For toll-free reservations, call: (800)822-2267. base rate...$10

Marina Dunes R.V. Park
9 mi. NE via CA 1 & Reservation Rd. at 3330 Dunes Dr. *384-6914*
The beach is a short stroll from this campground. Flush toilets, hot showers, and full hookups are available. Each large site has a picnic table, and there is a lawn area for tents. base rate...$12

SPECIAL EVENTS

Adobe Tour *downtown* *late April*
Attention is focused on historic buildings not normally open to the public during this one-day tour sponsored by the Monterey History and Art Association.

Monterey County Fair *Fairgrounds* *August*
Of special interest is the variety and quality of produce displayed and offered for sale in various forms in this major mid-summer event.

★ **Monterey Jazz Festival** *Fairgrounds* *mid-September*
The Monterey County Fairgrounds are jammed for three days in September with jazz buffs listening to "living legends" and stars of tomorrow. Reservations should be made well in advance for this renowned event.

★ **Wine Festival** *in town* *late November*
Many of the nation's finest wineries are represented at a prestigious series of tastings, banquets, and seminars in praise of the grape.

OTHER INFORMATION

Area Code: *408*

Zip Code: *93940*

Monterey Peninsula Chamber of Commerce
downtown at 380 Alvarado St. *649-1770*

Nevada City

Nevada City is the picturesque essence of the Mother Lode country. Handsome Victorian frame homes and brick businesses line narrow streets that wind up into the steep forested foothills of the Sierra Nevada. Countryside that once teemed with miners is host again to increasing numbers of visitors. This time, they're here to enjoy clear streams and scenic reservoirs folded into these gentle mountains, and to explore the residue of a tumultuous past. A relatively mild, but damp, four season climate supports a luxuriant combination of pine trees and broadleafs. Maples and other Eastern hardwoods brought in by Yankee argonauts contribute to the town's distinctive appearance. Brilliant displays of fall colors and pleasant temperatures make autumn the most appealing season. Yet the town is usually only crowded on weekends. Winters are cool and very wet. Snowfall is relatively light, so there are no major winter sports complexes in the immediate vicinity. Summer attracts the greatest numbers of visitors to spend their leisure time in the historic town and nearby forests, lakes, rivers, and mountains on uniformly hot sunny days.

Miners first settled here in 1849 with a few tents and log cabins along Deer Creek. Placer gold was abundant, and even richer gravels were soon discovered in an ancient stream bed. By the end of 1850, several thousand people called the newly named town of "Nevada" home. (Fourteen years later the town's name was stolen when the State of Nevada was admitted to the Union. Begrudgingly, residents added the word "City" after "Nevada" to distinguish their town from the younger state.) It became the seat of newly formed Nevada County in 1851. By 1856 it was California's third largest city with nearly ten thousand residents. After a disastrous fire that year, more substantial businesses were constructed of brick—with iron doors and shutters—and two fire companies were organized. A few years later, miners began to leave in great numbers for the new silver region in Nevada as the local gold placers and gravels began to play out. Thanks in part to its increasingly prosperous metal foundry, the town survived, albeit at a substantially reduced pace.

One of the West's most unspoiled Victorian business districts, still illuminated by gas lamps, is the priceless legacy of Nevada City's brief boom era. Impressive public buildings, historic theaters and churches, and a fine museum are all within an easy stroll of the heart of town. Other carefully restored and maintained brick and wood structures in the historic district house a growing number of specialty shops featuring Mother Lode artifacts, an unusual diversity of distinguised restaurants, and a captivating assortment of atmospheric theaters, bars, and saloons. There are surprisingly few places to stay, but the oldest operating hotel west of the Rockies is still the liveliest landmark in town.

Elevation:

2,535 feet

Population (1980):

2,431

Population (1970):

2,314

Location:

148 miles Northeast of San Francisco

Nevada City

WEATHER PROFILE

Vokac Weather Rating

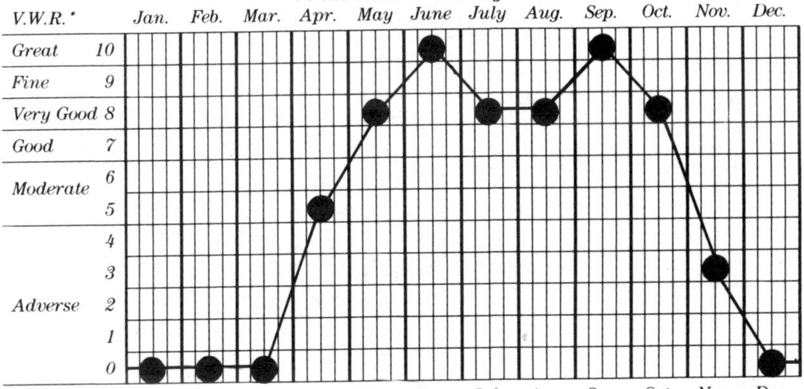

V.W.R.*	Jan.	Feb.	Mar.	Apr.	May	June	July	Aug.	Sep.	Oct.	Nov.	Dec.
Great 10						●			●			
Fine 9												
Very Good 8					●		●	●		●		
Good 7												
Moderate 6												
5				●								
Adverse 4												
3											●	
2												
1												
0	●	●	●									●

	Jan.	Feb.	Mar.	Apr.	May	June	July	Aug.	Sep.	Oct.	Nov.	Dec.
*V.W.R.**	0	0	0	5	8	10	8	8	10	8	3	0
Temperature												
Ave. High	52	54	58	65	70	81	90	89	82	72	62	54
Ave. Low	28	30	31	35	39	45	49	47	43	38	32	29
Precipitation												
Inches Rain	10.0	9.6	8.0	4.5	2.4	0.6	-	-	0.5	2.7	5.2	9.4
Inches Snow	13	8	6	-	-	-	-	-	-	-	-	3

**V.W.R. = Vokac Weather Rating: probability of mild (warm & dry) weather on any given day.*

Forecast

Month	*V.W.R.**		*Temperatures Daytime*	*Temperatures Evening*	*Precipitation*
Jan.	0	Adverse	cool	chilly	frequent snowstorms/downpours
Feb.	0	Adverse	cool	chilly	frequent downpours/snow flurries
Mar.	0	Adverse	cool	chilly	frequent downpours/snow flurries
Apr.	5	Moderate	warm	cool	occasional downpours
May	8	Very Good	warm	cool	infrequent rainstorms
June	10	Great	warm	cool	infrequent showers
July	8	Very Good	hot	warm	none
Aug.	8	Very Good	hot	warm	none
Sep.	10	Great	warm	cool	infrequent showers
Oct.	8	Very Good	warm	cool	infrequent downpours
Nov.	3	Adverse	cool	chilly	occasional downpours
Dec.	0	Adverse	cool	chilly	frequent downpours/snow flurries

Summary

Attractively situated in the Sierra foothills near the northern end of the Gold Camp country, Nevada City has a true four season climate. Almost all of the unfavorable weather is concentrated into the **winter** months, when cool days and chilly evenings are coupled with frequent snowfalls and heavy rainstorms that preclude most outdoor activities. During **spring**, temperatures increase rapidly. Unfortunately, the enjoyment of normally warm days is diminished by rainstorms that persist through much of the season. **Summer** is relatively pleasant. Days are typically hot and sunny, evenings are warm, and there is almost no rainfall to keep people indoors. Early **fall** offers faultless weather until heavy rainstorms begin again in earnest after Halloween. This is unquestionably the most delightful time of year, because the surrounding countryside is ablaze with one of the West's most spectacular fall foliage displays. As an added attraction, it is also harvest time in the many nearby apple orchards.

ATTRACTIONS & DIVERSIONS

★ **The American Victorian Museum**

downtown at 325 Spring St. *265-5804*

A unique museum occupies the historic Miners Foundry (1856), a group of stone, brick and frame buildings in which the Pelton Wheel (a key link between the water wheel and modern power generation) was first manufactured in 1878. Machine parts for mining operations were also made here, along with architectural iron used throughout the world. The museum is the only one in America devoted exclusively to displaying artifacts from the Victorian period (1840-1900). The complex also includes a popular theater, an unusual weekend restaurant and lounge, and a radio station.

★ ***Carriage Rides***

downtown at several "carriage for hire" signs *265-5348*

Visitors can tour the historic district in the nostalgic comfort of a horse-drawn carriage. Rides of up to a half hour are available daily—weather permitting.

★ ***Covered Bridge***

14 mi. W in Bridgeport

Built in 1862, the longest single-span wood covered bridge in America extends 225 feet across the South Yuba River near Bridgeport. Vehicles are shunted across a newer bridge nearby, so pedestrians can explore the well-preserved structure at their leisure. Scenic hiking trails continue along the canyon to secluded picnic sites and swimming holes.

★ **Empire Mine State Historic Park**

5 mi. S at 10791 E. Empire St. - Grass Valley *273-8522*

One of California's oldest and richest gold mines is also one of the deepest (9,000 feet) in the world. The grounds include a visitor center, exhibits reflecting more than a century of hard rock mining at this location, and the baronial Bourn Mansion. This former residence of the mine owner has been carefully restored and refurbished, as have the formal gardens surrounding the mansion. Guided tours are offered daily, except in winter.

Firehouse No. 1

downtown at 214 Main St. *265-5468*

The Nevada County Historical Society operates a museum in the photogenic 1861 structure. Pioneer implements and garb are exhibited.

Library

downtown at 211 N. Pine St. *265-4606*

The Nevada City Public Library has served the area since just after the turn of the century from this substantial building. The unspoiled old-fashioned interior is distinguished by polished wood trim. Browsers are tempted to linger in a couple of fine old wooden rocking chairs. Closed Sat.-Sun.

★ **Malakoff Diggins State Historic Park**
15 mi. NE off CA 49 at 23579 N. Bloomfield Rd. *265-2740*
Here was the world's largest hydraulic gold mine. The Malakoff Pit is an awesome testament to the destructive power of water under high pressure. It is a vast hole nearly 600 feet deep, 3,000 feet wide, and 7,000 feet long with a shallow lake at the bottom. Hydraulic mining was profitable, but it wrecked havoc with the environment. After a ten year legal battle, it was finally outlawed in California in 1884. Several interesting buildings still stand in the ghost town of North Bloomfield near the pit, including a former dance hall that is now a Park Museum with hydraulic mining exhibits. Nearby is the giant monitor nozzle that controlled the flow of water against the slopes. Wet winter weather closes the dirt access roads.

★ **North Star Mining Museum**
4.5 mi. SW on Allison Ranch Rd. - Grass Valley *273-9853*
A giant thirty-foot Pelton waterwheel displayed here was the largest of its type in the world when it was installed in 1895. The massive old powerhouse now also houses a substantial collection of artifacts depicting the history and methods of California gold mining. Closed November thru April except weekends.

Pioneer Park
.5 mi. E on Nimrod St. *265-2521*
A public outdoor swimming pool, tennis courts, playing fields, and shaded picnic tables are provided in this town park nestled in a fold of the hills.

★ **Tahoe National Forest**
N and E of town *265-4531*
All of the Sierra Nevada mountains between Tahoe City and Lake Tahoe are included in this spectacular forest. Features near town include numerous campgrounds, and miles of excellent trails for hiking and backpacking along the scenic canyons of the many-branched Yuba and Bear River drainages. Idyllic clear pools attract swimmers, and miles of whitewater rapids appeal to rafters and kayakers, especially in spring. In winter, an hour's drive east of town accesses the Royal Gorge Nordic Ski Resort, with perhaps the largest system of constantly maintained cross-country ski trails anywhere. Nearby, the historic Donner Pass area is the site of several fully developed downhill skiing complexes. An hour beyond lies Squaw Valley Ski Area, a magnificent legacy of the 1960 winter Olympics. The northwestern shore of Lake Tahoe, with facilities for every kind of winter sport, is the forest's supreme attraction.

Warm Water Feature

Misty Mountain Tubs & Things
downtown at 110 S. Pine St. *265-3149*
A Gold Camp update of the Saturday night bath furnishes private rooms with whirlpool tubs that can be rented by the hour. A sauna and a juice bar are other features. Massage can be arranged by reservation.

Winery

Nevada City Winery

downtown at 321 Spring St. *265-9463*

This small winery in the historic foundry complex is a first for the area. The tasting room is dramatically, and aromatically, perched at the top of the wine storage and aging area. Tasting and sales 12-5 daily.

SHOPPING

One of the West's most picturesque downtowns is a beguiling place to shop and stroll. The entire area is on the National Register of Historic Districts. Rows of pre-Civil War brick buildings line steep, narrow streets distinguished by wrought-iron gas lanterns and wooden street signs. Numerous specialty shops emphasize collectibles in arts, crafts, and artifacts related to the Mother Lode country.

Food Specialties

Apple Annie's

6.5 mi. S via CA 49 at 13895 CA 174 *273-9266*

Cider and homemade apple pie are served along with soups and sandwiches in a country roadside cafe, and at picnic tables in the orchard when weather permits. Fresh produce is sold in the adjoining market, including apples from their orchards harvested from September thru November.

The Apple Fare

downtown at 307 Broad St. *265-5458*

Several good, homemade pies are the specialty. Light meals are also served in this cheerful cafe.

★ **The Flour Garden Bakery**

2.5 mi. S at 11999 Sutton Way (in Gold Country Center) *272-2043*

It's part of a local chain, but quality and no preservatives are emphasized in a tantalizing array of baked goods ranging from raspberry walnut danish and scones, to cinnamon rolls and a good selection of bagels—even banana nut. It's all served to go or at tables with delicious Sierra Mountain house blend coffee.

★ **Friar Tuck's Wine Shop**

downtown at 111 N. Pine St. *265-9093*

A fine assortment of premium California wines is attractively displayed. Several reasonably priced tastes are offered each day at an inviting wine bar. Closed Mon.

★ **Grandma Hartung's Victorian Pantry**

downtown at 308½ Broad St. *275-3723*

Delicious homemade fudge and truffles, and muffins, plus fresh brewed coffee are featured in this tempting takeout.

★ **Happy Apple Kitchen**

11 mi. S via CA 49 on CA 174 *273-2822*

Apples are showcased year-round in an imaginative variety of delectable homemade foods like apple/cream cheese muffins, apple milkshakes, and old-fashioned or French apple pie. These specialties are served with sandwiches and light lunches in a little dining room or on an adjoining covered porch. An adjacent fresh produce stand is only open during the summer, but apples from the orchard are sold a short distance down the road during the fall harvest. Closed Sun.

★ **P.J.'s Meat**
.8 mi. S at 106 Argall Way *265-4267*
Hickory-smoked meats, beef jerky, and homemade sausages are highlights from the smokehouse of this new gourmet food store. It is a fine place for assembling a picnic. Gift packs are also available.

★ **Sierra Mountain Coffee Roasters**
downtown at 316 Commercial St. *265-5282*
A big, colorful in-room roaster and specially processed water suggest management's concern for producing the best possible coffees and expressos. Assorted premium beans, or coffees, are sold to go or with pastries at tables in a cozy new shop built into a historic structure. Closed Mon.

Tad's Apple-a-day Farm
2 mi. S via CA 49 at 10451 Pittsburg Rd. *273-6832*
Several varieties of apples are harvested from September to December and sold with cold and delicious fresh-pressed cider at a photogenic little hillside farm.

Specialty Shops

★ **Alpha**
downtown at 210 Broad St. *265-4503*
For more than a century, this large handsome store has been serving residents' houseware and hardware needs. It is still a great place to check out the latest in gold panning equipment, or at least to absorb the evolving spirit of the gold camps.

★ **Fur Traders**
downtown at 231 Broad St. *265-3300*
An impressive array of contemporary fur coats, slippers, and rugs are made and sold in this shop, and in another outlet down the block at 319 Broad St.

Grimblefinger
downtown at 242 Commercial St. *265-5592*
A good assortment of books plus periodicals and a gallery of prints and posters are invitingly displayed.

★ **Overtures**
downtown at 316 Broad St. *265-9604*
Whale tea, the Gold Camp's answer to spice teas everywhere, has found a home in this appealing new shop full of northern California collectibles.

NIGHTLIFE

An outstanding assortment of theaters and bars offering live entertainment, drinking and dancing is clustered in the historic district at the heart of town. Many of these places are "living showcases" of authentic architecture and decor of the Victorian period.

★ **American Victorian Museum**
downtown at 325 Spring St. *265-5804*
Live entertainment—plays, concerts, and more—takes place most weekends in "the great stone hall." This cavernous brick and stone room was once the heart of a century-old iron foundry.

Big Al's
downtown at 101 Broad St. *265-5808*
The largest dance floor in town and live entertainment most nights are reasons to check out this big new nightclub outfitted with unusual chrome and wood-toned decor.

Chief Crazy Horse Inn
downtownn at 230 Commercial St. *265-9933*
Pool tables and a dart alcove are featured in a funky old wood-trimmed saloon heated by a pot-bellied stove and a hooded fireplace. Closed Mon.-Tues.

Cirino's
downtown at 309 Broad St. *265-2246*
Live music and dancing are featured most nights. This comfortable newer lounge gives patrons a choice of sofas, tables and chairs, or padded bar stools by a handsome hardwood back bar.

Coach House
.9 mi. S at 754 Zion St. *265-5614*
Live country/western music is played nightly for dancing in a big, casual ranch-style lounge with comfortable armchairs. Closed Sun.

★ **Framastanyl's**
downtown at 235 Commercial St. *265-9292*
Dancing to live music is offered most nights in a contemporary saloon with a firelit conversation area, some stained glass, a distinctive bar with padded-backed stools, and abundant greenery. A padded booth area serves as a Mexican cafe during the day. A pleasant wood-decked courtyard is used when weather permits.

★ **McGees Annex**
downtown at 315 Broad St. *265-3205*
There is occasional live entertainment, but the sylish brick-and-wood saloon with many plush sofas, numerous paintings, and a handsome bar is a fine place for a drink and conversation anytime.

★ **National Hotel**
downtown at 211 Broad St. *265-4551*
An old upright piano is played frequently in the hotel's splendid Victorian saloon. With its magnificent polished hardwood bar, period pictures, and ornate fixtures, this is a living tribute to the spirit of the gold camps.

Nevada Theater
downtown at 401 Broad St. *265-6161*
California's oldest theater building (1865) has been carefully restored. It serves once again as the community's cultural center. Musical and dramatic productions and special concerts are regularly scheduled and enthusiastically supported.

RESTAURANTS

Most of the good restaurants are concentrated in the historic district, and contribute to its charm with appropriately Victorian decor. American fare prevails, with a few notable exceptions.

The Burrito Factory
downtown at 401 Commercial St. *265-6138*
L-D. *Low*
A good assortment of northern Mexican specialties is served in a casual, skylighted cafe, on a covered outdoor patio, or to go.

Cafe les Stace
downtown at 311 Broad St. *265-6440*
L-D. B on Sat.-Sun. Closed Tues. *Moderate*
American and Mexican dishes are served in a cheerful restaurant overlooking the main street. It is popular with families.

Coach House
.9 mi. S at 754 Zion St. *265-5614*
L-D. *Moderate*
Steaks highlight hearty American dishes served in a large casual dining room next to a big lounge with Western music for dancing.

Friar Tuck's
downtown at 111 N. Pine St. *265-9093*
D only. Closed Mon. *Moderate*
Some of the Gold Camp's finest steaks, seafood, chicken and fondues are offered in a historic building refitted in brick-and-wood wine-cellar decor. The charming little front room bar has a good street view and live entertainment, plus several tap beers and premium wine by the glass.

Jack's for Dinner
downtown at 101 Broad St. *265-3405*
D only. Closed Sun.-Tues. *Very Expensive*
Gourmet international cuisine is prepared from the freshest available ingredients. Five course dinners are presented at tables set with crystal, china, and silver in an elegant little dining room in an upstairs hideaway. Reservations are necessary.

Michael's Garden Restaurant
downtown at 216 Main St. *265-6660*
L-D. Closed Sun. *Moderate*
Creative adaptations of Continental dishes have gotten this new restaurant off to a notable start. A historic residence has been carefully re-outfitted with casually elegant dining rooms.

National Hotel
downtown at 211 Broad St. *265-4551*
B-L-D. Sun. brunch. *Moderate*
American fare is served in the authentically Victorian dining room of Nevada City's landmark hotel. Bentwood chairs grace tables set with fresh flowers and kerosene lamps in a large room distinguished by polished wainscoating on high walls accented by ornately framed old pictures.

★ **The Royal Garden**
downtown at 300 Commercial St. *265-6951*
L-D. Sun. brunch. Closed Wed. *Moderate*
Savory and authentic Thai cuisine is featured in a comfortably converted Victorian building. Outdoor seating amidst lush greenery (in season), or wood booths or low tables give patrons a choice of locales.

★ **Selaya's**
downtown at 320 Broad St. *265-5697*
D only. Closed Mon. *Moderate*
Continental dishes, and homemade soups and desserts, are specialties offered in a well-regarded Victorian-style dining room.

LODGING

Accommodations are surprisingly limited, considering the town's appeal. Visitors interested in staying in town should make reservations well in advance during summer and fall, and on weekends throughout the year. Winter and spring rates are usually at least 15% less than those shown. A few more lodgings are available in nearby Grass Valley.

Airway Motel
.3 mi. N at 575 E. Broad St. *265-2233*
This little old **bargain** motel with an outdoor pool is a pleasant walk from the historic district. Each modest room has cable color TV, and units #7 thru #10 are backed by a tiny stream.
regular room— D bed...$26

Gold Country Inn - Best Western
2.5 mi. S at 11972 Sutton Way- Grass Valley 95945 *273-1393*
The freeway is hard by this contemporary motel with an outdoor pool and whirlpool. Spacious rooms all have color TV and a phone. For toll-free reservations call (800)247-6590.
regular room— K bed...$41
regular room— Q bed...$39

Holiday Lodge Motel
3.5 mi. S at 1221 E. Main St. - Grass Valley 95945 *273-4406*
An outdoor pool (enclosed in winter), a whirlpool, and sauna are features of this modern motel. Each room has cable color TV with movies, and a phone.
regular room— K bed...$42

★ **National Hotel**
downtown at 211 Broad St. *265-4551*
Nevada City's three-story landmark, first opened in 1854, is the oldest continuously operated hotel in the state. Glimmerings of Victorian splendor flourish in the antique-filled public rooms. Modern amenities include an outdoor swimming pool, and private baths in most of the guest rooms.
#41—top floor corner, private tiny balcony,
B/W TV, private bath, town/mountain views, Q bed...$45
#20—suite, corner, public balcony, private bath,
some view, 4-poster D bed...$85
#34—parlor suite, public balcony, sitting room,
B/W TV, private path, antique K bed...$75
regular room—private bath, D bed...$45
regular room—shared bath, D bed...$35

Northern Queen Motel
.5 mi. S at 400 Railroad Av. *265-5824*
An outdoor pool and whirlpool distinguish this modern **bargain** motel. Each room has a color TV, a phone, and a refrigerator.
deluxe room— K waterbed...$36
regular room— Q bed...$28

Piety Hill Inn
.4 mi. S at 523 Sacramento St. *265-2245*
A tiny old auto court built around a handsome chestnut tree has been ingeniously remodeled into a fashionable motor inn. Each artistically furnished room has a color TV and a private bath.
#4—spacious, captivating painting of 3 ladies, K bed...$49
regular room— K bed...$39

★ **Red Castle Inn**
.3 mi. E at 109 Prospect Av. *265-5135*
A Victorian mansion built in 1860 in carpenter gothic style on a hill overlooking downtown is now the area's favorite bed-and-breakfast inn. Rooms have been faithfully restored and furnished in Victorian antiques. Most have private baths. A complimentary Continental breakfast is served.
Parlor Suite West—1 BR, sitting room, wood-burning
stove, private bath, D bed...$75
regular room—shared bath, D bed...$55

CAMPGROUNDS

There are many campgrounds in the area. The best are in forests by small rivers or reservoirs offering a good variety of water recreation.

Greenhorn Park
11 mi. SE via CA 20, Brunswick Rd. & CA 174 *272-6100*
This privately operated campground is on a gentle slope by Rollins Lake.

Boat rentals, a ramp, and a dock are provided, and swimming, fishing, and boating are popular on the small reservoir. Pit toilets, cold showers, and hookups are provided. Each site has a view of the lake and a picnic table. Some are shaded, and there is a separate tenting area.
base rate...$6

★ **Oregon Creek**
17 mi. NW via CA 49 *273-1371*
This small Tahoe National Forest campground is beautifully sited by the Middle Yuba River. Swimming, fishing, and gold panning are popular in the little river, and there are hiking trails nearby. Flush toilets are provided, but no showers or hookups. Each of the tree-shaded well-spaced sites has a picnic table. base rate...$4

★ **Scotts Flat Lake Recreation Area**
9 mi. E via CA 20 at 23333 Scotts Flat Rd. *265-5302*
A large private campground in a pine forest near a small reservoir has a sandy beach, boat rentals, and a (fee) dock and ramp. Boating, water-skiing, fishing, swimming, and hiking are popular. Flush toilets and hot showers, but no hookups, are available. Each site has a picnic table and a fire area. Some are pine-shaded with lake views. base rate...$7.50

South Yuba Campground
10 mi. NE on N. Bloomfield Rd. *985-4474*
The Bureau of Land Management operates this small campground in a rustic setting amidst pine and oak by the South Yuba River. Fishing, swimming, and gold panning are popular diversions, and a scenic trail through a rugged river canyon begins here. Only pit toilets have been provided. There are no showers or hookups. Each of the tree-shaded, well-spaced sites has a picnic table and fire area. no fee

SPECIAL EVENTS

★ **Fall Color Spectacular** *in/around town* *October - November*
When the sugar maples are ablaze, along with aspen groves, orchards, and a host of other deciduous trees that lend brilliance to the countryside, Nevada City becomes one of the West's most colorful destinations.

★ **Victorian Christmas** *downtown* *Wednesdays in December*
Each year, on the four Wednesday nights preceding Christmas, the town celebrates its heritage with special food, music, and entertainment under the picturesque gaslights downtown.

OTHER INFORMATION

Area Code: *916*

Zip Code: *95959*

Nevada City Chamber of Commerce
downtown at 132 Main St. *265-2692*

Tahoe National Forest Supervisor's Office
downtown at CA 491/Coyote St. *265-4531*

Ojai

Ojai is the West's Eden. In fact, when the novel *Lost Horizons* was made into a movie, overview scenes of "Shangri-La" were filmed of this narrow little valley sheltered by towering Coast Range mountains only a dozen miles inland from the ocean. At the heart of the defile lies Ojai, almost hidden among noble oaks and luxuriant vegetation that ultimately give way to fruit and nut orchards in every direction. The climate is almost as exceptional as the setting. While every season is appealing, spring and fall are the most notable. Ideal weather accompanies the beauty and fragrance of citrus blossom-time in the spring, and the fruit and nut harvest in the fall. With nearby ocean beaches, a large man-made lake, and several hot springs, all kinds of water sports are popular in the area, especially on weekends throughout the year. The surrounding mountains attract hikers, backpackers, horseback riders, and campers. In town, scenic golf courses and tennis complexes are enjoyed year-round along with shopping.

The Chumash Indians settled in the valley and named it Ojai, which means "The Nest," long before Spaniards ventured along the nearby coast. Sequentially, Indians, Spanish, Mexicans, and Americans laid claim to this favored hideaway. Since early in the twentieth century, the town has gradually evolved as both a secluded artists' colony and a serene resort. It was still a dusty little Western town by World War I, when a wealthy benefactor, Edward D. Libbey, began to translate his idea of simulating the architecture of southern Spain into the graceful reality of an arcade, post office, and other downtown buildings. Much of the town's distinctive Spanish-style charm is a result of his legacy.

Today, the picturesque and compact downtown area lends itself to relaxing strolls and unusual shopping excursions. It is an engaging combination of inspired architecture, interesting specialty shops, and luxuriant vegetation. Numerous sophisticated studios and galleries display local arts and crafts. Ojai is an early source of New California cuisine. One of the nation's first restaurants to feature this style, which emphasizes innovative dishes skillfully prepared with fresh local ingredients, has become a valley landmark. Several other similarly oriented gourmet restaurants have been added in recent years. Nightlife is scarce in town and limited throughout the area, but it is available in places as diverse as a plush resort or funky roadhouses. Accommodations are also relatively scarce. Almost all are sprinkled along the main approach in and out of town. The best of these facilities lend graceful elegance to the quiet grandeur of the area.

Elevation:

746 feet

Population (1980):

6,816

Population (1970):

5,591

Location:

80 miles Northwest of Los Angeles

Ojai

WEATHER PROFILE

Vokac Weather Rating

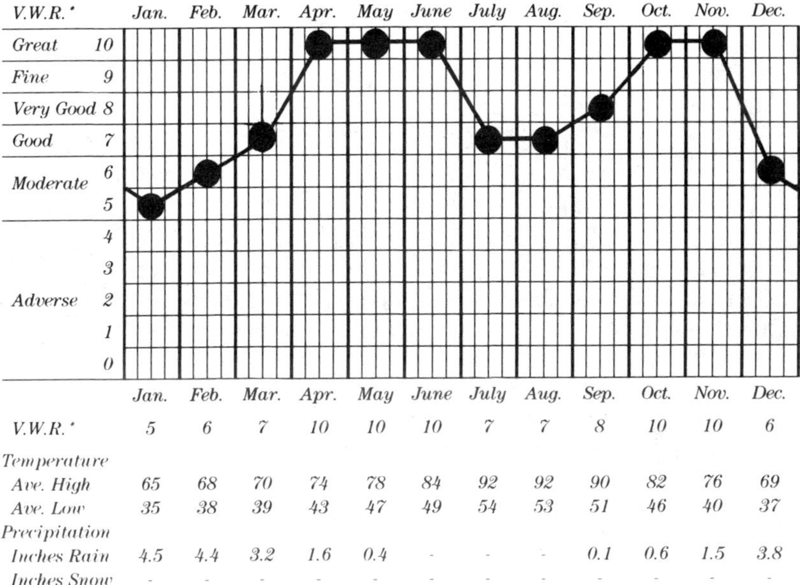

	Jan.	Feb.	Mar.	Apr.	May	June	July	Aug.	Sep.	Oct.	Nov.	Dec.
*V.W.R.**	5	6	7	10	10	10	7	7	8	10	10	6
Temperature												
Ave. High	65	68	70	74	78	84	92	92	90	82	76	69
Ave. Low	35	38	39	43	47	49	54	53	51	46	40	37
Precipitation												
Inches Rain	4.5	4.4	3.2	1.6	0.4	-	-	-	0.1	0.6	1.5	3.8
Inches Snow	-	-	-	-	-	-	-	-	-	-	-	-

**V.W.R. = Vokac Weather Rating: probability of mild (warm & dry) weather on any given day.*

Forecast

			Temperatures		
Month	*V.W.R.**		*Daytime*	*Evening*	*Precipitation*
Jan.	5	Moderate	warm	cool	infrequent downpours
Feb.	6	Moderate	warm	cool	infrequent downpours
Mar.	7	Good	warm	cool	infrequent downpours
Apr.	10	Great	warm	cool	infrequent downpours
May	10	Great	warm	cool	negligible
June	10	Great	hot	warm	none
July	7	Good	hot	warm	none
Aug.	7	Good	hot	warm	none
Sep.	8	Very Good	hot	warm	none
Oct.	10	Great	warm	cool	infrequent rainstorms
Nov.	10	Great	warm	cool	infrequent downpours
Dec.	6	Moderate	warm	cool	infrequent downpours

Summary

Ojai is a New World Shangri-La, with a climate to match. Even during the **winter**, warm days are the rule. Heavy rainstorms only infrequently hinder outdoor activity, while nurturing a superabundance of lush vegetation. **Spring** is outstanding. Warm days, cool evenings, and little or no rainfall are ideal for outdoor activities. The delicate beauty and fragrance of citrus and other blossoms is an unforgettable highlight of the little valley in this season. Surprisingly, **summer** is slightly less usable because of uniformly hot, sunny days. There is normally no rainfall to relieve the heat or deter any outdoor plans. **Fall**, like spring, is idyllic. Comfortably warm days, cool nights, and infrequent rainfalls are normal through Thanksgiving. It is a perfect time to explore the surrounding orchards while savoring the bounty of the fruit and nut harvest.

ATTRACTIONS & DIVERSIONS

★ ***Bicycling***

Open Spaces

.5 mi. E at 996 E. Ojai Av. 646-5205

Miles of flower-bordered paved byways provide access to all sections of the relatively flat little Shangri-La valley. In spite of the devastating fires of 1985, it is still brimming with subtropical orchards, luxurious gardens and grand old California live oaks sheltered by towering mountains. A good selection of bicycles can be rented by the hour or longer, and free route maps are available at this open-air shop behind a gas station. Closed Sun.

Golf

★ **Oiai Valley Inn Golf Course**

1 mi. W off CA 150 on Country Club Dr. 646-5511

Nationally known, this challenging, spectacularly beautiful 18-hole golf course is open to the public year-round, along with a pro shop, putting green, club and cart rentals, and a fine view restaurant and lounge.

★ **Soule Park Golf Course**

.8 mi. E at 1033 Ojai Av. 646-5633

This attractive county-owned 18-hole championship course is open to the public year-round with all necessary rentals and facilities.

★ ***Horseback Riding***

Chorro Grande Pack Station

25 mi. N on CA 150 at 22050 Maricopa Hwy. 646-6606

Guided hourly, all day, overnight, or extended horseback trips can be arranged into the high country wilderness of Los Padres National Forest.

★ **Ojai Valley Inn Riding Stables**

2 mi. W via CA 150 on Hermosa Rd. 646-2837

Horses may be rented here by the hour for guided rides along oak-shaded byways around town.

Lake Casitas Recreation Area

6.4 mi. SW on CA 150 649-2233

The site of the 1984 Olympic canoeing and rowing events is a many-armed freshwater reservoir surrounded by rolling grass-covered hills dotted with large oak trees. Its previous claim to fame has been as the source of state record bass and catfish. Scenic picnic sites plus many hundreds of campsites for tents and trailers overlook the lake. Because it is a domestic water supply, swimming, water-skiing, canoes, kayaks, and most inflatables are not allowed. Certain boats can be launched or rented, but only for fishing or sightseeing.

★ **Libbey Park**

downtown at Ojai Av./Signal St.

Noble oaks and giant old sycamores preside over lawns and gardens, a fountain court, picnic and play areas, eight tennis courts, and the famed music bowl in a lovely little park in the heart of town.

★ ***Library***
downtown at 111 E. Ojai Av. *646-1639*
The Ojai Library is in a distinctive little Spanish-style building. A working fireplace, comfortable sofas, and wooden armchairs grace the periodical reading room. An adjacent walled, oak-shaded patio is a tiny haven of tranquility with year-round flowers maintained by the Garden Club.

★ **The Loop**
for 10 mi. E of downtown
This ten-mile scenic drive suitable for either car or bicycle showcases the lush valley. It is an especially memorable tour when citrus groves fill the valley with an intoxicating fragrance during spring blossom-time. Miles of intriguing stone walls that line part of the road were built by Chinese labor during the 19th century. Drive east on Ojai Avenue 3.2 miles, then left on Reeves Road, McAndrew Road, and Thatcher Road.

★ **Los Padres National Forest**
starts 1 mi. N of town *646-8293*
This giant forest extends almost to the coast, and it includes all of the mountains towering above town to the north. The highest peaks reach pine-covered elevations nearly 9,000 feet above sea level. The last giant California condors outside of zoos lived, until 1986, in the Sespe Condor Sanctuary a few miles northeast of town. The mountainous San Rafael Wilderness, southern California's largest, is northwest of town. Horseback riding, hunting, backpacking, fishing, and camping are popular. Hikers especially enjoy the rugged scenic trails and natural swimming holes along Matilija Creek north of town and along Sespe Creek to the east.

Valley of "Shangri-La"
3.5 mi. E on CA 150
The panorama representing Shangri-La that was seen by Ronald Coleman years ago in the movie "Lost Horizons" is still magnificent from a small parking area near the top of the hill.

Warm Water Features

★ **Matilija Hot Springs**
5.5 mi. NW via CA 33 at 788 W. Hot Springs Rd. *646-7667*
Hidden away in a tiny scenic canyon, these hot springs were first developed as a health center and vacation resort in 1871. A large outdoor swimming pool is open during the summer, and an inviting picnic area overlooks a boulder-strewn creek. Meals are served in a rustic dining room. In a nearby health studio are several small private hot mineral pools, some with whirlpool features, that may be rented by the hour. Massage is available by appointment.

★ **Wheeler Hot Springs**
7.7 mi. NW via CA 33 *646-8131*
Part of this century-old spa has been refurbished and is open to the public. Redwood tubs can be rented in private rooms with skylights, both hot and cold mineral baths, and taped music. Massage is available by appointment.

SHOPPING

Ojai has one of the most compact and charming downtowns in the West. A cluster of Spanish-style buildings, many with graceful archways and landscaped courtyards, houses a full range of quality stores including a notable assortment of art galleries and antique shops.

Food Specialties

★ **Bill Baker's Ojai Bakery**
downtown at 457 E. Ojai Av. *646-1558*
A full line of breads, rolls, donuts, and pastries is displayed in this long-established bakery. The newly enlarged shop includes several coffee tables, as well as takeout service.

★ **Friend's Ranch**
5 mi. NW on CA 33 at 15150 Maricopa Hwy. *646-2871*
The finest local citrus, avocados, and nuts are sold at this roadside packing plant. Delicious fresh-squeezed orange juice is always available. Gift packs described in a free catalog will be shipped anywhere in the nation.

Good Taste
downtown at 206 N. Signal St. *646-2723*
Gourmet deli items like homemade pates, quiches, and desserts, plus international cheeses, wines, coffees, etc., are packaged to go. They may also be enjoyed on a flower-strewn little deck or in a casual dining room.

★ **Ojai Ice Cream & Candy Shoppe**
downtown at 210 E. Ojai Av. *646-6075*
Many flavors of outstanding homemade ice cream and sherbets, plus homemade chocolates, are displayed in this tantalizing takeout shop. The kiwi sherbet is a particularly innovative use of one of the locally grown exotic fruits.

Ojai Liquors
.3 mi. W at 301 W. Ojai Av. *646-5855*
An excellent selection of premium California wines is nicely displayed and stored. Periodic evening tastings are featured. International beers and liquors are also well represented in this modern store.

Rancho Arnaz
6.5 mi. SW on CA 33 at 9504 N. Ventura Av. - Oak View *649-2776*
From September to early November, you can pick your own apples. Several different kinds are grown. The ranch market also sells them packaged to go, plus cold cider, other seasonal fruits, nuts, and honey.

★ **Rancho Shangri-La**
5.4 mi. E on CA 150 at 9340 Ojai Rd. *646-1392*
Fresh walnuts, shelled or in the shell, may be purchased starting in October at a roadside stand or at the farm. You can pick your own during the harvest (October-November) if you wish.

★ **Village Pastry**
downtown at 217 E. Matilija St. *646-2232*
Delicious Danish pastries, donuts, specialties like scones, and assorted breads fill the tantalizing display cases of this popular bakery. Several coffee tables are indoors and on an oak-shaded patio.

Specialty Shops

★ **Bart's Corner**
.3 mi. W at 302 W. Matilija St. *646-3755*
Here is a remarkable outdoor bookstore. Tens of thousands of used books are shelved around a giant oak tree that shades customers as they browse or read while drinking tea or juice. After hours, customers may select books from shelves that line the sidewalk, and pay for them by tossing coins through the gate.

★ **Beatrice Wood Studio**
5 mi. E at 8560 CA 150 *646-3381*
A magical setting in the hills above town complements the museum-quality pottery in this studio/gallery. The ceramist is renowned for the lustrous sheens that she has developed. Her exotic and erotic primitives are unforgettable.

The Bookshop
downtown at 208 E. Ojai Av. *646-9047*
A good assortment of hard-cover and paperback books and magazines are displayed in this well-organized shop.

★ **The Pottery**
4 mi. E at 971 McAndrew Rd. *646-3393*
Quality dishes and vessels of all sorts are attractively displayed in an intriguing porcelain-stoneware studio/gallery. Closed Mon.

★ **Rain's**
downtown at 218 E. Ojai Av. *646-1441*
The centerpiece for the captivating Ojai arcade is this long-established specialty department store, where everyday merchandise is displayed with a genuine flair.

★ **Running Ridge Gallery**
downtown at 310 E. Ojai Av. *646-1525*
A contemporary collection of multimedia works by famous artists is beautifully showcased. An adjacent store bearing the same name features original-design clothing.

★ **Ruth H. Johnson Stoneware**
4 mi. SW at 335 Encino Dr. - Oak View *649-9787*
Fanciful stoneware birds and beasts created by an award-winning potter are displayed in her studio/home. Both indoor and outdoor sculptures are for sale.

NIGHTLIFE

The tranquil little valley has a surprising diversity of possibilities for an evening's entertainment, ranging from the plush and peaceful comfort of a lounge in a sophisticated resort to the rowdy and rustic vitality of a ramshackle roadhouse.

The Art Center
downtown at 113 S. Montgomery St. *646-0117*
Musicals, dramatic productions, dance performances, and lectures are presented in a small theater in the community art center on most Fri., Sat., and Sun. throughout the year.

Deer Lodge
2.5 mi. NW on CA 33 at 2259 Maricopa Hwy. *646-3813*
This rustic roadside tavern has an easygoing old-fashioned Western style that is a crowd-pleaser. Features include several kinds of tap beer, pool tables, darts, a patio, and short order home-cooked meals served all day.

The Firebird Lounge
.5 mi. E at 960 E. Ojai Av. *646-1566*
Dancers once again enjoy the sounds of live music on weekends in this recently reopened, casual lounge.

Flaming Duck
.4 mi. E at 815 E. Ojai Av. *646-7227*
Live country music is frequently played for dancing in a big, plain Western-style saloon.

★ **Ojai Valley Inn**
1 mi. W off CA 150 *646-5511*
There is usually live entertainment and dancing on weekends in the resort's comfortable lounge. Windows frame the lush valley, but the view from the adjoining terrace is even better.

The Wheel
7.7 mi. N on CA 33 at 16816 Maricopa Hwy. *646-4069*
Lively throngs are attracted by live music on weekends to this funky old roadhouse. A much-used free-standing stone fireplace and some comfortable booths highlight the really casual decor.

RESTAURANTS

Several gourmet restaurants have opened here in recent years, overseen by innovative chefs who take maximum advantage of the year-round availability of top quality, locally grown fruits and vegetables. As a result, the Ojai area has become a significant source of New California cuisine.

Antonio's
downtown at 106 S. Montgomery St. *646-6353*
L-D. *Low*
Authentic California-style Mexican food and atmosphere prevail. Don't be put off by the abundance of plastic and paper. The patio is pleasant and the food is good.

★ **Backstage Cafe**
downtown at 139 E. Ojai Av. *646-7266*
B-L-D. Sun. brunch. *Moderate*
Freshness is emphasized for contemporary American dishes including some of the best breakfasts in town. The recently opened restaurant has a comfortably furnished wood-toned dining room overlooking a covered and landscaped dining terrace.

The Firebird
.5 mi. E at 960 E. Ojai Av. *646-1566*
L-D. *Moderate*
Generous multicourse American meals are once again featured in this newly reopened landmark restaurant. The room is outfitted with comfortable booths and armchairs, and the table settings include full linen and fresh flowers.

Flaming Duck
4 mi E at 815 E. Ojai Av. *646-7227*
L-D. Sat. & Sun. brunch. Closed Wed. *Moderate*
Steaks broiled over an open pit are featured on a conventional American menu in a relaxed Western-style restaurant adjoining a popular saloon.

★ **Gaslight**
3.6 mi. SW on CA 33 at 11432 N. Ventura Av. *646-5990*
D only. Closed Mon. *Moderate*
Several kinds of delicious veal dishes, Old World specialties, and al dente vegetables are highlights of this attractive dinner house. There is also a dining patio, and the lounge offers entertainment and dancing on weekends.

★ **The Herb Garden**
downtown at 109 N. Montgomery St. *646-7065*
L only. D on Fri. & Sat. *Moderate*
Ojai's newest temple of lean cuisine accents carefully prepared light dishes with fresh, locally grown herbs, spices, and flowers. Savory and unusual meals and desserts will delight true believers and pleasantly surprise skeptics seated on a covered deck by a garden, or in the dining room. An adjoining herb store carries hundreds of herbs, spices, teas, and related items.

Landucci's
downtown at 206 N. Signal St. *646-8829*
L-D. No L on Sun.-Tues. No D on Wed. *Moderate*
Fish, chicken, and vegetarian specialties are carefully prepared with the freshest ingredients by the new owners of this restaurant. Fresh flowers and classical music accent the inviting dining room and an oak-shaded courtyard. An intimate lounge with an intriguing slate-mural and overstuffed armchairs adjoins.

★ **L'Auberge**
.3 mi. W at 314 El Paseo Rd. *646-2288*
D only. Sat. & Sun. brunch. Closed Tues. *Expensive*
French provincial cuisine emphasizing fresh ingredients is served in a

lovely old home that has been converted into a restaurant. In addition to a casually elegant dining room with a cozy fireplace, there is a wonderfully tranquil garden porch.

★ **The Nest**

downtown at 108 S. Montgomery St. — *646-8111*
L-D. Sat. & Sun. brunch. Closed Mon. — *Moderate*

The innovative soups, salads, sandwiches, and pastries made here fresh daily are classic presentations of New California cuisine. This highly regarded restaurant is Ojai's most sophisticated luncheon place. A first-rate gourmet deli adjoins in a front room.

Ojai Valley Inn

1 mi. W off CA 150 on Country Club Dr. — *646-5511*
B-L-D. — *Expensive*

Each of the resort's three large dining rooms offers distinctive views and classic American food served in comfortable surroundings. Daily buffet lunches on the terrace are outstanding because of the luxuriant vegetation and mountain-rimmed backdrop.

★ **The Ranch House**

3 mi. W on S. Lomita Av. — *646-2360*
L-D. Sun. brunch. Closed Mon.-Tues. — *Very Expensive*

The valley's most famous restaurant was one of the West's first to feature New California cuisine. Long before the regional style was widely known, the owner was creating unusual gourmet dishes with a light touch enhanced by locally grown herbs and vegetables, distinctive homemade breads, and premium California wines. Picture windows in the informally elegant, contemporary dining room overlook flower and herb gardens. Outside, tables shaded by noble oaks are set under heat lamps for year-round enjoyment of the gardens, pools, and fountains. Live chamber music is offered on Wednesday and Thursday evenings and on Sunday afternoons in spring and summer.

LODGING

Accommodations in Ojai are notably scarce, and there are no bargains on weekends. Visitors interested in staying in one of the town's few good lodgings should have reservations in advance on weekends year-round. Most places reduce their prices by at least 15% during the week.

Capri Motel

.8 mi. E at 1180 E. Ojai Av. — *646-4305*

A large, scenic outdoor pool and whirlpool in a tranquil garden setting are features of this modern motel. Each spacious room has a phone, cable color TV, and a private patio or balcony.

#210,#209—balcony with floor/ceiling view to mountains, — K bed...$45
regular room— — 2 D or K bed...$45

Casa Ojai - Best Western

.9 mi. E at 1302 E. Ojai Av. — *646-8175*

There is a large outdoor pool and a whirlpool in this modern motel.

Pastry and coffee are complimentary. Each well-furnished room has a phone and cable color TV. For toll-free reservations, call: (800)528-1234.

regular room— Q bed...$60

El Camino Lodge

.3 mi. W at 406 W. Ojai Av. *646-4341*

This modern motel is the most convenient to downtown, and has an outdoor pool. Each room has a phone and cable color TV.

regular room— 2 D, Q or K bed...$45

Los Padres Inn

.8 mi. E at 1208 E. Ojai Av. *646-4365*

Set back from the highway, this contemporary Spanish-style motel has a large outdoor pool and whirlpool. Each of the spacious well-furnished rooms has cable color TV and a phone.

deluxe room—newer, refrigerator, 2 Q or K bed...$65
regular room— 2 Q or K bed...$55

★ **The Oaks at Ojai**

downtown at 122 E. Ojai Av. *646-5573*

An old hotel and cottages have been converted into a popular health spa on beautifully landscaped grounds. Included in the price to guests are three skillfully prepared low calorie meals daily; all kinds of exercise, health, and self-awareness programs; plus an outdoor swimming pool, whirlpools, and saunas. Massage, facials, and other health and beauty services are also available for a fee. Each room has a cable color TV and a phone.

cottage—spacious, 2 D beds...$200
regular room—in lodge, 2 D beds...$160

★ **Ojai Valley Inn and Country Club**

1 mi. SW off CA 150 on Country Club Dr. *646-5511*

For many years, this has been the premier resort of Ojai Valley. Year-round facilities on the spectacularly landscaped grounds of the renowned hideaway include a beautifully sited large outdoor pool, plus (for a fee) an 18-hole golf course, putting green, lighted tennis courts, and horseback riding, as well as several dining rooms, a lounge, and shops. Spacious modern rooms, each with a phone and cable color TV, are in several levels of a mountain view complex near the main building, and in luxuriously furnished older bungalows with patios. Rates are American plan, with breakfast, lunch, and dinner included.

deluxe room—mountain or valley view, refrigerator, 2 T, D or Q bed...$175
regular room— 2 T or D bed...$135

Roseholm Inn

5 mi. S at 51 Sulphur Mountain Rd. *649-4014*

A rose-colored mansion built during the 1920s on a bluff near town became one of the West's most magnificent bed-and-breakfast country inns in 1984. Meticulously landscaped grounds include a large whirlpool, a steamroom, and wine cellar. Each room has a lavish private bath, and is beautifully decorated and furnished with antiques. Attention to details is reflected in luxurious towels and soaps, hand-painted rose tiles, and much more. Guests are greeted with fresh flowers, seasonal fruit, and premium champagne. A gourmet breakfast, and appetizers and wine, are complimentary, as are homemade desserts in the evening.

"Paradise"—top floor suite, fireplace, whirlpool, pvt. balcony, Q bed...$325
"Masquerade"—suite, fireplace, whirlpool, Q bed...$265
regular room "Tiffany"—whirlpool, D bed...$215

CAMPGROUNDS

There are several campgrounds in the area. The best provide a choice of either a large and complete facility by a reservoir, or a smaller rustic campground by a cool mountain stream.

Lake Casitas Recreation Area
6.4 mi. SW on CA 150 *649-2233*
The municipal water district operates an enormous campground located on two miles of landscaped slopes by Lake Casitas. Rentals/dock/ramps are available for fishing boats. Most other kinds of boats, water-skiing, and swimming are not allowed. The reservoir holds state records for bass and channel catfish. Flush toilets, (fee) hot showers, and hookups are available. Each of the closely spaced sites has a picnic table and a fire area. Most have a lakeshore view. base rate...$7

Wheeler Gorge
9 mi. N: 1 mi. W on CA 150 & 8 mi. N on CA 33 *646-4348*
The U.S. Forest Service has provided a picturesque campground in Los Padres National Forest by a stream deep in a narrow rugged canyon. Fishing, swimming, and hiking are popular. There are flush toilets, but no showers or hookups. Each site has a picnic table and a fire area.
base rate...$6

SPECIAL EVENTS

★ **Ojai Music Festival** *downtown in Libbey Park first weekend in June*
The area's most famous annual event takes place in a tree-shaded outdoor amphitheater where classical and jazz concerts are performed before large and enthusiastic audiences.

★ **Ojai Tennis Tournament** *downtown in Libbey Park* *late April*
Since the nineteenth century, amateurs have been competing in this oldest invitational tournament of its kind in the U.S.

OTHER INFORMATION

Area Code: *805*

Zip Code: *93023*

Los Padres National Forest - Ojai Ranger Office
.8 mi. E at 1190 E. Ojai Av. *646-8293*

Ojai Chamber of Commerce
downtown at 338 E. Ojai Av. *646-3000*

Pacific Grove

Pacific Grove is a seaside haven of tranquility. Situated along a strikingly beautiful coastline where the waters of the Pacific Ocean and Monterey Bay converge, the town has been evolving as a refined refuge for nearly a century. Lovingly maintained Victorian homes and businesses predominate amid manicured landscapes of mature trees and colorful gardens. Complementing the peaceful setting is a temperate year-round climate that is one of the West's finest. Spectacular displays of flowers and lush green hues in spring are especially memorable. Summer and fall are the busiest seasons, when warm, rainless days assure comfortable enjoyment of all area attractions. Carefully tended shoreline parks with resplendent gardens, sandy beaches, coves, and winding paths frame the entire ocean and bayside perimeters of town. Strolling, bicycling, beachcombing, sunbathing, scuba diving, sailing, and fishing are popular activities. Inland, browsing the old-fashioned business district, or exploring quiet neighborhoods, a notable small museum, or a historic lighthouse are other favorite pastimes. Nearby, outstanding facilities for golf and tennis draw players to some of the prettiest sites anywhere.

Methodists founded the town in 1875 when they started using the area as a summer retreat. Strict ordinances regulating dancing, drinking, swimming, and even profanity lasted until quite recently. In fact, it wasn't until 1969 that Pacific Grove residents voted to permit the sale of alcohol in what had been California's last "dry" town. The legacy of the austere early settlers was the creation of a genteel haven amidst extravagent surroundings.

Today, well-groomed Victorian houses and shops on quiet tree-shaded streets lend nostalgic distinction to the town. This is especially evident downtown, where the tidy appearance and feeling of a Northeastern village center before the turn of the century has been meticulously retained. Some sophisticated galleries and specialty shops are features of the classic district. Restaurants are numerous, varied, and typically plain. The best offer American or Old World cuisine in intimate settings. Not much happens to disturb tranquil evenings, but two plush bayside cocktail lounges frame unforgettable seascapes and sunsets through expansive picture windows. Accommodations range from some of the West's finest Victorian inns to comfortable motels. A number of lodgings are clustered in a shady forest that is the famed winter home of millions of monarch butterflies. Several others sprinkled along the town's marine drives offer views of waterfront parks and Monterey Bay or the ocean.

Elevation:

50 feet

Population (1980):

15,755

Population (1970):

13,505

Location:

132 miles Southeast of San Francisco

Pacific Grove

WEATHER PROFILE

Vokac Weather Rating

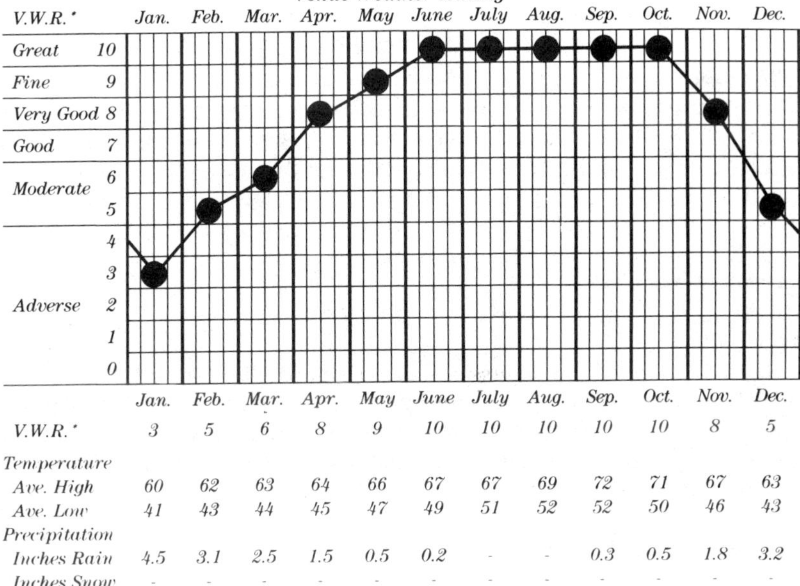

	Jan.	Feb.	Mar.	Apr.	May	June	July	Aug.	Sep.	Oct.	Nov.	Dec.
*V.W.R.**	3	5	6	8	9	10	10	10	10	10	8	5
Temperature												
Ave. High	60	62	63	64	66	67	67	69	72	71	67	63
Ave. Low	41	43	44	45	47	49	51	52	52	50	46	43
Precipitation												
Inches Rain	4.5	3.1	2.5	1.5	0.5	0.2	-	-	0.3	0.5	1.8	3.2
Inches Snow	-	-	-	-	-	-	-	-	-	-	-	-

**V.W.R.* = *Vokac Weather Rating: probability of mild (warm & dry) weather on any given day.*

Forecast

Month	*V.W.R.**		*Temperatures Daytime*	*Temperatures Evening*	*Precipitation*
Jan.	3	Adverse	cool	cool	frequent rainstorms
Feb.	5	Moderate	cool	cool	occasional rainstorms
Mar.	6	Moderate	cool	cool	occasional rainstorms
Apr.	8	Very Good	cool	cool	infrequent rainstorms
May	9	Fine	warm	cool	infrequent showers
June	10	Great	warm	cool	negligible
July	10	Great	warm	cool	none
Aug.	10	Great	warm	cool	none
Sep.	10	Great	warm	cool	negligible
Oct.	10	Great	warm	cool	infrequent showers
Nov.	8	Very Good	warm	cool	infrequent rainstorms
Dec.	5	Moderate	cool	cool	occasional rainstorms

Summary

Pacific Grove, at the northwestern tip of the Monterey Peninsula, shares one of the West's most desirable climates with Monterey and Carmel. Mild conditions prevail except during **winter**, when cool, frost-free weather is the norm, along with occasional rainstorms which contribute well over half of the average annual precipitation. In **spring**, shower activity diminishes, fog and sea breezes become more common, and continually warm days and cool evenings begin. Two fascinating natural phenomena occur during these seasons. Monarch butterflies by the millions return to their favorite trees on the west side of town for the winter, and the slopes along the bayfront parks become flamboyant masses of vivid purple as carpets of tiny iceplants salute spring. **Summer** is a continuation of warm days and cool nights. While this is the foggiest season, there is almost no rainfall. **Fall** offers the year's best weather. The highest annual temperatures normally occur at this time. Ideal conditions prevail until after Thanksgiving, when the rainy season begins again in earnest.

ATTRACTIONS & DIVERSIONS

★ ***Bicycling***

A separated bikeway was recently completed along the spectacular bayfront park. Additional miles of designated bike routes provide marine views, and close-ups of Victorian buildings and manicured gardens. Pacific Grove is also the northern terminus of the magnificent Seventeen Mile Drive. Various kinds of bicycles can be rented by the hour, half day, or day at the following locations:

Ocean View Bike Rentals *.7 mi. E at 121 Ocean View Blvd. 372-6055*

W.M. & M. Cyclery *downtown at 214 Forest Av.* *372-2552*

★ **Butterfly Trees**

.5 mi. W around Lighthouse Av. & Seventeen Mile Dr.

Pacific Grove is known as "Butterfly Town, U.S.A." because of the annual migration of hundreds of thousands of monarch butterflies to selected groves of trees (especially west of Seventeen Mile Drive and south of Lighthouse Avenue) between October and March.

Golf

★ **Pacific Grove Municipal Golf Course**

1.2 mi. NW at 77 Asilomar Blvd. *375-3456*

An oceanfront location has been outfitted with nicely maintained, relatively level fairways carved out of low sand dunes. This public 18-hole golf course is one of the most popular on the peninsula. Features include a pro shop, practice range, club and cart rentals, a restaurant, and one of the lowest greens fees on the peninsula.

Library

downtown at Central & Fountain Avs. *373-0603*

The Pacific Grove Library is housed in a modern building with high arched windows. An inviting periodical reading area has armchairs and numerous wall hangings. Closed Sun.

★ **Lover's Point**

.3 mi. N at the bay end of 17th St.

A small bayside park combines sandy coves, dramatic rock formations, Monterey cypress, and colorful landscaping into one of the peninsula's most romantic and photogenic highlights. Normally clear and safe, the water off Bathhouse Beach is a favorite destination for hearty swimmers in summer.

★ **The Magic Carpet of "Mesembryanthemum"**

N along the bay

This fanciful tongue-twister is the name for masses of ice plants that drape a stretch of Monterey Bay shoreline northwest of Lover's Point. From April through August, a solid lavender pink carpet of tiny flowers provides a brilliant accompaniment to green grass and shrubs above the rockbound bay.

★ **Pacific Grove Museum of Natural History**
downtown at 165 Forest Av. *372-4212*
Once singled out as the highest rated museum of its size in the United States, this free facility has a notable exhibit of butterflies. Also, a relief map of the peninsula and bay graphically depicts the great chasm of Monterey Bay, which plummets within a few miles from shore to 8,400 feet below sea level—far deeper than the Grand Canyon. Closed Mon.

★ **Point Lobos Lighthouse**
1.2 mi. W on Ocean View Blvd.
The oldest continuously operating lighthouse on the Pacific Coast has stood at the entrance to Monterey Harbor since 1855. It is open to the public only on Saturdays and Sundays between 1 and 4 p.m.

Shoreline Parks
N & W along Ocean View Blvd. & Sunset Dr.
One of the West's most picturesque coastline drives winds for four miles along a variously flower-bordered, rockbound, and sandy shoreline. The road is a boundary between the residential portions of town and a continuous series of seaside parks. Along Monterey Bay, beautifully landscaped parks provide access to numerous sandy beaches tucked into coves along the rocky headlands. Sunbathing, strolling, and picnicking are popular, and scuba diving is ideal when the bay is calm and clear. During the summer, glass-bottom boats take visitors out to marine gardens just offshore. On the ocean side, the rugged, rocky shoreline is flanked by low grassy sand dunes stopped short by a pine forest that never quite reaches the sea.

Warm Water Feature

Different Soaks
1 mi. S at 1157 Forest Av. *646-8294*
Hot tubs with whirlpool jets are the main attractions in private rooms with redwood decks, garden settings, showers, music, and a phone for ordering soft drinks. There is also a sauna. Tubs can be rented by the hour during the day or evening.

SHOPPING

Tidy Victorian structures dominate a compact central business district with a full range of distinctive shops. All of the colorful buildings are extensively landscaped and convenient to free parking areas.

Food Specialties

Bagel Bakery
1 mi. S at 1180C Forest Av. *649-6272*
A variety of good, locally produced bagels is served with coffee or to go.

★ **Cloris' Croissants**
.7 mi. E at 125 Ocean View Blvd. *372-3046*
Awesome plain and filled croissants are made fresh daily in an exhibition kitchen, and served to go with beverages and preserves at tables in this enticing shop in the American Tin Cannery. Closed Mon.

★ **Liquor Barn**
1 mi. S at 1170 Forest Av. *646-8571*
An outstanding selection of local and other California premium wines is sold at a worthwhile discount in a converted grocery store.

Portofino
downtown at Lighthouse/17th St. *373-7379*
Homemade New York-style ices, espresso, fresh-roasted coffee, and other light fare are served to go or in a casual room that is occasionally used for poetry readings and similar special events.

Scotch Bakery
downtown at 545 Lighthouse Av. *375-3569*
This place has been serving the area with a full line of baked goods and some specialties like scones for more than fifty years. Closed Mon.

Specialty Shops

★ **American Tin Cannery**
.7 mi. E at 125 Ocean View Blvd.
A cavernous old tin can manufacturing plant near Cannery Row has been ingeniously transformed. The original high ceilings and banks of skylights now impart a bright and spacious feeling to a series of specialty shops and restaurants amidst attractive fountains and plants.

★ **Bookworks**
downtown at 667 Lighthouse Av. *372-2242*
One of the peninsula's most complete bookstores also has a large selection of magazines and newspapers. A coffee bar features espresso and other hot beverages, plus croissants, bagels, and desserts from local sources in an atmosphere of classical music and all-you-can-read.

Ford's Department Store
downtown at 542 Lighthouse Av. *372-7131*
This old-fashioned department store has been providing full service in a downtown landmark for more than a half century. The top floor restaurant/deck has a superb view of town and Monterey Bay.

★ **Pacific Grove Art Center**
downtown at 568 Lighthouse Av. *375-2208*
A handsome building in the heart of town is now a lively art center. Displays of locally created arts and crafts in a variety of media are nicely showcased. A new exhibit with a reception is featured every five weeks. Closed Sun.-Mon.

★ **Vintage House**
downtown at 213 Forest Av. *649-6091*
Here is a one-stop shopping center for contemporary gourmet provisions—wines, cheese, chocolates, preserves, pates, and more. There are also a few small tables where you can enjoy a cup of first-rate freshly brewed coffee. Closed Sun.

NIGHTLIFE

Pacific Grove is still a haven of tranquility after dark, as it has been for over a century. While most of the action is in nearby Monterey, there are a couple of genteel places to enjoy live entertainment or a quiet drink.

★ **Old Bath House**
.3 mi. N at 620 Ocean View Blvd. *375-5195*
A historic bayside bathhouse has become an acclaimed restaurant and a lounge with plush romantic decor, a splendid Victorian back bar, and a memorable view of Monterey Bay.

★ **The Tinnery**
.3 mi. N at 631 Ocean View Blvd. *646-1040*
Easy-listening live music is featured nightly in this restaurant's elegant, contemporary lounge. The panoramic view of the landscaped coastline at Lover's Point is unforgettable.

RESTAURANTS

Several gourmet dining rooms have been added in recent years to a large assortment of restaurants serving primarily American dishes in pleasant surroundings. Several have fine bay views.

Deli-icious
.7 mi. E at 125 Ocean View Blvd. *649-5131*
B-L. *Moderate*
Deli specialties ranging from Chicago hot dogs to lox and bagels are served in a spacious dining room recently added to the American Tin Cannery. Patrons have a choice of padded soft-fabric booths or chairs set around hardwood tables, or alfresco dining when weather permits. Windows on three sides of the dining room provide a view of Monterey Bay and the Aquarium.

Fandango
downtown at 233 17th St. *373-0588*
L-D. Closed Mon. *Moderate*
Casually treated Basque specialties are among French-Spanish dishes offered. The mesquite broiler is a plus. Spanish country-themed decor is used in the dining areas.

★ **First Watch**
.7 mi. E at 125 Ocean View Blvd. *372-1125*
B-L. *Moderate*
Unusual egg dishes, many omelets, and pancakes are featured in a restaurant built into the American Tin Cannery. Cheerful rooms have been outfitted with comfortable booths and tables set with fresh flowers and jam pots. A small courtyard is used for alfresco dining in good weather.

★ **Hart Mansion**
downtown at Lighthouse/19th St. *373-6996*
D only. Closed Sun.-Wed. *Extremely Expensive*
Classic French cuisine is featured in multicourse prix fixe dinners

served amid elegant surroundings. The skillfully converted Victorian mansion, recently reopened by the new owners, is once again becoming a culinary landmark.

★ **La Maisonette**
downtown at 218 17th St. — *372-4481*
L-D. No D on Mon.-Wed. Closed Sun. — *Moderate*
A converted Victorian cottage has become a charming little French bistro that is especially popular for lunch. Selected French specialties are served in casual provincial atmosphere, and in a tiny courtyard.

La Provence
.7 mi. E at 105A Ocean View Blvd. — *649-0707*
L-D. — *Expensive*
The uncomplicated food and good-natured service live up to the restaurant's namesake area in France. The notion in the decor of the south of France is contrived, but the bay view isn't.

Monarch Restaurant
downtown at 162 Fountain Av. — *373-7911*
B-L-D. — *Moderate*
Homemade desserts and biscuits, and a variety of breakfast omelets, are specialties in this popular and unassuming coffee shop.

★ **Old Bath House Restaurant**
.3 mi. N at 620 Ocean View Blvd. — *375-5195*
D only. Sun. brunch. — *Very Expensive*
Continental cuisine is featured, along with homemade desserts. But, it is the magnificent view of Monterey Bay complemented by romantic, informally elegant decor in an ingeniously converted Victorian bathhouse that makes this restaurant special.

Old Europe Restaurant
downtown at 663 Lighthouse Av. — *375-1743*
D only. Closed Mon. — *Moderate*
Wild boar and tantalizing desserts are highlights among European specialties served in cozy Old World atmosphere.

Pasta Mia
downtown at 481 Lighthouse Av. — *375-7709*
D only. — *Expensive*
Homemade pastas, bread, dessert pastries, and gelato with a genuinely southern Italian flair are served in casual little dining rooms in a converted cottage.

★ **Pheasant's Eye**
.6 mi. E at 159 Central Av. — *372-7009*
D only. Closed Sun.-Mon. — *Expensive*
The gourmet menu changes weekly depending on the best seasonally available meats and produce. An old cottage has been artistically transformed into an elegant ultra-nouveau restaurant where the intimate decor is a perfect accompaniment for the New California cuisine.

Solarium Coffee Shop
downtown at 542 Lighthouse Av. *372-7131*
L only. Closed Sun. *Moderate*
Light American fare provides the excuse for enjoying the outstanding panoramic view of Monterey Bay and Pacific Ocean from this large pleasant dining room atop Ford's Department Store.

Tillie Gort's
.6 mi. E at 111 Central Av. *373-0335*
L-D. No L on Sun. *Moderate*
This natural food restaurant, coffee house, and art gallery does interesting things with homemade soups and baked goods. Rustic barnwood decor, far-out graphics painted on the ceiling, lacquered wood tables, and artifacts everywhere suggest the enduring Bohemian spirit of the place.

The Tinnery
.3 mi. N at 631 Ocean View Blvd. *646-1040*
B-L-D. Sun. brunch. *Moderate*
The menu offers a variety of international dishes, but the highlight of this nicely furnished contemporary restaurant is an expansive window-wall view of Lover's Point Park and Monterey Bay.

LODGING

Accommodations extol the natural beauty and serene Victorian spirit of Pacific Grove in individualistic facilities ranging from stylish contemporary motels to lovingly restored Victorian guest homes. None of the major motel or hotel chains are present. All of the lodgings are relatively small, except the specialized Asilomar Conference Center. Bargain rooms are nonexistent, and vacancies are unusual on any weekend and throughout summer. From late fall through spring, non-weekend rates are often reduced at least 25% below those shown.

Andril Fireplace Motel & Cottages
1.2 mi. W at 569 Asilomar Blvd. *375-0994*
These units are in the pines a short walk from an ocean beach. Each of the newer cottages has a wood-burning fireplace and full kitchen, plus cable color TV and a phone.
regular room— D & Q bed...$64

★ **Beachcomber Inn**
1.5 mi. SW at 1966 Sunset Dr. *373-4769*
This modern motel is the nearest to ocean beaches and sand dunes. A pool and a sauna, and complimentary bicycles, are popular features. Each room has cable color TV with movies, and a phone.
#24—end, top (2nd) floor, private patio,
refr., view to ocean, K bed...$73
regular room— Q bed...$53

Borg's Motel

.3 mi. N at 635 Ocean View Blvd. *375-2406*

This is one of the Monterey Peninsula's few waterfront motels. Some rooms have views across a street to a lovely park by Monterey Bay. Each modestly furnished room has cable color TV and a phone.

#50—spacious, corner of top (2nd) fl., bay view windows on 2 sides, Q bed...$77
regular room— Q bed...$53

Butterfly Grove Inn

.8 mi. NW at 1073 Lighthouse Av. *373-4921*

The adjacent woods are home to vast numbers of monarch butterflies from October to March each year. An outdoor pool and whirlpool are available to guests. Each room has cable color TV and a phone.

regular room— Q bed...$51

★ **Butterfly Trees Lodge - Best Western**

1 mi. NW at 1150 Lighthouse Av. *372-0503*

An outdoor pool and whirlpool, plus a sauna, are features of this skillfully remodeled/expanded motel a short walk from the ocean. A Continental breakfast and wine and cheese are complimentary. Each beautifully decorated unit has a phone and cable color TV. For toll-free reservations in California, call (800)822-8822.

#216/218,#115/117—1 BR suite, kit. with microwave, fireplace, balcony, ocean view, K bed...$161
#204—fireplace, balcony, ocean view, Q bed...$88
#206,#216—fireplace, balcony, ocean view, K bed...$96
regular room— Q bed...$66

Centrella Hotel

downtown at 612 Central Av. *372-3372*

Recently, a century-old building was meticulously restored and upgraded into a large bed-and-breakfast inn. Plush period furnishings and pastel colors are used in each individually decorated room. A complimentary Continental breakfast is served in the morning, and wine and sherry in the evening.

"Vera Franklin Suite"—pvt. bath, wet bar, color TV, some bay view, Q bed...$125
regular room #24—shares bath with one other room, Q bed...$70

The Executive Lodge

1 mi. SW at 660 Dennett St. *373-8777*

A small condominium complex in the pines was recently converted into overnight lodgings. Each of the large, attractively furnished units has a color TV, and phone, and most have a fully equipped kitchen, pressed-log fireplace, private deck, and garage. A Continental breakfast is free. For toll-free reservations, call (800)221-9323.

#10C,#8C—private forest-view balcony, pitched roof, K bed...$85
#10A,#8A—lg. suite, kitchen, pressed-log fireplace, pvt. balcony, K bed...$145
regular room—pvt. balcony, tree view, K bed...$85

★ **Gosby House Inn**
downtown at 643 Lighthouse Av. *375-1287*
An authentic Victorian mansion in the heart of town now serves as a bed-and-breakfast inn tastefully furnished with original antiques. A Continental breakfast is included, as is late afternoon tea or sherry. Bicycles are available for the asking.
#11—fireplace, private bath, Q bed...$115
#17—private bath, window seat, Q bed...$108
regular room—small, private bath, D bed...$80

★ **Green Gables Inn**
.5 mi. E at 104 5th St. *375-2095*
The bay is less than one hundred feet from a magnificent turn-of-the-century mansion that is now a bed-and-breakfast inn. Elegant period furnishings are used throughout. A complimentary breakfast is served in the dining room each morning, and wine is offered in the parlour each afternoon.
"Lacey Suite"—parlor with a fireplace, private bath, Q bed...$135
"Gable"—shared bath, ocean view windows, Q bed...$105
"Balcony"—shared bath, balcony, view to ocean, Q bed...$105
regular room "Garret"—shared bath, ocean view, D bed...$80

Larchwood Inn
1.1 mi. SW at 740 Crocker Av. *373-1114*
This newer motel is in a woodsy setting near Asilomar State Beach. Each of the spacious units has a duraflame log fireplace, color TV, and a phone.
#121—top floor, corner windows, pine view, Q bed...$55
regular room— Q bed...$55

★ **The Martine Inn**
.6 mi. E at 255 Ocean View Blvd. *373-3388*
A Victorian mansion across the street from Monterey Bay recently was converted into a large bed-and-breakfast inn. Each room features some authentic antiques, and has a private bathroom. A complimentary breakfast is served.
"Parke"—bay view windows on 3 sides, fireplace, bay view from both clawfoot tub and D bed...$165
"Eastlake"—bay view windows on 2 sides, bay view from both 7′ clawfoot tub and K bed...$150
"Marie's"—bay view windows on 2 sides, fireplace, Q bed...$135
regular room— D bed...$85

Olympia Motor Lodge
1 mi. NW at 1140 Lighthouse Av. *373-2777*
There is an outdoor pool in this contemporary wood-toned motel. Some of the spacious units have an almost Oriental simplicity, and balconies

with distant ocean views. Each has cable color TV and a phone.
#7A—corner, pitched roof, 2 decks, private
view to waves, K bed...$72
#8B—corner, pitched roof, view to waves, kitchenette, Q bed...$72
regular room— Q bed...$44

Pacific Gardens Inn
1.2 mi. W at 701 Asilomar Blvd. *646-9414*
This small, newer motel in the pines is a short walk from an ocean beach. There are two whirlpools. Each of the well-furnished rooms has a pressed-log fireplace, cable color TV, and a phone. A Continental breakfast and wine and cheese in the afternoon are complimentary. For toll-free reservations, call (800)822-8822.
regular room— K bed...$70
regular room— Q bed...$65

Roserox Country Inn
.3 mi. NE at 557 Ocean View Blvd. *373-7673*
A large turn-of-the-century home across the street from Monterey Bay has recently become a bed-and-breakfast inn. Each individually decorated room shares a bath with one other room. A sumptuous breakfast (served in bed on request) and afternoon appetizers and beverages are complimentary.
"Shenandoah"—fine bay view from clawfoot tub
and antique brass Q bed...$155
"Andorra"—fine views of Lover's Point/bay, D bed...$135
regular room— D bed...$85

★ **Seven Gables Inn**
.3 mi. NE at 555 Ocean View Blvd. *372-4341*
Monterey Bay is across the street from this handsomely restored Victorian mansion. Each room has a private bath and is lavishly decorated with an eclectic collection of mostly antique furnishings. A generous Continental breakfast is included, as is afternoon tea.
"W side of 2nd floor"—fine bay view, refrigerator, Q bed...$125
"NE side of 2nd floor"—fine bay views, Q bed...$125
regular room— D bed...$85

The Wilkie's Motel
.8 mi. NW at 1038 Lighthouse Av. *372-5960*
Most of the rooms in this attractively furnished modern motel have cable color TV and a phone.
#12—end of top floor, corner windows,
bay/pines view, K bed...$63
regular room— Q bed...$59

CAMPGROUNDS

No campground on the peninsula accommodates both tents and RVs, but there are two complete campgrounds within a half hour's drive inland.

Laguna Seca Recreation Area
10 mi. SE past Monterey via CA 68 *422-6138*
This large Monterey County campground near a small reservoir has boat rentals and ramps, and features boating and fishing. Flush toilets, hot showers, and hookups are available. Each of the sites has a picnic table, fire ring, and grill. base rate...$9.50

Saddle Mountain Recreation Park
9 mi. SE via Carmel Valley Rd. *624-1617*
This privately operated campground has a (fee) pool and a rec room. Flush toilets, hot showers, and hookups are available. Each site has a picnic table and fire area. base rate...$10

SPECIAL EVENTS

Good Old Days Celebration *several locations in town* *late April*
A classic Victorian homes tour is featured, along with an arts and crafts fair, a parade, and entertainment.

★ **Feast of Lanterns** *shoreline parks* *last week in July*
A lantern-lit procession along the shore accompanied by fireworks is the highlight of a unique celebration that also includes street dancing, sporting events, live entertainment, and a barbecue.

★ **Butterfly Festival** *downtown* *mid-October*
A parade where no commercial aspects are allowed, plus a carnival and bazaar, celebrate the arrival of hundreds of thousands of beautiful monarch butterflies that annually migrate hundreds of miles to their winter destination—groves of trees on the west side of town.

OTHER INFORMATION

Area Code: *408*
Zip Code: *93950*

Pacific Grove Chamber of Commerce
downtown at Forest & Central Avs. *373-3304*

Pacific Grove 667 Lighthouse
375-3121

Palm Springs

Palm Springs is America's desert showplace. A striking patchwork of low-profile buildings and lush manicured landscapes is interspersed with barren sand and rocks along the base of one of southern California's highest mountains. The precipitous bulk of this towering peak with its dazzling mantle of winter snow is a remarkable contrast to the flat desert floor. Mt. San Jacinto even affects the local climate by throwing a shadow over town while the rest of the desert to the east continues to bake in the afternoon, and by sheltering the town from strong winds that frequently sweep across the flatlands beyond. In this favored locale, spring and fall are appealing seasons with fine weather. But, Palm Springs has the unique distinction of being the only great town in the West where the best weather occurs in winter. Then, while the rest of the nation copes with snow or rain, a variety of special events are celebrated during warm sunny days enhanced by the intoxicating aroma of citrus and other fragrant vegetation. The desert in and around town offers memorable natural beauty—as undulating sand dunes; endless beaches without water; and barren rock and boulder gardens. Here also are America's most phenomenal oases in desert canyons where thousands of giant native fan palms provide an exotic backdrop to streams, pools, and waterfalls along the lower reaches of the San Jacinto Mountains. Nearby, irrigation has transformed hostile flatlands into mind-boggling numbers of golf courses, tennis courts, swimming pools, parks, and gardens. These facilities attract capacity crowds in winter and spring, and (thanks to centralized air conditioning) even attract bargain seekers during the area's long, relentlessly torrid summers.

By the late nineteenth century, U.S. government maps identified the tiny settlement in this area as "Palm Springs," recognizing both the hot springs and palm trees nearby. Around the turn of the century, the government granted many even-numbered sections along the base of the mountains to descendants of Cahuilla Indians who preceded the earliest white settlers to the area. Odd-numbered sections had been given earlier to the Southern Pacific Railway as incentive for developing a transcontinental railroad. Growth was slow until the 1950s, when effective air conditioning made the desert livable year-round, and super highways and improvement to air service made getting there easier. Meanwhile, celebrity golf tournaments and other star-studded events began to confirm Palm Springs' destiny as the heart of America's desert playground.

Today, stylish contemporary businesses along and near Palm Canyon Drive display the town's vitality, wealth, and an increasingly cosmopolitan flair. This beautifully landscaped area has some of the most extravagent specialty shops, galleries, restaurants, and entertainment places that money can buy. Lodgings in the area have long been superabundant. Thanks to an ongoing building boom, several opulent resort hotels with lavish facilities have been recently completed within an easy stroll of the heart of town.

Elevation:

448 feet

Population (1980):

32,271

Population (1970):

20,936

Location:

107 miles East of Los Angeles

Palm Springs

WEATHER PROFILE

Vokac Weather Rating

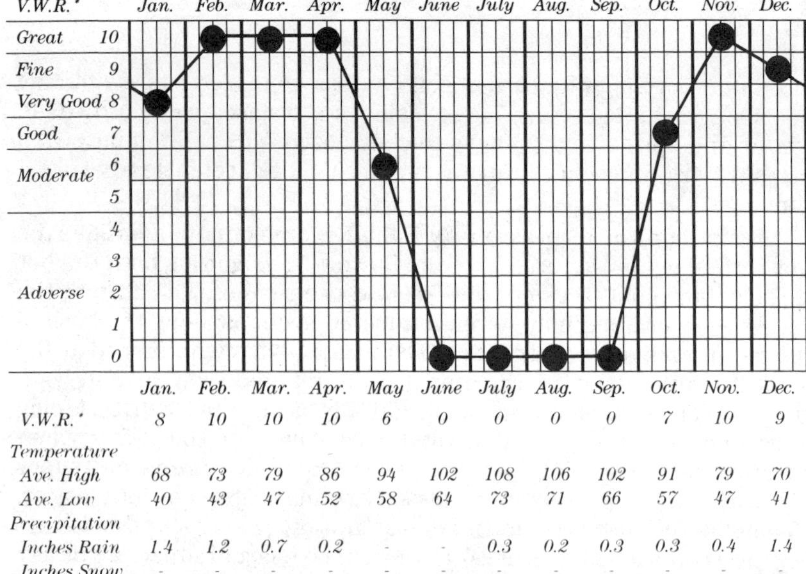

	Jan.	Feb.	Mar.	Apr.	May	June	July	Aug.	Sep.	Oct.	Nov.	Dec.
*V.W.R.**	8	10	10	10	6	0	0	0	0	7	10	9
Temperature												
Ave. High	68	73	79	86	94	102	108	106	102	91	79	70
Ave. Low	40	43	47	52	58	64	73	71	66	57	47	41
Precipitation												
Inches Rain	1.4	1.2	0.7	0.2	-	-	0.3	0.2	0.3	0.3	0.4	1.4
Inches Snow	-	-	-	-	-	-	-	-	-	-	-	-

**V.W.R. = Vokac Weather Rating: probability of mild (warm & dry) weather on any given day.*

Forecast

Month	*V.W.R.**		*Temperatures* *Daytime*	*Evening*	*Precipitation*
Jan.	8	Very Good	warm	cool	infrequent downpours
Feb.	10	Great	warm	cool	infrequent downpours
Mar.	10	Great	warm	cool	infrequent rainstorms
Apr.	10	Great	hot	warm	negligible
May	6	Moderate	hot	warm	none
June	0	Adverse	torrid	hot	none
July	0	Adverse	torrid	hot	negligible
Aug.	0	Adverse	torrid	hot	negligible
Sep.	0	Adverse	torrid	hot	negligible
Oct.	7	Good	hot	warm	negligible
Nov.	10	Great	warm	cool	negligible
Dec.	9	Fine	warm	cool	infrequent downpours

Summary

Only four hundred feet above sea level at the base of mountains that tower almost two miles above town, Palm Springs has one of the West's most awesome locations and its most distinctive climate. The outlook for comfortable **winter** weather is better here than anywhere in the West. With warm days and cool nights, sportswear and swimsuits are the rule in this desert playground. Rainfalls are scarce but heavy. Early **spring** is the most desirable season, when warm dry weather perfectly showcases the phenomenon of the desert in spectacular bloom. Later in the season, daytime temperatures become too hot to comfortably enjoy most outdoor activities. **Summer** is unusable because of consistently sweltering heat (even during the evenings) and almost no rainfall to even temporarily relieve the oppressive temperatures. In **fall**, however, temperatures decline rapidly and are ideal again before Thanksgiving. Warm days, cool evenings, and rare, unpredictable downpours continue through the season.

ATTRACTIONS & DIVERSIONS

★ ***Aerial Tramway***

6 mi NW via CA 111 & Tramway Rd *325-1391*

One of the world's most spectacular aerial rides transports passengers almost 6,000 feet up from the desert (the Valley Station is 2,643 feet above sea level in Chino Canyon) to the Mountain Station (8,516 feet above sea level on San Jacinto Mountain). Two eighty-passenger gondolas make the 2.5 mile trip in about fifteen minutes several times daily. Both stations have observation decks and picnic areas, plus a snack shop and lounge. The Mountain Station also has a restaurant. In the Mt. San Jacinto Wilderness State Park at the top of the tramway, hiking, backpacking, and wilderness camping are popular in summer. There is no extra charge for taking gear on the tram. In winter, cross-country skiing offers a startling contrast to warm weather sports in the desert below. Skiing and sledding equipment can be rented at the Nordic Ski Center on the mountain.

★ ***Balloon Flights***

Scenic balloon flights are a recent recreational innovation that offers an exciting new perspective on the desert and mountains. Passenger flights of approximately one hour can be arranged several places, including:

American Balloon Society *Palm Desert* *568-6700*
Desert Balloon Charters *Palm Desert* *346-8575*
Skysports Aviation *Palm Desert* *340-5545*
Sunrise Balloons *Thermal* *346-7591*

★ ***Bicycling***

Bicycle trails are scenic, flat, relatively safe (and occasionally separated), and well-marked by blue and white signs on more than thirty miles of streets in town. A bikeway map is available from the Convention & Visitors Bureau or the Leisure Services Department at City Hall. Bike rentals are available at:

Burnett's Bicycle Barn *1.2 mi. E at 429 S. Sunrise Way* *325-7844*
Mac's Bike Rentals *1.8 mi. SE at 700 E. Palm Canyon Dr* *327-5721*

★ ***Date Gardens***

15 mi. SE on CA 111

The Coachella Valley is America's date capital. Palm groves have thrived here since the turn of the century. Several groves have roadside shops with outdoor tables shaded by date and citrus trees. Visitors can buy various kinds of dates raw, in candy or baked goods, or in delicious date shakes.

Dune Buggy Rental

Dune Enterprises *325-0376*

The Windy Point area north of town is a popular nearby place for all-terrain vehicles (ATVs). You can rent a two, three, or four-wheeled ATV from these people, and pilot your own or leave the driving to them for one hour or longer desert excursions.

★ ***Golf***

Palm Springs is the "Winter Golfing Capital of the World." There are nearly fifty courses, including many of championship quality, within a fifteen mile radius of town. Several are open to the public, and others offer outside guest privileges. Collectively, they provide a wonderful variety of conditions and scenery for everyone interested in pursuing small white balls around picturesque oases. Additional information can be obtained at the Convention & Visitors Bureau, or at one of the nation's most beautiful and complete public 18-hole courses, the

Palm Springs Municipal Golf Course
5 mi. SE at 1885 Golf Club Dr. *328-1005*

Horseback Riding

★ **Smoke Tree Stables**
3.5 mi. SE at 2500 Toledo Av. *327-1372*

Horses of all types may be rented hourly with or without guides for rides on miles of safe desert trails up into the scenic Palm Canyon areas.

Libraries

★ **Palm Springs Library Center**
1 mi. E at Sunrise Way/Baristo Rd. *323-8291*

This large, contemporary building houses a comprehensive collection of books and audio-visual material. The periodical section is a fine place to relax in upholstered chairs near window walls overlooking a garden patio. Closed Sun.

Welwood Murray Memorial Library
downtown at 100 S. Palm Canyon Dr. *323-8296*

This small library occupies a charming older building that is a well-liked retreat with comfortable chairs for reading or playing chess or checkers. Closed Sat.-Sun.

★ **The Living Desert**
14 mi. SE at 47900 Portola Av. - Palm Desert *346-5694*

Almost two square miles have been set aside to preserve and depict several types of American deserts. In addition to botanical gardens, there is a visitor center with regional geological exhibits, an unusual "after-sundown" exhibit of live desert mammals and reptiles, an aviary, and several miles of self-guided trails. Picnic facilities are attractively located, and there is a gift shop. Closed mid-June thru mid-August.

★ **Moorten Botanical Garden**
1.4 mi. S at 1701 S. Palm Canyon Dr. *327-6555*

In this four acre arboretum, nearly two thousand varieties of desert plants from throughout the world have been arranged according to geographic regions. The gardens have been a landmark since 1938, and are also a sanctuary for birds and wildlife.

Palm Canyon
6 mi. S on Palm Canyon Dr.
The nation's largest stand of native Washingtonia palms lines this steep, narrow canyon for several miles. Hundreds of the giant fan palms can be seen from the rim parking lot at the end of the road. Hiking trails lead down to the canyon floor, where a stream meanders among palms estimated to be up to 2,000 years old. Nearby Andreas and Murray Canyons also have picturesque palm groves, spectacular rock formations, and streams with deep pools and waterfalls that are especially delightful in late winter and spring when they're filled with snow runoff. All canyons remain in a relatively natural condition as part of a reservation belonging to a tiny group of Indians, who may be among the world's wealthiest. The tribe charges an entrance fee to hike in or to drive to parking areas at the base of the canyons. Closed July thru September.

Palm Springs Desert Museum
downtown at 101 Museum Dr. *325-7186*
This strikingly handsome two-story cultural arts center was opened in 1976 on a twenty acre site against the San Jacinto Mountains. Five permanent collections and changing exhibits are displayed in several galleries. A 450-seat theater is used for lectures and concerts. Dancing fountains and sunken sculpture gardens embellish the beautifully landscaped grounds. The museum shop has a good selection of books and unusual gifts. Closed Mon.

Palms-to-Pines Highway
for 130 mi. W of town
A dramatically scenic paved highway climbs thousands of feet from desert date palm groves to pine forests and summer home areas high in the San Jacinto Mountains during a 130-mile loop drive. Take CA 111 south to Palm Desert; CA 74 west into the mountains; CA 243 through the pines to Idyllwild; and return via I-10 and CA 111.

Ruth Hardy Park
.8 mi. NE at Tamarisk Rd./Caballeros Av.
Tennis courts, elaborate play equipment, and shaded picnic tables with splendid mountain views are features of this large park with well-maintained lawns and gardens.

Salton Sea
41 mi. SE on CA 111
Sprawled for twenty-five miles along the lowest portion of the desert basin (235 feet below sea level) is a vast salty lake formed accidentally in 1905-1907 by Colorado River water that broke through irrigation canals. Water level is currently rising and raising havoc with shoreline facilities, but motor boating, water-skiing, and fishing are popular from fall through spring. The Salton Sea State Recreation Area also offers camping and picnic sites.

★ ***Sightseeing***

downtown

The Sun Special Bus Line provides convenient access around town aboard colorful two-level buses with fine visibility from topless upstairs seats.

Warm Water Features

★ **Cloverleaf Lake and R.V.Park**

9 mi. NE via Date Palm Dr. & Varner Rd.on Edom Hill Rd. *340-7101*

The world's longest water slide (750 feet) opened in 1986, along with shorter speed slides and a lazy river slide. Many shaded picnic tables overlook spectacular views of Mt. San Jacinto and Palm Springs.

★ **Oasis Waterpark**

4 mi. SE at 1500 Gene Autry Trail *327-0499*

Opened in 1986, this place lives up to its name. A half acre wave-pool, free-fall and speed slides, hydro-tubes, a lagoon, and three hot spas offer water-oriented fun for everyone. Dining, cocktails, fast foods, and a gift shop are also available.

★ **Palm Springs Swim Center**

1.2 mi. SE at Ramon Rd./Cerritos Dr. *323-8278*

An Olympic-sized fifty meter (fee) swimming pool with high diving boards is usually open to the public. A nicely landscaped half acre lawn and deck surround the pool and provide good mountain views.

★ **The Spa Hotel**

downtown at 100 N. Indian Av. *325-1461*

The public is invited (for a fee) to enjoy natural hot mineral waters at the Spa Hotel in indoor and outdoor pools and Roman tubs with whirlpool action. Massage, steam, exercise room, and related facilities are also lavishly available.

SHOPPING

Palm Springs has one of the West's most well-developed and photogenic downtowns. Architectural controls have resulted in human-scale buildings and luxuriant landscaping accented by garden courtyards, fountains, and sculptures. Off-street parking is plentiful and there are no parking meters. Although the main thoroughfare, Palm Canyon Drive, is a one-way street with heavy traffic flowing south, strolling and sightseeing are as popular as shopping. More than 1,200 large palm trees, illuminated nightly with individual spotlights, complement an abundance of major department and chain stores, distinctive specialty shops, galleries, entertainment places, and restaurants along this bustling thoroughfare.

Food Specialties

★ **Blue Chip Cookies**

downtown at 123 N. Palm Canyon Dr. *322-3111*

White chocolate macadamia nut cookies are one of the many innovative and tasty cookies sold at this new outlet of a California chain. Generous samples are provided.

★ **Frio-Frio**
downtown at 246 S. Palm Canyon Dr. *320-8787*
Various delicious gelato flavors are served to go or at a few indoor or outdoor tables in this classy new temple of frozen delights.

★ **Gaston's Patisserie**
.3 mi. E at 777 E. Tahquitz Way *323-0262*
Fine Continental pastries and breads are the attraction in this little carryout shop adjoining one of the desert's best restaurants.

★ **Grandma's Fudge Shop**
downtown at 130 N. Palm Canyon Dr. *325-9869*
Preparation of the many kinds of delicious homemade fudge, nut brittles, cookies, and candies sold here may be watched through display windows.

★ **Indian Wells Date Garden**
14 mi. SE at 74774 CA 111 - Indian Wells *323-3305*
This long-established date shop is located amidst forty acres of premium Medjool and Deglet Noir dates, and mature citrus orchards. Fresh date or orange shakes are a delicious specialty that can be enjoyed at outdoor garden tables. Dates, citrus, and dried fruit are sold in gift packs that will be shipped anywhere. The above specialties are also available at the downtown store at 364 N. Palm Canyon Drive.

★ **Jensen's Date & Citrus Gardens**
18.5 mi. SE at 80653 CA 111 *347-3897*
A small shop selling premium dates and a variety of citrus is tucked into one of the desert's loveliest orchards of mature citrus and date trees. Each plant is identified by signs along paths provided for visitors.

★ **Liquor Barn**
downtown at 350 S. Palm Canyon Dr. *325-6073*
Safeway has converted an old grocery store into a cavernous showroom for beer, liquor, and a fine assortment of premium California and other wine. Everything is sold at discount prices.

★ **Morrow's**
downtown at 222 N. Palm Canyon Dr. *320-9268*
The finest available nuts and candies, homemade Continental pastries, and gourmet gelato served in freshly made Danish cones make this classy, brassy store an easy winner.

★ **Penguin's**
downtown at 333 N. Palm Canyon Dr. *327-6455*
Yogurt-lovers will be delighted by this bright, tile-trimmed new outlet of a flourishing chain. Many styles, flavors, and various fresh fruit and other toppings are sold to go, or to enjoy at one of the comfortable indoor or outdoor tables overlooking the main street.

The Royal Bagel
downtown at 210 E. Arenas Rd. *322-4353*
At least a dozen varieties of well-made bagels are featured in this popular little takeout shop. Closed Mon.

★ **Shield's Date Gardens**
18 mi. SE at 80225 CA 111 - Indio *347-0996*
One of the world's largest date shops serves date shakes, and sells a wide selection of quality dates and fresh citrus to go or in gift packs to be shipped anywhere. The picturesque grounds around this venerable roadside landmark include a variety of mature date and citrus trees. The historic film "Romance and the Sex Life of the Date" is shown continuously.

Specialty Shops

★ **Alan Ladd Hardware & Gifts**
.4 mi. S at 500 S. Palm Canyon Dr. *325-1265*
This large, gleaming showcase of all that makes a house a home has become a Palm Springs tradition since its founding years ago by the Ladd family of film fame. Closed Sun.

Bookland
downtown at 102 N. Palm Canyon Dr. *325-1020*
This long-established shop has packed a good selection of best sellers, general and regional interest books, plus magazines into a popular little store on the main street.

★ **Brentano's**
downtown at 123 N. Palm Canyon Dr. *327-1338*
Palm Springs' newest and largest bookstore features well-organized selections of hardcover and paperbacks covering a broad range of subjects.

Crown Books
downtown at 368 S. Palm Canyon Dr. *320-0038*
Every book and a large selection of magazines in this newer outlet of a bookstore chain is discounted.

★ **Karen Asher Galleries, Ltd.**
downtown at 265 S. Palm Canyon Dr. *320-3333*
Fantasy plant and animal sculptures are showcased in a fascinating display. Sizes range from tiny to gigantic and materials vary from metal, wood, or rock through soft fabric to high-tech fiber optics.

★ **The Nelson Rockfeller Collection**
.3 mi. E at 707 E. Tahquitz Way *320-9554*
Exclusive fine art objects from life-sized bronzes to wall hangings, and from primitive to modern, are beautifully displayed.

★ **Other Galleries**
Almost forty art galleries in the Palm Springs area offer quality work in all media. Most are located downtown on Palm Canyon Drive. The Chamber of Commerce has free copies of "The Desert Arts Calendar" with a guide describing the collections in most of the area's galleries.

NIGHTLIFE

A while ago, Palm Springs was famous for its many piano bars. It still is. But, the town now also offers most of the evening diversions of major cities—with admissions and cover charges to match. Elaborate newer nightclubs and lounges (many clustered downtown) feature ultra-modern light-and-sound systems and high-tech decor. As a counterpoint, relaxed opulence and easy listening music are the hallmarks of many of the tony resort lounges scattered throughout the area.

★ **Balloons**
downtown at 440 S. Palm Canyon Dr. *320-7316*
There is fine music for dancing upstairs or downstairs amidst festive decor accented by hot-air balloon models, colorful helium balloons, and neon lighting. Patrons have a choice of padded bar stools, chairs, or bench-style sofas. Light meals are served.

Billy Reed's
1.6 mi. N at 1800 N. Palm Canyon Dr. *325-1946*
Live entertainment is showcased nightly in a large lounge that is comfortably outfitted with quality antiques and reproductions. One of the area's largest restaurants adjoins.

★ **Brandy's**
downtown at 238 N. Palm Canyon Dr. *327-1311*
An ultra-modern lounge with cushy booths and stools offers live music most nights and a "light show" dance floor. Pool, backgammon, and other games are also available.

★ **Canyon Hotel**
3 mi. S at 2850 S. Palm Canyon Dr. *323-5656*
This celebrated resort includes Raffles, a big well-furnished lounge with live music for dancing every night except Sunday.

★ **Cecils Disco**
2.4 mi. SE at 1775 E. Palm Canyon Dr. *320-4202*
This large and dazzling disco showplace "gets it on" with heavy sounds-and-lights every night. Next door, contemporary American dishes are served in a glitzy room dominated by disco dance floor decor.

★ **Doubles**
.3 mi. SW at 701 W. Baristo Rd. *323-3100*
A window wall view of luxuriant landscapes is a daytime feature, while live music for dancing is offered most nights in a plush contemporary lounge.

★ **L.N.0. Pompeii**
5.5 mi. SE at 67399 E. Palm Canyon Dr. *328-5800*
In the desert's most flamboyant fun center for adults, the volcano out front has cooled, and the full-sized, fully automated robot band has slowed to a crawl. However, patrons can still dance to a high-tech sound-

and-light show, or relax and enjoy a spectacular view of town and the mountains through a window wall beyond the dance floor. An adjoining contemporary restaurant offers simple American fare. Steep weekend cover charges are waived for those who eat in their dining room.

Sheraton Plaza
downtown at 400 E. Tahquitz Way *320-6868*
The first of the major new downtown hotels includes Harvey's Piano Lounge, a plush, comfortable hideaway with musical entertainment.

Valley Players Guild Theatre
downtown at 135 E. Tahquitz Way *324-4353*
Live theater is presented here on weekends throughout the year.

★ **Zelda's**
downtown at 169 N. Indian Av. *325-2375*
Here is a glittering landmark of space-age decor. Lots of flashing lights, chrome, and high-tech furnishings give pizzazz to the bars, dance floor, and lounge overlooking a center mall. Dancing to disco or the latest in live sounds is the main event nightly. Next door, a related club (Lips) features dance music of the 80s nightly.

RESTAURANTS

The Palm Springs area has a superabundance of dining rooms—including a surplus of both chain and hotel restaurants. Many feature expensively decorated "theme" dining rooms, while relatively few offer first-rate meals. Almost all of the area's gourmet restaurants have been added during the booming development of recent years. Unfortunately, prices have also accelerated rapidly, and are now generally higher than in any other great town except St. Helena.

Aerial Tramway
6 mi. NW via CA 111 & Tramway Dr. *325-1391*
L-D. *Expensive*
A popular ride-'n-dine special couples a family-style prime rib dinner with a spectacular view from a restaurant high on Mt. San Jacinto. An adjoining bar shares the view.

Banducci's Bit of Italy
1 mi. S at 1260 S. Palm Canyon Dr. *325-2537*
D only. *Moderate*
Authentic southern Italian fare is served in a long-established restaurant with a popular dining porch by the main thoroughfare.

Billy Reed's Restaurant
1.6 mi. N at 1800 N. Palm Canyon Dr. *325-1946*
B-L-D. *Moderate*
This huge coffee shop/restaurant/lounge complex is a favorite for hearty American fare and their own baked goods served amid a profusion of old-time bric-a-brac and plants.

Bistro
7 mi. SE at 70065 CA 111 - Rancho Mirage *328-5650*
D only. *Very Expensive*
Continental specialties are prepared to order. Pastel colors, soft lighting, and dramatic artwork are nicely coordinated with casually elegant furnishings.

Bit Of Country
downtown at 418 S. Indian Av. *325-5154*
B-L. *Low*
Plain homestyle cooking, some of the lowest breakfast prices in town, and a cozy sidewalk dining patio are features of this well-liked, unassuming coffee shop.

Buddy's Deli
downtown at 401 E. Tahquitz Way *325-6102*
B-L-D. *Moderate*
Smoked whitefish, fried kippers and onions, Nova lox, plus thick french toast and assorted distinctive omelets are among the deli-cacies served at booths or tables amidst lush greenery or on a sidewalk dining terrace.

★ **Cattails**
6 mi. SE at 68369 CA 111 - Cathedral City *324-8263*
D only. Closed Sun.-Mon. *Very Expensive*
A blackboard identifies half a dozen gourmet Continental entrees nightly in this romantic hideaway. The dining room is a study in contemporary elegance where pastel colors and soft fabrics complement beautifully appointed, well-spaced tables.

Cedar Creek Inn
1 mi. S at 1555 S. Palm Canyon Dr. *325-7300*
L-D. *Moderate*
Contemporary American fare is popular with families in this large and elaborate new restaurant. (The smaller original is in Palm Desert.) Decor is distinguished by lavish use of plants throughout.

The Chart House
7 mi. SE at 69934 CA 111 - Rancho Mirage *324-5613*
D only. *Expensive*
Fresh seafood, steaks, and an impressive salad bar are accompanied by a tour-de-force of free-form woodcraft architecture and contemporary decor in one of the best dining rooms representing a restaurant chain in the desert.

Chez Vous
downtown at 370 N. Palm Canyon Dr. *320-8989*
L-D. Closed Tues.-Wed. *Expensive*
Freshly prepared baked goods are featured on a short menu in a congested little French-style sidewalk cafe.

Chez Zizi
downtown at 276 N. Palm Canyon Dr. *320-3375*
L-D. *Expensive*
Very French dishes are served in a casual and colorful bistro or on a courtyard tucked away off the main street.

★ **The Croissant Connection**
downtown at 198 S. Palm Canyon Dr. *320-9666*
B-L. *Moderate*
A delicious assortment of croissants and other pastry is made on the premises. First-rate French-style omelets and other light fare are also available. Several of the tables in the cheerful dining room have picture window views of the main street and mountains.

★ **Dar Maghreb**
9.2 mi. SE at 42300 Bob Hope Dr. - Rancho Mirage *568-9486*
D only. *Expensive*
Traditional multicourse Moroccan feasts are served by a lavishly costumed staff amid extravagent Near Eastern atmosphere. Fanciful dining areas with low sofas and deep cushions overlook dramatically lighted gardens.

★ **David's Desert Greenhouse**
13 mi. S at 73725 El Paseo - Palm Desert *568-0300*
L-D. *Expensive*
Lamb is the highlight among American dishes skillfully prepared with a light touch. Plush booths and elegant table settings distinguish this sleek recent addition to desert dining.

Doubles at the Tennis Club
.3 mi. SW at 701 W. Baristo Rd. *323-3100*
L-D. Closed Mon. *Very Expensive*
Continental favorites are served amid quintessential Palm Springs decor. Window walls frame views of the luxuriant greenery of town one way, and stark desert vegetation is spotlighted on a mountain slope the other way. The large, split-level dining room is accented by a unique side-by-side rock wall fireplace-and-waterfall. A plush view lounge adjoins.

★ **Eveleen's**
.4 mi. N at 664 N. Palm Canyon Dr. *325-4766*
D only. Closed Tues. *Very Expensive*
Excellent French cuisine is presented in an intimate dining room that exudes gracious tranquility.

Fairchild's
3 mi. SE at 1001 S. El Cielo Rd. *327-3518*
L-D. Closed Mon. *Expensive*
Continental specialties are featured in a large and luxurious bistro-style dining room at Bel Air Greens. A dining terrace fronts on a picture-postcard backdrop—lush fairways by a small lake with a palm-studded island backed by snow-capped peaks.

★ **Flower Drum**
downtown at 424 S. Indian Av. *323-3020*
L-D. *Moderate*
Delicacies from five major regions of China are prepared with the utmost respect for quality and authenticity. A circular aquarium is mounted in the middle of a mirrored stage backdrop flanked by dramatic gilt dragons. The large, comfortably furnished dining room, opened in 1985, also includes a pond with golden koi and a bridge over a stream.

The French Quarters
13 mi. SE via CA 111 at 74155 El Paseo - Palm Desert *346-4460*
L-D. *Very Expensive*
A wide assortment of French dishes is served in several rooms in this large newer restaurant.

★ **Fuddruckers Restaurant**
downtown at 262 S. Palm Canyon Dr. *320-4889*
L-D. *Low*
This representative of a burgeoning burger chain is making a notable assault on the West's best burger competition by using meat ground in the restaurant's exhibition butcher shop and plenty of very fresh accompaniments. Multilevel dining areas offer a choice of main street and mountain views or scenes of the happy hubbub in the colorful interior.

★ **Gallery Louisiane**
13 mi. S at 73520 El Paseo - Palm Desert *346-8999*
D only. *Expensive*
Authentic Creole-style cooking arrived in the desert in 1985. These skillfully prepared renditions of Deep South dishes are delicious. Candlelight and full linen distinguish a dining room that becomes a cabaret later each evening.

★ **Gaston's**
.3 mi. E at 777 E. Tahquitz Way *320-7750*
L-D. *Very Expensive*
Acclaimed French cuisine is presented in a plush and pretty, contemporary dining room that is one of the desert's finest. Next door, a sleek, comfortable lounge provides grand piano music.

★ **Grill Le Ravel**
9.2 mi. SE at 42250 Bob Hope Dr. - Rancho Mirage *568-6800*
D only. *Extremely Expensive*
New California cuisine is a perfect complement to one of the desert's newest and most luxurious contemporary dining rooms. A pianist entertains nightly on the grand piano in the sophisticated adjoining lounge.

★ **Hamburger Hamlet**
downtown at 105 N. Palm Canyon Dr. *325-2321*
L-D. *Moderate*
American fast foods are treated with uncommon distinction in the desert's representative of one of California's finest and most popular coffee shop/restaurant chains.

La Cave
7 mi. SE at 70064 CA 111 - Rancho Mirage *324-4673*
D only. Closed Mon. *Very Expensive*
French cuisine is served in a formally elegant downstairs dining room. Background music is played on a grand piano nightly.

Las Casuelas Terraza
downtown at 222 S. Palm Canyon Dr. *325-2794*
L-D. *Moderate*
This recent addition to a very popular local restaurant chain offers a variety of conventional Mexican dishes amidst decor themed to a 19th century colonial hotel with several elaborately furnished dining rooms. Sidewalk patios combine alfresco dining with people-watching. Elsewhere, a lounge features large margaritas, twirling fans, and hanging plants.

Le Cafe de Paris
12 mi. S at 72820 El Paseo - Palm Desert *346-7356*
D only. Closed Mon. *Expensive*
French cuisine is the specialty in this tastefully decorated dining room.

★ **Le Paon**
13 mi. SE at 45640 CA 74 - Palm Desert *568-3651*
L-D. *Very Expensive*
Traditional and New Orleans-style French cuisine is graciously served amid candlelit elegance or on a heated patio.

★ **Le Vallauris**
downtown at 385 W. Tahquitz Way *325-5059*
L-D. Sun. brunch. Closed Mon. *Extremely Expensive*
French nouvelle cuisine with an emphasis on fresh seafood is served amid congested, formal elegance in an attractively restored house. The intimate, shady patio is a local favorite for lunch or brunch. A comfortable piano lounge adjoins.

Lord Fletcher Inn
7.5 mi. SE at 70385 CA 111 - Rancho Mirage *328-1161*
D only. Closed Sun. *Expensive*
Pot roast, chicken with dumplings, prime rib, and other dishes support the "Olde English" theme of this long-established restaurant. Costumed staff attend guests seated in several comfortable English country inn/ pub-style dining rooms.

Louise's Pantry
downtown at 124 S. Palm Canyon Dr. *325-5124*
B-L-D. *Low*
Homemade pies and pastries have been the specialties here for many years. The authentically old-fashioned coffee shop is so popular that people are inevitably lined up on the sidewalk waiting to get in.

★ **Mancuso's**
11 mi. SE at 72281 CA 111 - Palm Desert *340-6610*
D only. *Very Expensive*
Classic Northern Italian and French specialties are served in formally elegant dining areas enhanced by a showcased, well-played grand piano.

Medium Rare
7 mi. SE at 70064 CA 111 - Rancho Mirage *328-6563*
L-D. *Expensive*
Prime rib is the specialty among American and Continental dishes served in several dining rooms where comfortable armchairs and well-padded booths set the tone.

★ **Melvyn's Restaurant**
.4 mi. S at 200 Ramon Rd. *325-2323*
L-D. Sat. & Sun. brunch. *Very Expensive*
Highly regarded Continental cuisine and tableside cooking are featured in a handsomely appointed dining room and on a glass-enclosed patio of the beautifully restored old Ingleside Inn. Live entertainment is offered in an intimate and comfortable piano lounge nightly.

Mesquite's
12 mi. SE via CA 111 at 73030 El Paseo - Palm Desert *340-0999*
L-D. No L on Sun. *Moderate*
From fajitas to frittatas, and from blackened redfish to hangtown fry, this tribute to today's trends in tastes tries to do it all. Customers can watch what happens in a big, busy exhibition kitchen from casually outfitted booths, tables, or a counter in a dining room accented by a lot of gleaming chrome and tile. A glitzy bar adjoins. The desert's first designer diner opened in 1986.

Michael's
13 mi. SE via CA 111 at 73111 El Paseo - Palm Desert *340-4522*
L-D. Closed Sun. *Expensive*
American food with a French accent is served in a tiny new dining room with casual furnishings and a pink and white color scheme.

Nate's Deli and Restaurant
downtown at 100 S. Indian Av. *325-3506*
B-L-D. *Moderate*
New York-style deli specialties have dominated the very long menu of this casual deli/restaurant since 1948.

Our Place
13 mi. SE via CA 111 at 73260 El Paseo - Palm Desert *346-0744*
L-D. No L on Sun. *Moderate*
Authentic Yugoslavian dishes like meat-filled tender dumplings and beef in flaky pastry are featured in a tiny, colorful bistro that also has a sidewalk dining area.

Perrina's
downtown at 340 N. Palm Canyon Dr. *325-6544*
L-D. *Expensive*
Italian cuisine is served in dark-toned, intimate atmosphere in this restaurant/piano bar.

Raphael's
.5 mi. S at 691 S. Palm Canyon Dr. *320-8221*
D only. *Expensive*
Italian dishes are served in a candlelit dining room with comfortable booths and crisp linen.

Revels
14 mi. SE at 74985 CA 111 - Indian Wells *346-8811*
B-L-D. *Moderate*
The flaky pastries are excellent among an otherwise conventional full line of baked goods that can be enjoyed with omelets and other light fare. Lush greenery and sleek wood-and-brass decor further enhance this new bakery/restaurant/lounge.

★ **Riccio's**
2 mi. N at 2155 N. Palm Canyon Dr. *325-2369*
D only. *Very Expensive*
Classic Italian specialties achieve gourmet distinction and are presented by tuxedoed waiters in an exuberant and congested dining room. A baby grand piano in the adjoining bar is played nightly.

★ **Rockwell's**
13 mi. SE at 73705 El Paseo - Palm Desert *568-0091*
L-D. Closed Tues. *Expensive*
Old-fashioned all-American recipes make a nostalgic comeback in a handsome restaurant that opened in mid-1985. Cushioned armchairs and fully linened tables are set in a high-ceilinged dining room enhanced by singular art objects and an exhibition kitchen.

Siamese Gourmet
4.5 mi. SE at 4711 E. Palm Canyon Dr. *328-0057*
L-D. *Moderate*
Thai specialties are featured, including several using homemade curry paste. Linen, and hardwood-and-wicker chairs, lend interest to the simply furnished dining room in a shopping center.

Sorrentino's
1 mi. N at 1032 N. Palm Canyon Dr. *325-2944*
D only. Closed June-Sept. *Moderate*
This popular seafood house features inviting Mediterranean decor and a lounge with live entertainment.

★ **Tai Ping Restaurant**
13 mi. SE at 45299 Lupine Lane at El Paseo - Palm Desert 340-1836
D only. Expensive
Outstanding Szechwan, Mandarin, Hunan, and Cantonese cuisine is served nightly to patrons seated at tables set with full linen, plus a flower and candle in silver. An intricate, hand-wrought gilt temple casting is showcased to one side of the expansive dining room, while giant prints of beautiful Orientals grace the opposite wall. Exotic Polynesian drinks are prepared in the adjoining Peacock lounge.

Tony Rama's
downtown at 450 S. Palm Canyon Dr. 320-4297
L-D. Moderate
Barbecued baby back ribs and a loaf of onion rings are the specialty on a limited American menu. This branch of a casual restaurant chain is one of the few places in town that serves past midnight every night, and there is live music.

The Velvet Turtle
14 mi. SE at 74700 CA 111 340-2499
L-D. Sun. brunch. Expensive
A contemporary American menu is offered in the desert's first representative of this well-regarded restaurant chain. A large, casually elegant dining room with Mediterranean-style furnishings opens onto a dining patio overlooking a well-landscaped courtyard.

★ **Wally's Restaurant**
9 mi. SE at 71755 CA 111 - Rancho Mirage 568-9321
L-D. Closed Sun. Very Expensive
Gourmet Continental cuisine is formally presented in the desert's definitive showcase of contemporary opulence. Careful attention was paid to every detail in the large multilevel dining room, on the delightful patio, and in the luxurious lounge with a grand piano bar.

★ **The Wilde Goose**
6 mi. SE at 67938 CA 111 - Cathedral City 328-5775
D only. Closed Mon. Expensive
Fine Continental cuisine is given a contemporary styling in this well-regarded restaurant. There is piano entertainment most evenings in the casually elegant dining room.

LODGING

America's foremost desert destination has an appropriately outstanding assortment of accommodations. Major resort hotels are the area's most spectacular landmarks. Each is architecturally distinctive, elaborately landscaped, and includes a range of recreation, entertainment, drinking, and lodging facilities. More than 150 lodgings dot the area, but during the winter season there are usually few vacancies and almost no bargains in town. From June through September, however, remarkable discounts of 50% or more from the winter rates shown below are normally available. Even the major resorts that stay open reduce their prices by as much as fifty percent.

Allstar Inns
7 mi. SE at 69570 CA 111 *324-8475*
A fast-growing economy lodging chain recently added this large motel with an outdoor pool and whirlpool. Each of the nicely furnished units has a cable color TV and phone.
regular room— Q bed...$33

★ **Americana Canyon Hotel**
3 mi. S at 2850 S. Palm Canyon Dr. *323-5656*
Palm Springs' most complete resort is the only one in town with a private 18-hole championship golf course. The beautifully landscaped grounds also include three swimming pools, three whirlpools, ten (fee) tennis courts (several night-lighted), and a health club with sauna and steam baths. ***Perry's*** is an informally elegant dining room with a mesquite grill and seafood bar, plus an outstanding champagne brunch. ***Bogie's*** is a nostalgic nightclub, and the ***Greenhouse*** is a bright, plant-filled lobby lounge. Each spacious, well-furnished room has a balcony or patio, a phone, and cable color TV. The resort is closed during the summer. For toll-free reservations, call: (800)228-3278.
suite—separate BR with wet bar, K bed...$235
regular room— K bed...$180

Casa de Camero
1.4 mi. N at 1480 N. Indian Av. *320-1678*
This tiny single-level motel has a large outdoor pool with a fine mountain view. Each of the small, plain rooms has cable color TV.
regular room— D bed...$35

Casa Del Camino
1.4 mi. N at 1447 N. Palm Canyon Dr. *325-9018*
An outdoor pool and whirlpool on nicely landscaped grounds are features of this unassuming, older single-level motel. Each room has a cable color TV.
regular room— D, Q or K bed...$35

★ **Desert Princess**
5.5 mi. NE at Vista Chino/Landau Blvd. *322-7000*
Princess Cruises' lavish desert resort officially opened in January 1986. A spacious and elegant four-story hotel is the main building on a flat, nearly half square mile site with a panoramic view of southern California's highest peaks. Amenities include a large swimming pool and whirlpools; plus (for a fee) an 18-hole championship golf course; ten tennis courts (five lighted); two racquetball/handball courts; a fitness center; and bicycle rentals. The elegant ***Princess Restaurant*** features Continental specialties, and the ***Oasis Lounge*** offers live entertainment and dancing. Each beautifully decorated, spacious room has a refrigerator, patio or balcony, phone, and remote-controlled cable color TV.
#482,#382,#282—windows on 2 sides with pool/golf course/mt. views, huge balc., K bed...$240
regular room—desert view, K bed...$150

★ **Embassy Suites**
14 mi. SE at 74700 CA 111 - Palm Desert *340-6600*
This large full-service hotel opened in 1985. A complex of three-story Spanish-style buildings surrounds a landscaped courtyard with a big outdoor pool and a whirlpool. Six lighted tennis courts and a putting green are also available. The casually elegant ***Velvet Turtle*** restaurant and lounge overlook the courtyard. Each spacious two-room suite has two phones, two cable color TVs, and a refrigerator/wet bar. A full American breakfast and two-hour afternoon cocktail party are complimentary. For toll-free reservations, call: in California (800)223-1679; elsewhere (800)633-2834.
regular room— 2 D or K bed...$160

★ **Gene Autry Hotel**
4 mi. SE at 4200 E. Palm Canyon Dr. *328-1171*
One of the area's long-established large resort hotels is on nicely landscaped grounds with three outdoor pools, two whirlpools, six lighted (fee) tennis courts, plus a gift shop. The ***Sombrero Room*** offers Continental and Mexican selections, and the ***Red Cantina Lounge*** has live entertainment. Each well-furnished room has a phone and cable color TV.
"Executive Wing"—adults only, spacious, refr., some have pvt. patio, K bed...$165
regular room— K bed...$105

Holiday Lodge
downtown at 227 N. Indian Av. *325-7810*
A large outdoor pool is surrounded by the guest rooms of this small, older motel near the heart of town. Table tennis, a pool table, and an exercise room are also free to guests. Each simply furnished room has cable color TV and a phone.
#201—large, pitched roof, windows on 2 sides, view over balc. to mts., K bed...$75
regular room—small, D bed...$55

Hotel 6 Palms
1.6 mi. SE at 595 E. Palm Canyon Dr. *327-2044*
The Motel 6 economy chain is represented by a large, renamed motel (the word "motel" is not used in Palm Springs) that is the best **bargain** in town. Typically reserved months in advance in winter, it is conveniently located and has a landscaped outdoor pool. Each room has a (pay) TV.
regular room— D bed...$25

Ingleside Inn
.4 mi. S at 200 W. Ramon Rd. *325-0046*
This handsomely restored small hotel is wonderfully overgrown with bouganvilla and flowering trees. There is a small outdoor pool and a whirlpool in a garden. ***Melvyn's*** Restaurant and the ***Casa Blanca*** Lounge are among the best in town. Each room is individually furnished with antiques, and has a phone, cable color TV, a refrigerator, plus an in-

bath steam bath and whirlpool. A Continental breakfast is complimentary.

#V1,#V2,#145—fireplace, sitting area, pvt. terrace, K bed...$195
Penthouse #4—end unit, private mountain view, K bed...$115
regular room—some have mountain view, Q bed...$95

International Resort Hotel

2.5 mi. SE at 1800 E. Palm Canyon Dr. *323-1711*

A landscaped courtyard with a big outdoor pool and two whirlpools is surrounded on all sides by three floors of rooms in this large, modern full-service hotel. Saunas and (fee) massage are also available, along with a restaurant, lounge, and coffee shop. Each nicely remodeled room has a phone, cable color TV, and private balcony or patio. For toll-free reservations, call: in California (800)245-6904; elsewhere (800)245-6907.

#345—2-room suite, top floor, refr., mt. view beyond pool, K bed...$150
#346 thru #355—spacious, top floor, 2 Q beds...$129
regular room— Q bed...$89

★ **La Mancha**

1 mi. NE at 444 N. Avenida Caballeros *323-1773*

The premiere of a new generation of ultra-plush "personal" resorts is this Spanish-style villa complex. Amenities include a beautifully landscaped outdoor pool and whirlpool, plus a sauna, gym, and tennis courts. Bikes and motorbikes are available. Each spacious, luxuriously furnished suite has a phone, cable color TV, fully equipped kitchen, living room and dining room, and a private patio.

"private villa"—1 BR, outdoor whirlpool, gas fireplace, wet bar, gas barbecue, K bed...$185
"casitas"—1 BR, gas fireplace, wet bar, pvt. walled yard with small pool, gas BBQ, K bed...$285
regular room—no kitchen, K bed...$110

★ **La Quinta**

19 mi. SE at 49499 Eisenhower Dr. (Box 69) - La Quinta *564-4111*

After sixty years, the most celebrated resort in the desert retains all of its unique charm. Remote and serene, the sprawling oasis includes four large outdoor pools; whirlpools; and (for a fee) a top-rated 18-hole championship golf course; a putting green; thirty tennis courts (some lighted); and rental bicycles. Acres of date groves are nearby, and lovely formal gardens and citrus trees surround gracious public rooms, including an elegant dining room with a renowned buffet brunch, and a lounge with live entertainment and dancing. Each beautifully furnished adobe bungalow unit has a refrigerator, phone, and cable color TV. The resort is closed during the summer.

"deluxe" rooms—newer, 1 BR, wet bar, fireplace, 2 T, Q or K bed...$195
"superior" rooms—newer, cozy, fireplace, 2 T, Q or K bed...$165
regular room— 2 T or Q bed...$115

Lexington Hotel Suites
6.8 mi. SE at 69151 E. Palm Canyon Dr. - Cathedral City 324-5939
Opened in 1985, this large motel has an outdoor pool and whirlpool. Each of the attractively furnished suites has a kitchen, cable color TV, and a phone.
large suite—2 BR, 2 Q beds...$119
small suite—1 BR, Q bed...$104
regular room—studio, Q bed...$94

★ **Marriott's Rancho las Palmas**
9.5 mi. S at 41000 Bob Hope Dr. - Rancho Mirage 568-2727
The current state of the art in luxury desert resorts, this monumental early California-style hotel has three big outdoor pools and two whirlpools in a flower-filled garden setting, saunas, a game room, and (for a fee) a spectacular 27-hole golf course with small lakes, a putting green, twenty-five tennis courts (eight lighted), and rental bicycles. The multilevel ***Cabrillo*** dining room serves Continental fare amid elegant early-California decor. In the ***Fountain Court***, all meals are served in a delightful tropical courtyard setting. The ***Sunrise Terrace*** offers patio dining and fine mountain views. ***Miguel's*** is a comfortable lounge with live entertainment and dancing. Each of the spacious, well-furnished guest rooms has a phone, cable color TV with movies, refrigerator, and a patio or balcony. For toll-free reservations, call (800)228-9290.
Bldgs. #10 & #28—lakeside, superb golf course/mt. view, K bed...$200
regular room—garden view, 2 D or K bed...$185

★ **Maxim's Suite Hotel**
downtown at 285 N. Palm Canyon Dr. 322-9000
Opened in 1986, this grandiose full-service hotel rises six stories above a prime location at the heart of town. A long outdoor pool, indoor and outdoor whirlpools, sauna, and (for a fee) a complete health spa are amenities surrounding the desert's most striking atrium lobby. The sophisticated ***Le Jardin*** offers Continental specialties for dinner, while all meals are served in the casual, comfortably appointed ***Palm Canyon Cafe***. The ***Palm Court Lounge*** shares the airy ambiance of the beautifully decorated atrium with the cafe, and features grand piano entertainment. Each spacious, beautifully furnished room has two phones, remote-controlled cable color TV, a mini-bar, private balcony, and a marble bath. For toll-free reservations, call: in California (800)533-3556; elsewhere (800)222-8112.
regular room—request 6th fl. mountain side for max. privacy/view, K bed...$225

Mira Loma Hotel
1.4 mi. N at 1420 N. Indian Av. 320-1178
This small, single-level older motel has a large outdoor pool. In February and March, citrus trees surrounding the pool and guest rooms have an intoxicating fragrance. Each room has a phone, cable color TV, and a

refrigerator.
regular room—poolside, Q bed...$56
regular room—small, by busy street, D bed...$31

Monte Vista Hotel
.3 mi. N at 414 N. Palm Canyon Dr. *325-5641*
This nicely landscaped older motel features an outdoor pool and whirlpool, plus many mature citrus trees. Each room has a cable color TV.
regular room— 2 T or D bed...$36

Mountain View Inn
downtown at 200 S. Cahuilla Rd. *325-5281*
Two outdoor pools and a whirlpool are enhanced by a garden setting in this older single-level motel. Bicycles are furnished. Each of the well-maintained rooms has a cable color TV and kitchenette.
#13—fireplace, by pool, K bed...$60
#11—end unit, fireplace, private patio, 2 T beds...$60
#16—spacious, 1 BR, kitchen, fireplace in LR, K bed...$75
regular room— 2 T beds...$40

Palm Springs Biltmore Hotel
2 mi. SE at 1000 E. Palm Canyon Dr. *323-1811*
Public rooms, cottages, and bungalows occupy twelve acres of landscaped grounds. This older resort has a large landscaped pool and whirlpool with fine mountain views, plus tennis courts. The ***1000 East*** is an attractive dining room with a garden view, and there is a lounge and coffee shop. Each room has a phone and cable color TV. For toll-free reservations, call: in California (800)826-4162; elsewhere (800)772-6655.
#15,#12,#10,#8,#6—spacious, sunken tile bath/spa, refr., K bed...$115
regular room— Q or K bed...$95

Palm Springs Hilton Riviera Hotel
1.5 mi. N at 1600 N. Indian Av. *327-8311*
Palm Springs' largest resort hotel, a sprawling Las Vegas-style convention facility, was renovated in 1985. Seventeen landscaped acres also include an Olympic-sized outdoor pool; a huge whirlpool; fifteen (fee) tennis courts (several night-lighted); plus the casually elegant ***Veranda Grill*** and lounge. Each redecorated room has a patio or balcony, a phone, and cable color TV. For toll-free reservations in California, call (800)367-3296.
suite—larger, wet bar/refrigerator, 2 D or K bed...$185
regular room— 2 D or K bed...$135

Palm Springs Hotel
.4 mi. N at 515 N. Palm Canyon Dr. *325-2591*
This older motel has a large outdoor pool and whirlpool on landscaped grounds. Each unit has cable color TV with movies.
poolside unit— K bed...$65
regular room—in rear, D or K bed...$45

★ **Palm Springs Marquis**
downtown at 150 S. Indian Av. *322-2121*
Opened in 1985, this elaborate full-service hotel sprawls across two downtown blocks. Landscaped courtyards include two outdoor pools, two whirlpools, and two tennis courts. There is also a (fee) health club with saunas and massage. In addition to a specialty restaurant, live entertainment is featured in the lounge. Each well-furnished room has cable color TV with movies, two phones, and a private balcony or patio. For toll-free reservations, call: in California (800)223-1050; elsewhere (800)458-6679.
villa—1 BR, spacious, kitchen, gas fireplace, wet bar, sunken Roman tub, pool/mt. view, K bed...$275
regular room— 2 D or K bed...$175

★ **Royce Resort Hotel**
7 mi. SE at 34567 Cathedral Canyon Dr. *321-9000*
This large newer all-suite hotel on landscaped grounds offers ten tennis courts (seven lighted); a large outdoor pool; plus (a fee for) a championship 18-hole golf course. The large dining room, ***Arthur's***, serves all meals. A piano bar adjoins. Each nicely furnished unit has a living room/dining room, complete kitchen, and bedroom, plus a phone, cable color TV, and a balcony or patio. For toll-free reservations, call: in California (800)824-8224; elsewhere (800)321-9000.
regular suite—1 BR, 2 D or K bed...$180

Sandcastle Inn
2 mi. N at 2330 N. Palm Canyon Dr. *325-2212*
This plain, modern motel has a large outdoor pool and whirlpool, plus a sauna. Each simply furnished unit has cable TV.
regular room— D, Q or K bed...$35

Sandstone Inn
2 mi. N at 2395 N. Indian Av. *325-7191*
A large outdoor pool is the center of attention in this tiny, single-level older motel. Each modest room has a cable color TV and refrigerator.
regular room— Q bed...$39

★ **Sheraton Oasis Hotel**
downtown at 155 S. Belardo Rd. *325-1301*
This large modern full-service hotel has one of the best locations downtown. The nearby mountains provide a towering backdrop to luxuriant landscaping in a garden courtyard containing an outdoor pool and a whirlpool. ***Hank's Cafe Americain*** is an exotic dining room reminiscent of Casablanca. Live entertainment and dancing are available in a comfortable lounge. Each spacious well-furnished unit has a phone, cable color TV, and a private balcony or patio. For toll-free reservations, call (800)325-3535.
#375,#373,#371,#369—top floor, mt. & pool view, K bed...$145
#374,#368—mt. & pool view, K bed...$145
regular room— 2 T or K bed...$115

★ **Sheraton Plaza - Palm Springs**
downtown at 400 E. Tahquitz Way *320-6868*
The first of the 1980s' downtown resort hotels is a showcase of contemporary architecture and decor. A flower-filled interior courtyard has a large outdoor pool, two whirlpools, and a sea of deck chairs with splendid mountain views. There is a fully equipped spa with a sauna, plus (for a fee) massage and other services, and six lighted tennis courts. The ***Tapestry*** offers Continental cuisine in an elegant ultra-modern setting. The ***Terrace Cafe*** is a glass-enclosed dining room serving all meals. ***Harvey's Bar*** is a comfortable, plush lounge with entertainment. Each spacious, beautifully furnished room has a phone, cable color TV with movies, refrigerator, and a balcony or patio. For toll-free reservations, call (800)325-3535.
#340,#345,#366,#367—fine mt. views beyond courtyard pool, K bed...$225
#339,#346,#365—1 BR suites, fine mt. views beyond courtyard pool, K bed...$275
regular room— K bed...$145

★ **Spa Hotel and Mineral Springs**
downtown at 100 N. Indian Av. *325-1461*
Palm Springs' only mineral springs facility is a big modern five-story hotel in the heart of town. A large outdoor pool, a hot mineral whirlpool, and still pools (all with mountain views) are free to guests. In addition, (for a fee) there are three lighted tennis courts and a lavish health spa with mineral springs whirlpools, steam baths, massage, and a co-ed gym. All meals are served in the casually elegant ***Agua Restaurant***, and there is live entertainment for dancing in the ***Agua Lounge***. Each of the recently remodeled, nicely furnished rooms has a phone, cable color TV, and a private patio or balcony. The best views are on the upper floors on the west side above the pool. For toll-free reservations, call: in California (800)472-4371; elsewhere (800)854-1279.
regular room—poolside (ask for 5th floor), fine pool/mt. view, K bed...$180
regular room—window-wall view, D bed...$140

★ **Sundance Villas**
2.5 mi. NW at 378 W. Cabrillo Rd. *325-3888*
Here is a quintessential example of personalized luxury in the Palm Springs life style. All of the units share a beautifully landscaped outdoor pool, whirlpool, sauna, and a lighted tennis court. But the real attraction is the spacious, sybaritic two- or three-bedroom villas. Each has a private outdoor pool and whirlpool in an enclosed yard, plus a gas fireplace, wet bar and stocked liquor cabinet, large sunken tub in master bath, kitchen, phone, and cable color TV. A jug of fresh orange juice, fruit, and pastries are provided on arrival, along with a bottle of wine, in addition to other pleasant surprises.
villa—3 BR, 3 baths, 2 Q & K beds...$325
regular suite—2 BR villa, 2 baths, Q & K beds...$295

CAMPGROUNDS

There are several relatively elaborate recreation vehicle and trailer parks around town. However, there is no campground that provides tent sites anywhere in the area.

SPECIAL EVENTS

★ **Bob Hope/Chrysler Classic Golf Tournament** *mid-January*
This 90-hole Pro-Am competition has been attracting huge crowds to watch celebrities and professionals play charity golf on some of the world's most beautiful courses for more than a quarter of a century.

★ **Palm Springs Mounted Police Rodeo** *downtown* *late January*
One of the West's few mid-winter rodeos is a major two-day competition, preceded by the largest equestrian parade in California.

★ **National Date Festival** *22 mi. SE in Indio* *mid-February*
The Arabian Nights (and days) atmosphere at the fairgrounds in Indio—"The Date Capital of the World"—is the right setting for this unique and popular ten-day celebration that includes parades, cultural exhibits, and live entertainment—even camel races.

OTHER INFORMATION

Area Code: *619*

Zip Code: *92262 (and others)*

Palm Springs Chamber of Commerce
downtown at 190 W. Amado Rd. *325-1577*

Palm Springs Convention & Visitor Bureau
2 mi. E at 255 N. El Cielo Rd. (the airport) *327-8411*

St. Helena

St. Helena is the heart of America's most illustrious wine-producing valley. In every direction beyond the compact town, a sea of vineyards splashes against steep-sided oak-covered mountains that frame the flat valley floor. An appealing blend of bucolic charm and urbane diversions is complemented by a temperate climate. The excellent weather of spring is usually perfect for viewing the greening of endless vineyards and for savoring wineries' new releases. Idyllic weather returns again in the fall, and coincides with the harvest and crush. Especially during this season, visitors arrive in overwhelming numbers to experience the beauty of grapes on the vine, to observe the harvest, and to taste new premium wines. Crowds also fill the handsome little valley to capacity during the hot, sunny days of summer. Hiking, bicycling, ballooning, and boating are enjoyed, but the most popular activities are associated with the grape. In winter, the disadvantages of cool wet days are offset by the leisurely pace and absence of crowds throughout the area.

The town was founded in 1853 by an Englishman, J.H. Still, who opened a general store and offered free land for potential businesses. Within a few years, St. Helena was flourishing as a farming and milling center. Shortly after the Civil War, grape growing and wine production began near town. A combination of talented wine makers and ideal conditions soon established Napa Valley as the center of California's premium wine production. It is still the nation's most renowned wine making region.

Today, a wonderful diversity of landmark wineries welcome visitors in beautifully maintained Victorian mansions and in distinctive contemporary structures on the approaches to town. St. Helena retains much of the charm of a Victorian farming village in spite of rapid growth in recent years. The unspoiled heart of the compact business district features romantic settings for picnics in delightful little parks with noble shade trees. In addition, many carefully restored historic buildings house specialty and gourmet shops. One of the West's newest major concentrations of gourmet restaurants is another attraction downtown. After dark, tranquility reigns as it always has in this pastoral setting. In lieu of live entertainment, lounges offer atmospheric, quiet surroundings well suited to conversation, and a variety of local wines by the glass. Lodgings are in surprisingly short supply. There are no large conventional hotels or clones of motel chains. Visitors can, however, choose from a fascinating assortment of uniquely furnished rooms in one of the West's finest concentrations of stylish bed-and-breakfast inns. As an added bonus, contemporary motor lodges in the vicinity are romantic havens that cater to adult fantasies with plush facilities and manicured gardens tucked away amidst the ubiquitous vineyards.

Elevation:

256 feet

Population (1980):

4,898

Population (1970):

3,173

Location:

65 mi. North
of San Francisco

St. Helena

WEATHER PROFILE

Vokac Weather Rating

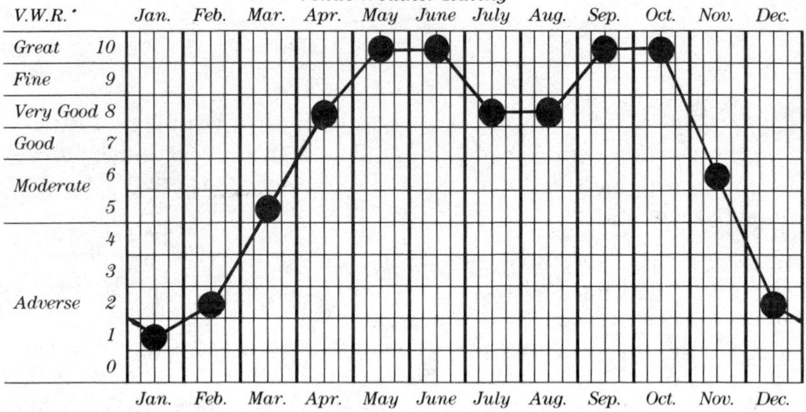

	Jan.	Feb.	Mar.	Apr.	May	June	July	Aug.	Sep.	Oct.	Nov.	Dec.
*V.W.R.**	1	2	5	8	10	10	8	8	10	10	6	2
Temperature												
Ave. High	56	60	65	71	77	85	90	89	86	77	67	58
Ave. Low	36	38	39	42	45	49	50	49	48	44	39	37
Precipitation												
Inches Rain	7.1	6.3	4.3	2.4	1.0	0.3	-	-	0.3	1.7	3.1	6.6
Inches Snow	-	-	-	-	-	-	-	-	-	-	-	-

**V.W.R. = Vokac Weather Rating: probability of mild (warm & dry) weather on any given day.*

Forecast

Month	*V.W.R.**		*Temperatures Daytime*	*Evening*	*Precipitation*
Jan.	1	Adverse	cool	chilly	frequent downpours
Feb.	2	Adverse	cool	chilly	frequent downpours
Mar.	5	Moderate	warm	cool	occasional downpours
Apr.	8	Very Good	warm	cool	infrequent downpours
May	10	Great	warm	cool	infrequent rainstorms
June	10	Great	hot	warm	negligible
July	8	Very Good	hot	warm	none
Aug.	8	Very Good	hot	warm	none
Sep.	10	Great	hot	warm	negligible
Oct.	10	Great	warm	cool	infrequent rainstorms
Nov.	6	Moderate	warm	cool	infrequent downpours
Dec.	2	Adverse	cool	chilly	frequent downpours

Summary

St. Helena is the heart of Napa Valley, where weather is moderated by marine air pouring through a gap in the Coast Range at the Golden Gate and spreading northward beyond San Francisco Bay. As a result, there is almost no snow. Instead, **winter** is cool and very damp with frequent heavy rainfalls providing well over half the year's normal precipitation. **Spring** is delightful. Warm days, cool evenings, plus fewer and lighter rainfalls contribute to easy enjoyment of the luxuriant green valley. **Summer** days are usually hot and sunny and evenings are warm. There is no precipitation to disrupt outdoor activities. **Fall** signals the return of mild weather. Warm days, cool evenings, and infrequent rainfalls assure final vine ripening prior to the normally bountiful grape harvest and add to the visitors' pleasure in sampling the fruits of this labor.

ATTRACTIONS & DIVERSIONS

Bale Grist Mill State Historical Park
3.2 mi. N on CA 29 942-4575
Built in 1846, this picturesque mill provided flour for upper Napa Valley farmers until 1879. It was acquired by the State in 1974, and has been meticulously reconstructed. Shady picnic sites have been provided nearby, overlooking a creek.

★ ***Ballooning***
Fine weather and lovely countryside make the Napa Valley a natural for hot-air balloon flights. Several companies now offer guests champagne flights with a unique vantage point to both the sights and sounds of the area, including:
Napa Valley Balloons, Inc. *Box 2860 - Yountville* 253-2224
Silverado Balloon Co. *1356 Sulphur Springs Av.* 963-5515

★ ***Bicycling***
St. Helena Cyclery
downtown at 1156 Main St. 963-7736
The relatively flat terrain, fine wine country scenery and attractions, and good weather are all reasons for the enormous popularity of bicycle touring in Napa Valley. Rentals by the hour and longer can be arranged here. Closed Sun.

★ **Bothe-Napa Valley State Park**
4.8 mi. N on CA 29 942-4575
Marked hiking trails in this 1,800 acre park pass through some of the most easterly stands of Coast redwoods as well as a luxuriant forest of oak and madrone. Wildflower displays are particularly beautiful in spring. An outdoor swimming pool is open to the public in summer. Tree-shaded picnic tables and creekside campsites are available year-round.

★ ***Library***
downtown at 1492 Library Lane 963-5244
The St. Helena Public Library occupies an architecturally unusual newer building. Attractively furnished reading areas with upholstered armchairs and cushioned window wells have picture window views of adjacent vineyards. The Napa Valley Wine Library is also here. Closed Sun.-Mon.

Lyman Park
downtown on Main St.
This pretty little tree-shaded park near the heart of town is a perfect spot for a picnic.

Moped Rental
9 mi. SE off CA 29 in Vintage 1870 - Yountville 252-0180
An easy, breezy way to tour the wine country is on a moped that can be rented here by the hour, half day, or full day.

★ **Silverado Museum**
downtown at 1490 Library Lane 963-3757
One of the world's largest collections of Robert Louis Stevenson

memorabilia is attractively displayed in a handsome extension of the St. Helena Public Library Center. Closed Mon.

Wineries

St. Helena is the heart of the world famous Napa Valley wine district. It is now surrounded by well over one hundred wineries and about 29,000 acres of premium vineyards. Following is a cross-section of large, well-known wineries that encourage visitors to drop in for tours, tastes and sales. Many smaller premium wineries throughout the valley offer personalized tours and tasting. Some require an appointment. The Chamber of Commerce, bookstores,and specialty shops have detailed guides and maps.

★ **Beaulieu**

4 mi. SE at 1960 S. CA 29 *963-2411*

Founded in 1900 by Georges de Latour, this became one of California's grand old family wineries. It is still a landmark, although now owned by a conglomerate. A handsome wood-crafted visitor center at one side of the winery is the beginning point for tours, and where selected wines may be tasted. Tasting, tours, and sales 10-4 daily.

★ **Beringer**

.6 mi. N at 2000 N. CA 29 *963-7115*

This winery has been in continuous operation since it was founded in 1876. An impressive seventeen-room Rhine House mansion was built by the Beringer brothers in 1883 as a tribute to their homeland. Inside is a gift shop. The gracious tasting center is normally only available to those who take the tour that features nearby cellar caves and hand-carved wine casks. Tasting, tours, and sales 9:30-4:30 daily.

★ **Domaine Chandon**

10 mi. SE via CA 29 on California Dr. - Yountville *944-2280*

A heroically scaled, strikingly modern winery was built by Moet-Hennessy of France to make sparkling wines from California grapes in the traditional manner of French champagne production. You can judge how well they've succeeded by tasting the premium red or white styles of sparkling wines in the salon, or, weather permitting, on a lovely garden terrace adjoining the spectacular restaurant complex. Tasting (for a fee), tours, and sales 11-6 daily. (Closed Mon.-Tues. from Nov. thru Apr.)

★ **Inglenook**

4.5 mi. SE at 1991 S. CA 29 *963-7184*

The heart of this historic winery is a stately 1880s-vintage stone building that houses a museum and a tasting room offering a broad sampling of wines made here. The winery is now part of a conglomerate. Tasting, tours, and sales 10-5 daily.

★ **Louis M. Martini**

1.1 mi. SE at 254 S. CA 29 *963-2736*

Founded in 1933, this remains a family operation all the way. The winery has perhaps the most generous attitude about tasting in the Napa Valley with the complete roster of Martini wines available for sampling. Tasting, tours, and sales 10-4:30 daily.

★ **Robert Mondavi Winery**
5.5 mi. SE at 7801 S. CA 29 963-9611
Many of California's state-of-the-art advances in premium wine making originated in this mission-style complex founded in 1966. The spacious lawn at the junction of the two wings of the building is the site of acclaimed summer concerts, plus art shows and special tastings. Limited selections are available for tasting only to those who take the tour. Tasting, tours, and sales 9-5 daily (10-4 daily Nov. thru Mar.).

★ **Yountville**
9 mi. SE off CA 29
This town was a bustling village by 1855. It is now the site of some of the region's finest shops and restaurants. The town park on the north side has pleasant, tree-shaded picnic spots.

SHOPPING

St. Helena has a compact downtown where handsome Victorian buildings house a small but growing number of specialty and gourmet shops, in addition to the kinds of stores that have served an agricultural economy for more than a century. Today, utility wires are underground, downtown streets are tree-shaded, and there are still no parking meters or traffic lights.

Food Specialties

★ **The Bottle Shop**
downtown at 1321 Main St. 963-3092
The area's original wine store has been impressively updated. Premium Napa Valley wines are beautifully displayed in a mirrored back room.

★ **Chutney Kitchen**
9.5 mi. SE off CA 29 in Vintage 1870 - Yountville 944-2788
A variety of outstanding locally-made chutneys is displayed for tasting and purchase at a carryout counter next to the restaurant.

The Cook's Corner
9.5 mi. SE off CA 29 in Vintage 1870 - Yountville 944-8100
Local products are emphasized in an excellent assortment of specialty foods, including mustards, olives, breads, cheeses, and pates. The selection of gourmet cookware is equally impressive.

The Croissant Place
9.5 mi. SE off CA 29 at 6528 Washington St. - Yountville 944-8096
This bright little carryout shop offers several kinds of croissants made here daily, plus gelato. An adjoining tree-shaded courtyard has several picnic tables.

★ **Fantasie au Chocolat**
9.5 mi. SE off CA 29 at 6528 Washington St. - Yountville 944-8096
Beautifully displayed in this chocoholic's downfall is an awesome selection of hand-dipped chocolate truffles, molded dark chocolates, and freshly baked pastries and cakes.

★ **Groezinger Wine Co.**
9.5 mi. SE off CA 29 in Vintage 1870 - Yountville *944-233*
Well over one hundred California wineries' bottlings are convenient displayed in a refurbished, massive old stables. There is also a tasting ba and an instant wine bottle chiller.

★ **The Model Bakery**
downtown at 1357 Main St. *963-819*
Karen Mitchell & Co. produces a delicious assortment of French-sty pastries and breads in this enticing little carryout. Closed Sun.-Mon.

★ **Napa Valley Olive Oil Mfg. Co.**
.5 mi. SE at 835 McCorkle Av. *963-417*
Fine olive oil has been produced here for nearly a century. All kinds o quality cheeses, ripe olives, sausages, and other California gourme groceries are also sold at surprisingly low prices in this unabashedly olc fashioned store.

★ **Oakville Grocery Co.**
6 mi. SE at 7856 S. CA 29 - Oakville *944-880*
This little roadside grocery store is justifiably renowned for the mos tantalizing selection of sophisticated international gourmet foods to b found in any store this size.

★ **St. Helena Wine Merchant**
1.5 mi. S at 699 S. CA 29 *963-788*
A mind-boggling array of California wines is sold here. Small premiu wineries are a specialty, and there is a good selection of wines fro around the world. Wine tastings are available for a small fee daily.

★ **Vintage Patissiere**
9.5 mi. SE off CA 29 in Vintage 1870 - Yountville *944-213*
Splendid Continental pastries are served with coffee at a few marble topped tables set with fresh flowers indoors, on a scenic patio, or to g

★ **V. Sattui Winery**
1.5 mi. S off CA 29 on White Lane *963-777*
The winery's bottlings are available for tasting and sale here onl Equally impressive are the outstanding selection of cheeses, plus pate sausages, specialty breads, and other gourmet items. Inviting picni grounds are adjacent to the handsome new winery headquarters.

★ **Wineworks Inc.**
2.4 mi. N at 3111 N. CA 29 *963-948*
Napa Valley and other California premium wines are the highlight of a expansive shop in the Cement Works. About a dozen wines are feature daily by the taste or glass. In addition, gourmet cheeses, pates, smoke meats, exotic local mushrooms, and other provisions are nicel displayed in this showcase of the area's culinary endowment Purchases can be enjoyed at tile-topped tables in an adjoining courtyar shaded by a picturesque grape arbor.

Specialty Shops

Bah Humbug
downtown at 1201 Main St. *963-7423*
This handsome culinary emporium features truffles and premium wines, plus a notable assortment of cookware and recipe books. Closed Sun. Closed Sun.-Mon. in winter.

Cement Works
2.4 mi. N at 3111 N. CA 29 *963-9484*
An abandoned cement works has become the valley's newest complex of fine shops. Quality arts and crafts, gift items, gourmet foods, premium wines, restaurants, and lounges are housed in stylish wood-toned buildings on well-landscaped grounds. Acres of tree-shaded picnic sites are nearby.

Freemark Abbey Complex
2.1 mi. N at 3020 N. CA 29 *963-7211*
The Hurd Beeswax Candle Factory is a highlight of a shopping complex in this converted stone winery. Also of interest are a big gourmet-and-gift shop (with a fine selection of books of regional interest and wine accessories) plus the large Abbey Restaurant.

Vintage 1870
9.5 mi. SE off CA 29 - Yountville *944-2451*
A fascinating complex of quality specialty shops occupies a massive brick and timber complex that was the valley's second oldest winery—Groezinger's. There are many delightful touches—large sculptures, a gazebo, colorful garden areas, and so on.

NIGHTLIFE

After dark, peace and quiet prevail. Still, there are a few enticing places to go for a nightcap.

Fox & Hound
2.4 mi. N at 3111 N. CA 29 *963-0256*
As many as ten beers (including Anchor Steam) are on tap in a comfortable reproduction of a traditional English pub. There is also live music several nights each week, plus darts and comfortably upholstered armchairs, in this novel addition to the Cement Works.

Hotel St. Helena Wine Bar
downtown at 1309 Main St. *963-4388*
Sixteen different types of wine by the glass are offered for tasting daily in the hotel's comfortable little lounge. Plush furnishings include pillow sofas. An extensive California wine list is complemented by a variety of appetizers.

Mama Nino's
9.1 mi. SE off CA 29 at 6772 Washington St. - Yountville *944-2112*
A cheery fireplace and chrome-and-wood armchairs highlight this pleasant and popular lounge. The wine list is limited to Napa and Sonoma wineries, and several wines by the glass are featured. Closed Wed.

Pastime Club
downtown at 1351 Main St. *963-4045*
This stylish "locals" bar in a handsome, refurbished old building with an interesting rock wall interior and comfortable furnishings is a good place for a quiet nightcap.

★ **St. George**
.3 mi. S at 1050 Charter Oak Av. *963-7930*
Adjoining a distinguished restaurant is a one-of-a-kind lounge filled with authentic baroque antiques including a carved, polished hardwood-and-brass bar, an ornate working fireplace, and towering walls graced with pictures of colossal nudes in rococo gold leaf frames. It is a memorable place for drinks and conversation. During the day, another bar serves patrons seated in the tree-shaded courtyard.

RESTAURANTS

Nowhere is the change from farming village to urbane community more apparent than in the sophisticated restaurants which have opened in the St. Helena area in recent years. Some of the West's finest (and most expensive) dining rooms are now in or near town. Almost all of the best restaurants have notable wine lists with an appropriately chauvinistic emphasis on California wineries.

Anestis Grill
9.5 mi. SE off CA 29 at 6518 Washington St. - Yountville *944-1500*
B-L-D. No B on Mon.-Fri. *Expensive*
Duckling and suckling pig turn on a European-style rotisserie, and homemade sausage is cooked on the mesquite grill. Crisp white linen and sleek chrome chairs were used to outfit the recently remodeled, purple-toned dining room.

★ **Auberge du Soleil**
5 mi. SE at 180 Rutherford Hill Rd. *963-1211*
L-D. Closed Wed. *Extremely Expensive*
Prix fixe meals are stylish presentations of nouvelle cuisine in the valley's most monumental culinary landmark. An imposing chateau-style structure provides panoramic views of the vineyards from a hillside on which it was recently constructed. Cocktails or wine are particularly memorable when savored on the deck by the plush lounge.

California Cafe
2.4 mi. N at 3111 N. CA 29 *963-5300*
L-D. *Expensive*
Shoestring potatoes and dried breadsticks accompany most of the New California-style entrees. The big, bright restaurant offers 1980s moderne decor, plus a vineyard view from a few tables or the covered deck.

★ **Chutney Kitchen**
9.5 mi. SE off CA 29 in Vintage 1870 - Yountville *944-2788*
L only. *Moderate*
This long-time favorite luncheon spot offers excellent homemade soups,

sandwiches, fresh salads, and their own delicious chutneys. Fresh flowers and linen grace the tables in this bustling corner of a converted winery building. Alfresco lunches are served on a vine-covered patio overlooking a vineyard during spring and summer.

The Diner

9.6 mi. SE off CA 29 at 6476 Washington St. - Yountville *944-2626*
B-L-D. Closed Mon. *Moderate*

Fresh ingredients and homestyle cooking are at their best in this simply furnished, old-fashioned diner. Breakfasts can be remarkably good, and evening Mexican dinners in "El Diner" are also well-liked. A covered wooden deck was recently added, overlooking the main street.

Domaine Chandon

10 mi. SE off CA 29 on California Dr. - Yountville *944-2280*
L-D. No D Mon.-Tues. No L Mon.-Tues. in winter. *Very Expensive*

The French have produced a gastronomic showplace for their sparkling wines made here. The restaurant is a modern architectural tour de force of wood, glass, and concrete surrounded by charming pastoral scenery. Gourmet lunches are served on a flower-strewn outdoor patio during warm months. Disciplined French haute cuisine, including grand pastries, is served in dining rooms that are usually fully reserved well in advance.

French Laundry

9.2 mi. SE off CA 29 at 6440 Washington St. - Yountville *944-2380*
D only. Closed Mon.-Tues. *Very Expensive*

Memorable country-style French cuisine prepared with the freshest ingredients is served to one seating of guests each evening. The stone and redwood building was a French laundry at the turn of the century. It has no signs identifying it as a restaurant and it is not listed in the yellow pages. Nevertheless, it is a real "find." The vineyard view from the casually elegant upstairs dining room is especially pleasant in summer, while the fireplace downstairs has a warm, romantic appeal in winter.

La Belle Helene

downtown at 1345 Railroad Av. *963-1234*
L-D. Closed Tues.-Wed. Sun. brunch. *Very Expensive*

Highly regarded French haute cuisine and splendid homemade baked goods are accompanied by casually elegant atmosphere and classical background music in a charming enhancement of a Victorian stone building.

Le Chardonnay

9.5 mi. SE off CA 29 at 6534 Washington St. - Yountville *944-2521*
L-D. Closed Mon. *Expensive*

Delicious French cuisine is served in a beautifully proportioned room with a canopied ceiling and arched windows. Floral displays, crystal, and china lend elegance to each table.

Le Rhone
downtown at 1234 Main St. *963-0240*
D only. Closed Mon.-Tues. *Extremely Expensive*
French cuisine is served prix fixe or a la carte in this small, thoroughly French dinner house. The intimate, country-elegant dining room is entered through a courtyard.

★ **Mama Nino's**
9.1 mi. SE off CA 29 at 6772 Washington St. - Yountville *944-2112*
L-D. Closed Wed. *Expensive*
Fresh homemade pasta is the specialty on an appealing Italian menu. Dining rooms are outfitted with fresh flowers and plants set amidst wood-and-chrome decor. Patio dining is popular during the warm months. A cheerful fireplace lounge adjoins.

★ **Meadowwood**
2 mi. E at 900 Meadowwood Lane *963-3646*
D only. Sun. brunch. Closed Mon.-Tues. *Very Expensive*
Here is serious competition for the ultimate New California cuisine. Fresh and unusual ingredients are skillfully used in exciting new entrees. A feeling of quiet country elegance in the beautiful new dining room is complemented by picture window views through nearby oaks to a golf course and heavily wooded hills. A redwood view deck is used for alfresco dining when weather permits.

★ **Miramonte**
downtown at 1327 Railroad Av. *963-3970*
D only. Closed Mon.-Tues. *Very Expensive*
Renowned nouvelle cuisine is the attraction in a picturesque old hotel that has been restored with a dining room decorated in the style of a baronial hunting lodge—complete with a large working fireplace. The menu is constantly changing according to the freshest seasonally available ingredients. Prix fixe five-course meals are delicious, artful presentations.

★ **Mustards Grill**
7.5 mi. S at 7399 S. CA 29 *944-2424*
L-D. *Moderate*
The creative New California cuisine prepared in this contemporary dinner house is a smash hit. Mesquite-broiled and brick oven-smoked meats are flavorful hallmarks of the new style here. Support dishes are given a wonderfully light touch, and many wines are available by the glass. A profusion of crisp white linen complements wood-tones and prints in the dining room and the whitewashed openness of a cool, screened porch.

★ **Palmer's**
downtown at 1313 Main St. *963-1788*
B-L-D. Only brunch on Sun. Closed Mon. *Moderate*
Homemade pastries are featured at all meals, along with carefully

prepared light fare. Selected wines are poured by the taste or the glass. The quality of the food compensates for the relaxed, place-your-own-order setting of this simply furnished little cafe.

Rancho Caymus Kitchen
4 mi. SE near CA 29 on CA 128 *963-1777*
B-L. *Very Expensive*
A short menu of distinctive-sounding dishes is given casual treatment in an attractively furnished wood-toned coffee salon in the new Rancho Caymus Inn.

Rose et le Favour
downtown at 1420 Main St. *963-1681*
D only. Closed Mon.-Tues. *Extremely Expensive*
There is only one seating at the seven tables in this intimate, opulent restaurant where a prix fixe multi-course dinner of fearlessly eclectic New California cuisine is presented each evening. Every dish is prepared with skill and imagination from the freshest and choicest ingredients. The intimate dining room is lavishly furnished with flowers and paintings, and each table is meticulously appointed with starched white linen and fine china.

St. George
.3 mi. S at 1050 Charter Oak at Main St. *963-7930*
L-D. *Expensive*
Distinguished Italian cuisine is served amid museum-quality baroque decor—antique marble busts, brass chandeliers, polished woodwork, jumbo mirrors, and monumental nude paintings in a sumptuous, high-ceilinged dining room. Lunch is served on a tree-studded, walled, brick terrace in summer. The firelit lounge is also furnished with baroque antiques.

Spring Street Restaurant
downtown at 1245 Spring St. *963-5578*
B-L-D. Closed Sat.-Sun. *Moderate*
Carefully prepared soups, salads, sandwiches, and desserts are all popular with regulars who frequent the pleasant dining room and dining porch of a converted house on a side street.

Washington Street Restaurant
9.4 mi. SE off CA 29 at 6539 Washington St. *944-2406*
L-D. No L on Mon. & Tues. *Expensive*
A recently updated menu describes an adventurous array of New California cuisine. The spacious, firelit dining room occupies most of a converted historic brick mansion. Picture windows provide intimate views of adjacent vineyards. A wood-trimmed lounge separates the two handsomely furnished dining rooms. A veranda overlooking gardens is also used.

LODGING

In recent years, St. Helena has become one of the country inn capitals of the West. These bed-and-breakfast lodgings have restored some of the area's finest residences into distinctive showplaces filled with authentic Victorian charm. Visitors can also select from a few motels and motor lodges. Several feature remarkably plush furnishings. The town carefully protects its distinction of having no large-scale accommodations. There are no bargain rooms in the area. However, rates are often reduced by 20% and more on weekdays during winter and spring.

★ **Auberge du Soleil**

5 mi. SE at 180 Rutherford Hill Rd. - Rutherford 94573 *963-1211*

One of the West's most lavish hideaways is nestled in an olive grove on a hillside overlooking the Napa Valley. Tennis courts, a large outdoor pool, and a renowned restaurant are features of this gracious new facility. Each beautifully furnished room has a fireplace, wet bar, cable color TV, and a deck overlooking the wine country. A Continental breakfast is complimentary.

suite—living room, bedroom, 2 Q beds...$250
regular room—1 bedroom, Q bed...$180

★ **Bordeaux House**

9.3 mi. SE at 6600 Webber (Box 2766) - Yountville 94599 *944-2855*

This modernistic little brick inn has rooms impeccably decorated with Continental-contemporary furnishings and private, sunken baths. Each of the elegant, uncluttered rooms has a fireplace. Some have a private balcony. Complimentary Continental breakfasts and an evening glass of wine are offered.

"Chablis"—end, top (2nd) fl., tree view from pvt. balc., Q bed...$120
"Sherry"—end, some view, Q bed...$115
regular room— 2 raised T beds...$100

Chalet Bernensis

1.2 mi. S at 225 S. CA 29 *963-4423*

An impressive century-old Victorian mansion with landscaped gardens has been converted into a bed-and-breakfast inn. All rooms are furnished with antiques, and share a bath. In adjacent water tower and carriage house replicas, each room has antique furnishings, a private bath, and a gas fireplace. A Continental breakfast is included, and sherry is served in the sitting room.

#9 "Water Tower"—top floor, private bath, gas fireplace, some view, Q bed..$79
#3—corner, windows on 2 sides, shared bath, view past giant camellia bush, Q bed...$64
regular room—small, shared bath, Q bed...$54

Cinnamon Bear

downtown at 1407 Kearney St. *963-4653*

Each of the rooms in this large, homey old bed-and-breakfast residence has a private bathroom, some Victorian furnishings, and dozens of teddy bears. A country-style breakfast is served (on the porch in warm weather). Wine and cheese (also complimentary) are served in the afternoon.

downstairs room—spacious, footed tub with shower, Q bed...$85
regular room— Q bed...$85

Creekside Inn

.3 mi. S at 945 Main St. *963-7244*

A pleasant, newer home adjacent to a creek in the shade of an enormous oak now serves as a bed-and-breakfast inn with several nicely furnished rooms. A complimentary full breakfast is served indoors or on a creekside patio. Baths are shared.

queen bed room—large, windows on 3 sides, Q bed...$65
regular room—corner, windows on 2 sides, D bed...$65

El Bonita Motel

.8 mi. S at 195 Main St. *963-3216*

A landscaped outdoor pool is an attraction of this small, nicely maintained single-level motel. Each room has a phone and cable color TV.

#23—spacious, in quiet back section, refrigerator, K bed...$65
regular room— D bed...$39

★ **Harvest Inn**

1.1 mi. S at 1 Main St. *963-9463*

Situated in a twenty acre working vineyard is one of the West's ultimate fantasy lodgings. Amid carefully tended gardens with a large outdoor pool and a whirlpool is an imposing, newer Tudor-style motor inn lavishly furnished with antiques and quality reproductions. Each spacious, beautifully appointed room has a refrigerator, cable color TV, and a phone.

#30 "Knight of Nights"—grandiose suite, grand curved staircase, wet bar, in-room whirlpool, 2 fireplaces, balcony, pvt. vineyard view, K bed...$300
#32 "Lord of the Manor"—grandiose suite, wet bar, in-room whirlpool, 2 fireplaces, balcony, private vineyard views, K bed...$310
#23 "Vin Rose"—wet bar, raised stone fireplace, balcony, vineyard view, K bed...$140
#1 "Gamay"—wet bar, raised stone fireplace, K bed...$135
regular room— Q or K bed...$85

Hotel St. Helena
downtown at 1309 Main St. *963-4388*
This century-old hotel was recently reopened after being completely refurbished. Most of the lushly carpeted rooms have Victorian accents and private baths. A Continental breakfast and glass of wine are complimentary.
"North Wing" room—private bath, Q bed...$65
regular room—shared bath, Q bed...$50

★ **Magnolia Hotel**
9.5 mi. SE off CA 29 at 6529 Yount - Yountville 94599 *944-2056*
In the 1960s, this century-old three-story inn was completely renovated with period furnishings, and a private bath was added to each room. There is a whirlpool in an enclosed redwood patio, and a large pool in a garden area. Complimentary full breakfasts are served in the dining room.
"Magnolia"—spacious, gas fireplace, view windows, balcony, K bed...$145
"Cabarnet"—spacious, view windows on 2 sides, window seat, K bed...$115
"Chardonnay"—intimate, view windows, Q bed...$90
regular room—small, D bed...$75

★ **Meadowwood**
2 mi. E at 900 Meadowwood Lane *963-3646*
Five championship tennis courts, a large outdoor pool, whirlpool, a Parcours circuit, and (for a fee) a 9-hole golf course, plus a Continental breakfast and the morning paper are all part of the daily fare in this exclusive retreat. A new world class restaurant overlooks the golf course and majestic oaks in a secluded canyon. In California, call toll-free: (800) 458-8080.
"suite"—fireplace, wet bar, deck, private views, K bed...$190
regular room "studio"—private views, wet bar, deck, Q bed...$140

★ **Napa Valley Lodge - Best Western**
9 mi. SE off CA 29 on Madison St. - Yountville 94599 *944-2468*
The area's first major motel was recently completely upgraded. A large swimming pool and a whirlpool are immediately adjacent to vineyards. Each nicely decorated room has a cable color TV, phone, and a refrigerator. In California, call toll-free: (800) 528-1234.
#15—spacious, end unit, gas fireplace, vineyard view, K bed...$98
regular room—many have vineyard view, K bed...$92

Rancho Caymus Inn
4 mi. SE on CA 128 (Box 78) - Rutherford 94573 *963-1777*
One of the wine country's newest fantasy lodgings is a small, Spanish-style motor hotel encircling a private garden. Each artistically decorated

unit has a wet bar/refrigerator, cable color TV, and a phone.
"Master Suites"—2-level, kitchen, in-bath whirlpool, private balcony, fireplace, Q bed...$250
"Rancho Suites"—2-level, private balcony, fireplace, Q bed...$125
regular room—2-level with living/dining downstairs, Q bed...$120

★ **Vintage Inn**
9.3 mi. SE at 6541 Washington St. - Yountville 94599 *944-1112*
The wine country's largest deluxe motel inn recently opened a short stroll from the Vintage 1870 shopping complex. An attractively landscaped courtyard includes a swimming pool and whirlpool. Tennis courts for guests are nearby. Each of the stylish units has a fireplace, an in-bath whirlpool, a wine bar, an individual balcony or veranda, and cable color TV. Continental breakfast with champagne is complimentary, as is afternoon tea. In California, call toll free: (800) 351-1133.
regular room— 2 Q or K bed...$129

★ **Wine Country Inn**
2 mi. N at 1152 Lodi Lane *963-7077*
Hidden away on a slope above a vineyard is a charming bed-and-breakfast motor inn, constructed in 1975. Individually decorated rooms have antique furnishings, good vineyard views, and private baths. Many of the spacious, well-furnished units have fireplaces. A complimentary Continental breakfast is served.
#24—large suite, Franklin fireplace, private balcony, panoramic vineyard view, canopied Q bed...$130
#26—large suite, fireplace, private deck, vineyard view, Q bed...$105
regular room— D bed...$ 85

CAMPGROUNDS

The area's best campground with complete facilities is by a picturesque creek near town. Several additional campgrounds are a half hour drive east at a reservoir (Lake Berryessa).

★ **Bothe-Napa Valley State Park**
4.8 mi. N on CA 29 *942-4575*
This large, state-operated facility is in a luxuriant forest of oaks, pines, and coastal redwoods. Fishing in tiny Ritchie Creek, a beautifully sited outdoor swimming pool (in summer), plus hiking and marked nature trails, are attractions. Flush toilets and hot showers are available. There are no hookups. All of the well-spaced sites are shaded by large broadleaf trees. Each site has a picnic table, grill/fire pit, and a wooden storage locker. There are a few walk-in tent sites. base rate...$6

Spanish Flat Resort
22 mi. E via CA 128 & Knoxville Rd. *966-2101*
This large, privately operated campground is located on an oak-and-grass-covered slope by Lake Berryessa. Boat rentals, plus a ramp and dock, are provided. The big reservoir is used for boating, water-skiing, fishing, and swimming. Flush toilets, hot showers, and hookups are available. Each site has a picnic table, fire ring, and grill. Some sites are shaded and have lake views. base rate...$7

SPECIAL EVENT

★ **Napa Valley Wine Crush** *Early August - early November*
From late summer into fall, premium grapes are heavy on vines throughout Napa Valley, and wineries are at their busiest. Visitors in great numbers come to experience the harvest and crush. To learn what, where, and when things happen, a 24-hour toll-free hot line is available from August into November—call (800)86-CRUSH.

OTHER INFORMATION

Area Code: *707*
Zip Code: *94574*
St. Helena Chamber of Commerce
downtown at 1508 Main St. *963-4456*

San Luis Obispo

San Luis Obispo is a classic California town. It is an architectural showcase for a multicultural heritage that includes a centuries-old Spanish mission in the heart of town surrounded by an engaging mixture of Victorian and modern structures. Geographically, it is at the center of a picturesque valley bordered by Coast Range mountains only a few miles from the ocean. Vast sand dunes, miles of hard sand beaches, secluded ocean coves, large scenic reservoirs, picturesque hot springs, and a mountain wilderness are among noteworthy features within a short drive. The area also benefits from one of the nation's finest year-round climates. Crowds are heaviest on weekends in every season and daily throughout summer. For some, the best season is spring, after winter rains have restored lush green hues to countrysides accented by masses of wildflowers. Fall is also favored, because there are fewer visitors and a slower pace, and because warm sunny days linger until very late in the year.

Father Junipero Serra correctly sensed the site's desirability and established Mission San Luis Obispo de Tolosa here in 1772 as the fifth in the chain of California's missions. During the next century, Spaniards and Indians were joined by an admixture of Mexican farmers, Portuguese fishermen, Chinese railroad builders, Japanese vegetable growers, and Swiss dairymen, among others. Architectural contributions of these early pioneers are still evident downtown. American settlers from the East and Midwest began arriving in large numbers before the turn of the century. They built substantial businesses and homes similar to the ones they had left back home. A surprising number of Victorian remnants still serve their original purpose. Many others have been creatively adapted to contemporary uses.

The town's economic vitality and diversity is apparent in one of the West's most handsome business districts. Its centerpiece is the beautifully preserved old adobe mission that overlooks a sunny plaza and lush greenery along the banks of San Luis Creek. Footpaths, bridges, and attractive landscaping have turned this small meandering stream into a unique feature lined by inviting restaurants, galleries, and specialty shops. In recent years, a remarkable number of gourmet food specialty stores—collectively featuring everything from bagels to beef jerky—have opened downtown and nearby. Areawide, restaurants and nightlife are relatively abundant and surprisingly conventional. Accommodations are plentiful both in town and along nearby beaches. As added attractions, the nation's first motel is still operating in San Luis Obispo, as is the most unusual motel anywhere.

Elevation:

230 feet

Population (1980):

34,252

Population (1970):

28,036

Location:

195 miles Northwest of Los Angeles

San Luis Obispo

WEATHER PROFILE

Vokac Weather Rating

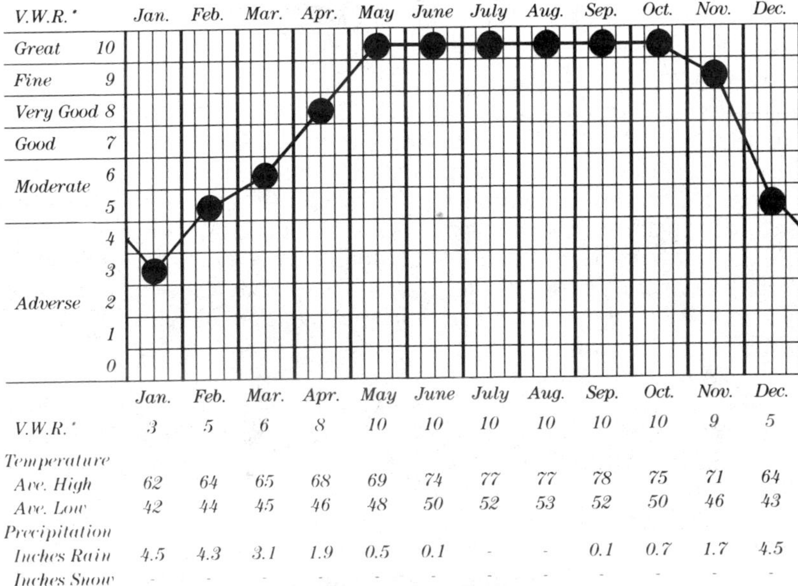

	Jan.	Feb.	Mar.	Apr.	May	June	July	Aug.	Sep.	Oct.	Nov.	Dec.
*V.W.R.**	3	5	6	8	10	10	10	10	10	10	9	5
Temperature												
Ave. High	62	64	65	68	69	74	77	77	78	75	71	64
Ave. Low	42	44	45	46	48	50	52	53	52	50	46	43
Precipitation												
Inches Rain	4.5	4.3	3.1	1.9	0.5	0.1	-	-	0.1	0.7	1.7	4.5
Inches Snow	-	-	-	-	-	-	-	-	-	-	-	-

**V.W.R. = Vokac Weather Rating: probability of mild (warm & dry) weather on any given day.*

Forecast

Month	*V.W.R.**		*Temperatures Daytime*	*Temperatures Evening*	*Precipitation*
Jan.	3	Adverse	cool	cool	frequent rainstorms
Feb.	5	Moderate	cool	cool	frequent rainstorms
Mar.	6	Moderate	warm	cool	occasional rainstorms
Apr.	8	Very Good	warm	cool	occasional rainstorms
May	10	Great	warm	cool	negligible
June	10	Great	warm	cool	none
July	10	Great	warm	cool	none
Aug.	10	Great	warm	warm	none
Sep.	10	Great	warm	warm	none
Oct.	10	Great	warm	cool	infrequent showers
Nov.	9	Fine	warm	cool	infrequent rainstorms
Dec.	5	Moderate	cool	cool	occasional downpours

Summary

San Luis Obispo, with a mountain-sheltered location near the ocean, is just far enough inland to escape much of the winter fog of coastal areas and the extreme heat of summer common to most interior locations. The temperate climate is one of the town's most appealing features, and one of the best in the West. **Winter** is cool, with no frost of any consequence, and wet, with frequent rainstorms contributing well over half of the annual precipitation. **Spring**, while often breezy, usually offers warm days, cool evenings, and diminishing rainfalls. There is an exhilarating allure about this season, when the senses are rewarded by lavish displays of lovely and aromatic new blooms, including certain flowering trees that lend to the pervasive fragrance of the lush green scene. In **summer**, consistently warm weather and no rainfall assure comfortable enjoyment of all outdoor activities. Warm sunny days continue through late **fall**, until the rainy season begins again in earnest after Thanksgiving.

ATTRACTIONS & DIVERSIONS

★ **Avila Beach**

10 mi. SW via US 101 on Avila Rd.

This raffish little town is unique along the central coast for its combination of a south-facing shoreline and a sheltered harbor. Fine sunbathing and ocean swimming can be enjoyed along a safe beach where the water occasionally gets above 70°F in summer. Facilities include a plain little beachfront park with picnic tables and fire rings. Nearby are a fishing pier; launching ramp; charter boats and gear rental concessions; and a remote, sheltered shoreline that has been unofficially adopted as a very popular swimming-suits-optional beach.

★ **Cal Poly**

1 mi. N on California Blvd. *544-6084*

California State Polytechnic University is the fifth oldest unit (1901) of the California state university system. It occupies more than 5,000 acres of rolling hills at the base of the Santa Lucia Mountains at the northern edge of town. About 15,000 full time students use the attractive campus, distinguished by tropical and subtropical landscaping and a number of impressive new buildings. The schools of agriculture and architecture are among the nation's largest. A schedule of intercollegiate athletics, music, theater, art and craft productions, and special events is available at the University Union.

Cuesta Ridge Road

6 mi. N off US 101

A spectacularly scenic drive begins just south of the Cuesta Grade Summit of US 101 at a dirt turnout space for trucks. A poorly paved, narrow road rewards courageous drivers with awesome town, mountain, and ocean panoramas as it winds upward for 2.5 miles. Just below the TV transmitters at the top of Cuesta Ridge are a dirt parking lot, rugged picnic sites (no tables), and hiking trails. The Cuesta Grade Botanical Area, an interesting dwarf pine forest of the rare Santa Lucia fir, is half a mile beyond.

Dune Buggy Rental

★ **The Sand Center**

13 mi. S via CA 1 at 307 Pier Av. - Oceano *489-6014*

Large sand dunes back a wide hard sand beach for several miles at Pismo Dunes State Vehicular Recreation Area. This place adjoins the main entrance and is the most convenient of several that rent three-wheeled sand vehicles by the hour or longer for trips down the beach and over the dunes. Closed Wed.

Golf

Morro Bay Golf Course

12 mi. NW in Morro Bay State Park *772-4341*

This 18-hole course on a landscaped slope overlooking Morro Bay is open to the public with all necessary services and rentals.

★ **San Luis Bay Inn Golf Course**
10 mi. SW off US 101 - Avila Beach *595-2307*
The resort's challenging 18-hole course is beautifully sited along a creek near the ocean. A driving range, club and cart rentals, and food and beverage service are open to the public as well as guests.

Sea Pines Golf Club
12 mi. NW via Los Osos Rd. at 250 Howard Av. *528-1788*
The public is invited to use this pretty little 9-hole course overlooking Morro Bay and the ocean. A driving range, food and beverages, and all necessary services and rentals are provided.

★ ***Hiking***

Mountain Air Sports
downtown at 6670 Marsh St. *543-1676*
All types of backpacking gear can be rented here in summer to enjoy nearby mountains, camping, and beach trails. Both downhill and cross-country skis can be rented in winter for sojourns to more distant winter sports areas. Topographic maps are sold, along with sportswear and sports gear.

Horseback Riding

★ **The Livery Stable**
15 mi. S via CA 1 at 1207 Silver Spur Pl. - Oceano *489-8100*
The stable is located at the base of the lee side of the vast Pismo Dunes. Here is the only place where you can rent a horse by the hour or longer any day for unguided rides across the dune to miles of hard sandy ocean beaches.

Library
downtown at 888 Morro St. *549-5991*
The San Luis Obispo City Library is a big, conventional facility with a good selection of newspapers and periodicals, and a few armchairs in the second floor reading area. Closed Sun.

★ **Lopez Lake Recreation Area**
18 mi. SE via CA 227 & Lopez Canyon Rd. *489-2095*
Open year-round, this picturesque 956-acre reservoir with twenty-two miles of shoreline offers a remarkable diversity of recreation possibilities. Segregated campsites for tents and trailers are attractively located on oak-studded, grassy slopes near the lake. A food and supplies store, picnic areas, barbecue facilities, restrooms, playgrounds, and a museum are also available. For offbeat excitement, the Mustang Water Slide is the area's best onshore feature, with two 600-foot water slides and four hot whirlpools. The main attraction, however, is the lake, with designated swimming areas, good trout and bass fishing, a marina with a paved boat launch, and boat rentals. (Call 489-1006 for information or rentals of motor boats, sailboats, sailboards, canoes, patio boats, bumper or paddle boats.) Sailing is also very popular, and this is one of the best freshwater wind surfing sites in the West.

★ **Mission San Luis Obispo de Tolosa**
downtown at Chorro/Monterey Sts. *543-6850*
The "Prince of Missions" is the fifth of the California missions, founded in 1772 by Father Junipero Serra. It was built of adobe brick by the Chumash Indians with walls up to five feet thick. Completed in 1794, this mission was the first with a tiled roof in California. The restored building still serves as a parish church and also includes an eight-room museum and gardens. The adjacent beautifully landscaped plaza, recreated in 1971, is the town's focal point and the center of many community events throughout the year.

★ **Montana de Oro State Beach**
17 mi. W via Los Osos Valley Rd. *772-2560*
Hiking in rugged hills and headlands above unspoiled sandy beaches and secluded coves is the major attraction in this largely undeveloped park where wildlife and spring wildflowers abound. Beachcombing, clamming, skin diving, and shore fishing are other possibilities. A boat launch, campsites, and picnic tables are provided.

Morro Bay Embarcadero
12 mi. NW via CA 1 - Morro Bay
A tourist attraction with a lively nautical atmosphere has developed along the little bay, with many family-oriented gift shops and restaurants. Midway is a tiny park that features a giant outdoor chess board with two-to-three-foot tall pieces, available free to the public by reservation through the Morro Bay Parks and Recreation Department (772-2214 ext. 226). Charter boats are readily available for ocean fishing year-round, and for whale watching tours during the annual winter migration of the great grey whales (January thru March).

★ **Morro Bay State Park**
11 mi. W via CA 1 & State Park Rd. - Morro Bay *772-2560*
Facilities in this outstanding marine area include a large campground, shady picnic sites, a scenic golf course, nature walks and hiking trails, a museum, plus boat and bicycle rentals. Pismo clamming and fishing, good surfing, skin diving, and cold water swimming are also enjoyed. Remote sand dunes and beaches on the peninsula between the ocean and bay are well worth the walk, or boat trip. To get to Sand Spit Wild Area, take Los Osos Valley Road and Pecho Valley Road to the first dirt road to the west.

Morro Rock
12 mi. W via CA 1 - Morro Bay
A solid rock monolith, Morro Rock, juts 576 feet above Morro Bay. Unfortunately, the natural grandeur of this geological phenomenon is marred by the adjacent giant Morro Bay Power Plant and its three towering 450-foot stacks. Several larger but less precipitous morros create a dramatic "backbone" down the middle of the Los Osos Valley that extends back to San Luis Obispo and beyond.

Nude Beach

★ **Pirate's Cove**

10 mi. SW via US 101 & Avila Rd.

Steep hills shelter a curving half-mile-long sandy shoreline that has been unofficially adopted as a very popular swimming-suits-optional beach. It is accessible from a dirt parking area .3 mile south of the oil tank farm overlooking the town of Avila Beach.

Path of History

downtown

A two-mile self-guided tour past many nicely maintained and restored Victorian homes and businesses is made easy by a green line painted on downtown streets. The Chamber of Commerce has a many-stop brochure that identifies some of the best of these nostalgic remnants.

★ **Pismo Dunes State Vehicular Recreation Area**

13 mi. S via US 101 on CA 1 *489-2684*

Auto driving on the beach is permitted for six miles south of the town of Pismo Beach. This is one of the few places in California where you can experience smooth, hard beach sand under your wheels. Renting a three-wheeled sand vehicle is the most exhilarating way to explore the miles of dunes that lie just beyond the beach. There are plenty of places for sunbathing and picnicking, and you can easily get away from the crowds in the fenced dunes area reserved for hikers. The casual carnival atmosphere in this sandy paradise entices fun-lovers of all ages to try Pismo clamming, swimming, surfing, fishing, or even horseback riding on the beach.

Santa Lucia Wilderness

9 mi. NE via US 101 *543-4244*

The crest of the Santa Lucia Range with peaks towering 3,000 feet above the nearby ocean lies just east of town. It has been designated as a wilderness area in the Los Padres National Forest, with an area about fifteen miles long and two miles wide. Backpacking, camping, hiking, and hunting are popular.

Sportfishing

Port San Luis Sportfishing

11.3 mi. SW via US 101 at W end of Avila Rd. *595-7200*

Charter boats and gear can be rented for rock cod trips daily, and for albacore and salmon fishing trips in season.

Virg's Fish'n

12 mi. W via CA 1 at 1215 Embarcadero *772-1222*

Full day or twilight fishing trips with rental equipment can be chartered any time. Fall albacore fishing, and winter whale watching trips,can also be reserved.

Warm Water Features

Avila Hot Springs

8 mi. S at US 101/Avila Rd. *595-2359*

This venerable family-oriented hot springs spa has a 50′ x 100′ warm swimming pool and a small hotter pool outdoors. These and indoor private hot mineral baths and massage facilities are open year-round.

★ **Mustang Water Slide**
18 mi. SE via CA 227 & Lopez Canyon Rd. *489-8898*
In Lopez Lake Recreation Area, visitors are treated to the excitement of two 600-foot curving warm water slides and four hot mineral whirlpools on an oak-studded hillside above the lake. Open daily June thru Sept.

★ **Sycamore Mineral Springs**
9 mi. SW via US 101 at 1215 Avila Beach Rd. *595-7302*
Open twenty-four hours every day, this unique facility rents redwood hot tubs by the hour in seductive natural settings on a steep oak-covered hillside. Among the more than two dozen tubs, the ones named "Shangri-La" and "Rendezvous" are in especially remote sylvan settings. An adjoining motel has hot mineral whirlpools on private, oak-shaded decks next to the bedrooms.

Wineries

Many good wineries have been developed within an hour's drive to the north around Paso Robles and to the south near Solvang. Complete information and a map of all central coast wineries can be obtained at the Chamber of Commerce or local bookstores. In recent years, a major newly recognized wine growing district has been established within a few miles of town to the southeast in Edna Valley. Several wineries have opened, with more on the way. Currently, the most impressive local facility is:

★ **Corbett Canyon Vineyards**
8 mi. SE at 2195 Corbett Canyon Rd. *544-5800*
The largest south-central coast winery only dates back to the late 1970s. A limited variety of premium wines is produced with grapes from regional vineyards. The knowledgable staff is friendly and generous with tastes. Shaded picnic tables occupy alcoves of the big Spanish-style building overlooking much of the Edna Valley. Tasting, tours, and sales 10-4:30 daily, except Sun. 12-4:30.

SHOPPING

Downtown is a fascinating blend of preservation and progress, with many early buildings still serving their original commercial purposes, while several large older buildings have been converted into appealing mini-malls. An unusual variety of both shops and merchandise is complemented by luxuriant rows of trees, an abundance of flowers, and street furniture. A landscaped stream provides a wonderfully strollable center of attention for this vital district.

Food Specialties

★ **The Bakery Cafe**
downtown at 1040 Broad St. *549-0551*
An array of splendid croissants is displayed in one of the West's outstanding newer bakeries. Other delicious baked goods and light

meals are also served to go, inside, or on a tranquil deck over a landscaped creek.

Boston Bagel Company
downtown at 1127 Broad St. *541-5134*
Outstanding bagels (as many as two dozen varieties), including some delicious specialties like whole wheat apple walnut bagels, are served with a choice of toppings and coffee at a few tables, or to go.

Burnardo'z
downtown at Montgomery & Osos Sts.
The region's outstanding native ice cream is now available at a conveniently located new branch downtown.

Burnardo'z Candy Kitchen
15 mi. S at 114 W. Branch St. - Arroyo Grande *481-2041*
Deliciously rich ice creams famed throughout central California are served in a handsome old-time ice cream parlor, along with candies and pastries. Individual scoops and cones may be purchased at a little carryout counter in front of the ice cream factory just down the street.

Cattaneo Bros.
1 mi. S at 769 Caudill St. *543-7188*
Some of the best beef jerky in the West is made here in all styles (thin cut, thick cut, hand cut, peppered, etc.). It can be purchased here, and it is shipped to customers nationwide. Closed Sat.-Sun.

Cowboy Cookies
downtown at 1035 Chorro St. *543-2096*
Delicious cookies, brownies, quiches, and muffins are available in this little carryout. Closed Sun.

Delite Bakery
downtown at 723 Higuera St. *543-5842*
This enduring bakery offers an impressive assortment of old-fashioned breads, pastries, and donuts, mostly to go.

Eclair Bakery
11 mi. S via US 101 at 221 Pomeroy - Pismo Beach *773-4145*
In this delightful European-style bakery/deli, first class pastries, sausage rolls, and sandwiches are served at a few tables, or to go. Closed Mon.-Tues.

A Gourmet Touch
downtown at 600 Marsh St. *549-9111*
Gourmet pastas, pates, desserts, and specialty foods are packaged to go in this classy little shop. Closed Sun.-Mon.

Lauren's Cookies
downtown at 778 Higuera St. *541-2253*
Tempting cookies and brownies, and Linn's fruit pies, plus ice cream, are sold in this handy takeout shop in the Network and can be enjoyed on the sunny back deck by the creek. Fresh-baked hot pretzels are another feature.

Nothing But The Best
downtown at 1117 Chorro St. *541-8086*
Croissants, scones, cookies, muffins, and sandwiches are featured in this small carryout shop.

★ **Old Country Deli**
downtown at 600 Marsh St. *541-2968*
The showcases in this newer deli are packed with home-cured ham, sausage, jerky, and other meats, plus cheeses, gourmet foods, and local wines. Ribs are barbecued over oak wood in front of the store every Saturday. Closed Sun.

★ **Rocky Mountain Chocolate Factory**
downtown at 848 Higuera St. *541-2221*
Fresh-made chocolate specialties, hand-dipped fruits, truffles, fudge, and other gourmet confections are sold in this snazzy newer representative of a Western candy chain.

★ **San Luis Sourdough Co.**
downtown at 717 Higuera St. *546-9609*
Some of the best sourdough-based baked goods in the West, plus fine traditional breads and croissants, are displayed in this outstanding carryout bakery. Samples are offered.

★ **Wine Street Wines**
downtown at 774 Higuera St. *543-0203*
Many styles of regional and other California premium wines are attractively displayed and well stored in a large downstairs shop in the Network. Closed Sun.

Specialty Shops

Art Center Art Association Gallery
downtown at 1010 Broad St. *543-8562*
Local artists are featured in a variety of media, with emphasis on paintings and sculpture. Closed Mon.

Bookland
downtown at 787 Higuera St. *544-0150*
This shop offers a large selection of hard-cover and paperback books.

The Gabby Book Store
downtown at 894 Monterey St. *543-9035*
Books, calendars, posters, and games are displayed in the brightly lighted new location of this long-established business.

★ **Law's Hobby Center**
downtown at 855 Marsh St. *544-5518*
Home hobbyists of all ages and inclinations will be fascinated by this vast two-level supply center for artists and craftsmen; model ship, plane, and train buffs; weavers and sewers; etc.

Mission News
downtown at 1030 Chorro St. *543-3169*
A surprisingly large number of magazines and newspapers, plus paperback books, are well organized in this bright little shop.

The Network
downtown at 774 Higuera St.
An old department store was carefully converted into an appealing two-level arcade of boutiques and restaurants with a choice of creekside or wine cellar dining. Free live entertainment is an added attraction on the rear dining patio by the creek most weekends.

Norwood Books
downtown at 942 Chorro St. *543-4391*
This shop carries a full line of books, including many of local and regional interest.

NIGHTLIFE

A variety of noteworthy bars and lounges throughout the area feature live entertainment and dancing. Several of the best are concentrated downtown. Most are associated with major restaurants.

Champions
downtown at 1009 Monterey St. *541-1161*
The area's newest high-tech sports bar features giant-screen TVs in the corners of an airy, split-level bar/restaurant. Polished wood-and-metal decor is used throughout. The raised bar area is separated by a railing from comfortable, casual seating around hardwood tables in the dining area where snacks or full-course lunches and dinners are served.

Dark Room
downtown at 1037 Monterey St. *543-5131*
This small hideaway is often crowded because of its good reputation for folk and rock music. Light meals are also served.

J.P. Andrews Saloon
downtown at Monterey & Osos Sts. *541-1888*
Live easy listening music is offered most nights in a historic building that has been remodeled into an upbeat, updated saloon trimmed with abundant greenery, brass, and wood.

Madonna Inn
1 mi. W at 100 Madonna Rd. *543-3000*
An old-fashioned orchestra plays big band sounds for dancing most nights in the spacious one-of-a-kind ballroom of the West's most flamboyant motel.

F. McLintock's Saloon
downtown at 686 Higuera St. *541-0680*
You'd never guess that this comfortable Old Western-style saloon loaded with period paintings and paraphernalia isn't a carry-over from those golden days of yesteryear. There's hearty food as well as drink, and live entertainment usually packs the place on weekends.

Motel Inn
1 mi. E at 2223 Monterey St. *543-4000*
Popular groups play music for dancing nightly in the Branding Iron Lounge, a casual outpost of "early modern" decor in the world's first motel.

★ **Olde Port Inn**
11.3 mi. S via US 101 & Avila Rd. - Avila Beach *595-2515*
Well-known names occasionally provide the live music for dancing on weekends in a casual nautical lounge with picture window views of the waterfront. A popular seafood restaurant shares the building on Port San Luis pier.

The Rose and Crown
downtown at 1000 Higuera St. *541-1911*
Well-lighted dart boards, an upright piano, and a cozy fireplace, plus comfortable armchairs and booths, all contribute to the lively atmosphere in San Luis Obispo's first authentic pub, opened in 1985. Almost a dozen beers are on tap to wash down shepherd's pie, cornish pasties, bangers and mash, and other tasty pub grub.

★ **The Spirit**
2.5 mi. SW by US 101 at 1772 Calle Joaquin *544-6078*
A good mix of popular groups, including some "name" acts, provides live entertainment for dancing. The roomy nightclub, perched on a hill, gives patrons a panoramic view of town.

Tortilla Flats
downtown at 1051 Nipomo *544-7575*
Live entertainment and dancing are offered most nights in a large Mexican cantina-style lounge next to a dining room featuring Mexican dishes.

RESTAURANTS

Conventional dining places are abundant. Several distinctive restaurants have opened in and around town in recent years. Many of the best are themed to the historical merits of the area, and concentrate on hearty American dishes using fresh, quality ingredients. The regional specialty—oakwood barbecue—is deservedly gaining widespread acclaim.

Angelo's
downtown at 969 Monterey St. *544-5888*
L-D. No L on Sun. *Low*
Fresh ingredients are emphasized for pizzas, calzones, and other southern Italian dishes served in a nifty new wood-booth dining room, or to go.

Apple Farm
.9 mi. E at 2015 Monterey St. *544-6100*
B-L-D. *Moderate*
This very large, country-themed restaurant serves their own baked goods with American fare that is extremely popular with traveling families.

Assembly Line
downtown at 970 Higuera St. *544-6193*
L-D. No L on Sun. *Moderate*
An elaborate salad bar accompanies the house specialty of tender

barbecued ribs. The cozy dining room is well outfitted with booths and plants.

The Bakery Cafe

downtown at 1040 Broad St. *549-0551*

B-L. *Moderate*

Several kinds of delicious oversized croissants plus other fine pastries and desserts complement light fare including nicely prepared omelets and specialties like walnut chicken salad. Pastries, cheeses, and pate plates are served in the afternoon, and box lunches can be packaged to go. Tables on a balcony over the landscaped creek are set with linen and fresh flowers.

Cafe Roma

.5 mi. SE at 1819 Osos St. *541-6800*

L-D. Closed Sun.-Mon. *Expensive*

Homemade pasta and other Italian fare are offered in a well-regarded, congested trattoria.

Carmel Beach Restaurant

downtown at 450 Marsh St. *541-3474*

L-D. Sun. brunch. *Moderate*

Fresh fish is emphasized on an ambitious contemporary menu offered in casually elegant dining rooms in a newly converted residence.

Chocolate Soup

downtown at 980 Morro St. *543 7229*

L-D. Closed Sun. *Low*

A nightly special accompanies a salad bar and homemade soups (including "chocolate soup" which is a dessert), breads, and desserts. Patrons order cafeteria-style, then are seated at tables with director chairs or in high-gloss blue booths.

Cigar Factory

downtown at 726 Higuera St. *543-6900*

D only. *Moderate*

Contemporary American fare is served in an old cigar factory that was recycled as one of the area's first theme restaurants. A popular Victorian-style bar downstairs features live music nightly.

Coffee Pot Restaurant

13 mi. N at 2770 N. Main St. - Morro Bay *772-3176*

B-L. *Moderate*

Big homemade cinnamon rolls, biscuits, and muffins accent all-American meals served amid the homespun warmth of a little old-fashioned roadside cafe with a view of Morro Rock.

★ **The Custom House**

10 mi. SW at 324 Front St. - Avila Beach *595-7555*

B-L-D. *Moderate*

Highly regarded breakfasts, like specialty omelets using seafoods and fresh local produce, are prepared in a tiny beachfront cafe, and served in a heated garden patio in the back.

Del Monte Cafe
.5 mi. SE at 1901 Santa Barbara St. *541-1901*
B-L-D. No D Sun.-Tues. *Moderate*
American fare is served amid handcrafted Art Deco decor in a converted historic cottage.

★ **Dorn's Original Breakers**
12 mi. NW at 801 Market Av. - Morro Bay *772-4415*
B-L-D. *Moderate*
Fresh seafood is carefully prepared in this big casual restaurant on a bluff above the Embarcadero. Breakfasts are especially noteworthy, with a variety of crepe-style omelets, homemade muffins, pancakes, waffles, and more. The area's best views of Morro Rock and Morro Bay also contribute to the restaurant's abiding popularity.

1865
.8 mi. E at 1865 Monterey St. *544-1865*
L-D. No L Sat.-Sun. *Moderate*
Prime rib is the specialty of this large, contemporary restaurant. Loft dining is a feature, and the decor is accented by lots of natural wood beams, hanging plants, and tapestries. The comfortable lounge offers live music by popular groups most nights.

Golden China Restaurant
downtown at 1085 Higuera St. *543-7354*
L-D. *Moderate*
Mandarin and Szechwan dishes, including fresh seasonal specialties, are served to tables set with crisp white linen at dinner in this large new restaurant. The original location (675 Higuera) is now primarily buffet.

Hudson's Grill
downtown at 1005 Monterey St. *541-5999*
L-D. *Moderate*
Here's a lively new update of the 1950s. Both the short order ("something for everyone") menu and "the gang's all here" atmosphere recall the spirit of that era.

Louisa's Place
downtown at 964 Higuera St. *541-0227*
B-L. *Moderate*
Good, all-American food continues to draw knowledgable natives to an enduring cafe where the service is friendly and the decor is unabashedly homespun.

Madonna Inn
1 mi. W at 100 Madonna Rd. *543-3000*
B-L-D. *Expensive*
The fairly ambitious menu and elaborate homemade pastries might go unnoticed by first-timers. In a remarkable motel that is a paean to pink, both the coffee shop and dining room are flamboyant fantasies that have added new dimensions to restaurant decor. Even the restrooms are so unique that women occasionally sneak into the men's room when the coast is clear just to see the incomparable fixtures.

★ **F. McLintock's Dining House**
9 mi. S via US 101 at 750 Mattie Rd. *773-1892*
L-D. *Moderate*
The region's most famous restaurant is one of the best places to go for very complete meals highlighting central California's gourmet specialty, oak-pit barbecued steaks and ribs. The Western outfits of the staff match the rustic decor of the big dining room in a historic roadhouse that was restyled years ago. Live country/western music is featured nightly in an adjoining saloon.

F. McLintock's Saloon
downtown at 686 Higuera St. *541-0686*
B-L-D. Closed Sun. *Moderate*
Beef is the specialty on a casual all-American menu that also includes buffalo burgers. Both food and drinks are served in a comfortable reproduction of a Western-style saloon dining room.

Michael's Deli
downtown at 785 Higuera St. *544-4040*
B-L. *Moderate*
The only New York-style deli cafe in the area has been a source of lox and bagels (among many other things) for years.

Plessas Tavern
11 mi. S via US 101 at 891 Price St. - Pismo Beach *773-2060*
L-D. *Moderate*
Since 1921, this unassuming seafood house has specialized in baked clams on the half shell au gratin. The old-fashioned durable dish is still featured, and tables are still set with crisp white linen in plain dining rooms.

Rhynos
downtown at 698 Higuera St. *546-9066*
L-D. *Moderate*
Half pound hamburgers and a generous condiment bar, milkshakes, and other all-American fast foods are featured in a simply furnished room with a picture window view of downtown.

The Rose and Crown
downtown at 1000 Higuera St. *541-1911*
L-tea-D. *Moderate*
Shepherd's pie, cornish pasties, bangers and mash, and other examples of English pub grub attest to the owner's interest in authenticity, along with almost a dozen English and other tap beers offered. Comfortable booths and armchairs give diners an opportunity to enjoy the fireplace and the action around the upright piano and the dart boards.

San Luis Bay Inn
10 mi. SW via US 101 - Avila Beach *595-2097*
B-L-D. *Expensive*
Continental specialties are served with some formality in the resort's centerpiece—a large, casually elegant bay-view dining room. An adjacent firelit lounge offers live entertainment and dancing.

Sebastian's
downtown at Monterey/Chorro Sts. *544-5666*
L-D. Sun. brunch. *Moderate*
Steak and seafood are served in a nicely furnished dining room or on a terrace overlooking the Mission. There is also a comfortable lounge with easy listening music most evenings.

Spike's Place
downtown at 570 Higuera St. *544-7157*
L-D. *Low*
Potato skins served a dozen ways, fresh deep-fried artichokes and veggies, and other eclectic enticements are offered amidst wood and greenery indoors or on a back deck.

The Spindle
downtown at 778 Higuera St. *543-5555*
L only. Closed Sun. D on Thurs. *Low*
Casual foods, beer, and wine are especially enjoyable on the sunny rear deck of San Luis Obispo's original creekside cafe in the Network. Live music on Friday and Saturday afternoons is another alfresco attraction.

Spyglass Inn Restaurant
9.5 mi. S at 2705 Spyglass Dr. - Shell Beach *773-4855*
B-L-D. *Moderate*
Contemporary American dishes are served in the motor hotel's comfortably furnished dining room. Picture windows overlook the ocean from the blufftop location. An adjoining piano bar/lounge has similarly impressive ocean views.

★ **This Old House**
3 mi. NW at 740 W. Foothill Blvd. *543-2690*
D only. *Moderate*
Crowds love the smells and flavors that oak-pit barbecue cooking gives to the very complete steak and ribs dinners served in this sprawling steakhouse. Rustic ranch decor is well brought off in several dining rooms and in a wood-toned firelit lounge.

Wine Street Inn
downtown at 774 Higuera St. *543-4488*
L-D. No L on Sun. *Moderate*
Savory fondues are the specialty. Beef, chicken, and seafood dishes are also served in a relaxed dining room situated in the middle of a cellar wine shop.

LODGING

San Luis Obispo gave the world the word "motel" more than half a century ago. Today, most of the major motel chains have joined the "historic" Motel Inn in town to share the growing demand for overnight accommodations in this locale. A small but increasing number of really noteworthy lodging places reflects the town's expanding role as a vacation destination. Most of the area's lodgings are concentrated on Monterey Street east of downtown. There are almost no bargains in summer and on Saturday night—when "no vacancy" signs are the rule. Rates are usually reduced at least 20% apart from those times.

Campus Motel
.5 mi. N at CA 1/404 Santa Rosa *544-0881*
A large heated pool is available to guests in this conveniently located two-story motel by a freeway. Each nicely furnished room has a cable color TV and phone.
#218,#219,#220—in-bath whirlpool/steambath, K bed...$64
regular room—some have refrigerator, Q or K bed...$50

Discovery Motor Inn
.8 mi. E at 1800 Monterey St. *544-8600*
This large contemporary motor hotel offers a large outdoor pool and whirlpool, plus an unusually well-decorated greenhouse-style restaurant and lounge. Each tastefully furnished room has cable color TV with movies and a phone.
regular room— 2 D, Q or K bed...$62

Heritage Inn
.5 mi. N at 978 Olive St. *544-7440*
The first bed-and-breakfast facility in town is located in a recently restored, antique-filled Victorian inn. Guests enjoy Continental breakfasts and complimentary wine, fresh flowers, and a delightful parlor with a fireplace. Clubfoot tubs are down the hall.
Magnolia—gas fireplace, mt. view, windows on 2 sides, D bed...$73
Del's Room—gas fireplace, shared bath, Q bed...$73
regular room—some have private bath, D bed...$73

Homestead Motel
.5 mi. N at 920 Olive St. *543-7700*
An outdoor pool is a feature in this modern single-level motel. Each room has a phone and cable color TV with movies.
#25—spacious, private view of trees over a creek, 2 T & K beds...$55
#22,#23—spacious, some view above creek, T & Q beds...$50
regular room— Q bed...$45

★ **Kon Tiki Inn**
10.7 mi. S via CA 1 at 1621 Price St. Pismo Beach 93449 *773-4833*
A large outdoor view pool and whirlpool, plus easy access to the beach, are features along with a restaurant and lounge in this large modern four-story motor hotel on a bluff by the ocean. Each room has a phone, cable color TV, and a private balcony.
#401-#404—free-standing fireplace, pvt. ocean view balc., K bed...$70
regular room—many have an ocean view, 2 D or K bed...$56

★ **Madonna Inn**
1 mi. W at 100 Madonna Rd. *543-3000*
San Luis Obispo's most fantastic lodging is unique in all of the West. For more than a quarter of a century, this place has been delighting travelers with its outrageous flamboyance. The more recently completed guest rooms are so popular that they must be reserved well in advance. Each room has a phone and cable color TV.
#137—rock ceilings, walls, floors & rock waterfall in bathroom, K bed...$105
#130—lush greens, natural rock walls, huge fireplace, K bed...$105
#143—massive rocks everywhere, even in the bathroom, K bed...$95
#146—subdued pink & grey decor, massive rock fireplace, K bed...$105
#138—most elaborate rock waterfall in bath, stained glass, K bed...$95
#183—paean to pink, spiral staircase, K bed...$115
#128—large, contemporary room in blue tones, K bed...$62
#125—spacious, contemporary decor, muted shades of blue, D & K beds...$70
regular room— Q bed...$62

Motel Inn
1 mi. E at 2223 Monterey St. *543-4000*
The world's first motel is a curiously contemporary "antiquity" that has been refurbished through the years. Attractively landscaped grounds include a variety of mature citrus trees and banana palms, and a large outdoor pool, plus a dining room and lounge. Most of the rooms are in quiet, single-level buildings, and have phones and cable color TV.
"Al","G4","L5"—nicely furnished, K bed...$40
regular room— D bed...$38

Motel 6
2 mi. SW by US 101 at 1433 Calle Joaquin *544-8400*
The **bargain** motel chain is represented by a modest, modern facility close to the freeway with an outdoor pool. Each simply furnished room has a (fee) TV.
regular room— D bed...$25

★ **Quality Inn Sea Venture**
11.5 mi. S at 100 Ocean View - Pismo Beach 93449 *773-4994*
One of the area's newest beachfront motor hotels has covered parking and a panoramic view restaurant. Each well-decorated room has cable color TV with movies, phone, wet bar, and refrigerator. For toll-free reservations, call (800)228-5151.
#251,#249,#247,#245, etc. to #237—
oceanfront view balcony with private whirlpool, K bed...$128
regular room— K bed...$84

★ **San Luis Bay Inn**
10 mi. SW via US 101 and Avila Rd. - Avila Beach 93424   595-2333
This self-contained resort is on a promontory across a highway from a sandy beach. Amenities include a splendid (fee) 18-hole golf course, plus lighted tennis courts, a large outdoor pool, and a well-regarded dining room and lounge. Each spacious room has a phone, cable color TV, and a private balcony.
ocean view room— Q or K bed...$124
regular room—mountain view, Q bed...$94

★ **Sea Crest**
10.3 mi. S via US 101 at 2241 Price St.-Pismo Beach 93449 773-4608
This large, modern motel has a beautifully sited big outdoor pool and whirlpool at the crest of a bluff above the sea, and private access to the beach. Each room has a phone, cable color TV, and an ocean view.
regular room—many have an ocean view, K bed...$58

★ **Shore Cliff Lodge - Best Western**
10 mi. S at 2555 Price St. - Pismo Beach 93449   773-4671
A large outdoor pool, sauna, whirlpool, and two lighted tennis courts on a bluff above the ocean, plus a stairway to the beach, are amenities on the well-landscaped grounds of this large contemporary motor hotel. An ocean view dining room and a lounge are also provided. Each spacious well-furnished room has a phone, cable color TV, and a private patio or balcony.
#304,#306—top floor, floor-to-ceiling whitewater view, K bed...$70
regular room—many have ocean view, 2 D or K bed...$66

Somerset Manor Motel
.8 mi. E at 1895 Monterey St.   544-0973
A large outdoor pool and a whirlpool by a banana palm, plus a coffee shop, enhance this modern two-story motel. Each room has a phone and cable color TV.
#36—private side view of mountains beyond pool, 2 D beds...$43
regular room— 2 D or Q bed...$43

Spyglass Inn
9.5 mi. S at 2705 Spyglass Dr. - Shell Beach 93449   773-4855
This large modern motor hotel is on a bluff over the beach. Landscaped grounds include an outdoor pool, whirlpool, and miniature golf course, plus a restaurant and lounge. Each attractively furnished room has a cable color TV and a phone. For toll-free reservations, call: (800)824-2612.
#226,#126—floor-to-ceiling ocean view, pvt. balc., refr., K bed...$95
regular room—floor-to-ceiling ocean view, 2 D beds...$80
regular room—hill view, 2 Q beds...$75

Sunbeam Motel

.6 mi. E at 1656 Monterey St. *543-8141*

In this small, older motel, each modest room has a cable color TV and phone.

regular room— D bed...$36

Sycamore Mineral Springs

9 mi. S via US 101 at 1215 Avila Beach Dr. *595-7302*

On the oak-shaded grounds are (for a fee) two dozen secluded hot tubs and a new outdoor pool. In addition, a plain two-story motel has cable color TV and one major amenity—most of the simply furnished rooms have a private whirlpool on an enclosed tree-view deck.

"Ultra"—spacious, tranquil, oak branches view from pvt. whirlpool, Q bed...$60

regular room—whirlpool in room or on private deck, Q bed...$60

Villa San Luis Motel

.7 mi. E at 1670 Monterey St. *543-8071*

An outdoor pool is a feature of this small motel. Each of the rooms has a phone and cable color TV with movies.

regular room— Q bed...$42

CAMPGROUNDS

Several nearby campgrounds showcase the town's remarkable variety of water-oriented features. Campers can select sites next to the ocean, Morro Bay, Lopez Lake, or Avila Hot Springs pool.

Avila Hot Springs Spa & RV Park

8 mi. S on US 101 at 250 Avila Beach Dr. *595-2359*

A big outdoor hot springs pool is the attraction at this privately operated campground. Swimming, hot mineral baths, and massage are offered (for a fee). Flush toilets, hot showers, and hookups are available. Each of the closely spaced sites has a picnic table and grill. There is a separate grassy tenting area. base rate...$10

★ **Lopez Lake Recreation Area**

18 mi. SE via Orcutt Rd. & Lopez Dr. *489-2095*

This huge park is one of the most outstanding county-operated recreation facilities anywhere. Located on gentle, grassy oak-dotted slopes by a large picturesque reservoir, it features rentals/docks/ramps for boating, sailing, water-skiing, fishing, lake swimming, a (fee) water slide and whirlpool complex, and hiking trails. The enormous campground has flush toilets, hot showers, and hookups. Each well-spaced, oak-shaded site has a picnic table and fire area. Many have a fine view of the lake. For toll-free reservations, call: (800)822-CAMP.

base rate...$7

★ **Montana de Oro State Park**

16 mi. W via Los Osos Valley *528-0513*

A state-operated campground is beautifully situated near unspoiled ocean beaches and coves in a remote section of the park. Beachcombing, fishing, skin diving, swimming, clamming, and hiking are popular. Only pit toilets are available. There are no showers, hookups, or drinking water. Each of the sites has a picnic table and a fire area. base rate...$3

★ **Morro Bay State Park**
12 mi. NW via CA 1 & South Bay Blvd. *489-2784*
This large state-operated park is adjacent to Morro Bay. Boat rentals; a (fee) dock and ramp; saltwater swimming, boating, and fishing; bicycle rentals; a museum; a (fee) golf course and driving range; hiking trails; and a remote sand dune area across the bay are features. Flush toilets, hot showers, and hookups are available. Each site has a picnic table and fire area. base rate...$6

SPECIAL EVENTS

★ **Poly Royal**
California Polytechnic State University *last weekend in April*
An unusual two-day "country fair on a college campus" is hosted by the students of Cal Poly. Features include a rodeo, a tractor pull and other sporting events, live theater and dance, a carnival, educational exhibits, plus a delicious array of international and all-American foods prepared with locally-grown produce.

★ **La Fiesta de San Luis Obispo** *downtown* *third weekend in May*
In celebration of the town's Spanish heritage, there are three days of parades, dances, barbecues, a Spanish market place, and live music by costumed participants.

★ **Mozart Festival** *Cal Poly campus and the Mission* *first weekend in August*
Guest musicians from all over the country join local talent for six days of indoor and outdoor concerts—including recitals, orchestra concerts, choral music, and chamber music.

OTHER INFORMATION

Area Code: *805*

Zip Code: *93401*

San Luis Obispo Chamber of Commerce
downtown at 1039 Chorro St. *543-1323*

Solvang

Solvang is the Danish capital of America. The sights, sounds, and delicious aromas of an authentic Danish village are present here in the heart of the lovely Santa Ynez Valley. All around, lush pasturelands are accented by noble oak trees. A massive ridge of Coast Range mountains towers to the south, and the ocean is only a few miles away. The peaceful setting is also favored by one of the West's most delightful climates. Mild daytime temperatures and cool evenings prevail year-round. Since most outdoor activities are enjoyable in every season, Solvang is usually teeming with visitors on weekends throughout the year. Shopping and strolling in town, bicycling and wine touring in the valley, hiking and camping in the Coast Range, plus sailing and fishing in southern California's largest lake are popular leisure time pursuits. Spring may be the most desirable season. Then, fields of wildflowers highlight the verdant countryside, new releases are offered for sampling in the valley's many wineries, and crowds are usually light. As the exclusive feature of summer, the nearby ocean warms sufficiently that it can be comfortably used for swimming and surfing off the fine state park beaches a short drive west of town.

There has been a settlement on this site since 1804, when the Spanish built Mission Santa Ines with the Chumash Indians. For more than a century, however, little development occurred. Early in the twentieth century, a group of Danes established a school and village next to the mission as a place where immigrants from Denmark could be educated. After World War II, visitors began to discover this unique cultural enclave as a source of Scandinavian specialties. As a result, merchants and homeowners were encouraged to further emphasize their heritage with more consistently "Danish" architecture to replace the earlier Spanish and Yankee styles.

Careful attention is still paid to nostalgic Old World details as new structures are added. This is especially apparent in the unique central business district, which is a recreated corner of Denmark. Creaking windmills, steep tiled and thatched roofs, cobblestone courtyards, gas street lamps, traditional guard booths, and other fanciful embellishments are everywhere. Significantly, descendants of the Danish-Americans who started all this still preside in a large and growing number of Scandinavian import shops, gourmet food stores, bakeries, and restaurants. After dark, peace and quiet reign. Good live theater during the summer festival is the most noteworthy evening diversion in town. Several places nearby offer drinking and entertainment with distinctive Old Western atmosphere. Both the architecture and contemporary appointments of lodging places in town also reflect the Danish heritage. Little touches like complimentary Continental breakfasts further distinguish these inns and display the friendly spirit of the townsfolk. Most of the best lodgings are an easy stroll from the heart of town.

Elevation:

480 feet

Population (1980):

3,091

Population (1970):

2,004

Location:

130 miles Northwest of Los Angeles

Solvang

WEATHER PROFILE

Vokac Weather Rating

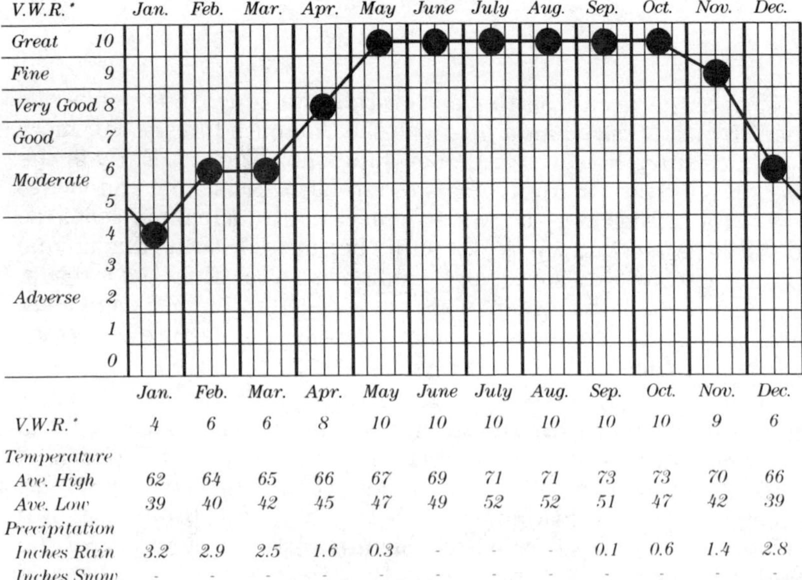

	Jan.	Feb.	Mar.	Apr.	May	June	July	Aug.	Sep.	Oct.	Nov.	Dec.
*V.W.R.**	4	6	6	8	10	10	10	10	10	10	9	6
Temperature												
Ave. High	62	64	65	66	67	69	71	71	73	73	70	66
Ave. Low	39	40	42	45	47	49	52	52	51	47	42	39
Precipitation												
Inches Rain	3.2	2.9	2.5	1.6	0.3	-	-	-	0.1	0.6	1.4	2.8
Inches Snow	-	-	-	-	-	-	-	-	-	-	-	-

**V.W.R. = Vokac Weather Rating: probability of mild (warm & dry) weather on any given day.*

Forecast

Month	*V.W.R.**		*Temperatures Daytime*	*Evening*	*Precipitation*
Jan.	4	Adverse	cool	cool	occasional rainstorms
Feb.	6	Moderate	cool	cool	occasional rainstorms
Mar.	6	Moderate	warm	cool	occasional rainstorms
Apr.	8	Very Good	warm	cool	infrequent rainstorms
May	10	Great	warm	cool	negligible
June	10	Great	warm	cool	none
July	10	Great	warm	cool	none
Aug.	10	Great	warm	cool	none
Sep.	10	Great	warm	cool	none
Oct.	10	Great	warm	cool	infrequent showers
Nov.	9	Fine	warm	cool	infrequent rainstorms
Dec.	6	Moderate	warm	cool	occasional rainstorms

Summary

Solvang has a beautifully pastoral location in a broad luxuriant valley flanked on the south by the Coast Range. With the ocean only a few miles away, the town also benefits from one of the West's most desirable climates. The only season when light sportswear might be unsuitable is **winter**, which is usually cool. Snow and frost are rare, but occasional rainstorms sweeping in from the Pacific provide more than half of the annual precipitation. Rainfall diminishes rapidly in **spring**, which is the beginning of many months of warm days and cool evenings. This is the best time for exploring the countryside while it is emerald green from earlier rains. **Summer** is ideal, with warm sunny days, cool evenings, and no rain. As an added attraction, ocean water temperatures along the beaches a few miles to the south are comfortably warm for swimming and other water sports during the season. Excellent weather usually continues through **fall**, with more warm days and cool evenings. Occasional rainstorms are routine after Thanksgiving.

ATTRACTIONS & DIVERSIONS

Bethania Lutheran Church
downtown at 603 Atterdag Rd. *688-4637*
This church typifies Danish provincial architecture. It's worth a quiet visit to see the model of a full-rigged ship hanging from the ceiling in accordance with Scandinavian seafaring tradition.

Bicycling

Dr. J's Bicychiatry
downtown at 1661-B Fir Av. *688-6263*
The less-traveled highways and byways throughout the pastoral Santa Ynez Valley provide unlimited opportunities for leisurely bicycling. Bicycles can be rented here by the hour or longer. A recommended route map is free. Closed Sun.

El Capitan State Park
26 mi. SE on US 101 *968-0019*
Sunbathing, surfing, and warm ocean swimming (in summer only); pier fishing (which doesn't require a license); boating and sailing (there is a boat hoist); and camping are enjoyed in this well-furnished park.

Gaviota State Park
15 mi. SW on US 101 *968-0019*
The fine sandy beach is the nearest to town. Sunbathing, surfing, and warm ocean swimming (in summer only) are enjoyed, along with fishing, boating, and sailing. The sheltered cove also includes a shady campground.

Horseback Riding

Circle Bar B Ranch
28 mi. SE via US 101 at 1800 Refugio Rd. *968-5929*
The Reagan ranch is relatively near this guest ranch where the owner has turned Secret Service agents into occasional cowboys. It is the only rental stables for many miles where horses tailored to each rider's ability can be reserved for unescorted trail rides. Waterfalls and natural swimming holes up nearby canyons provide idyllic destinations.

Lake Cachuma Recreation Area
11 mi. SE via CA 246 & CA 154 *688-4658*
The largest freshwater reservoir in southern California provides excellent fishing, boating, and sailing opportunities. Motorboat and sailboat rentals are available (phone: 688-4040). Swimming is not permitted in the lake, but there is an outdoor pool at the recreation center, plus a roller skating rink and miniature golf. Picnic tables and barbecue grills are attractively sited under big oak trees and there is a large campground. Horses may be rented for guided trail rides near the entrance to the dam (phone: 668-3018).

★ **Mission Santa Ines**
just E of downtown at 1760 Mission Dr. *688-4815*
Established in 1804, this "hidden gem" was the nineteenth in the chain of twenty-one California missions. Skillfully restored, the large adobe building is used as a church. The grounds also include a picturesque arched colonnade and a garden.

★ **Nojoqui Falls County Park**
6.5 mi. S on Alisal Rd. *688-4217*
An impressive natural waterfall is reached by a well-worn trail through a serene forest of oak and sycamore. This county park is a great place for picnics during the winter and spring—the waterfall dries up during the summer! There are also some campsites.

★ ***Nude Beaches***
starting 18 mi. S via US 101
At the base of a picturesque sandstone bluff is a sandy beach that (at low tide) extends for miles. It is ideal for sun, surf, and sandy hikes. The usually uncrowded swimming-suits-optional portion of the coast starts approximately 2.5 miles southeast of Gaviota State Park. To reach it, look for parked cars just off the west side of the highway by the railroad tracks. Numerous well-worn trails extend via gullies from the blufftop to the secluded shoreline.

★ **Refugio Beach State Park**
24 mi. SE on US 101 *968-1350*
A sandy beach in a sheltered cove is backed by palm-shaded lawns. Conditions are excellent for warm ocean swimming, surfing, and scuba diving during the summer. Surf fishing, camping, and a play area are enjoyed all year.

Sightseeing
downtown at Alisal Rd./Copenhagen Dr.
Guides in Scandinavian attire take visitors on tours of the village in a replica of a turn-of-the-century Danish streetcar. The colorful red trolley is pulled by two Clydesdale horses.

Warm Water Feature
Las Cruces Hot Springs
12 mi. SW via US 101 near CA 1
A naturalized pool dug out of a hillside overflows with hot mineral water from an adjoining spring. It's not deep enough for a swim, but the ooze on the bottom is soothing, and the lush green surroundings can be delightfully tranquil. From the small parking area on the east sides of US 101 at CA 1, it's a pleasant .7 mile hike.

Wineries
Solvang is the center of the largest concentration of premium wineries in southern California. The Santa Ynez Valley is well on its way to

becoming a famous wine-producing district. The premium wineries identified below are perhaps the most fully developed to accommodate visitors. You can also enjoy the leisurely pursuit of fine wine discoveries in several other young wineries in vineyards near town (some require calling ahead). The Chamber of Commerce has maps and details about all wineries in the area.

The Firestone Vineyard

11 mi. N via US 101 & Zaca Station Rd. *688-3940*

Established in 1972, the massive winery is housed in a dramatically contemporary wooden structure on a blufftop promontory. A unique view of both the flourishing vineyards below and of barrels aging wine is provided from different sets of windows in the tasting room. Several estate-bottled wines are offered. Tasting, sales, and tours 10-4. Closed Sun.

The Gainey Vineyard

3 mi. E at 3950 E. CA 246 *688-0558*

Completed in 1984, the valley's newest premium winery is housed in a large Spanish-style building. A handsome tasting room overlooks extensive vineyards on the rolling hills. Picnic tables are located on an adjoining manicured lawn. Regimented tastings are available every fifteen minutes. Tasting, sales, and tours 10-5 daily.

Rancho Sisquoc Winery

27 mi. N via Foxen Canyon Rd. *937-3616*

This small redwood and stone winery was bonded in 1977. Located at the picturesque headquarters of a large, diversified ranch in the pastoral Sisquoc River Valley, the winery uses only grapes produced in the ranch's vineyards. Premium variety wines are sold exclusively at the winery. Large trees shade a secluded picnic area near a tasting room where the entire line is offered. Tasting and sales 10-4 daily.

Santa Ynez Valley Winery

3.5 mi. SE via CA 246 at 365 N. Refugio Rd. *688-8381*

Since it opened in 1976, this has become one of the valley's best known wineries. While the specialty is primarily white wine, a notable blanc de cabernet is also produced. A pleasant view deck with picnic tables adjoins a tasting room where the entire line of premium wines is offered. Tasting, sales, and tours 10-4 daily.

Vintage House

downtown on Mission Dr. at 511 Atterdag Rd. *688-1815*

The downtown tasting room for the Ballard Canyon Winery (built in 1978 at 1825 Ballard Canyon Rd.) generously offers tastes of the winery's entire line of premium wines. Appetizers may be purchased to enjoy with wine in a pleasant, flower-strewn patio. Tasting and sales 12-5 daily (until 5:30 on Sat. & Sun.).

★ **Zaca Mesa Winery**
15 mi. N via Ballard Canyon/Foxen Canyon Rds. *688-3310*
The original 1978 cellar of this young winery has already been expanded into a very large barn-like building where several premium wines are produced. A limited number are offered for tasting. Shaded picnic tables are next to the winery building. Regimented tastings are available every twenty minutes. Tasting, sales, and tours 10-4 daily.

SHOPPING

Downtown Solvang is a pleasure for drivers and pedestrians. All of the town's attractions are within comfortable walking distance of numerous large free parking lots that even include public toilets. On-street parking is also free. The entire downtown area has a Danish motif brimming with little architectural surprises. Cobblestone sidewalks beneath old-fashioned gas lamps, fanciful gables, wood-shingled and copper-tiled rooftops, creaking windmills, hand-carved benches, fountains, and statues abound. So do ersatz thatched rooftops, stork nests and birds, and colorful royal guard boxes. Collectively, these embellishments provide a unique pedestrian-scaled showcase for the West's most remarkable collection of Scandinavian import shops, restaurants, and bakeries.

Food Specialties

★ ***Bakeries***
all over downtown
Tempting aromas drift from bakeries scattered throughout downtown Solvang. Here is the largest concentration of European specialty bakeries in the West. Each is marked by a guild sign showing a kringle—a pretzel-shaped pastry—with a crown. Sampling baked goods to "discover" the best in town is a delight of any visit. Most of the bakeries are open every day, and also serve outstanding Danish coffee in casual dining areas near tantalizing display counters.

Copenhagen Cellars
downtown at 448 Alisal Rd. *688-4218*
Local premium wines are displayed in this cheerful little cellar shop. Tastes of Stearns Wharf wines are offered.

The Great Danish Cone Company
downtown at 441 Alisal Rd. *688-1718*
This popular little ice cream takeout features delicious Danish cones freshly made by a window near the front of the shop.

H & P's Vinhus Ltd.
downtown at 440 Alisal Rd. *688-7117*
Many international cheeses are displayed, and some tastes are offered. A fine assortment of premium wines and gourmet foods is also featured.

★ **Jim Garrahy's Fudge Kitchens**
downtown at 1696 Copenhagen Dr. *688-7048*
Solvang may well be the fudge capital of the West. Visitors to this shop and several others in the downtown area can watch it being made, taste free samples, or make a purchase of excellent custom packed fudges.

★ **The Little Mermaid**
downtown at 1546 Mission Dr. *688-6141*
Aebleskiver is the most popular and distinctively Scandinavian pastry in Solvang. Pancake-like batter is cooked in special pans which turn out little round treats described as the Danish version of a donut. They are the specialty of this Danish restaurant. Visitors can watch them being made at various times in an exhibition kitchen in a front dining room.

Pretzel N Cheese Inc.
downtown at Alisal Rd./Copenhagen Dr. *688-0980*
Fresh hot pretzels are made all day and served with a notable cheddar cheese spread in this little carryout shop. Cheese spread samples are available.

★ **Rocky Mountain Chocolate Factory**
downtown at 1455 Copenhagen Dr.
Delicious fudges and other chocolates of all kinds are beautifully displayed in this outlet of an excellent regional chain. Visitors can watch fudges being made the old way on a giant marble slab.

★ **The Solvang Bakery**
downtown at 1682 Copenhagen Dr. *688-5713*
This bakery displays the full line of fine European specialty pastries and breads sold in numerous bakeries downtown. A colorful coffee room in back and handsome show windows and glass cases brimming with tantalizing baked goods suggest why Solvang's bakeries are renowned.

★ **Solvang Sausage Shop**
downtown at 490-A 1st St. *688-4044*
Excellent European and Danish-style sausages are made and sold in this long-established shop, along with home-smoked Black Forest ham.

Specialty Shops

The Book Loft
downtown at 1680 Mission Dr. *688-6010*
A well-organized selection of hard-cover and paperback books is attractively displayed in the several rooms of this bookstore.

★ **Copenhagen Galleri**
downtown at 1618 Copenhagen Dr. *688-4422*
Solvang's premier art gallery is a multilevel showcase for first-rate wall hangings and sculptures.

NIGHTLIFE

Professional live theater in summer and a few restaurant lounges provide the only nightlife in town. However, there are a few notably atmospheric saloons nearby.

Belle Terrasse Pub
downtown at 1564 Copenhagen Dr. *688-2762*
Live music is provided most nights in an intimate pub setting next to a popular restaurant.

★ **Cold Spring Tavern**
21 mi. S via CA 154 at 5995 Stagecoach Rd. *967-0066*
Live music attracts swarms of ultra-casual "regulars" and fascinated "first timers" to look, listen, and dance most nights. But, it is the authentic, unspoiled old stagecoach stop high in the mountains south of town that is the real attraction. The rustic Old West atmosphere in the firelit bar is unforgettable.

★ **Solvang Theaterfest**
downtown at 420 2nd St. *922-8313*
One of the oldest repertory theaters on the West Coast presents a mixture of dramas and musicals in an appealing, half-timbered open air theater. The season runs from mid-June through September. For details, the theaterfest box office can be called toll-free: (800)221-9469.

The Valhalla Lounge
downtown at 400 Alisal Rd. *688-8000*
Live music for dancing or listening is featured most nights in a casual lounge with a stone fireplace in the new Sheraton Royal Scandinavian Inn.

Zaca Creek Saloon
5.5 mi. NW at 1297 N. US 101 - Buellton *688-2412*
Live entertainment and dancing draw crowds from miles around on weekends to this big, comfortable Western-style saloon. The adjoining steak house is also popular.

RESTAURANTS

Most of the restaurants in town feature Scandinavian dishes. A few take pride in authentic Old World specialties. Several fine restaurants tucked away in the surrounding countryside reflect a surprisingly long tradition of thoroughly Yankee charm.

Andersen's Restaurant
4 mi. W at US 101 - Buellton *688-5581*
B-L-D. *Moderate*
Since it opened in 1924, this place has evolved into a huge family-oriented tourist stop. Their famous split pea soup is still a crowd-pleaser. Free cheese samples and wine tastes are offered in a complex of shops adjoining the dining rooms.

★ **Ballard Store**
3.8 mi. NE via Alamo Rd. at 2449 Baseline Av. *688-5319*
D only. Closed Mon.-Tues. *Expensive*
This is the premier restaurant of the Santa Ynez Valley. Continental cuisine is prepared with the highest quality meats and the freshest

vegetables accompanied by homemade sauces, soups, bread, and desserts. Reservations are essential, often days in advance. Recently enlarged dining rooms still convey the Yankee charm of what once was a country general store. Delicious appetizers and desserts, plus wines by the glass, are served in a stylish little wine bar between the casually posh dining rooms.

Belgian Cafe
downtown at 475 1st St. *688-6316*
B-L. *Moderate*
Assorted fresh-baked Belgian waffles and crepes are served by costumed waitresses in a cheerful little coffee shop, or in an umbrella-shaded garden courtyard that is usually jammed on sunny days.

★ **Belle Terrasse**
downtown at 1564 Copenhagen Dr. *688-2762*
L-D. *Expensive*
Northern Italian specialties, especially veal and seafood with a "light touch," are served in several casually elegant small dining areas in a handsome newer restaurant adjoining the Tivoli Inn.

★ **Cold Spring Tavern**
21 mi. S via CA 154 at 5995 Stagecoach Rd. *967-0066*
L-D. *Moderate*
Hearty American fare, including wild game, is skillfully prepared and accompanied by delicious homemade bread. All of the charm of a bygone era is present in this historic stagecoach stop. The buildings have a ramshackle authenticity unmatched in southern California. The tiny firelit bar is particularly romantic.

Danish Inn Restaurant
downtown at 1547 Mission Dr. *688-4813*
L-D. *Expensive*
This large restaurant produces the most celebrated of Solvang's Danish smorgasbords, in addition to an extensive assortment of Danish/Continental dishes. Comfortable armchairs, crisp linens, and fireplaces enhance the informally plush Old World atmosphere of the dining room and a small lounge.

Equestrian Restaurant
3.5 mi. W at 406 E. CA 246 - Buellton *688-3737*
D only. *Moderate*
American dishes—especially seafood and steaks—are barbecued over oakwood, and served in a casual wood-toned dining room with a fireplace.

Federico's Mexican Restaurant
4 mi. W at 585 McMurray Rd. - Buellton *688-0606*
L-D. *Moderate*
The valley's newest large restaurant features mesquite broiling and homemade tortilla chips. An ambitious menu includes unusual

Mexican-style entrees and desserts. Comfortable, padded booths in a spacious multilevel dining room surround a dramatic life-sized sculpture of three horses.

The Little Mermaid

downtown at 1546 Mission Dr. *688-6141*
B-L-D. *Low*

Authentic aebleskiver with homemade raspberry jam and Danish sausage, the best dishes here, are served all day in casual, Danish-style dining rooms. The pleasant little restaurant also has Danish beer on tap.

Mattei's Tavern

6 mi. N on CA 154 - Los Olivos *688-4820*
D only. *Moderate*

In continuous operation since 1886, this valley landmark is now operated as a restaurant by the Charthouse chain. Good steaks, plus seafood and a salad bar, are offered in carefully restored Old Western dining rooms. An authentic saloon and parlor with working fireplaces contribute to the warmly nostalgic atmosphere.

Mollekroen

downtown at 435 Alisal Rd. *688-4555*
L-D. *Low*

Well-prepared Danish specialties and a bountiful smorgasbord attract enthusiastic crowds to this casual and congested upstairs restaurant. Downstairs, a congenial lounge provides live entertainment on weekends.

The Mustard Seed

downtown at 1655 Mission Dr. *688-1318*
B-L. Closed Mon. *Moderate*

Omelets and some homemade pastries are served in a bright little coffee shop, and on a pleasant patio overlooking the main street and town park.

Remington Restaurant

5.5 mi. N at 2860 Grand Av. - Los Olivos *688-7788*
L-D. *Very Expensive*

The chef's efforts with New California cuisine are overshadowed by the near-elegance of the Los Olivos Grand Hotel's pricey new dining room. Expensive fabric-and-hardwood armchairs are set around tables outfitted with crisp white linen and fresh flowers. A dramatic Remington bronze and a working fireplace highlight the spacious surroundings.

Yorick's

downtown at 443 2nd St. *688-4822*
B-L. *Moderate*

In this colorful sidewalk cafe, fresh croissants and muffins accompany a large variety of omelets and other light fare served indoors or out. Several premium wines are poured by the glass.

Zaca Creek Restaurant
5.5 mi. NW at 1297 N. US 101 - Buellton *688-2412*
D only. *Moderate*
Oak-pit broiled steaks are the specialty on a contemporary American menu. This large newer restaurant gets a warm country feeling from natural wood decor and a lot of plants. The comfortable adjacent lounge features music and dancing on weekends.

LODGING

Motor lodges in more-or-less Danish architectural styles have proliferated throughout the downtown area. Most are well-furnished and offer complimentary Continental breakfasts. From spring through fall and on weekends year-round, it is not uncommon for every room in town to be full. Nearby Buellton has a little motel row that serves as a backup, and offers near-bargains midweek. Rates are usually reduced at least 10% in winter and from Sunday thru Thursday except in summer.

★ **The Alisal**
2.6 mi. S on Alisal Rd. (P.O. Box 26) *688-6411*
One of the most luxurious guest ranches in California is in a pretty little canyon near town. Beautifully maintained single-story bungalows are set amidst flowers, oaks, and sycamores in 10,000 acres of rolling green foothills of the Santa Ynez Mountains. Facilities (available to guests only) include tennis courts, a picturesque 18-hole golf course, stables for guided horseback rides, the resort's own tiny lake for sailing and fishing, a large landscaped pool, whirlpool, plus a fine dining room and lounge. Each spacious, beautifully decorated room has a wood-burning fireplace. Rates are for two people on a modified American plan—breakfast and dinner included.
regular room—studio, 2 T or K bed...$176

★ **The Ballard Inn**
3.8 mi. NE via Alamo Rd. at 2436 Baseline Rd. *688-7770*
The most meticulous decor in the valley is part of the charm of this new bed-and-breakfast inn. Each room has a complete bath, and celebrates an aspect of the area's past with skillfully coordinated furnishings and decorations. Complimentary breakfast and afternoon tea are served in a lovely dining room.
"The Mountain Room"—spacious, pvt. balc., view on 3 sides, fireplace, Q bed...$150
"The Wildflower Room"—cozy, fireplace, Q bed...$130
"The Fiesta Room"—cheerful, fireplace, Q bed...$130
"Cynthia's Room"—the bridal suite, spacious, fireplace, Q bed...$150
regular room— Q bed...$120

★ **Chimney Sweep Inn**
downtown at 1554 Copenhagen Dr. *688-2111*
This Danish contemporary motor inn is backed by an intimate flower-filled garden with a secluded whirlpool. A complimentary Continental breakfast is offered. Each spacious, lavishly furnished unit has a phone and cable color TV. For toll-free reservations, call: (800)824-6444.
#2 "The Dawn Treader"—2-story fantasy cottage, kitchen, patio with private whirlpool, 2 fireplaces, K bed...$175
#1 "The Tree House"—2-story fantasy cottage, kitchen, private tree branch balcony, fireplace, pvt. patio with stream, K bed...$175
#50,#49—split-level suite, raised K bed...$100
regular room— Q bed...$60

★ **The Danish Country Inn**
downtown at 1455 Mission Dr. *688-2018*
A whirlpool overlooking an oak grove and a small outdoor pool are features of this large motor inn, along with a sauna and a charming oak view dining room—used for complimentary breakfast and cocktail hour for guests. Each spacious, well-furnished room has a phone and cable color TV with movies. For toll-free reservations, call: (800)44 RELAX.
deluxe room—E side of 2nd fl. has pvt. balc. with oak views, K bed...$87
regular room— K bed...$67

Los Olivos Grand Hotel
5.5 mi. N at 2860 Grand Av. - Los Olivos 93441 *688-7788*
The valley's first small hotel in the European tradition of intimate elegance opened in 1985. Landscaped grounds include an outdoor pool and whirlpool, and there is a handsome dining room. Each luxuriously appointed room has cable color TV, a phone, a refrigerator, and complimentary wine upon arrival.
suite—spacious, in-bath whirlpool, K bed...$210
regular room— Q or K bed...$150

Meadowlark Motel
2 mi. E on CA 246 at 2644 Mission Dr. *688-4631*
This modern single-level motel has spacious lawns and a small outdoor pool in a rural setting. Each large, quiet room has cable color TV.
regular room— Q bed...$48

Motel 6
4 mi. W at 333 McMurray Rd. - Buellton *688-3293*
The **bargain** motel chain has a modest, modern facility with an outdoor pool adjacent to the freeway in nearby Buellton. There is a (fee) TV.
regular room— D bed...$25

The Petersen Inn
downtown at 1583 Mission Dr. *688-3121*
One of Solvang's newest Danish-style motor inns is built around a charming fountain courtyard. Each of the well-furnished rooms has cable color TV and a phone. A nearby bakery serves a Continental breakfast complimentary to guests. For toll-free reservations, call: (800)321-8985.

"Tower Suite"—spacious, wet bar, in-bath whirlpool, gas fireplace, 4-poster K bed...$150
"courtyard view" (several)—spacious, canopy K bed...$90
#312—in garret, vaulted ceiling, balcony, Q bed...$65
"Garden Garret"—small, vaulted ceiling, balcony, D bed...$55
regular room—street view, Q bed...$70

San Marcos Motel
4 mi. W at 536 Av. of Flags - Buellton *688-5511*
This small single-level motel has an outdoor pool. Each room includes a color TV.

regular room— K bed...$46
regular room— D bed...$38

Sheraton Royal Scandinavian Inn
downtown at 400 Alisal Rd. *688-8000*
Solvang's largest motor hotel opened in 1984 near the heart of town on a bluff overlooking the Santa Ynez river valley. The conventional facility includes an outdoor pool and whirlpool, a sauna, plus an instantly-Old-World restaurant and lounge. Each spacious, well-furnished room has a phone and cable color TV. For toll-free reservations: in California (800)624-5572; elsewhere (800)325-3535.

#311,#309—large room, overlooks pool & countryside, K bed...$85
regular room— Q bed...$65

Sleepy Hollow Motel
4 mi. W at 550 Av. of Flags - Buellton *688-6638*
This small single-level motel on motel row has cable color TV with movies in each plainly furnished room.

regular room— Q bed...$38
regular room— D bed...$32

Solvang Gaard Lodge
downtown at 293 Alisal Rd. *688-4404*
This small single-level motel is the only real **bargain** in town, and it is conveniently located on the quiet side of downtown. Each large, well-maintained room has a cable color TV.

regular room— Q bed...$26

★ **Svendsgaard's Lodge**
downtown at 1711 Mission Dr. *688-3277*
An outdoor pool and whirlpool are located in a courtyard of this Danish-style motel in the heart of town. Each unit has a phone, cable color TV,

and a refrigerator. A free Continental breakfast is served.

#40,#51—suite, spacious, village/mt. view,
gas fireplace, kit., K bed...$75
#24—spacious, gas fireplace, wet bar, K bed...$54
regular room— Q bed...$40

★ **Tivoli Inn**
downtown at 1564 Copenhagen Dr. *688-0559*

One of Solvang's most picturesque Danish-style complexes was recently remodeled to include some of the valley's finest accommodations. The small hotel with an Old World flair features uniquely decorated rooms. Each is luxuriously furnished with a (pressed wood) fireplace; remote controlled cable color TV; a phone; and a sunken tiled bath. Fruit and champagne upon arrival are complimentary, as is a Continental breakfast which is brought to the room.

#214 "Honeymoon"—spacious, in-bath whirlpool, K bed...$190
#305 "Midnight"— wet bar, same mt. view, raised K bed...$125
#309 "Love"—spacious, symphony of blues, K bed...$105
#301 "Joyful"—multi-sloped walls, tile roof views, K bed...$105
#310 "Moonlight"—spacious, round K bed...$105
regular room— Q bed...$95

Viking Motel
downtown at 1506 Mission Dr. *688-4827*

This tiny, no-frills, single-level motel is convenient to everything in town. Each unit has a cable color TV.

regular room— K bed...$48
regular room— Q bed...$38

CAMPGROUNDS

Three of the West's finest California-subtropical campgrounds have choice oceanfront locations less than a half hour drive from town. Even nearer inland, southern California's largest reservoir is the site of a huge and popular campground.

★ **El Capitan State Beach**
27 mi. SE on US 101 *968-1411*

This large, state-operated campground occupies a picturesque area by a sandy ocean beach. Sunbathing, swimming (in summer), fishing, and hiking are favorite pastimes. There are flush toilets and hot showers, but no hookups. Each site has a picnic table, fire ring, and grill.
base rate...$8

★ **Gaviota State Beach**
15 mi. SW on US 101 *968-0019*

A sheltered cove by a sandy ocean beach has been developed into a popular state-operated campground. Sunbathing; swimming, surfing, and skin diving (in summer); fishing; and boat rentals/hoist are features. Flush toilets and hot showers, but no hookups, are available. Park officials advise bringing drinking water. Each of the closely spaced sites has a picnic table, fire ring, and grill. base rate...$8

Lake Cachuma Recreation Area
11 mi. SE on CA 154 *963-7108*
An enormous county-operated campground is attractively sited on oak-shaded slopes above Lake Cachuma. Lake swimming is not allowed in southern California's largest reservoir, but fishing, boat rentals/ramps, an outdoor pool (in summer), and horseback riding rentals are popular. Flush toilets, hot showers, and hookups are available. Each site has a picnic table and a fire area. In California, call toll-free: (800)822-CAMP
base rate...$7

Refugio State Beach
25 mi. SE via CA 246 & US 101 *968-1350*
This state-operated campground is in a beautifully landscaped sheltered cove by a sandy ocean beach. Sunbathing; swimming, surfing, and skin diving in summer; and fishing are popular. Flush toilets and hot showers, but no hookups, are available. Each site has a picnic table, fire ring, and grill.
base rate...$8

SPECIAL EVENT

Danish Days Festival *throughout town* *third weekend in September*
Residents wear Danish costumes and celebrate their heritage in the town's biggest event. Highlights include parades, a feast and ball, theatrical productions, and other live entertainment.

OTHER INFORMATION

Area Code: *805*

Zip Code: *93463*

Solvang Chamber of Commerce
downtown at 1623 Mission Dr. *688-3317*

Sonoma

Sonoma is the treasury of northern California history. For more than 150 years, the heart of town has been a large, beautifully landscaped plaza. It is still almost completely surrounded by carefully preserved nineteenth century buildings. Beyond, gentle grass-and-oak-covered hills define the southern end of "The Valley of the Moon" a few miles north of San Francisco Bay. Majestic rows of eucalyptus shade the orchards and vineyards that fill the valley around town. In addition to the lush pastoral setting, Sonoma also benefits from a temperate climate. Spring is an idyllic time to experience Sonoma, when blossoms everywhere accent emerald green landscapes, vintners are pouring their new releases, and crowds are usually light. The town is usually filled with visitors throughout summer and fall. Normally dry sunny days of those seasons are popular for winery touring, for picnics and hiking in the hills, or for bicycling, golf, or tennis in the valley. Since the area's finest attractions are all indoors—in historic buildings, distinctive shops, or wineries—even winter appeals to visitors willing to accept cool damp weather in exchange for a slower pace and absence of crowds.

Sonoma, "the birthplace of California viticulture," was founded in 1823 by Franciscan fathers as the twenty-first of their El Camino Real chain of missions. It was also the last and most northerly of these historic Spanish settlements. California's first vineyards were planted here by the padres in 1824 so wines for sacramental purposes would be available. Within a decade, jurisdiction of the area was passed to Mexico. That country's commander, Mariano Guadalupe Vallejo, planted other grape varieties for table wines. Mexican control ended when the short-lived California Republic was born in Sonoma with the raising of the Bear Flag on the plaza in 1846. Four years later, California became an American state. During the Civil War, Sonoma once again made viticultural history when America's first big experimental vineyard was established by a Hungarian nobleman, Count Agoston Haraszthy, at Buena Vista.

The wine industry remains the key to the town's prosperity. Vineyards dating from those momentous times endure as charming reminders of a rich heritage. Downtown, the spacious plaza is a continuing delight for strollers and picnickers. It provides a picturesque counterpoint to historic structures all around which now house an outstanding array of specialty shops, gourmet food stores and restaurants, and atmospheric bars and lounges. Accommodations are surprisingly scarce in the valley. Clones of motel chains or large conventional hotels are nonexistent. Instead, all of the best lodgings are in skillful restorations of historic structures. Several romantic small hotels and bed-and-breakfast inns are on or within a stroll of the plaza.

Elevation:

81 feet

Population (1980):

6,054

Population (1970):

4,259

Location:

47 mi. Northeast of San Francisco

Sonoma

WEATHER PROFILE

Vokac Weather Rating

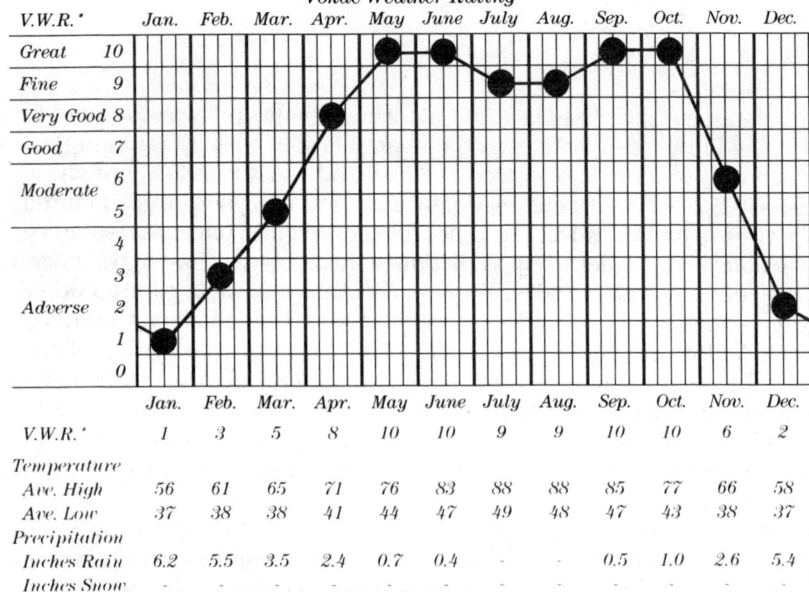

	Jan.	Feb.	Mar.	Apr.	May	June	July	Aug.	Sep.	Oct.	Nov.	Dec.
*V.W.R.**	1	3	5	8	10	10	9	9	10	10	6	2
Temperature												
Ave. High	56	61	65	71	76	83	88	88	85	77	66	58
Ave. Low	37	38	38	41	44	47	49	48	47	43	38	37
Precipitation												
Inches Rain	6.2	5.5	3.5	2.4	0.7	0.4	-	-	0.5	1.0	2.6	5.4
Inches Snow	-	-	-	-	-	-	-	-	-	-	-	-

**V.W.R. = Vokac Weather Rating: probability of mild (warm & dry) weather on any given day.*

Forecast

Month	*V.W.R.**		*Temperatures* *Daytime*	*Evening*	*Precipitation*
Jan.	1	Adverse	cool	chilly	frequent downpours
Feb.	3	Adverse	cool	chilly	frequent downpours
Mar.	5	Moderate	warm	cool	occasional downpours
Apr.	8	Very Good	warm	cool	infrequent rainstorms
May	10	Great	warm	cool	infrequent showers
June	10	Great	hot	warm	negligible
July	9	Fine	hot	warm	none
Aug.	9	Fine	hot	warm	none
Sep.	10	Great	hot	warm	negligible
Oct.	10	Great	warm	cool	infrequent rainstorms
Nov.	6	Moderate	warm	cool	occasional rainstorms
Dec.	2	Adverse	cool	chilly	frequent downpours

Summary

Located near the southern end of the Valley of the Moon, Sonoma is only a few miles north of San Francisco Bay. Marine air pouring through the Coast Range gap at the Golden Gate is a major influence. While there is normally almost no snow, **winter** is cool and very wet, with frequent downpours providing well over half the year's normal precipitation. **Spring** is the beginning of a long period of comfortable weather. Warm days, cool evenings, and fewer and lighter rainfalls encourage casual enjoyment of the verdant countryside. **Summer** days are typically fairly hot, evenings are warm, and there is remarkably little precipitation. **Fall** is outstanding. Warm days, cool evenings, and infrequent rainfalls assure the final ripening of grapes. The weather is perfect for observing the transformation of grapes into wine, and for savoring the fruits of this labor.

ATTRACTIONS & DIVERSIONS

Ballooning
A champagne flight in a hot-air balloon is a unique way to achieve a serene perspective on the sights and sounds of the "Valley of the Moon."
Airborn of Sonoma County *P.O. Box 4887* *528-8133*
Sonoma Thunder, Inc. *P.O. Box 641 - El Verana 95433* *996-3665*

Bear Flag Monument
NE corner of plaza
A heroic bronze figure holding a Bear Flag marks the site where thirty American horsemen rode into Sonoma, captured General Vallejo without a struggle, and proclaimed the "California Republic" on June 14, 1846.

★ ***Bicycling***
Sonoma Wheels Bicycle Shop
just S of plaza at 523 Broadway *935-1366*
Fat-tired bicycles may be rented here by the hour or day to tour the pastoral countryside. A short and scenic separated bikeway on the north side of town supplements well-marked highways and byways in the relatively level Valley of the Moon. Closed Tues.

Blue Wing Inn
just off NE corner of plaza on Spain St.
Built in 1840 by General Vallejo for travelers, this structure is probably Sonoma's oldest remaining building. While the part that is not in a state of atmospheric disrepair is now occupied by shops, its ancient register includes such famous names as John C. Fremont, U.S. Grant, and Kit Carson.

Golf
Sonoma National Golf Club
3.3 mi. NW at 17700 Arnold Dr. *996-0300*
This attractive 18-hole championship course on the gentle west slope of the Valley of the Moon is open to the public year-round. Facilities include club and cart rentals, plus a clubhouse, driving range, and restaurant.

★ **Jack London State Historic Park**
9 mi. NW via CA 12 - Glen Ellen *938-5216*
The park is part of the famed author's "Beauty Ranch" where he resided from 1905 until his death in 1916. The "House of Happy Walls," a large fieldstone structure built in 1919 by his widow, has an excellent collection of his memorabilia, and is the park interpretive center. A half-mile trail leads through woods to the ruins of the ill-fated "Wolf House." Stark walls and massive chimneys of native volcanic stone are all that remain of the imposing structure that was destroyed by fire shortly before the Londons could move in. The author's grave is nearby. A three-mile trail to the summit of Sonoma Mountain offers impressive views of the Valley of the Moon.

Library
.8 mi. W at 755 W. Napa St. *996-5217*
The Sonoma Regional Library occupies a large, contemporary building. Upholstered armchairs draw browsers to a well-lighted periodical reading area. Closed Sun.

★ **The Plaza**
downtown
This National Historic Landmark is a delight to visitors and residents alike. Surrounding the old City Hall are well-landscaped, expansive lawns with paths, monuments, a fountain, ponds, and shade trees ideally suited to picnickers and strollers.

★ **Sonoma State Historic Park**
N side of plaza *928-1578*
A number of major historic structures have been restored downtown. Casa Grande, the first adobe home of General Vallejo, was built in 1836 and destroyed by fire in 1867. Only the Indian servants' wing remains. The Mission San Francisco de Solano was the last (1823) of California's twenty-one missions built by Father Junipero Serra. The chapel no longer serves a religious purpose, but it is nicely preserved. Other rooms in the long adobe structure house a large collection of historic relics. The Sonoma Barracks, erected in 1836 of redwood timbers and adobe brick, housed General Vallejo's troops when he was the last Mexican governor of California. The building has been restored to resemble its original appearance, right down to the dusty rear courtyard.

★ **Spring Lake Regional Park**
17 mi. NW via CA 12 & Montgomery St. *539-8092*
A small reservoir in a lovely rural setting has been ingeniously converted into a superb water recreation facility by the county and local water district. Well-landscaped, tree-shaded grounds include an expansive warm spring-fed swimming lagoon with a sandy beach, open from Memorial Day through Labor Day. On the lake itself, boating (electric motors only), rental boats, a ramp and dock, and fishing are available. Hiking trails, bicycle paths, picnic tables, and a campground are other attractions.

★ **Vallejo Home ("Lachryma Montis")**
.5 mi. NW on 3rd St. W *938-1578*
This stately Carpenter Gothic home of General Mariano Vallejo was built in 1852. "Lachryma Montis," as it was called; the adjoining Swiss chalet; and several outbuildings are now state-owned museums housing his momentoes. The carefully maintained grounds reflect Vallejo's fascination with horticulture. A giant old pommelo tree in front of the chalet is especially spectacular early in the year when the huge grapefruit-like fruit is ripe.

Warm Water Features

Agua Caliente Springs

2.8 mi. NW via CA 12 at 17350 Vailetti Dr. *996-6822*

A large warm mineral springs pool, open to the public, is the centerpiece of a historic facility that includes picnic tables under shade trees on an adjoining lawn area. Closed Tues.-Wed.

Morton's Warm Springs

11.5 mi. NW via CA 12 at 1651 Warm Springs Rd. *833-5511*

A large outdoor mineral springs pool in a scenic location is open to the public daily in summer. Many picnic tables are located on an adjoining tree-shaded lawn.

Wineries

Sonoma is the birthplace of America's premium wine industry. Grapes were first grown here in 1823 to make wine for sacramental purposes. Soon, secular wines were also being produced. After the Civil War, Sonoma became the state's largest wine producer. This area remains one of California's most illustrious producers of premium wine. For detailed information and a map of all wineries in the area, contact the Chamber of Commerce, a bookstore, or most food specialty shops.

Buena Vista Winery

1 mi. E at 18000 Old Winery Rd. *938-1266*

Founded in 1857 by Count Agoston Haraszthy, this is the oldest winery in the valley and a state historic landmark. A self-guided tour of the 1857 cellar and wine caves dug into the hillside is a must. Shaded picnic grounds in front of the ivy-covered old stone building are set amidst ancient eucalyptus by a creek. Tasting, tours, and sales 10-5 daily.

Chateau St. Jean

11.6 mi. NW at 8555 CA 12 *833-4134*

This young winery (1974) is one of the outstanding producers of premium wine in the nation. Visitors are free to enjoy informative self-guided tours of the impressive, recently added wine production and storage complex. Nearby, a splendid old Mediterranean-style chateau includes a wood-paneled room where selected tastes are offered. The attractively landscaped grounds include romantic, shady picnic areas. Tasting, tours, and sales 10-4:30 daily.

Grand Cru Vineyards

10 mi. N via CA 12 at 1 Vintage Lane *996-8100*

In 1970 this small premium winery was established on a much older winery estate. An A-frame tasting room and a grassy, oak-shaded picnic area adjoin stainless steel tanks on an attractive site overlooking vineyards and hills. Tasting and sales 10-5 daily.

Hacienda Wine Cellars

1 mi. E at 1000 Vineyard Lane *938-3220*

This small winery, occupying a Spanish colonial-style building on part of the original Buena Vista estate, concentrates on a limited selection of premium wines. An informative display of premium grapevine varieties is adjacent to the tasting room entrance. Nearby, a spacious picnic area offers charming tree-shaded or sunny views of the vineyards and valley. Tasting and sales 10-5 daily.

★ **Kenwood Vineyards**
10.5 mi. N at 9592 CA 12 *833-5891*
A rustic redwood building is used to house a congenial tasting room with stained glass windows and a ceiling of grape stakes. Tastes of all varieties are offered. This outstanding little winery set in old-fashioned wood barns has been notably successful in recent years in developing premium quality wines. Tasting and sales 10-4:30 daily.

★ **St. Francis Vineyards**
11.6 mi. NW at 8450 CA 12 *833-4666*
The plush new tasting room of this young (1979) premium winery has a fireplace and picture window views of surrounding vineyards. Several picnic tables are on a pleasant adjoining patio. Tasting and sales 10-4:30 daily.

★ **Sebastiani Vineyards**
.4 mi. E at 389 4th St. E *938-5532*
The largest wine maker in the valley, this historic landmark is still a family operation. Many wines are produced and most are generously available for tasting. The cellars include a fascinating collection of carved casks. Tasting, tours, and sales 10-5 daily.

SHOPPING

A unique, vital central business district completely surrounds the large plaza that has been the heart of town for more than one hundred and fifty years. Picturesque nineteenth century facades invite closer inspection of a fascinating collection of specialty and gourmet shops, dining and drinking places, and secret courtyards like Place des Pyrenees and El Paseo de Sonoma with their clusters of boutiques around cobblestone walkways and secret gardens.

Food Specialties

★ **Brundages**
E side of plaza at 492 1st St. E *938-4388*
A large historic building now serves as a delightfully eclectic deli. Foot-long hot dogs, piroshki, even pot stickers are among the items served at well-worn tables, or to go. There's also a complete turn-of-the-century soda fountain, and a good selection of premium California wines, plus gourmet coffee beans and teas.

The Cherry Tree
4 mi. S on CA 12 & CA 121 at 1901 Fremont Dr. *938-3480*
Fruit spreads and a variety of natural juices like cherry cider are featured in this enduring roadside shop.

★ **Fantasie au Chocolat**
N side of plaza at 40 W. Spain St. *938-2020*
An irresistible selection of chocolate candies, pastries, and cookies is displayed and sold. The shop has a pleasant seating area where coffee and a variety of other beverages are served with the delicious chocolates.

Fruit Basket
25 mi. NW at 18474 CA 12 *996-7433*
A very good assortment of fresh fruits and vegetables, gourmet nuts and other produce, plus California wines are displayed and sold in a rambling roadside stand.

★ **Homegrown Bagels**
near SW corner of plaza at 122 W. Napa St. *996-0166*
The various well-made bagels produced here daily can be enjoyed at a few plain tables with coffee or taken out.

★ **Ma Stokeld's**
E side of plaza at 464 1st St. E *935-0660*
Delicious puff pastries, bangers, and pies are made fresh daily in a new, authentic little shop tucked away in the Place de Pyrenees.

★ **Moosetta's**
2 mi. W at 18976 CA 12 *996-1313*
Piroshki—pastry dough filled with meat or vegetables—is the delicious house specialty. Tempting casseroles and small sweet pastries are also displayed and sold in this unusual little carryout shop. Closed Sun.-Mon.

★ **Simmons Pharmacy**
S side of plaza at 29 E. Napa St. *996-3696*
An authentic solid marble soda fountain is the highlight of this quintessential village pharmacy. Visitors have enjoyed ice cream, sundaes, phosphates, and cold lemonade here for more than eighty years. Closed Mon.

★ **Sonoma Cheese Factory**
N side of plaza at 2 W. Spain St. *996-1931*
Visitors can watch superb Sonoma Jack cheese being made. It and many other cheeses can be purchased to eat indoors in the deli or on a patio, to go, or for shipment. Other local gourmet deli specialties along with wines, and a wine-by-the-glass bar, are also available. Unfortunately, cheese is no longer available for sampling without asking.

★ **Sonoma Creamery**
NE corner of plaza at 400 1st St. E *938-2938*
A converted creamery building houses an ice cream fountain with a full range of locally made ice cream treats. Service is at the counter or at tables set amidst plant-laden decor accented by a weeping rock wall. The adjacent deli features a good assortment of cheeses, meats, sandwiches, and wines.

★ **Sonoma French Bakery**
NE side of plaza at 468 1st St. E *996-2691*
Here is a gastronomic shrine for all lovers of genuine sourdough French bread. Since the 1950s, this enormously popular bread has been captivating all who discover it. Other breads, pastries, and cookies are also sold in a disarmingly plain little carryout bakery. Closed Mon.-Tues.

★ **Sonoma Sausage Co.**
W side of plaza at 453 1st St. W *938-8200*
Dozens of different kinds of top-quality 100% pure meat sausage plus smoked meats are produced locally and sold in a handsomely restored historic building.

Sonoma Wine Shop
E side of plaza at 412 1st St. E *996-1230*
Local California wineries are well represented in this attractive little shop, along with a full line of wine accessories. Several local wines are usually available for tasting at the wine bar in the back room. Closed Mon.

★ **Vella Cheese Co.**
.3 mi. NE at 315 2nd St. E *938-3232*
The fresh jack, cheddar, and other cheeses that have been made here for more than fifty years are very good, and reasonably priced. Tastes of any of the cheeses are provided.

Specialty Shops

★ **Arts Guild of Sonoma**
E side of plaza at 460 1st St. E *996-3115*
Guild members' works in a variety of media are beautifully displayed in a well-lighted little gallery.

Bookends Book Store
.3 mi. W at 201 W. Napa St. *938-5926*
A large selection of books includes many of local and regional interest. There is also a good selection of topographic and other maps, and magazines.

NIGHTLIFE

Live music is scarce in the Valley of the Moon. While there are several distinctive places to enjoy a drink on the plaza, most of the action (such as it is) is in the string of tiny villages a few miles northwest of town.

Gino's in Sonoma
E side of plaza at 420 1st St. E *996-4466*
This friendly "locals" bar has a wood-toned interior accented by plants, stained glass lamps, and a view of the plaza. Light meals are also served.

Little Switzerland
2 mi. NW at Grove & Riverside Dr. - El Verano *938-9990*
A live band plays polka and waltz music for dancing and listening on

Friday through Sunday nights in a turn-of-the-century roadhouse tavern with Old World decor and a patio. European and American food is also served. Closed Mon.-Thurs.

London Lodge

8 mi. NW at 13740 Arnold Dr. - Glen Ellen *996-3100*

Visitors can relax in bentwood chairs in a saloon from the Jack London era that still sports a well-worn wood floor, a handsome old bar, and brick walls adorned by nostalgic pictures. A popular restaurant is in the next room.

★ **Marioni's**

N side of plaza at 8 W. Spain St. *996-6866*

The intimate lounge area fronting on the plaza with a raised adobe fireplace and director chairs is a fine place for a quiet drink. A contemporary bar adjoining the restaurant inside is also popular. Closed Mon.

★ **Sonoma Hotel**

NW corner of plaza at 110 W. Spain St. *996-2996*

A good place for a quiet drink is the beautifully restored saloon in this historic hotel. A high ceilinged room with polished wood floors and hardwood trim is outfitted with stained glass, shiny brass, fine period paintings, a handsome hardwood front and back bar, and fresh flowers on antique tables.

RESTAURANTS

Sonoma enjoys a starring role in the dramatic expansion of fine dining in the wine country. Several fine newer restaurants, along with established favorites, inevitably feature local seasonally fresh ingredients and first class regional wines. With an emphasis on creative California cuisine, Sonoma is becoming one of the gourmet capitals of the West. In a region where restaurant prices have recently skyrocketed, visitors will be pleasantly surprised by uniformly reasonable prices throughout the Valley of the Moon.

★ **Au Relais**

.3 mi. S at 691 Broadway *996-1031*

L-D. Sun. brunch. *Moderate*

Country French cuisine is served in a charming cottage filled with stained glass, polished hardwoods, prints, and plants. This long-established restaurant also has a pleasant brick patio for alfresco dining, and a cozy lounge.

★ **Capri**

9 mi. N at 9900 CA 12 - Kenwood *833-6326*

D only. Sun. brunch. Closed Mon. *Moderate*

Full course Continental dinners are featured. Guests seated at tables accented by fresh flowers and crisp linens have a picture window view of the countryside.

★ **El Dorado Inn**
NW corner of plaza at 405 1st St. W — *996-3030*
L-D. — *Expensive*
Contemporary American fare is featured in the casually elegant spacious dining room or in a shady courtyard of a carefully restored historic hotel. A variety of homemade desserts, as well as drinks, are also served in the plush Victorian lounge.

★ **Garden Court Cafe**
6.5 mi. N at 13875 CA 12 - Glen Ellen — *935-1565*
B-L. Closed Mon.-Tues. — *Moderate*
The best breakfasts in the valley are a highlight on a limited menu of all-American dishes carefully prepared from scratch. The cheerful little roadside cafe is as plainly appealing as the food, with fresh flowers and jam pots gracing each table.

★ **Grist Mill Inn**
7.8 mi. NW at 14301 Arnold Dr. - Glen Ellen — *996-3077*
L-D. No L on Tues. Closed Mon. — *Moderate*
California cuisine is given a disciplined light touch in one of the valley's most charming restaurants. A pre-Civil War grist mill was recently skillfully transformed to include a dining room overlooking a creek with tables set with linen, crystal, and fresh flowers.

La Casa
near NE corner of plaza at 121 E. Spain St. — *996-3406*
L-D. — *Low*
An extensive menu of well-prepared traditional Mexican specialties is served amidst colorful Mexican furnishings. An inviting cantina in the next room emphasizes imported beers and margaritas.

★ **La Vina**
just S of plaza at 599 Broadway — *938-8788*
L-D. — *Moderate*
Delicious and unusual Mexican and Spanish dishes are the feature of this plain little, recently opened dining room.

London Lodge
8 mi. NW at 13740 Arnold Dr. - Glen Ellen — *996-3100*
L-D. Closed Tues.-Wed. — *Moderate*
Hearty American and Italian fare is served in a well-furnished large dining room and (seasonally) on a deck overlooking picturesque Sonoma Creek. The adjoining nostalgic bar has pictures and furnishings that capture the flavor of Jack London's era.

Marioni's
N side of plaza at 8 W. Spain St. — *996-6866*
L-D. Closed Mon. No L on Sun. — *Moderate*
Steak and seafood are served amidst colorful contemporary Southwestern decor. A tiled courtyard with an adobe fireplace that fronts on the plaza is especially charming, and the decor and multilevel dining areas inside are striking.

Pasta Nostra
near SE corner of plaza at 139 E. Napa St. *938-4166*
D only. Closed Tues.-Wed. *Moderate*
Freshly made pasta and sauces plus veal and chicken dishes are featured in a colorful, congested trattoria.

Peterberry's
near SE corner of plaza at 140 E. Napa St. *996-5559*
B-L. *Moderate*
Coffees, espresso, and local wines are served with a variety of locally made pastries and light fare. This casual coffee house offers dining in several cozy areas, and some tables by picture windows overlooking the street.

★ **Pilou**
E side of plaza at 464 1st St. E *996-2757*
L-D. Sat. & Sun. Brunch. No D Sun.-Tues. Closed Mon. *Moderate*
Hidden away in a cobblestone courtyard, this lovely little restaurant is a notable addition to gourmet dining in Sonoma. Fresh local produce is used extensively and creatively in French and New California cuisine.

★ **Sharl's**
near SW corner of plaza at 136 W. Napa St. *996-5155*
L-D. Closed Tues. *Expensive*
An unusual selection of updated Continental cuisine is offered in an expansive dining room enhanced by skylights, a fireplace, plants, and tables set with full linen and fresh flowers. A shaded patio is also used in summer. An adjacent sunken bar offers comfortable armchairs and slick, modern decor.

★ **Sonoma Hotel**
NW corner of plaza at 110 W. Spain St. *996-2996*
L-D. Closed Wed.-Thurs. Sun. brunch. *Moderate*
Fresh and homemade ingredients are skillfully used to prepare a limited number of creative New California dishes offered on a menu that changes weekly. A century-old hotel has been carefully restored to its former status as a Victorian landmark with an artistically refurbished dining room and saloon and a tranquil garden patio.

Sonoma Mission Inn
2.5 mi. W at 18140 CA 12 *938-9000*
B-L-D. *Expensive*
"Spa food" is the new highlight of the stylishly restored Sonoma Mission Inn. Gracious table settings and padded armchairs lend to the tranquil feeling of the pretty pink and white dining room overlooking the pool.

Stein's of Sonoma
just S of plaza at 522 Broadway *935-0853*
B-L. *Moderate*
The only place in town serving complete breakfasts throughout the week is a casual spot that features hearty fare (like Sheboygan bratwurst) reminiscent of the new owner's Midwestern roots.

★ **Vineyards Inn**
11.7 mi. N at 8445 CA 12 — *833-4500*
D only. Closed Tues. — *Low*
Delicious Mexican specialties like shrimp enchiladas and chile verde with marinated pork are served in a lively little roadside cantina, and in a covered heated patio. A large stone fireplace lends warmth in winter to the cozy bar and dining room.

★ **Willabe's**
near SE corner of plaza at 133 E. Napa St. — *996-4663*
L-D. Closed Mon.-Tues. No D on Wed. — *Moderate*
Fresh seafoods and New California specialties are prepared on a mesquite charcoal grill and served with homemade pastas in this well-regarded restaurant. Diners can choose between a casually elegant firelit room or a tranquil tree-shaded fountain court.

LODGING

Accommodations in and around Sonoma are relatively scarce and expensive. There is only one bargain motel in the area. Visitors interested in staying in any of the noted lodgings should make reservations well in advance from spring through fall. Rates are often reduced by at least 20% during the winter, except on weekends.

Au Relais Inn
.3 mi. S at 691 Broadway — *996-1031*
A Victorian home has been carefully restored to serve as a charming bed-and-breakfast. A Continental breakfast is offered to guests. Each room is attractively furnished with antique accents.
#4—spacious, cheerful decor, pvt. bath & entrance, Q bed...$75
regular room—shared bath, Q bed...$65

★ **Beltane Ranch**
8.5 mi. NW at 11775 CA 12 (Box 395) - Glen Ellen — *996-6501*
An authentic Victorian-era ranch offers fine pastoral views of the Valley of the Moon from porches that surround second floor rooms in an unspoiled building that now serves as a bed-and-breakfast country inn. Period antiques, ceiling fans, and private baths are featured in each room. A Continental breakfast often including home-grown food is complimentary.
"Fireplace Room"—sitting room with a view, iron fireplace, K bed...$70
regular room— D bed...$70

★ **Chalet Bed and Breakfast**
1.2 mi. NW at 18935 5th St. W (Box 595) — *938-3129*
Cows graze on the hillside next to a quaint old chalet that has been made into a bed-and-breakfast country inn. Features include a hot tub with a tranquil pastoral view, an upstairs sitting room warmed by a pot-bellied stove, and peacocks strolling among citrus trees on lush grounds. A real

country breakfast is complimentary.

"New Cottage"—spacious, pvt. bath, wood-burning stove, refr., view on 3 sides, D bed...$90
"top floor front"—shared bath, spacious, private views, D bed...$70
regular room—shared bath, D bed...$70

El Dorado Inn
NW corner of plaza at 405 1st St. W *996-3030*

A pre-Civil War landmark has been artistically reconstructed into a small hotel with an atmospheric restaurant and saloon. Upstairs, each room has been comfortably outfitted with quality contemporary furnishings. A Continental breakfast is served in the beautifully appointed lobby.

#28—corner of top floor, town/hills view, private bath, Q bed...$95
regular room—shared bath, 2 T or Q bed...$65

El Pueblo Motel
1.2 mi. W at 896 W. Napa St. *996-3651*

This is the nearest conventional modern motel to the plaza. Each room has color TV and some have a phone. There is a large outdoor pool.

regular room— 2 D beds...$46

★ **The Hidden Oak**
near SE corner of plaza at 214 E. Napa St. *996-9863*

A classic California Brown Shingle Bungalow is the newest first-rate bed-and-breakfast in Sonoma. Nicely landscaped grounds include a deck and a large outdoor pool. Bikes are free to guests. Each of the three spacious rooms includes carefully chosen antiques and a private bathroom. A complete breakfast with homemade pastry is complimentary, as are wine and appetizers in the afternoon.

"Delft Room"—beautifully coordinated blue-toned antiques and decor, Q bed...$90
regular room— Q bed...$80

London Lodge Motel
8 mi. NW at 13740 Arnold Dr. (Box 488) - Glen Ellen *938-8510*

An outdoor pool and a quiet, scenic location by Sonoma Creek are features of this modern motel. Each room has cable color TV and a phone.

#34,#23—end, large, K bed...$45
regular room— 2 Q or K bed...$45

★ **Sonoma Hotel**
NW corner of plaza at 110 W. Spain St. *996-2996*

This three-floor, century-old landmark was recently thoroughly renovated, including the restaurant, bar, and lobby. Each room is furnished with authentic Victorian antiques. A Continental breakfast is included.

#1—spacious, corner overlooking the plaza, bathtub, brass D bed...$68

#3 "Vallejo Room"—spacious, clawfoot bathtub, monumental carved rosewood — D bed...$79
#4—good view, unique armoire, clawfoot tub, small — D bed...$68
#20—overlooks Sonoma plaza, antique armoire, shared bath, — D bed...$49
regular room—shared bath, — 2 T or D bed...$49

★ **Sonoma Mission Inn**
2.5 mi. NW at 18170 CA 12 — *938-9000*

A large old Spanish-style landmark was recently transformed into an exclusive resort hotel. Soft pastel colors and natural fabrics are used throughout to create understated contemporary elegance. Lighted tennis courts, an Olympic-sized outdoor pool, and (for a fee) a complete health spa, plus a restaurant and lounge, are provided. Private baths, color TV, phones, and canopy beds are featured in all of the small, beautifully decorated rooms and in larger suites. A Continental breakfast is offered. Call toll-free: (800)862-4945—California. (800)358-9022—nationwide.

turret room—rounded room, private sundeck, — K bed...$155
regular room— — 2 T or Q bed...$110

Thistle Dew Inn
near NW corner of plaza at 171 W. Spain St. — *938-2909*

This bed-and-breakfast inn offers turn-of-the-century ambiance in two ingeniously converted older buildings close to everything. A complimentary buffet-style Continental breakfast is served in the morning, and sherry is offered each evening by the fireplace.

#4 "Back House"—spacious, private bath, — Q bed...$85
regular room—shared bath, — Q bed...$60

★ **Victorian Garden Inn**
.3 mi. SE at 316 E. Napa St. — *996-5339*

A secluded bed-and-breakfast inn occupies a historic farmhouse and water tower surrounded by picturesque gardens. A small stream runs through the property, and there is a large outdoor pool. A Continental breakfast and afternoon wine or sherry are complimentary.

"Woodcutters Cottage"—spacious, vaulted ceiling, private entrance, big bath, fireplace, by stream, — Q bed...$110
"Tower"—private entrance & bath, by stream, at top of water tower, — D bed...$79
"Garden"—private entrance & bath, by stream, — Q bed...$89
regular room—in main house, shared bath, — Q bed...$69

Vineyard View Village
4.5 mi. S on CA 121 at 23000 Arnold Dr. — *938-2350*

This single-level older motel is the only **bargain** for many miles. Each small, modest room has a color TV.

regular room— — Q bed...$28
regular room— — D bed...$27

CAMPGROUNDS

There are two notable campgrounds within easy driving distance of town, providing a choice between rustic facilities in a scenic canyon or complete facilities near a picturesque little reservoir.

★ **Spring Lake Regional Park**
19 mi. NW via CA 12 *539-8092*
Sonoma County and a local water district operate this campground by a lovely little reservoir with a swimming lagoon by a long sandy beach, rental boats, a ramp and dock, boating (no motors allowed), fishing, and hiking and bicycle paths. Flush toilets and hot showers are available, but there are no hookups. Each site has a picnic table and a fire area.
base rate...$6

Sugarloaf Ridge State Park
15 mi. NE at 2605 Adobe Canyon Rd. - Kenwood *833-5712*
This state-operated campground is in a secluded pine-and-oak-shaded canyon, where Sonoma Creek begins. The tiny stream, and hiking and riding trails, are attractions. Only pit toilets are available—no showers or hookups. Each shady site has a picnic table and a fire ring/grill.
base rate...$6

SPECIAL EVENT

★ **Valley of the Moon Vintage Festival** *on the plaza* *late September*
A weekend of parades, pageants, art shows, dances, music, and entertainment coincides with the annual grape harvest for the year's biggest and liveliest event. Light-hearted homage is paid to the valley's most famous product in the blessing of the grape, grape stomping, and wine tasting parties.

OTHER INFORMATION

Area Code: *707*
Zip Code: *95476*
Sonoma Valley Chamber of Commerce
on the plaza at 453 1st St. E *996-1033*

Sonora

Sonora is the robust "Queen of the Mother Lode." Well-tended Victorian homes and businesses still lend a gold camp flavor to this thriving hub in the foothills of the high Sierra. With a relatively mild four season climate, little snow falls in town during the winter. But, an hour away, there is plenty in the higher mountains for every kind of snow sport. The best weather usually occurs during late spring and early fall. Yet, crowds are only noticeable in summer, when long, hot days create great demand for the remarkable assortment of lakes, reservoirs, and rivers in the oak-and-grass-covered foothills and pine-forested mountains surrounding town. Swimming, boating, sailing, fishing, river running, and gold panning lead a long list of outdoor recreation opportunities. The most popular year-round attraction, however, is the historic town itself and other nearby well-preserved Mother Lode towns.

Mexican miners established an encampment here in 1848 and named it the "Sonoran Camp." A short time later, when gold was discovered, Americans quickly supplanted Mexican and Chilean miners in the area. When California became a state in 1850, Sonora was named the Tuolumne County seat. After a disastrous fire in 1852, the town was rebuilt more substantially with stone, brick, adobe, and iron. The big Bonanza Mine, located just north of downtown, was perhaps the richest pocket mine in the Mother Lode. The high school now stands on land that gave up some of the largest pure nuggets ever found in this part of the state. The mines played out many decades ago, but Sonora continued to grow as a commercial center because of its convenient location. Recently, it has also become a leisure destination as a result of increasing awareness of the area's historic significance and recreation opportunities.

Sonora stretches across several hills that are lightly forested with a pleasing combination of broadleaf and pine trees. Downtown, lush vegetation shades the courthouse plaza, and a little creek running through the business district is showcased in a landscaped minipark. Many notable Victorian buildings remain. Some still serve their original purpose as churches, public buildings, saloons, or stores. Others have been carefully transformed into specialty shops, galleries, and restaurants. Several distinctive Western-style entertainment spots are clustered in the heart of town. The collection of Victorian homes surrounding the business district is one of the best in the Mother Lode country. Lodgings are not abundant. There are several conventional motels. However, the most noteworthy accommodations are in historic hotels including two landmarks downtown and several handsome restorations with atmospheric gold camp furnishings in the vicinity.

Elevation:

1,825 feet

Population (1980):

3,247

Population (1970):

3,100

Location:

132 miles East of San Francisco

Sonora

WEATHER PROFILE

Vokac Weather Rating

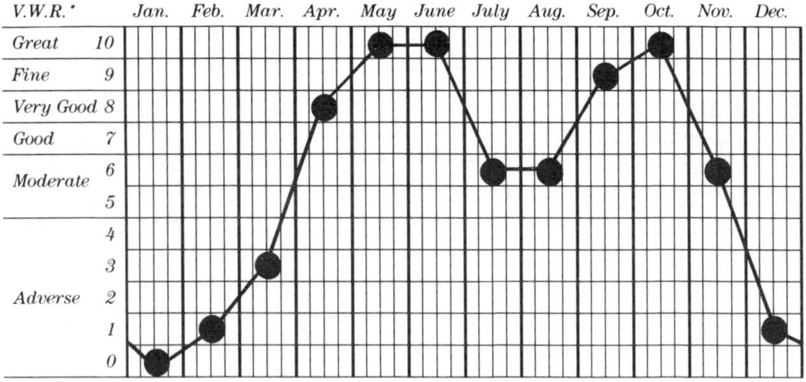

*V.W.R.**		*Jan.*	*Feb.*	*Mar.*	*Apr.*	*May*	*June*	*July*	*Aug.*	*Sep.*	*Oct.*	*Nov.*	*Dec.*
Great	*10*												
Fine	*9*												
Very Good	*8*												
Good	*7*												
Moderate	*6*												
	5												
Adverse	*4*												
	3												
	2												
	1												
	0												

	Jan.	*Feb.*	*Mar.*	*Apr.*	*May*	*June*	*July*	*Aug.*	*Sep.*	*Oct.*	*Nov.*	*Dec.*
*V.W.R.**	*0*	*1*	*3*	*8*	*10*	*10*	*6*	*6*	*9*	*10*	*6*	*1*
Temperature												
Ave. High	*54*	*58*	*62*	*70*	*77*	*86*	*94*	*93*	*88*	*76*	*65*	*57*
Ave. Low	*34*	*36*	*39*	*43*	*48*	*53*	*60*	*59*	*54*	*47*	*39*	*35*
Precipitation												
Inches Rain	*6.0*	*6.0*	*5.0*	*2.8*	*1.3*	*0.3*	-	-	*0.4*	*1.6*	*3.0*	*5.6*
Inches Snow	*3*	*2*	*1*	-	-	-	-	-	-	-	-	*1*

**V.W.R. = Vokac Weather Rating: probability of mild (warm & dry) weather on any given day.*

Forecast

			Temperatures		
Month	*V.W.R.**		*Daytime*	*Evening*	*Precipitation*
Jan.	0	Adverse	cool	chilly	frequent downpours/snow flurries
Feb.	1	Adverse	cool	chilly	frequent downpours/snow flurries
Mar.	3	Adverse	cool	cool	occasional downpours
Apr.	8	Very Good	warm	cool	infrequent downpours
May	10	Great	warm	cool	infrequent rainstorms
June	10	Great	hot	warm	negligible
July	6	Moderate	hot	warm	none
Aug.	6	Moderate	hot	warm	none
Sep.	9	Fine	hot	warm	negligible
Oct.	10	Great	warm	cool	infrequent rainstorms
Nov.	6	Moderate	warm	cool	infrequent downpours
Dec.	1	Adverse	cool	chilly	occasional downpours

Summary

Sonora is located in the scenic Sierra foothills near the southern end of the Gold Camp country. The area has a relatively mild four season climate. All of the unfavorable weather is concentrated in **winter**. Heavy frosts and cold days are rare, but typically cool days and chilly evenings are frequently accompanied by heavy rains and some snow flurries which provide more than half the year's total precipitation. **Spring** is the most pleasant season, as days grow warmer and there are fewer and lighter rainstorms. **Summer** days are hot, evenings are warm, and there is usually no rainfall. While these conditions reduce the comfortable enjoyment of some outdoor activities, they are perfect for river running, swimming, and other popular water sports available in abundance in surrounding lakes and rivers. During **fall**, mild warm days, cool evenings, and infrequent rainstorms last into November, when the rainy season normally begins again in earnest.

ATTRACTIONS & DIVERSIONS

★ **Columbia State Historic Park**

4 mi. N off CA 49 on Parrotts Ferry Rd. *532-4301*

Part of the old business district in Columbia has been faithfully restored to its appearance in gold rush days. For a few years during the 1850s, thousands of people lived here while fabulously rich placer mines were yielding $87 million in gold. The state has restored several buildings that may be viewed on a self-guided walking tour including: the firehouse (and an 1852 two-cylinder fire engine); an 1860 two-story brick schoolhouse; St. Anne's Church (1856); the Wells Fargo Express office (1858), now a museum; the Fallon House Theater (1860); and the City Hotel (1857). A tour of a gold mine, stagecoach rides, and gold panning are some of the unusual activities offered during the summer and on most weekends year-round.

★ **Don Pedro Lake**

15 mi. S on CA 49 *989-2383*

The Mother Lode country's largest water body is a twenty-six-mile-long reservoir with a shoreline of 160 miles reaching into scenic woodland foothills. Houseboats and fishing boats can be rented at either of two full service marinas. Sailing is also popular. Swimming coves are numerous and a large sandy beach area has been provided. Picnic and camping areas are located at several scenic sites near the lake.

Flying

Columbia Airport

4 mi. N via CA 49, Parrotts Ferry & Airport Rds. *533-5685*

Scenic flights over the southern Mother Lode country or above Yosemite Valley can be reserved at one of the aviation services here any day.

★ ***Gold Panning***

There is still enough gold left in the once-fabulously-rich placer deposits of nearby streams to provide an occasional thrill for latter-day argonauts. You can learn to pan, dredge, and separate gold at the Columbia Mine Supply Store (532-9693) in Columbia State Park where for a price, you're guaranteed to get some gold. Or, you can buy a pan here and hike up one of the nearby streams. Closed Mon.-Tues. in winter.

Hiking

Sonora Mountaineering

downtown at 173 S. Washington St. *532-5621*

Sonora is a base camp for hiking trails of all kinds, from easy walks among gold camp relics in and around town or amidst awesome nearby sequoia groves, to extended backpacks into remote canyons and crystal-clear lakes in the high Sierra. This place rents (and sells) all of the gear you'll need. They also sell a good assortment of U.S.G.S. maps and books about the outdoors. In winter, cross-country skis and gear can be rented.

★ **Jamestown**
3.5 mi. SW via CA 49
A narrow main street accented by two-story balconied buildings and a park with a gazebo are highlights of this little Victorian relic. The photogenic town has been used as the setting for several classic Hollywood westerns. A few shops and several restaurants and bars are well worth visiting.

Library
downtown at 465 S. Washington St. *533-5707*
The Tuolumne County Library is a modest facility in a refurbished older building with a nicely displayed selection of magazines and newspapers. Closed Sun.

Moaning Cave
14 mi. NW at 5150 Moaning Cave Rd. *736-2708*
Discovered around 1850, this is California's largest public cavern. A guided tour descends a 100-foot spiral staircase into a gigantic chamber with impressive formations.

Railtown 1897 State Historic Park
3.5 mi. SW off CA 49 at 9th St./5th Av. *984-3953*
Since 1982, the state has operated steam-powered passenger trains over a historic twelve-mile route through oak-studded hill country each weekend in summer. The old roundhouse and shop complex is open to the public daily in summer (weekends only in winter).

★ ***River Running***
Sonora is between two of the most famous whitewater streams in the West—the Stanislaus and the Tuolumne Rivers. Some of the best rapids are now submerged beneath the waters of huge downstream reservoirs. However, exciting one or two day raft trips can still be enjoyed further upstream on the remaining scenic portions of the rivers. Several guide services operate between April and November. Among the most popular are:

OARS, Inc. *P.O. Box 67 - Angels Camp 95222* *736-4677*
Zephyr River Expeditions *P.O. Box 3607* *532-6249*

★ **St. James Episcopal Church**
downtown at Washington & Snell Sts. *532-7644*
This picturesque Episcopal church, built in 1859 on a rise at the north end of downtown, may be California's oldest. Many consider it the most beautiful frame building in the Mother Lode. A Victorian mansion across the street is also notable.

★ **Stanislaus National Forest**
starts 5 mi. E of town *532-3671*
All of the Sierra Nevada mountains between Sonora and Yosemite National Park are included in this extraordinary forest. Features near town include numerous campgrounds and miles of hiking, backpacking, and horseback riding trails along the splendid canyons of the Tuolumne and Stanislaus river drainages. The upper reaches of these rivers include

some of the West's great whitewater rafting opportunities. In the calmer stretches, swimmers are attracted to crystal-clear natural pools,with sandy beaches. A magnificent stand of sequoia gigantea, the Calaveras Big Trees, has been famous since its discovery in 1852. It is less than an hour by car from town. A similar distance to the east are trailheads for the Emigrant Wilderness bordered by Yosemite to the south and the crest of the Sierra to the east. This forest of pine and aspen, interspersed with broad meadows and numerous small lakes and streams, is a favorite with fishermen, hunters, and backpackers. In winter, Sonora is an easy drive from Dodge Ridge Ski Area, which was recently expanded into a major winter sports center. Mt. Reba and Bear Valley Ski Areas are somewhat farther to the northeast.

Tuolumne County Museum

downtown at 158 W. Bradford Av. *532-1317*

Gold Camp photographs and memorabilia are displayed, along with an authentically furnished jail cell, in a building that housed the local jail well over a century ago.

Warm Water Feature

Sierra Hot Tub

1.5 mi. SE on CA 108 at 1255 Mono Way *532-1522*

Private hot tub enclosures, indoors or outdoors under oak trees, are rented by the hour until late each evening. Guests may bring in their choice of beverages.

★ ***Water Features***

A remarkable variety of lakes, streams, and reservoirs are within an hour's drive of town. During the uniformly sunny and hot months of summer, Sierra waters are a compelling attraction for swimmers, as well as fishermen, water-skiers, sailers, river runners, and all others who enjoy cool, clear water recreation. Public parks with sandy beaches and private coves abound on Don Pedro, New Melones, McClure, Woodward, Modesto, Turlock, and other nearby man-made lakes. There are also excellent swimming holes and sandy beaches on the Stanislaus and Tuolumne Rivers and other nearby rivers flowing through the Sierra foothills.

★ **Weird Wanda's**

3.6 mi. SW off CA 49 at 10365 9th St. - Jamestown *984-4149*

This unique store easily lives up to its name with bizarre displays of coyote claws; rare bird pelts, wings, and feathers; demonic masks; and other strange stuff for sale.

Wineries

Shenandoah Vineyards

4 mi. N at 2260B Parrotts Ferry Rd. - Columbia *532-3771*

In the Columbia Tasting Room, visitors may sample and buy the full line of wines made at a small family winery in Plymouth, sixty miles north on CA 49. An impressive array of spices is also packaged and sold here. Tasting and sales 10-5 daily.

★ **Stevenot Winery**
21 mi. N on Sheep Ranch Rd. - 2 mi. N of Murphys *728-3436*
The small winery and vineyards are tucked away at the bottom of a deep gorge. Modern, quality equipment is housed in a restored 110-year-old hay barn. Zinfandel is the Mother Lode's most famous contribution to wine, and visitors may sample a notable example here, along with other premium varietals in an atmospheric tasting room. The little valley is ideal for a pastoral picnic. Tasting, tours, and sales 10-5 daily.

Winter Sports

★ **Dodge Ridge Ski Area**
33 mi. NE off CA 108 on Dodge Ridge Rd. *965-3474*
The vertical drop was recently increased to approximately 1,600 feet, and the longest run is more than a mile. Two triples and five double chairlifts serve the area. Concessions include ski rentals and school, a cafeteria, and a bar. Open daily from mid-November to mid-April. For toll-free ski conditions: (800)233-SNOW.

★ **Leland Meadows Resort**
30 mi. NE off CA 108 - Pinecrest *965-3745*
This is a popular snow play area. Features include a tobogganing hill where toboggans, saucers, or inner tubes can be rented—or bring your own. There is also a cross-country ski area with designated trails. Lessons can be arranged. Hourly or daily snowmobile rentals and sleigh rides are also available. Open daily from December to April.

★ **Yosemite National Park**
52 mi. SE via CA 49 & CA 120 *372-4605*
Well over two million people visit this world famous national park each year. Its magnificent waterfalls and sheer granite domes are unsurpassed. Giant sequoia groves, vast high country wilderness areas, snowfields, and crystal-clear lakes and streams are some of the attractions that have won the acclaim of increasing hordes of recreation enthusiasts since before the turn of the century.

SHOPPING

Sonora's business district is a distinctive combination of historic and new buildings that exists in spite of an outsize string of shopping centers along the highway southeast of town. The narrow main business thorofare—Washington Street—is a delight for strollers as well as shoppers. A barber shop with a much-used pot-bellied stove, an unspoiled old-time grocery store with a wooden floor and a beer bar, and a sporting goods store serving tap beer over a well-worn back bar illustrate the amiable authenticity of this still-vital commercial district.

Food Specialties

★ **Hershey Chocolate Plant**
35 mi. SW on Albers Rd. - Oakdale *847-0381*
Sprawling aromatically on wide-open farmlands just south of Oakdale is

a giant factory that supplies the entire West with Hershey chocolate. Half-hour guided tours pass mind-boggling, fully automated facilities used for making Hershey candies. Each visitor is given a Hershey milk chocolate bar at the end of the tour. Closed Sat.-Sun.

Riverbank Cheese Co.
39 mi. SW at 6603 2nd St. - Riverbank *869-4533*
Several cheeses are made here, including Teleme—a delicious creamy jack cheese first made by Greek-Americans. Visitors can purchase cheese to go or in gift packs in this modern little factory. Tours and samples are available on request.

★ **Sonka's Apple Ranch**
8 mi. SE via Tuolumne Rd. at 19200 Cherokee Rd. *928-4689*
Magnificent mile-high apple pie and other outstanding homemade apple pies, pastries and preserves, plus many varieties of apples (in season) are sold at this old-fashioned roadside farm.

Stanislaus Cheese Co.
39 mi. SW at 3141 Sierra Av. - Riverbank *869-2558*
Greek, Italian, and American cheeses, including Teleme, a delicious soft creamy Jack cheese, are made and sold in this casual little old-fashioned cheese factory, to go, or in gift packs. Tours and samples are available upon request.

Specialty Shops

★ ***Antiques***
The area is still a bonanza for antique hunters. A list of the many shops that feature Mother Lode memorabilia and antiques can be obtained at the Chamber of Commerce.

Charley's Washington Hall Books
downtown at 77 N. Washington St. *532-6242*
An amazing jumble of books and magazines is crammed into this tiny shop.

Heritage Books and Coffee Mill
downtown at 52 S. Washington St. *532-6261*
Books about the region are featured, and there is a casual coffee and pastry bar in the back. Closed Sun.

NIGHTLIFE

The Old West lives on in several remarkably authentic saloons in the historic downtown sections of Sonora, Murphys, Jamestown, and Columbia.

Fallon House Theatre
4 mi. N at Broadway/Washington Sts. - Columbia *532-4644*
Musicals, comedies, and dramas are staged by a repertory company in a historic restoration from spring thru fall. Closed Mon.-Wed. in winter.

★ **Gunn House**
downtown at 286 S. Washington St. *532-3421*
Hidden away in the back of the historic inn is a romantic and intimate bar with an impressive stone fireplace, plush Victorian furnishings and an ornate hardwood back bar.

★ **Hotel Willow**
3.5 mi. SW at Main & Willow Sts. - Jamestown *984-4388*
There is no hotel, but the building houses one of the most picturesque barrooms in the Mother Lode country. The authentically restored room includes an outstanding back bar and front bar that gold miners bellied up to well over a century ago, an ornate working Franklin stove, well-worn floorboards, hardwood bar stools, and period pictures.

★ **The Murphys Hotel Saloon**
18 mi. N on Main St. - Murphys *728-3444*
This classic saloon in a landmark hotel that has operated since 1856 is a Mother Lode favorite. Natives and visitors alike flock in on weekends for live music and to enjoy authentic Gold Camp atmosphere enhanced by a pot-bellied stove, a beautiful old back bar, an upright piano, and hardwood armchairs.

The 90s
downtown at 131 S. Washington St. *532-9963*
Poker, Lo-Ball, pool, and shuffleboard attract players into a casual, comfortable saloon dominated by one of the most splendid back bars anywhere.

Rawhide Saloon
3.5 mi. SW on CA 49 - Jamestown *984-5113*
Live music on weekends and the area's largest dance floor draw throngs. A large fireplace and several pool tables are other attractions of this rustic and rowdy roadhouse.

★ **St. Charles Saloon**
4 mi. N at 22801 Main St. - Columbia *533-4656*
This authentically restored old saloon is a fine place to drop in for a drink, to shoot pool, or to just relax in a wooden armchair and contemplate the handsome old back bar, the pot-bellied stove, or the well-worn hardwood floor.

Sonora Inn
downtown at 160 S. Washington St. *532-7468*
Live music and dancing are featured on weekends in the comfortably updated lounge of Sonora's landmark hotel.

RESTAURANTS

Most of the area's best restaurants are located in the historic downtown sections of Sonora and the tiny nearby Gold Rush towns. Hearty

American fare is emphasized, with a few cosmopolitan exceptions.

Bonavia's Yosemite Inn
9 mi. SW on CA 108 at Yosemite Jct. — *984-5847*
D only. — *Moderate*
Abundant American meals that include a relish plate, soup, salad, entree, beverage, and dessert are served in the casual dining room of a big modern roadhouse. In the next room is a relaxed firelit bar.

★ **City Hotel**
4 mi. N via Parrotts Ferry Rd. on Main St. - Columbia — *532-1479*
L-D. Closed Mon. — *Expensive*
Outstanding French cuisine is skillfully prepared from seasonally fresh ingredients and presented amid beautifully restored Victorian elegance in one of the most significant heirlooms of the Gold Rush days. A classic old-time saloon adjoins.

★ **Country Kitchen Cafe**
3.5 mi. SW at 18231 Main St. - Jamestown — *484-3326*
B-L. — *Moderate*
Assorted tasty croissants are given a tempting display and served with omelets and other breakfast specialties. Fudges and ice creams are also available, but the delicious homemade pies are the real crowd-pleasers in this cheerful cafe with a main street view.

The Eproson House Restaurant
12 mi. E on CA 108 - Twain Harte — *586-5600*
B-L-D. — *Moderate*
American and traditional Continental dishes are featured. A polished knotty pine interior, a wood-burning fireplace, and old-fashioned table settings give the dining room a feeling of country charm. Live entertainment and dancing are offered most nights in the firelit lounge.

Europa Coffee Shop
downtown at 275 S. Washington St. — *532-9957*
B-L-D. — *Low*
A large selection of very basic American dishes including homemade pies, plus a few Greek pastries, are prepared simply and served twenty-four hours every day in a homespun, old-fashioned coffee shop that hasn't changed much in more than forty years.

★ **Good Heavens - a Restaurant**
downtown at 51 N. Washington St. — *532-3663*
L only. D on Sat.-Sun. only. Closed Tues. — *Moderate*
The imaginative entrees, unusual soups and sandwiches, and homemade desserts offered on a short menu and on a frequently changing chalkboard are delicious. The warmly nostalgic atmosphere in this handsome little place is just right for a recently restored historic building on the main street.

★ **Hemingway's**
downtown at 362 S. Stewart Av. *532-4900*
L-D. Closed Sun.-Mon. *Expensive*
Creative Continental cuisine on a menu that changes daily has gotten this new restaurant off to a fine start. An older frame building was remodeled and expanded into casually elegant dining rooms.

Hotel Willow Restaurant
3.4 mi. SW on Main St. - Jamestown *984-4388*
L-D. No L on Sat. *Moderate*
American and Continental dishes are served in two plainly furnished dining rooms that still display glimmerings of their Victorian origins in polished wainscoating, wooden booths, and dark bentwood chairs. The outstanding saloon in the next room is a genuine reflection of the era.

★ **Il Refugio**
18 mi. N on CA 4/Main St. - Murphys *728-3964*
D only. Sun. brunch. Closed Tues.-Wed. *Moderate*
First-rate Northern Italian cuisine is the specialty in a sophisticated restaurant that recently relocated into larger quarters by the main highway. Intimate country decor has been retained.

Jamestown Hotel
3.5 mi. SW off CA 49 on Main St. - Jamestown *984-3902*
L-D. Sun. brunch. *Moderate*
International specialties are served in a dining room furnished in updated period decor and on a large, screened, street-front patio. Victorian-style reproductions are also used in an adjoining bar and in the small upstairs guest rooms of this recently remodeled hotel.

Kinland Cove Restaurant
2.5 mi. E at CA 108/Tuolumne Rd. *532-0193*
L-D. No L on Sat.-Sun. Closed Mon. *Moderate*
A fish market out in front sells seasonally fresh fish and shellfish which are also the specialties served in the casual, nautically themed dining room. The modern bar in the next room is a tribute to ballooning.

The Kitchen
3.5 mi. SW off CA 49 at 18258 Main St. - Jamestown *984-3573*
B-L. *Low*
American favorites are given a down-home treatment in this humble, popular little cafe.

Manzanita Bar & Grill
downtown at 83 S. Stewart St. *533-8224*
L-D. *Moderate*
In this new downtown restaurant, a chalkboard menu describes offerings of seafoods and meats prepared on a mesquite grill. Desserts are tantalizingly displayed to one side of a well-furnished dining area that is also bordered by a well-stocked salad bar and an exhibition kitchen.

The Miners Shack
downtown at 157 S. Washington St. *532-5252*
B-L. *Low*
Many omelets are offered all day as the feature among all-American short order foods served in this plain little cafe.

Murphys Hotel
18 mi. N on Main St. - Murphys *728-3444*
B-L-D. *Moderate*
Steaks and other American dishes (like liver and onions) are emphasized in the remodeled dining room of a restored pre-Civil War hotel.

National Hotel
3.4 mi. SW off CA 49 on Main St. - Jamestown *984-3446*
L-D. Closed Tues. *Moderate*
American and Italian dishes are served amid mining camp decor in the large dining room of a carefully restored pre-Civil War hotel, or in a tranquil vine-covered courtyard when weather permits. An authentic little Gold Camp saloon is next door.

★ **The Smoke Cafe**
3.4 mi. SW off CA 49 on Main St. - Jamestown *984-3733*
D only. Closed Mon. *Low*
Specialties from all regions of Mexico are carefully prepared and enthusiastically enjoyed by patrons in a spiffy update of a Victorian dining room and a charming adjoining bar in a historic building.

★ **Villa d'Oro**
12 mi. NE at 23036 Joaquin Gulley Rd. - Twain Harte *586-2182*
L-D. No L on Sat. & Sun. *Moderate*
Generous Italian dinners with antipasto, soup, salad, entree, and dessert are skillfully prepared and served in a casually furnished split-level dining room accented by a wood-burning fireplace and hanging plants. Low priced smaller dinners are also available.

LODGING

There aren't many places to stay in the Sonora area. But, visitors do have a real choice among authentically furnished historic hotels, bed-and-breakfast inns, or modern motels with contemporary amenities. Rates are usually at least 10% lower than those shown during the fall-to-spring off-season, except on weekends.

Barretta Gardens Inn
.5 mi. S at 700 S. Barretta St. *532-6039*
A new bed-and-breakfast inn has been created from a turn-of-the-century home on a hillside overlooking Sonora and the inn's lovely gardens. A full-course breakfast and afternoon beverage are

complimentary.
"Periwinkle"—spacious, downstairs, private bath, Q bed...$56
"Iris"—bright upstairs room, tranquil view, shared bath, Q bed...$56
regular room—upstairs, shared bath, Q bed...$50

City Hotel
4 mi. N on Main St. (Box 1870) - Columbia 95310 *532-1479*
Built in the midst of the Gold Rush, this small two-story brick hotel remains a landmark of that era. Several years ago the building was completely restored. It once again serves as a gracious Victorian hotel with one of the West's finest dining rooms and an atmospheric Old West saloon. Each bedroom has a toilet and marble sink, and there is a hall shower. A complimentary Continental breakfast is offered.
"Balcony Suite"—corner, above bar, main street view, elaborately woodcrafted antique D bed...$65
#9—end, quiet, 2 large windows with private hill view, D bed...$55
regular room— 2 T or D bed...$55

★ **Gunn House**
downtown at 286 S. Washington St. *532-3421*
Many additions have been made to the original two-story adobe built in 1851, including a large landscaped oval pool and a plush intimate bar. Each room is furnished with some Gold Rush era antiques—plus an unobtrusive phone, cable TV, and a bathroom. A Continental breakfast is complimentary.
#18,#22—corner, windows on 2 sides, balc. walkway, Q bed...$41
regular room— D bed...$35

★ **Jameson's**
9.3 mi. E via CA 108 at 22157 Feather River Dr. *532-1248*
A modern wood-trimmed home in a near-wilderness shaded by majestic oak and pine trees is now a tranquil bed-and-breakfast inn. Small waterfalls flow under the house which was built on top of enormous boulders. A complimentary Continental breakfast usually includes fresh Irish soda bread or scones fresh from the oven. Each room shares a bath and is beautifully furnished.
"Bridal Suite"—spacious, exotic Arabian Nights decor, Q bed...$60
"Charmaine"—French decor, overlooks a waterfall, Q bed...$45
regular room— D or Q bed...$45

Mountain View Motel
2 mi. SE on CA 108 at 1642 Mono Way *532-4961*
This frayed, older single-level motel is a **bargain**. There is an outdoor pool, and each room has a TV.
regular room— D or Q bed...$29

The National Hotel
3.5 mi. SW on Main St. (Box 502) - Jamestown 95327 *984-3446*
One of the Mother Lode's oldest continuously operated hotels (1859)

has been nicely restored. Downstairs are an atmospheric dining room and saloon, and a garden courtyard where a free Continental breakfast is served when weather permits. Each comfortably furnished room has a brass bed and an antique washbasin. TVs are available upon request.

#3,#2—corner windows, private bath, public balcony, Q bed...$45
regular room—shared bath, T or Q bed...$35

Oasis Motel

4 mi. E on CA 108 at 3535 Mono Way *533-1886*

This tiny old single-level motel is a **bargain** with an outdoor pool and whirlpool. Each of the recently refurbished, plainly furnished rooms has a B/W TV.

regular room— D bed...$30

Rail Fence Motel

5 mi. E at 19950 CA 108 *532-9191*

In a country setting, this modern little motel has a pool and a hot tub. A Continental breakfast is offered. Each room has a color TV.

regular room— Q bed...$39

Royal Hotel

3.5 mi. SW off CA 49 on Main St. - Jamestown 95327 *984-5271*

This newly restored little 1920s hotel in the heart of Jamestown features plush blue carpet and attractive wallpaper, updated furnishings, plus some private bathrooms. A Continental breakfast is complimentary.

"Royal Room"—private bath, corner, balcony above main street, town view windows, Q bed...$55
regular room—private bath, D bed...$49
regular room—shared bath, 2 T or D bed...$44

The Ryan House

downtown at 153 S. Shepherd St. *533-3445*

A classic pre-Civil War frame home has been skillfully restored and converted into a picturesque bed-and-breakfast inn in a rose garden. Each of the four guest rooms is furnished in antiques and handsome reproductions. A complimentary Continental breakfast is served in the dining room or outdoors in summer.

"Sun Room"—private bath, bright & cheerful, D bed...$60
"Garden Room"—shared bath, pleasant view, Q bed...$55
regular room—shared bath, D bed...$45

Sonora Inn

downtown at 160 S. Washington St. *532-7468*

In an era when downtown hotels are being converted or replaced, this big old landmark still serves as the county's only full service hotel. Amenities include an outdoor pool, an indoor whirlpool, and a large, nicely refurbished restaurant and lounge. The hotel units are well-worn, but there is an upgraded motel section across a street by a creek. Each

room has a phone, color TV, and bathroom.
#31,#32—in newer motel section, only rooms with creek view/sound, K bed...$43
#201—corner, spacious, in hotel, overlooking main street, K bed...$43
regular room—in hotel, small, frayed, D bed...$36

Sonora Oaks Motor Hotel - Best Western
3.5 mi. E on CA 108 at Hess Av. *533-4400*
The area's newest motor hotel is located in gentle hill country. A noble oak shades a courtyard pool and whirlpool. A restaurant and lounge are adjacent. Each of the spacious, nicely appointed rooms has a balcony or patio, cable color TV with movies, and a phone. For toll-free reservations, call (800)528-1234.
regular room— Q bed...$60

Sonora Towne House I & II
downtown at 350 S. Washington St. *532-3633*
Sonora's largest accommodation is a modern motel complex with two outdoor pools, a hot tub, and coffee shop. Each nicely furnished room has a phone and cable color TV with movies. For toll-free reservations in California, call (800)251-1538.
regular room— K bed...$49
regular room— D bed...$45

CAMPGROUNDS

There are several campgrounds in the area. Outstanding water-oriented campgrounds have been provided on nearby Don Pedro reservoir.

★ **Flaming Meadows**
25 mi. S via CA 108 & La Grange Rd. *852-2396*
The Don Pedro Recreation Area operates a spacious campground on grassy oak-and-pine-shaded slopes near the dam on Don Pedro reservoir. An unusually attractive sandy beach and swimming lagoon, boating (plus rentals, ramp, and dock), houseboating, sailing, water-skiing, and fishing attract campers to this end of the big, popular lake. Flush toilets, hot showers, and hookups are available. Each tree-shaded site has a picnic table and fire area. base rate...$7

★ **Moccasin Point**
15 mi. S on CA 49 at Jacksonville Rd. *852-2396*
The Don Pedro Recreation Area operates this sprawling campground on grassy oak-and-pine-shaded slopes above scenic Don Pedro reservoir. Boating (plus rentals, ramp, and dock), water-skiing, sailing, houseboating, swimming, and fishing are enjoyed on the big lake, and there are hiking trails on the adjoining oak-and-pine-studded hills. Flush toilets, hot showers, and hookups are available. Each well-spaced, tree-shaded site has a lake view, picnic table, raised fireplace, grill, and food storage box. base rate...$7

SPECIAL EVENT

Mother Lode Round-up *fairgrounds* *early May*
The Sheriff's Posse sponsors a colorful weekend of Western festivities, including a parade, rodeo, and live entertainment to celebrate Mother's Day.

OTHER INFORMATION

Area Code: *209*

Zip Code: *95370*

Tuolumne County Visitors Bureau
downtown at 16 W. Stockton Rd. (Box 4020) *984-4636*

Stanislaus National Forest - Supervisor's Office
1.5 mi. E at 19777 Greenley Rd. *532-3671*

South Lake Tahoe

For sheer exhilaration, South Lake Tahoe is matchless. This sprawling boom town is ideally situated in a lush pine forest along the southern shore of one of nature's most sublime high mountain lakes. Here is the greatest concentration anywhere of outdoor and indoor leisure pursuits. To the delight of some and the dismay of others, the civilization of that urbane enclave is so complete that fun-lovers can keep busy twenty-four hours a day, year-round—indoors. Fortunately, even more attention has been given to providing recreation facilities and access to the magnificent surroundings, which are perfectly complemented by the right weather during two notable seasons. Warm, sunny days with very little chance of rain attract teeming hordes of visitors to the Lake Tahoe area every summer. In town, there are long sandy beaches for swimming and sunbathing. Several marinas offer outstanding sportfishing, boating, water-skiing, and sailing, plus a remarkable variety of sightseeing cruises. Nearby state parks, national forests, and a wilderness area provide a diversity of other outdoor recreation opportunities in inspiring lake shore and mountain settings. Scenic golf and tennis facilities, miles of separated bicycle paths, and an aerial tramway ride are among diversions in town that compete with a cluster of grandiose casinos just across the Nevada state line. Winter is the other peak season. Usually enormous snowfalls are well-suited to downhill and cross-country skiing and a wealth of other snow sports. Excellent facilities have been provided throughout the area. In-town facilities range from a first-rate snow play hill to the base of the nation's largest alpine skiing complex. The wide-angle view of the lake and Sierra from the top of the lifts is spellbinding in winter or summer.

Development occurred slowly along the south shore after the first settlement in the late nineteenth century. It wasn't until the 1950s that construction of major casinos at the state line signaled the beginning of year-round action, and development of an enormous skiing complex soon established the town as a winter sports capital. More than two-thirds of the total population surrounding the lake now lives in South Lake Tahoe.

Fortunately, much of the sylvan beauty of the setting has been retained. Towering pines are still abundant, even along the business strip. There is no traditional heart of town where business and government are focused. Instead, a tight cluster of high-rise casinos on the Nevada side of the state line anchors an awesome proliferation of visitor-related facilities at the town's eastern extremity. As a result, the hustle and bustle of around-the-clock gambling and big-name entertainment are only a stroll away from the relative tranquility of one of the West's largest and most sophisticated concentrations of lodgings. Restaurants are also abundant. A small but increasing number offer gourmet cuisine or spectacular views. Shops are surprisingly ordinary and scattered, but there are some good sources of outdoor recreation equipment.

Elevation:

6,260 feet

Population (1980):

20,681

Population (1970):

12,921

Location:

192 miles Northeast of San Francisco

WEATHER PROFILE

Vokac Weather Rating

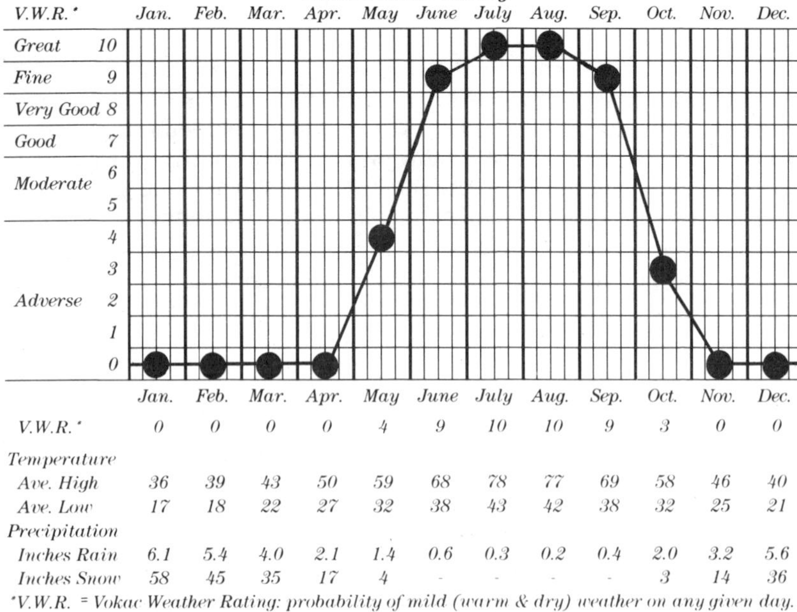

	Jan.	Feb.	Mar.	Apr.	May	June	July	Aug.	Sep.	Oct.	Nov.	Dec.
*V.W.R.**	0	0	0	0	4	9	10	10	9	3	0	0
Temperature												
Ave. High	36	39	43	50	59	68	78	77	69	58	46	40
Ave. Low	17	18	22	27	32	38	43	42	38	32	25	21
Precipitation												
Inches Rain	6.1	5.4	4.0	2.1	1.4	0.6	0.3	0.2	0.4	2.0	3.2	5.6
Inches Snow	58	45	35	17	4	-	-	-	-	3	14	36

**V.W.R. = Vokac Weather Rating: probability of mild (warm & dry) weather on any given day.*

Forecast

Month	*V.W.R.**		*Temperatures* *Daytime*	*Evening*	*Precipitation*
Jan.	0	Adverse	chilly	cold	frequent snowstorms
Feb.	0	Adverse	chilly	cold	frequent snowstorms
Mar.	0	Adverse	chilly	cold	occasional snowstorms
Apr.	0	Adverse	cool	chilly	occasional snowstorms
May	4	Adverse	cool	chilly	infrequent rainstorms/snow flurries
June	9	Fine	warm	cool	infrequent rainstorms
July	10	Great	warm	cool	negligible
Aug.	10	Great	warm	cool	none
Sep.	9	Fine	warm	cool	negligible
Oct.	3	Adverse	cool	chilly	infrequent downpours/snow flurries
Nov.	0	Adverse	chilly	chilly	occasional snowstorms
Dec.	0	Adverse	chilly	cold	occasional snowstorms

Summary

Well over a mile high on the southern shore of one of the world's most beautiful big alpine lakes, South Lake Tahoe has a classic two season climate. **Winter** is chilly, snowy, and ideal for all winter sports. In fact, snowfalls are usually heavier than in any other great town except Tahoe City, at the other end of the lake, which shares the same winter wonderland. **Spring** is a continuation of winter weather until May, when there is a short muddy transition with cool breezy days and occasional snowfalls through Memorial Day. All of the best weather is concentrated into **summer**. In this splendid season, warm sunny days, cool evenings, and inconsequential rainfall assure hassle-free comfort while exploring America's most renowned lake-and-mountain playground. With the arrival of **fall**, the weather quickly becomes unusable. Temperatures cool rapidly; and unpredictable, increasingly heavy rainfalls are replaced by snowstorms that normally provide the base for outstanding skiing after Thanksgiving.

ATTRACTIONS & DIVERSIONS

Aerial Tramway

Heavenly Valley Ski Resort
2 mi. S via Ski Run Blvd. on Saddle Rd. *544-6263*

An enclosed gondola lifts passengers more than 2,000 feet above the lake via an aerial tramway. Panoramas of the lake and mountains are magnificent. Indoor and outdoor view dining is featured at the Top of the Tram Restaurant (L-D June-Sept.; L only Nov.-Apr.).

★ ***Bicycling***

There are several miles of exclusive bike paths in and near town over relatively flat, safe, and scenic terrain. The best segment is almost four miles of paved trail through a pine forest near south shore beaches. There are several bike rental shops. Among these are:

Anderson's Bicycle Rental *6 mi. SW at 645 CA 89* *541-0500*
The Clean Machine *1.6 mi. SW at 3542 Lake Tahoe Blvd.* *544-2453*
The Outdoorsman *4 mi. SW at 2358 US 50* *541-0224*
Sierra Cycle Works *1.7 mi. SW at 3430 US 50* *541-7505*

★ ***Boat Rentals***

Every kind of boating imaginable can be enjoyed on more than two hundred square miles of crystal-clear water. Visitors can rent an extraordinary assortment of craft—fishing boats, ski or cruising boats, sailboats, catamarans, canoes, or windsurf boards—by the hour or longer at several marina facilities, including:

Camp Richardson *8 mi. W at 1900 Jameson Beach Rd.* *541-1777*
Jet and Sail Rentals *1 mi. SW at foot of Ski Run Blvd.* *544-7240*
Moped Place (skeeterboats) *1.7 mi. SW at 3131 Harrison* *544-7160*
Ski Run Marina (para-sailing) *1 mi. SW on Ski Run Blvd.* *544-0200*
Timber Cove Marina *1.7 mi. SW at 3411 US 50* *544-2942*
Windsurf, Tahoe *1 mi. SW at foot of Ski Run Blvd.* *544-7240*
Zephyr Cove Sailing Center *4 mi. N - Zephyr Cove* *(702)588-3369*

Boat Rides

★ **Lake Tahoe Cruises**
1 mi. SW at foot of Ski Run Blvd. *541-4652*

Large modern sightseeing boats with glass bottom windows cruise four times daily, including a dinner-dance cruise, to Emerald Bay.

★ **Miss Tahoe Cruises**
downtown at 828 Park Av. *541-3364*

This big modern vessel has a glass bottom window. There are daily trips to Emerald Bay and a sunset dinner-dance cruise each evening. The ship operates year-round.

★ **M.S. Dixie**
4 mi. N off US 50 on Zephyr Av. *(702)588-3508*
A paddlewheeler with a 350-passenger capacity offers live music for dancing in the cocktail lounge, and steak dinners for evening cruises to Emerald Bay. The glass-bottom view is popular on morning and afternoon trips daily from May thru October.

★ **Woodwind**
4 mi. N off US 50 on Zephyr Av. *(702)588-3000*
Sailing excursions are scheduled four times daily to Emerald Bay aboard a large trimaran with glass bottom windows. A sunset cruise features complimentary champagne.

★ **Desolation Wilderness**
12 mi. W off CA 89 *544-6420*
Approximately eighty named lakes lie amid a "desolation" of huge boulders and glacier-polished granite slopes nearly devoid of trees in mountains that reach almost 10,000 feet above sea level. There are also clear streams, vast pine forests, and fields of wildflowers accessed by more than fifty miles of trails. Summer backpacking and camping are so popular that a campsite reservation system is in effect from mid-June to Labor Day. Horses and guides are available nearby for overnight, and longer, pack trips into the wilderness. Information and permits are available at the Eldorado National Forest Visitor Center.

★ **D.L. Bliss State Park**
15 mi. NW on CA 89 *525-7277*
The park offers excellent hiking trails and swimming off one of the lake's finest beaches. A large forested campground is situated by the lake just north of Emerald Bay.

★ **Eldorado Beach**
2 mi. SW at US 50 & Harrison Av. *544-3317*
This half-mile long sandy beach is a favorite place for sunbathing and swimming with splendid views of the magnificent mountain-rimmed lake.

★ **Emerald Bay State Park**
11 mi. NW on CA 89 *541-3030*
The most famous landmark of Lake Tahoe is Emerald Bay, which includes the lake's only island—Fannette. Cut into mountain slopes high above the water, the highway around the bay provides panoramic views that are unforgettable. A mile-long footpath from Inspiration Point leads steeply down to the shore, where Vikingsholm, a thirty-eight room mansion, can be toured during the summer. It was built in 1929 as a summer residence patterned after a Viking's castle. At the head of the bay is a parking area for a worthwhile shore hike up to Eagle Falls. Scenic picnic sites are nearby. On the bay's east side is a large sylvan campground, with fishing, boating, and a swimming beach nearby.

★ ***Flying***

Executive Aero Systems

6 mi. SW via US 50 at South Lake Tahoe Airport — *541-7820*

Thrilling overviews of Lake Tahoe and the High Sierra can be reserved here daily. A longer (1.5 hour) flight gives passengers an unforgettable bird's-eye view of both Tahoe and Yosemite Park.

Golf

★ **Edgewood Tahoe Golf Course**

.3 mi. N on Loop Rd. — *(702)588-3566*

Between the lake and the casino district, this scenic and relatively level 18-hole championship golf course is open to the public with all facilities, rentals, and services.

★ **Lake Tahoe Country Club**

8 mi. S on US 50 — *577-0788*

A relatively flat and well-tended 18-hole championship golf course on the upper Truckee River is open to the public with complete facilities, rentals, and services.

★ ***Hiking***

Hundreds of miles of scenic hiking trails have been provided by the U.S. Forest Service and the State Parks Department to give visitors access to magnificent wilderness valleys, mountain peaks, and sandy beaches. Maps, information, backpacks, and tents (no sleeping bags) can be rented at:

The Outdoorsman

4 mi. SW at 2358 US 50 — *541-1660*

★ ***Horseback Riding***

Quiet, wooded trails are found throughout the Tahoe basin. Several riding stables are located near town. All offer horse rentals by the hour, half day, or day. Most also provide guides for riders on breakfast, dinner, or moonlight rides, and for fishing or pack trips.

Camp Richardson's Corral *8 mi. W on CA 89* — *541-3113*
Cascade Stables *11 mi. NW via CA 89 on Cascade Rd.* — *541-2055*
Stateline Stable (guide optional) *downtown on US 50* — *541-0962*
Sunset Corral (guide optional) *7 mi. SW on US 50* — *541-9944*
Zephyr Cove Stables (guide optional) *4 mi. N* — *(702)588-6136*

★ **Lake Tahoe**

the northern border of town

Straddling the California/Nevada state line 6,229 feet above sea level is a mountain-rimmed lake that is one of nature's grandest achievements. The water is said to be so pure that a white dinner plate can be seen at a depth of well over one hundred feet. Lake Tahoe is the largest deep alpine lake on the continent. In fact, with its twenty-two mile length, twelve mile width, and maximum depth of 1,645 feet, the lake's volume would cover the entire state of California with more than a foot of pure water. But statistics can't do justice to this serious contender for the world's most beautiful water body. It's also one of the most usable, with a remarkable assortment of watercraft available for rent, charter, or tours, plus a proliferation of onshore recreation facilities to better enjoy the forests, sandy beaches, dramatic bouldered coves, and the river, streams, and mountains that surround the lake. A seventy-two mile highway loop around the lake is immodestly described by the South Lake Tahoe Visitor's Bureau as "The Most Beautiful Drive in America" on their map and guide describing points of interest along the route.

★ **Lake Tahoe State Park**

starts 13 mi. NE via US 50 on NV 28 *(702)588-4180*

Several miles of the lake's northeastern shoreline are included in this large Nevada park. Pine-shaded picnic grounds near picturesque granite boulders and sandy beaches are popular, along with fishing and boating—launching facilities are provided.

★ **Lake Tahoe Visitor Center**

8 mi. W on CA 89 *544-6420*

The U.S. Forest Service provides an ingeniously designed underground stream profile chamber here, giving visitors an opportunity to look through glass windows into a large pool on Taylor Creek to watch trout pass. Also in summer months, self-guided trails and guided nature walks originate from here. In winter, guided cross-country ski tours are featured. This is the best place to get information about the Eldorado National Forest and the Desolation Wilderness Area.

★ ***Library***

2 mi. SW at 1000 Rufus Allen Blvd. *544-4416*

The South Lake Tahoe branch of the El Dorado County Library is in a large contemporary building with picture window views through a pine forest to the lake. The well-furnished facility includes an inviting periodical reading area with fabric-backed armchairs and sofas. Closed Sun.-Mon.

★ ***Moped Rentals***

An exhilarating, relatively effortless way to enjoy the scenic roads around the lake is on a moped. Hourly and longer rentals can be arranged at several shops in town, including:

Country Moped, Inc. *5.5 mi. SW at 800 CA 89* *544-3500*
The Moped Place *2 mi. SW at 3131 US 50* *544-7160*

★ ***Nude Beaches***

starting 17 mi. NE via US 50 & NV 28

More than two miles of the lake's remote northeastern shoreline is a popular swimming-suits-optional area. Picturesque granite boulders and numerous tiny sandy beaches are backed by steep forested hills. Park off the road wherever there are clusters of cars. Sandy trails lead down to the beach from these informal parking areas.

★ **Regan Beach**
2.5 mi. SW at the foot of Sacramento Av. *541-4611*
A grassy area above this sandy beach is a favorite for sunbathing and sightseeing.

South Lake Tahoe Recreation Center
2 mi. SW at 1180 Rufus Allen Blvd. *541-4611*
A large heated swimming pool (enclosed in winter) is open to the public year-round. This impressive contemporary center also includes a gymnasium, game room, and exercise room. Closed Sun.

★ ***Sportfishing***
Several sportfishing boats are available daily (year-round) for guided excursions in search of big trout and kokanee. The following operators offer all necessary services and equipment:

Dennis's Fishing Charters *577-6834*
Lake Tahoe Excursions *541-7177*
Tahoe Sportsfishing *541-5448*

Warm Water Features

★ **Nephele Restaurant**
1 mi. SW at 1169 Ski Run Blvd. *544-8130*
Hot tubs with whirlpool jets can be rented hourly in attractively furnished private rooms with stereo music and towels. Cocktail service is on-call. Each of the roofless rooms has a fine pine-top view.

★ **Shingle Creek Hot Tubs**
1 mi. SW at 1142 Ski Run Blvd. *544-5400*
Patrons can select any of six nicely decorated private outside enclosures, each with a pine-top view, hot tub with therapy jets, piped-in stereo music, and towels. Cocktails may be ordered through room service.

Winter Sports

★ **Hansen's Resort**
1.5 mi. S at 1360 Ski Run Blvd. *544-3361*
A toboggan and saucer hill with banked turns and packed runs is open daily in winter with a mechanical lift to return toboggans to the top of the hill. All equipment can be rented.

★ **Heavenly Valley Ski Resort**
2 mi. S via Ski Run Blvd. on Saddle Rd. *541-1330*
America's largest ski area sprawls into two states and covers more than twenty square miles of varying terrain with runs up to seven miles long. Spellbinding views of both Lake Tahoe and the Carson Valley are accessed by sixteen chairlifts (including two triple chairs) and a gondola. The vertical drop is more than 4,000 feet. Both day and night skiing are available on well-groomed slopes designed for every range of ability. Helicopter skiing can be arranged, and excellent cross-country trails are nearby. The aerial tramway also operates during summer months to a scenic observation platform and restaurant.

★ ***Skiing***

Three downhill ski areas surround town, and twenty-two are within a fifty mile radius. Four cross-country skiing centers are located near the south shore. The remarkable number and quality of facilities is closely correlated to the breathtakingly beautiful and endlessly varied terrain. Ski rental equipment and lessons for both downhill and cross-country skiing are available at most of the major ski areas. In addition, almost a dozen places in town sell and rent all kinds of skiing equipment, and have maps and information on all areas.

Sleigh Rides

downtown near the High Sierra Hotel *541-2953*

During the winter months, visitors can bundle up for a forty minute horse-drawn sleigh ride to a high plateau for a panoramic lake view.

Tahoe Paradise Snowmobiles

9 mi. S on US 50 *577-2121*

Snowmobiles can be rented for use on an area that is groomed daily.

SHOPPING

South Lake Tahoe has no central business district or conventional downtown. Instead, a full range of shops is strung out along a five-mile strip between the "Y" (intersection of US 50 and CA 89) and the state line where huge hotel/casinos in Nevada border the largest concentration of businesses in South Lake Tahoe. Because the skyscraper hotels are the area's dominant visual reference, the state line area is referred to as "downtown."

Food Specialties

★ **The Cork & More**

2.4 mi. SW at 1032 Al Tahoe Blvd. *544-5253*

Wine tastings and an impressive selection of all-California wines are featured, along with gourmet foods and accessories, in a large new culinary haven.

★ **Cream Puff Bakery**

3.9 mi. SW at US 50/Sierra Blvd. *544-2090*

Delicious and distinctive pastries, cakes, cookies, and breads, plus some fine European specialties, are sold to go, or with coffee at a few tables. Another outlet is located downtown in the Crescent V Center.

★ **Dart Discount Liquors**

.4 mi. N at US 50/NV 19 *(702)588-5187*

More than 700 wine labels, plus hundreds of liquors, are deeply discounted in this big, modern store.

Dunk-N-Spice Donuts

4.4 mi. SW at 2122 US 50 *541-2029*

A distinctive assortment of delicious donuts is displayed in this independently owned little carryout.

Holland's Donut Factory
4.3 mi. SW at 2180 US 50 — *541-6044*
This large new donut factory offers all kinds of donuts to go or with coffee at several tables.

★ **Liquor Barn**
1.6 mi. SW at 3473 US 50 — *541-6063*
Hundreds of premium California and other wines, plus liquors, are discounted in this big, bright store.

Sweet Inspiration
5 mi. SW on US 50/CA 89 — *542-1906*
Tucked away in the South Y Shopping Center is a small store with many cheeses, smoked meats and sausages, other gourmet foods, and a good selection of beer and wine.

Specialty Shops

Hot Gossip
1 mi. SW on US 50 at 1007 Ski Run Blvd. — *541-4823*
This tiny shop caters to a variety of needs with a thoughtful mixture of magazines and newspapers, plus assorted coffees, espresso, and pastries that can be enjoyed at a few tables.

M's Books & Gifts
downtown at 1075 Park Av. — *544-3262*
Good selections of regional interest and travel books are nicely displayed in this store. Closed Sun.

★ **The Outdoorsman of Lake Tahoe**
4 mi. SW at 2358 US 50 — *541-1660*
One of the West's largest and most complete sporting goods stores sells everything the recreationist could desire including clothing, equipment, and reading material. They also rent selected backpacking, bicycling, and skiing gear in season. The store's awesome centerpiece is a nine-foot tall trophy polar bear.

Sierra Bookshop
5 mi. SW on US 50 at 1072 Emerald Bay Rd. — *541-6464*
A large selection of books and topographic maps are for sale in this shopping center store, and at the Bijou outlet at 3443 US 50.

NIGHTLIFE

The third largest and most compact cluster of casinos in the West (after Reno and Las Vegas) is only a stroll from dozens of motels in town. As a result, there is non-stop gambling action, and more "name" entertainment year-round in major showrooms than in any other great town. Also, drinking and dancing places are notably diverse, ranging from elegant to rustic and from rowdy to relatively serene.

★ **Caesar's Tahoe**
downtown on US 50 at Stateline — *(702)588-3515*
This huge hotel/casino, clone of the Las Vegas operation, has a

prodigious assortment of extravagent facilities offering live entertainment, dancing, and non-stop gambling. Name entertainment is featured in the elaborate Cascade Showroom, while the Crystal Cabaret offers revues, comedy, and music.

★ **Christiania Inn**
2 mi. SW via Ski Run Blvd. on Saddle Av. *544-7337*
A charming little inn at the Heavenly Valley Ski Area offers a perfect place for a peaceful respite from the casino action. Several intimate areas have been created in a multilevel lounge with a handsome stone fireplace, an intriguing wine cellar window wall, and a posh assortment of sofas and easy chairs.

★ **Harrah's Tahoe**
downtown on US 50 at Stateline *(702)588-6611*
The superstar of Tahoe resort casinos has an outstanding array of entertainment facilities, in addition to a cavernous high-tech gambling casino. The South Shore Room is a first-class, big-name dinner theater. The Stateline Cabaret features quality lounge acts nightly. Above it all, the Summit Lounge offers live background music and breathtaking panoramas of the lake and mountains from the contemporary opulence of an 18th floor hideaway that is an unforgettable setting for a romantic interlude.

★ **Harvey's Resort Hotel**
downtown on US 50 at Stateline *(702)588-2411*
This large hotel/casino offers non-stop gambling on the ground floor. On the top floor (11th), the Top of the Wheel features cocktails, dining, and dancing nightly, plus good views of Lake Tahoe. Exotic Polynesian drinks and decor are offered in the adjacent Tiki Lounge.

★ **High Sierra Hotel/Casino**
downtown on US 50 at Stateline *(702)588-6211*
In addition to an improved name (it was once the Tahoe Sahara), this high-rise hotel/casino has an impressive variety of entertainment facilities as well as non-stop gambling. The Pine Cone Lounge offers cabaret-style acts nightly. Lily's Dance Hall features music for dancing and listening.

RESTAURANTS

An abundance of restaurants in and near town offer casually prepared fare in a variety of styles. Gourmet cuisine is surprisingly scarce. However, several dining rooms provide stylish high-country decor, and several have splendid views of Lake Tahoe.

Caesar's Tahoe
downtown on US 50 at Stateline *(702)588-3515*
Within the grandiose hotel/casino complex are several major specialty restaurants. The ***Edgewood*** *(D only. Closed Sun.-Mon.—Very Expensive)* features New California cuisine and plush decor. The

Evergreen buffet *(D only. Sat. & Sun. brunch.—Low)* is a bargain. The most innovative restaurant is the posh ***Alpine Cafe*** *(Sat. & Sun. brunch only—Moderate)* located in a fanciful boulder-strewn corner of a bright and airy room that includes a large lagoon-style swimming pool with an impressive swim-under intermittent waterfall.

The Chart House
1.5 mi. NE on NV 207 — *(702)588-6276*
D only. — *Expensive*
Contemporary American fare (prime rib, steaks, seafood, salad bar) is offered at this first-rate representative of a restaurant chain. But, the main attraction is an awe-inspiring view of Lake Tahoe from picture windows in the big stylish dining room high on a hill east of town. The view from the comfortable lounge is also impressive.

★ **Chez Villaret**
6 mi. SW at 536 CA 89 — *541-7868*
D only. — *Very Expensive*
Nouvelle French cuisine is skillfully prepared and served in an intimate, formally elegant dinner house.

★ **Christiania Inn**
2 mi. S via Ski Run Blvd. on Saddle Rd. — *544-7337*
D only. — *Expensive*
Skillfully prepared Continental cuisine is complemented by romantic contemporary furnishings including a picture window view of a wine cellar and a great stone fireplace. There is also an outstanding handcrafted lounge.

The Cook Book
5.5 mi. W at 787 CA 89 — *541-8400*
B-L. D in summer only. — *Expensive*
An elaborate menu of big, expensive omelets is served with uninspired accompaniments amidst casual country decor. A selected few diners may enjoy the wood-burning fireplace in this once-highly-regarded roadside restaurant.

★ **Cuckoos Nest Cafe**
3.9 mi. SW at 2502 US 50 — *541-0873*
L-D. No L fall-spring. — *Expensive*
Ample portions of European specialties are carefully prepared from scratch, and served in small, informally elegant dining rooms where the tables are unusually well spaced.

The Dory's Oar
2 mi. SW at 1041 Fremont Av. — *541-6603*
L-D. No L on Sat. & Sun. — *Moderate*
Live Maine lobsters, soft shell Maryland crabs, blue point oysters, and steamed clams are featured with a limited salad bar in a casual, family-oriented seafood restaurant.

★ **The Driftwood Cafe**
downtown at 4115 Laurel Av. — *544-6545*
B-L. Closed Wed. — *Moderate*
Distinctive omelets and some unusual specialties like cashew banana nut waffles highlight the light fare offered in this pleasant little cafe where breakfast is featured all day.

Frank's Restaurant
6 mi. SW at 1207 US 50 — *544-3434*
B-L. — *Moderate*
A huge menu describes all kinds of waffles, hot cakes, and omelets in an old-fashioned all-American roadside coffee shop.

The Fresh Ketch
5.5 mi. SW via Tahoe Keys Blvd. at 2435 Venice Dr. E — *541-5683*
L-D. Sat. & Sun. brunch. — *Expensive*
Seafood is emphasized in a large handsome restaurant with several casually elegant rooms overlooking Tahoe Keys Marina and the lake. The marina-view lounge has plush seating and a wood-burning fireplace.

The Greenhouse
downtown at 4140 Cedar Av. — *541-5800*
D only. — *Expensive*
Old-fashioned Continental fare is served amidst decor highlighted by a gas-lit fireplace, stained glass, and hanging plants. A copper-top bar lends interest to an adjoining cozy lounge.

★ **Harrah's Tahoe**
downtown on US 50 at Stateline — *(702)588-6611*
Lake Tahoe's most distinguished hotel/casino has eight restaurants. Three are especially notable. The ***Summit*** *(D only—Very Expensive)* presents Continental cuisine with a nouvelle touch in a formal, opulent setting with a magnificent 18th floor view of Lake Tahoe and the high Sierra. The ***Forest*** *(B-L-D. Only brunch on Sun.—Moderate)* features the finest buffet on the lake amidst unusual gilded forest decor in an 18th floor dining room with panoramic mountain and lake views. The ***South Shore Room*** *(D only—Expensive)* combines dinner with exclusively "big name" entertainment in a grandiose showroom. ***Friday's Station Steak House*** *(L-D—Expensive)* highlights brick oven gourmet pizza for lunch, plus steak and seafoods and wine by the glass.

Harvey's Resort Hotel
downtown on US 50 at Stateline — *(702)588-2411*
Three specialty restaurants highlight the area's oldest major hotel/casino. The ***Top of the Wheel*** *(D only. Sun. brunch—Expensive)* offers Polynesian and American dishes with a panoramic lake view. The ***Sage Room Steak House*** *(D only—Expensive)* features beef in an atmosphere of Western elegance. The ***El Dorado*** buffet *(B-L-D—Low)* displays a tempting array of American specialties and desserts in a large, pleasant dining room.

Heavenly Valley Ski Resort
2 mi. SW via Ski Run Blvd. on Saddle Rd. *544-6263*
L-D. *Moderate*
The Top of the Tram is the ski area's restaurant. It is reached by an aerial tram ride to more than 2,000 feet above Lake Tahoe. American fare is served with a truly wide-angle view from those tables by the windows.

Heidi's Pancake House
1.6 mi. SW at 3485 US 50 *544-8113*
B-L-D. *Expensive*
Plain hearty breakfasts of all kinds are served in a big, casual wood-trimmed coffee shop. Other meals are moderately priced.

High Sierra Hotel/Casino
downtown on US 50 at Stateline *(702)588-6211*
Several restaurants are located in this big hotel/casino. ***Stetson's*** *(D only—Expensive)* features mesquite-broiled American fare and plush booths amidst casually elegant decor. The ***Chuckwagon*** buffet *(L-D—Low)* provides an abundance of food in a large Western-style dining room accented by a dramatic mural.

Le Bon Creole
5.7 mi. W at 681 CA 89 *541-0405*
L-D. No L fall-spring. Closed Mon. *Moderate*
The lively flavors of creole dishes are authentically preserved by the New Orleans family that operates this new restaurant. The simply furnished little dining rooms are enhanced by a wood-burning fireplace and tables set with crisp linens.

Maison Marguite
downtown at 901 Park Av. *542-1072*
B-L-D. *Very Expensive*
Contemporary American fare is offered on a pricey menu in a beautiful, wood-tone and fabric dining room where linens and fresh flowers grace each table for breakfast as well as dinner. Diners in comfortable armchairs have a picture window view of the surrounding pine forest.

Nephele
1 mi. SW at 1169 Ski Run Blvd. *544-8130*
D only. *Moderate*
International cuisine is the highlight of an intimate contemporary dining room that is a delightful blend of wood tones and stained glass.

Oglebee's
1 mi. SW at US 50/Ski Run Blvd. *544-2429*
B-L-D. *Moderate*
Various four-egg specialty omelets are featured for breakfast, and contemporary American fare is offered at other meals in this comfortably furnished restaurant.

Red Hut Cafe
3.5 mi. SW at 2723 US 50 — *541-9024*
B-L. — *Low*
Outstanding waffles and the best prices in town on an assortment of omelets and other breakfast specialties account for the enduring popularity of this rustic little roadside cafe.

Ristorante Tre Fontane
9 mi. SW at 3140 US 50 - Tahoe Paradise — *577-2016*
D only. — *Very Expensive*
Carefully prepared Italian and French cuisine is served in an informal little roadside dinner house.

Swiss Chalet
3.9 mi. SW at US 50 & Sierra Blvd. — *544-3304*
D only. Closed Mon. — *Moderate*
Old-fashioned European and American dishes accompany European-themed decor in a large, long-established dinner house.

Tep's Villa Roma
3.8 mi. SW at 2588 US 50 and Reno Av. — *541-8227*
D only. — *Moderate*
Old-fashioned Italian dishes and a help-yourself antipasto bar are featured in the casual, congested dining room of this long-established restaurant.

Waterwheel South
downtown at Pine/US 50 — *544-4158*
D only. — *Moderate*
A good assortment of Cantonese and Szechwan dishes is offered in the Crescent V Shopping Center outpost of a Tahoe area restaurant chain. Tables are set with crisp linens amidst casual Chinese decor in spacious dining rooms.

LODGING

South Lake Tahoe boasts one of the West's greatest concentrations of accommodations. There are more than 7,000 rooms in lakefront or forest locations to suit every taste and budget. In addition, there are nearly 2,000 rooms in the four casino/hotel towers clustered at the state line. (These rooms are not included in this listing. While the entertainment and dining facilities in the big hotels are notable, accommodations in the hotel towers are both more expensive and more remote from the lake and forest than are the first-class lodgings in town.) During the summer, bargains are almost non-existent and reservations should be made in advance, especially on weekends. However, most places offer discounts from October to May of at least 10% on Friday and Saturday and 30% or more on weekdays. The South Lake Tahoe Visitors Bureau operates a nationwide toll-free reservation system ((800)822-5922) which allows direct contact with most of the listed properties.

Chateau L'Amour
1.1 mi. SW at 3620 US 50 (Box 17527, zip: 95706) *544-6969*
Hedonism hit the high country when a modern little motel was converted into a complex of uninhibited romper rooms for adults only. Guests have a choice of bright reds, blues, or browns as the color scheme for flamboyant furnishings that include cable color TV with X-rated movies, mirrored walls and ceilings, and carpeted floors and walls.
#9 "Honeymoon Suite"—red decor, in-room big heart-shaped whirlpool, champagne, 8′ round K waterbed...$95
#10—blue decor, in-room whirlpool, 8′ round K waterbed...$80
regular room—in-room whirlpool, K waterbed...$75
regular room— K waterbed...$60

★ **Christiania Inn**
2 mi. S at Heavenly Valley Ski Area (Box 6870, zip: 95729) *544-7337*
Overlooking the base of Heavenly Valley Ski Area, this classic little bed-and-breakfast inn offers spacious, beautifully furnished units with private baths, cable color TV, and dramatic ski glope views. A Continental breakfast and decanter of brandy are complimentary. Because of the ideal location in ski season, winter rates are substantially higher than the prices quoted.
#4 suite—split level, wet bar, fireplace, high window wall with slope view, round K bed...$120
suite—wet bar, fireplace, in-bath steam bath, K bed...$120
regular room— Q bed...$60

★ **Eagles' Nest Inn**
4 mi. E via US 50 at 472 Needle Peak Rd. *(702)588-6492*
New in 1984, this elegant little motor inn is a skier's delight, with a grand view of the lake in the distance from a choice location on a ridge between two ski lifts. There is skiing in and out of Heavenly Valley North, some covered parking, a handsome dining room and lounge, and privileges to use the facilities at the Ridge Club. Each beautifully furnished room has a large in-bath whirlpool, cable color TV, a phone, and a private balcony.
regular room—request lake view, K bed...$125

★ **Fantasy II**
downtown at 924 Park Av. (Box 6008, zip: 95729) *544-6767*
This modern motel has a small outdoor pool. It is near the beach and the casinos. The real distinction, though, is the decor—intended exclusively for adults interested in accommodations unlike anything back home. Rooms are decorated in flamboyant reds, browns, or blues with carpet and mirrors everywhere—even on the walls and ceiling. Each room has X-rated movies on adult closed-circuit color TV, a phone, and a stereo radio.

#127—blue, spacious, in-room heart-shaped whirlpool, heart-shaped K bed...$96
regular room—in-room heart-shaped whirlpool, water or regular K bed...$88
regular room— round water K bed...$72

Frontier Lodge
.5 mi. SW at 3880 Pioneer Trail (Box 5467, zip: 95729) 541-6226
This big modern motel has a large outdoor pool (covered in winter) and a redwood hot tub in the pines. Each spacious room has cable color TV and a phone.
regular room— Q bed...$42

Hansen's Resort
2 mi. SW at 1360 Ski Run Blvd. (Box 316, zip: 95705) 544-3361
Adjacent to a toboggan lift in a quiet forested location is a rustic motel and several cabins.
Cabin #6—2 BR, LR with fireplace, kitchen, 2 D & Q beds...$80
regular room—in motel, Q bed...$40

Holiday Lodge
downtown at 4095 Laurel Av. (Box 4007, zip: 95729) 544-4101
Near the casinos and a short stroll from the beach, this big modern motel has large indoor and outdoor pools, a whirlpool, and saunas. Each room has a phone and cable color TV.
regular room— K bed...$65

★ **Inn by the Lake**
1.8 mi. SW at 3300 US 50 (Box 849, zip: 95705) 542-0330
The lake and a fine public beach are across the highway from this contemporary motel which has a large outdoor pool, two whirlpools, and a sauna. Each nicely furnished room has a phone, cable color TV with movies, and a small balcony or patio. For toll-free reservations in California, call: (800)535-0330.
deluxe room—lake view, wet bar, refrigerator, K bed...$95
regular room—mountain view, Q bed...$75

★ **Lakeland Village**
1.2 mi. SW at 3535 US 50 (Box A, zip: 95705) 541-7711
Nestled among nineteen acres of pines is a large condo complex adjoining Lake Tahoe on a thousand feet of private sandy beach that is ideal for swimming and sunning. A fishing pier, rental boats, two landscaped outdoor pools, a whirlpool, saunas, and two tennis courts are also available to guests. Each unit has a phone, cable color TV, a kitchen, fireplace, and a private balcony. Unfortunately, only units with three or more bedrooms have lakefront views. For toll-free reservations in California, call: (800)822-5969.
townhouse—1 BR, two-level, wood-burning fireplace, Q bed...$124
regular unit—studio, hideabed, gas fireplace, Q bed...$75

Motel 6

4 mi. SW at 2375 US 50 (Box 7756, zip: 95731) *541-6272*

The West's biggest **bargain** chain of motels is represented by a very large facility with an outdoor pool, and (fee) TV.

regular room— D bed...$27

★ **Pacifica Lodge**

downtown at 931 Park Av. (Box 4298, zip: 95729) *544-4131*

In addition to a convenient location near both the beach and casinos, this modern motel has a large outdoor pool and an enclosed whirlpool. Each room has a phone and cable color TV. Coffee and donuts are brought to the rooms daily. The real attraction, however, is the assortment of stylishly decorated, feature-filled adult rooms.

#117 "Queen of Hearts"—spacious, wet bar, fireplace, raised in-room heart-shaped whirlpool, K waterbed...$80

#118 "Captain's Quarters"—spacious, nautical decor, wet bar, fireplace, raised in-room heart-shaped whirlpool, K waterbed...$80

#311,#312—spacious, nautical or Egyptian decor, raised in-room heart-shaped whirlpool, wet bar, pine view from K bed...$75

#508,#511,#517—spacious, blue, red, or orange tones, raised stone fireplace, private balcony, K bed...$65

regular room— K bed...$50

Pioneer Trail Motel

.5 mi. S at Pioneer Trail/Moss Rd. (Box PP, zip: 95729) *544-5705*

This small two-story motel has an outdoor pool. Each simply decorated, spacious room is furnished with cable color TV with movies and a phone.

special room—in-bath choice of steambath or whirlpool, Q bed...$50

regular room— Q bed...$45

Play Chalet Motel

1 mi. SW at 1200 Ski Run Blvd. (Box 4504, zip: 95729) *544-4661*

A recently refurbished motel a few blocks from the ski slopes has a large outdoor hot tub in the pines. Each of the spacious rooms has a cable color TV.

special room—raised heart-shaped in-room whirlpool, Q bed...$65

regular room— Q bed...$40

★ **Royal Valhalla Motor Lodge**

.3 mi. W at 4401 Lake Shore Dr. (Drawer GG, zip: 95729) *544-2233*

This contemporary lakefront motel has guest privileges at a splendid private beach across the street. There is also a large outdoor pool. Each spacious room has a private balcony (most overlook the lake), cable

color TV, and a phone.
lakefront room—view overlooks the lake, Q bed...$6
regular room— Q bed...$5

Ski Inn
1 mi. SW at 3641 US 50 (Box 1267, zip: 95705) *544-201*
An outdoor pool and hot tub are available in a motel that is only a bloc from the beach. Each room has cable color TV.
#23—cabin, fireplace, kit., in-room raised whirlpool, Q waterbed...$6
#29—fireplace, kitchen, K bed...$5
regular room— D bed...$3

Tahoe Hacienda Motel
1 mi. SW at 3820 US 50 (Box 815, zip: 95705) *541-38C*
A large outdoor oval-shaped pool and a whirlpool are features of th pine-shaded single-level motel. Each room has a phone and cable colc TV.
#5,#6—spacious, fireplace, K waterbed...$7
#29,#30—spacious, in-room heart-shaped whirlpool, refr., Q bed...$8
regular room— K bed...$5

★ **Tahoe Marina Inn**
1.8 mi. SW at US 50 & Bal Bijou Rd. (Box 871) 95705 *541-218*
This contemporary condominium resort includes five hundred feet private sandy beach, a large outdoor pool with a fabulous lakeside view and a sauna. Each of the spacious, beautifully furnished units in th motor inn or adjacent condos has a phone, cable color TV with movie and a lakeside balcony or deck.
#318,#315,#212,#114—inn room, corner, fine lake views, kit., 2 Q beds...$9
#230,#234—upstairs condo, fine lake views, fireplace, kit., 2 T & Q beds...$11
regular room—inn room, Q bed...$8

★ **Tahoe Seasons Resort**
2 mi. SW at Keller & Saddle Rds. (Box 5656, zip: 95729) *541-67C*
Near the aerial tramway at Heavenly Valley, this large resort opened 1984 with an outdoor pool, two whirlpools, two tennis courts, paddleba courts, and an exercise room. A garage, restaurant, and lounge are als available. Each nicely decorated unit has both a living area an bedroom; wet bar/refrigerator; a large in-bath whirlpool; a gas fireplac two cable color TVs, and a phone. For toll-free reservations in Californ call (800)722-9144; elsewhere, (800)822-5922.
regular room—some have slope view, Q bed...$12

★ **Timber Cove Lodge - Best Western**
1.7 mi. SW at US 50 & Bal Bijou Rd. (Box AC) 95705 *541-67*
This large contemporary motor hotel is on attractively landscape

lakefront grounds and six hundred feet of private sandy beach next to one of the best public beaches on the lake. In addition to fine lake swimming, there is a fishing pier, a marina with boat rentals, a large outdoor pool and two whirlpools, plus an attractive fireplace lobby/lounge and dining room. Each spacious, well-furnished room has cable color TV and a phone. For toll-free reservations, call: (800)528-1234.

#512,#508,#504,#269,#245,#221—end rooms, fine lakefront view, semi-private balcony, K bed...$75

regular room— 2 D or K bed...$70

Villa Montreux

1 mi. SW at 971 Ski Run Blvd. (Box 638, zip: 95705) *544-3224*

A half block from the beach in a quiet location, this modern motel has a large outdoor pool. Each room has a phone and cable color TV with movies.

regular room— Q bed...$42

regular room— D bed...$38

CAMPGROUNDS

Numerous campgrounds are located on or near the south shore of Lake Tahoe. The best provide complete camping and recreation facilities in luxuriant pine forests by beaches along the majestic lake.

Camp Richardson

8 mi. W via US 50 & CA 89 *541-1801*

This huge campground is located in a pine forest next to a fine beach along Lake Tahoe. Sunbathing, swimming, boating (plus a ramp and dock), water-skiing, fishing, bicycle trails (plus rentals), and tennis courts are among the attractions and diversions. Flush toilets, hot showers, and hookups are available. Each pine-shaded site has a picnic table and fire area. Some have a lake view. base rate...$7

El Dorado Recreation Area

2 mi. SW on US 50 *573-2059*

Across the highway from one of the lake's finest sandy beaches is a large municipal campground. Sunbathing, swimming, boating (plus a ramp and dock), water-skiing, and fishing are very popular. A large municipal (fee) indoor/outdoor pool is adjacent. Flush toilets, hot showers, and hookups are available. Each of the pine-shaded sites has a picnic table and a raised fire grill. base rate...$7

Emerald Bay State Park

11 mi. W via US 50 & CA 89 *541-3030*

On a peninsula between the south shore of picturesque Emerald Bay and Lake Tahoe is a large state-operated campground. Sunbathing, swimming, boating (plus a dock), fishing, and hiking are popular activities. Flush toilets and hot showers, but no hookups, are available. Each pine-shaded site has a picnic table and fire area. base rate...$7

Nevada Beach Campground
2.6 mi. N via US 50 & Elks Point Rd. *544-6420*
This national forest campground by Lake Tahoe is just inside Nevada. Activities include swimming, sunbathing, boating, and fishing. Flush toilets are available, but there are no showers or hookups. Each site has a picnic table and a fire area. base rate...$7

SPECIAL EVENTS

South Lake Tahoe Winter Carnival *in town* *first week in January*
This week-long event features races, games, contests, food, and live entertainment in a mid-winter celebration of ice and snow for both skiers and non-skiers.

Tahoe Wild West Week *in town* *third week in June*
A draft horse pulling contest, buffalo chip throwing contest, cowboy polo, mudbath tug-of-war, haystack scramble, Wild West show, parade, and chili cook-off are some of the events in this wild and woolly week-long celebration.

OTHER INFORMATION

Area Code: *916*
Zip Code: *95702 & 95706 (plus others)*

South Lake Tahoe Chamber of Commerce
2 mi. SW at 3066 US 50 *541-5255*

Eldorado National Forest Visitor Center
8 mi. W at 870 CA 89 *544-6420*

Tahoe City

Tahoe City is the outdoor recreation hub of the Sierra high country. It is situated in a thriving pine forest along the northern shore of one of the world's most beautiful high mountain lakes. Two seasons perfectly complement this splendid natural environment. Summer usually provides warm sunny days that are ideal for enjoying both Lake Tahoe, the Sierra's greatest natural attraction, and the Truckee River which flows out of the lake through town. Some of the finest sections of the lakeshore, river, and nearby mountains have been set aside for public use in an outstanding assortment of parks, forests, and wilderness areas. In town, splendid beaches attract swimmers and sunbathers; marinas offer cruises, sailing, boating, water-skiing, and sportfishing; and guides and equipment are available for river running. Bicycle paths, hiking trails, campgrounds, golf, and tennis facilities are also heavily used by capacity crowds all summer. Winter is the other peak season. Because snowfalls are usually enormous, downhill and cross-country skiing and a full range of other snow sports entice throngs to a remarkable number of major facilities in the mountains around town.

Summer resorts began to develop along the north shore of Lake Tahoe during the 1870s. In part because of its unique location at the only river outlet of the lake, Tahoe City became the terminus for a small railroad that served the lake near the turn of the century. Growth was slow until the late 1950s when the development of the first major ski areas and casinos began to turn the Tahoe basin into a year-round attraction. Since that time, Tahoe City has become the hub for eight ski areas within a dozen miles. It is also a tranquil alternative to the faster pace generated by several substantial casinos in the Crystal Bay area fifteen miles eastward on the Nevada side of the northern lake shore. With so much to do nearby, the north shore's first downtown finally began to develop in the heart of Tahoe City in a picturesque location near the lake between the Truckee River and Tahoe State Recreation Area.

Today, this is the best defined business district on the entire lake. Several distinctive shopping complexes share the wood-toned "Tahoe style" of architecture that blends nicely with the luxuriant pine forest along the lake shore. Excellent sportswear and sporting goods stores are numerous, and there are several unusual specialty shops and galleries. Downtown is also the core of one of the West's noteworthy concentrations of gourmet restaurants. After dark, nightlife is primarily oriented toward comfortable lake view lounges, but several places also offer live entertainment. A full range of gambling action and "name" entertainment are only a short drive away in Nevada. Lodgings in town are surprisingly scarce but diverse, ranging from some luxuriously furnished lakeview units to several motels and bed-and-breakfast inns.

Elevation:

6,253 feet

Population (1980):

1,840

Population (1970):

1,400

Location:

200 miles Northeast of San Francisco

Tahoe City

WEATHER PROFILE

Vokac Weather Rating

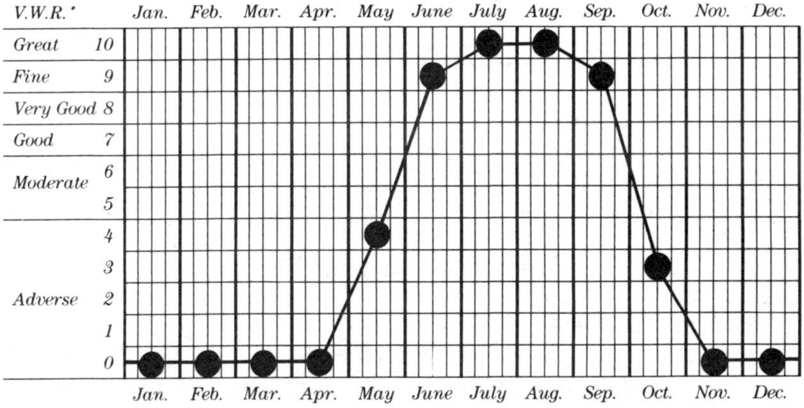

	Jan.	Feb.	Mar.	Apr.	May	June	July	Aug.	Sep.	Oct.	Nov.	Dec.
*V.W.R.**	0	0	0	0	4	9	10	10	9	3	0	0
Temperature												
Ave. High	36	39	43	50	59	68	78	77	69	58	46	40
Ave. Low	17	18	22	27	32	38	43	42	38	32	25	21
Precipitation												
Inches Rain	6.1	5.4	4.0	2.1	1.4	0.6	0.3	0.2	0.4	2.0	3.2	5.6
Inches Snow	58	45	35	17	4	-	-	-	-	3	14	36

**V.W.R. = Vokac Weather Rating: probability of mild (warm & dry) weather on any given day.*

Forecast

Month	*V.W.R.**	*Temperatures Daytime*	*Temperatures Evening*	*Precipitation*
Jan.	0 Adverse	chilly	cold	frequent snowstorms
Feb.	0 Adverse	chilly	cold	frequent snowstorms
Mar.	0 Adverse	chilly	cold	occasional snowstorms
Apr.	0 Adverse	cool	chilly	occasional snowstorms
May	4 Adverse	cool	chilly	infrequent rainstorms/snow flurries
June	9 Fine	warm	cool	infrequent rainstorms
July	10 Great	warm	cool	negligible
Aug.	10 Great	warm	cool	none
Sep.	9 Fine	warm	cool	negligible
Oct.	3 Adverse	cool	chilly	infrequent downpours/snow flurries
Nov.	0 Adverse	chilly	chilly	occasional snowstorms
Dec.	0 Adverse	chilly	cold	occasional snowstorms

Summary

On the northern shore of one of the world's most beautiful big alphine lakes at an elevation well over a mile high, Tahoe City has a climate with two desirable seasons. **Winter** is one—cold, snowy, and perfect for almost all winter sports. Snowstorms during this season are frequent and among the heaviest in the West, which normally assures many months of quality skiing. **Spring** is a continuation of winter until May, when a short, sloppy transition gives way to mild weather after Memorial Day. **Summer** is the other outstanding season. Warm sunny days, cool evenings, and little rainfall are a perfect accompaniment to unlimited water and mountain sports. **Fall** is another brief transitional season. Shortly after Labor Day the area's outdoor attractions become relatively unusable as temperatures cool rapidly, and unpredictable rainfalls give way to expected snowstorms that mormally provide the base for outstanding skiing after Thanksgiving.

ATTRACTIONS & DIVERSIONS

Aerial Tramway

★ **Squaw Valley Tram**
8.5 mi. NW via CA 89 & Squaw Valley Rd. *583-6985*
Visitors are whisked 2,000 feet up from the valley floor to the top of one of the nearby ridges where the High Sierra provide a memorable backdrop to lunch or cocktails on an outdoor view deck in summer. Hikers can walk to Shirley Lake and cool off with a swim.

Alpine Slide

★ **Boreal Alpine Slide**
24 mi. NW via CA 89 & I-80 - Castle Peak exit *426-3666*
A scenic chairlift up a mountain is followed by a half mile of exciting curves and straight-aways on the fiberglass track of an alpine slide. The speed of the sled is controlled by the rider. (Summer only.) The slide is also lighted for night use.

★ ***Bicycling***
Miles of separated bike paths have been constructed in and around town that are relatively flat, safe, and scenic. Both regular and mountain bicycles can be rented by the hour or longer at:

Basecamps' Bike Shop *downtown at 255 N. Lake Blvd.* *583-9530*
Olympic Bike Shop *downtown at 620 N. Lake Blvd.* *583-6415*
Wray's Rentals *.6 mi. S at 315 CA 89* *581-3030*

★ ***Boat Rentals***
Every kind of boating imaginable is enjoyed on Lake Tahoe. Several places along the north shore rent watercraft, including fishing, pleasure, ski and sail boats, canoes, kayaks, or jet skis. Following are some of the more convenient.

High Sierra Boat Rental *6.5 mi. S at 5180 CA 89* *525-5589*
Obexer's *6.8 mi. S at 5355 CA 80 - Homewood* *525-7962*
Sierra Jet Sports *downtown* *583-6292*
Sunnyside (parasailing, too) *2.5 mi. S at 1850 CA 89* *583-7417*
Tahoe Water Adventures *downtown at 120 Grove St.* *583-3225*

Boat Rides

★ **North Tahoe Cruises**
downtown at 700 N. Lake Blvd. *583-0141*
Sightseeing cruises along the north shore of Lake Tahoe aboard a new paddle wheel boat with a glass bottom window, or on the fifty-passenger "Sunrunner," are offered daily from May to October. From December to April, the "Sunrunner" transports skiers to Heavenly Valley.

Fanny Bridge
downtown on CA 89 just S of CA 28
Everyone looks from this bridge into the crystal-clear Truckee River to

see the big rainbow trout waiting below to snap up food that's tossed down to them. Nearby are the Lake Tahoe outlet gates which are used to control the flow of water into the Truckee River—the lake's only outlet.

Flying

★ **Cal-Vada Aircraft Inc.**
6.5 mi. S at 5165 CA 89 - Homewood *525-7143*
Chartered scenic sea plane rides are one unusual and exciting way to view the lake and mountains.

Gatekeeper's Cabin Museum
downtown at Truckee River outlet
The North Lake Tahoe Historical Society has restored the cabin once used by the person who controlled the flow of water out of Lake Tahoe. It now contains historic Tahoe photos and relics. Adjacent pine-shaded picnic tables are beautifully located overlooking the Truckee River outlet. Closed Tues.-Wed. and in winter.

Golf

★ **Incline Golf Course**
15 mi. NE at 955 Fairway Dr. - Incline Village *(702)832-1144*
This beautifully landscaped 18-hole championship golf course was designed by Robert Trent Jones. It is open to the public and offers all facilities and services.

Tahoe City Golf Course
downtown at 251 N. Lake Blvd. *583-1516*
Conveniently located downtown, this relatively level pine-studded 9-hole golf course is open to the public. There is also a putting green, bar, and restaurant.

★ ***Hiking***

The U.S. Forest Service and the California State Parks Department maintain many miles of scenic hiking trails near town.

Basecamp
downtown at 255 N. Lake Blvd. *583-5306*
Topo maps, information, and backpack and tent rentals are available here.

Wray's Rentals
.6 mi. S at 315 CA 89 *581-3030*
Backpackers' tents, stoves, lanterns, day packs, and sleeping bags are rented here, along with bicycles, inflatable boats, and many other kinds of recreation equipment.

★ ***Horseback Riding***

Several stables in the area rent horses by the hour or longer for guided trail rides into the pristine high country from late May through September. Pack trips can also be arranged. The nearest stables are:

Alpine Meadows Stables *5 mi. NW on Alpine Meadows Rd.* *583-3905*
Squaw Valley Stables *8 mi. NW at 1525 Squaw Valley Rd.* *583-1130*

★ **Lake Tahoe**

the eastern border of town

One of the world's most beautiful lakes straddles the California/Nevada border 6,229 feet above sea level. This water wonderland is twenty-two miles long and twelve miles wide. As much as 1,645 feet deep, it is the second deepest lake in the United States. In spite of massive development along the shoreline, it is said that the lake is still so clear that a white dinner plate can be seen at a depth of well over one hundred feet. A splendid assortment of recreation facilities contributes to the appeal of forests, streams, river, sandy beaches, and dramatic bouldered coves that surround the mountain-rimmed lake. Even though the maximum water temperature normally only reaches 68°F, swimming is popular on warm summer days. A seventy-two-mile highway loop around the lake is immodestly described as "The Most Beautiful Drive in America." Visitors can judge for themselves using a map and guide describing points of interest along the route—available at the Chamber of Commerce.

★ ***Library***

downtown at 740 N. Lake Blvd. *583-3382*

The Tahoe City branch of the Placer County Library is in a contemporary building with a large working fireplace and comfortable reading chairs near an extensive display of current magazines and newspapers. When the weather is pleasant, outdoor lake-view seating is also provided. Closed Sun.

★ ***Moped Rentals***

Kings Beach Moped Rental

4.6 mi. NE at 8700 N. Lake Blvd. - Kings Beach

The scenic roads around the lake are perfectly suited to the relatively effortless and slow pace of a moped. This is the only licensed/insured moped rental on the California north shore.

★ ***Nude Beach***

21 mi. E off NV 28

Swimming suits are optional at Chimney Beach, where secluded, sandy alcoves are scattered along a shoreline of dramatic granite outcroppings. Visitors can park on dirt turnouts by the road (starting 2.3 miles south of the car entrance to Sand Harbor on the lake's northeast side) and take well-worn trails to the lake.

★ ***River Running***

The Truckee River offers some small rapids and scenic calm stretches through a beautiful pine forest for almost four miles below the Lake Tahoe outlet in town. You can do-it-yourself with rental equipment and transportation provided by:

Fanny Bridge Rafts *downtown at Fanny Bridge* *583-3021*
Mountain Air Sports *downtown at 205 CA 89* *583-5606*
Truckee River Raft Rentals *downtown at 185 CA 89* *583-9724*

★ ***Sportfishing***
Trout and kokanee salmon fishing can be excellent on Lake Tahoe and the Truckee River. Professional guides have charter sportfishing boats and the latest in fishing equipment to improve visitors' luck year-round.
Hooker for Hire *downtown* *525-5654*
King Fish Guide Service *downtown* *583-0350*
Mickey's Guide Service *downtown* *583-4602*

★ **Sugar Pine Point State Park**
10 mi. S on CA 89 *525-7982*
In a dense forest of sugar pines, this very popular park offers more than one mile of beaches for swimming and sunbathing, plus picnic sites, hiking trails, and camping in summer. The imposing Ehrman Mansion, the former vacation residence of a wealthy San Francisco family, is now an interpretive center and museum with Tahoe memorabilia. In winter, cross-country skiing, snowshoeing, and winter camping attract visitors.

★ **Tahoe City Public Beach**
downtown
Adjacent to the business district is a lawn with picnic tables and play equipment. Just beyond is a photogenic sandy beach where swimming and sunbathing are enormously popular in summer.

★ **Tahoe State Recreation Area**
.3 mi. N on CA 28 *583-3074*
The little beach is nearly always crowded in summer, as is the neighboring campground, because of the pine-forested lakefront location at the north end of the business district.

Winter Sports

★ ***Helicopter Skiing***
Sierra Helicopter Ski *587-4573*
This outfit serves both downhill and cross-country skiers. With daily operation out of Squaw Valley, it is the fastest way to get to remote locales and pristine slopes.

★ ***Skiing***
With eight downhill ski areas within a dozen miles of town, this is one of the most thoroughly developed alpine skiing regions in the world. In addition, cross-country ski touring centers are numerous. The attraction is the awesome snowpack each winter and breathtakingly beautiful mountain and lake scenery. Ski equipment rentals, sales, maps, and information can be obtained at any of the ski areas or from several sporting goods stores downtown.

Sleigh Rides
Squaw Valley Riding Stables
8 mi. NW via CA 89 at 1525 Squaw Valley Rd. *583-0419*
Sleigh rides can be arranged here any day in winter.

★ ***Snowmobiles***
Tahoe City Recreation Area
downtown at 251 N. Lake Blvd. *583-1516*
In winter, the downtown golf course becomes part of a recreation area where snowmobiles can be rented by the hour or half hour.

Snow Play Area
Granlibakken
1.2 mi. SW via CA 89 on Tonopah Dr. *583-4242*
A rope tow and poma lift take beginner skiers up gentle-to-intermediate slopes at the oldest established ski resort in the Tahoe basin. Plastic saucers, plus downhill and cross-country rentals, are provided. The lodge has a restaurant and lounge.

★ **Squaw Valley U.S.A.**
8 mi. NW off CA 89 on Squaw Valley Rd. *583-5585*
The site of the 1960 Winter Olympics is the largest downhill ski area in north Tahoe. This world-class complex has an outstanding variety of downhill slopes. A vertical drop of 2,700 feet is served by twenty-seven lifts, including an aerial tram, gondola, and five triple chairs. A major cross-country ski center, night skiing, and a free shuttle bus on the north shore are other features. All rentals and services are provided along with restaurants, bars, and lodging at the base that includes a plush resort hotel opened in 1983 as the first phase of a major new alpine village.

★ **Tahoe Nordic Ski Area**
2.5 mi. NE via CA 28 at 925 Country Club Dr. *583-9858*
More than thirty miles of groomed trails provide spectacular views of Lake Tahoe from pine-forested slopes and brilliant meadows. Rentals, lessons, guided tours (both day and moonlight), and a day lodge are at the area.

SHOPPING

Several architecturally distinctive shopping complexes built in recent years have given the town an unusual lakefront business district. Excellent sporting goods stores and several fine art galleries are especially worth discovering.

Food Specialties

Carroll's
downtown at 255 N. Lake Blvd. *583-8896*
Hawaiian snow (shaved ice) is an alternative to the ice cream served here. Light breakfasts and lunches are also available.

The Cork & More
downtown at 760 N. Lake Blvd. *583-2675*
An impressive collection of California premium wines is complemented by regular wine tastings and gourmet deli items in an upstairs shop at the Boatworks Mall.

★ **Gourmet Chalet**
downtown at 521 N. Lake Blvd. *583-2292*
A large selection of well-stored wines, plus a variety of cheeses, coffees, teas, and other gourmet items are sold. An adjoining pub and patio features wine by the glass with luncheon dishes and dinner on weekends.

Pennypacker's
downtown at 760 N. Lake Blvd. *583-1315*
An inviting assortment of cookies is made here daily.

Starz Bakery
downtown at 115 W. Lake Blvd. *581-5078*
Selected donuts and pastries and coffee are featured in this takeout bakery. Closed Mon. except in summer.

Tahoe City Bakery
downtown at 950 N. Lake Blvd. *583-8918*
Oversized cinnamon rolls and apple fritters are highlights among traditional pastries and breads served to go, or at a few coffee tables with a lake view.

Specialty Shops

★ **The Boatworks Shopping Mall**
downtown at 760 N. Lake Blvd. *583-1488*
A two-level, enclosed structure of natural wood design by the lake features three fine small art galleries among an inviting assortment of specialty shops and several restaurants. There are fine lake and mountain views from rear decks.

★ **The Cobblestone Center**
downtown at 475 N. Lake Blvd.
This small shopping complex sports a Tyrolean motif, complete with a clock tower. It has several notable specialty shops, including an excellent (upstairs) kitchenware and gourmet provisions gallery. There is also a fascinating collection of pre-electric slot machines displayed for sale in an antique shop, and a first-rate sheepskin and leather garment shop.

The Lighthouse Center
downtown at 850 N. Lake Blvd. *583-3471*
Rustic wood-trimmed buildings maximize a lakeshore site and house a variety of good shops, and services, including the chamber of commerce.

★ **The Potter's Wheel**
downtown at 560 N. Lake Blvd. *583-5457*
Distinctive handcrafted pottery made predominantly by northern California artisans, and genuine Navajo rugs, are displayed in a handsome little gallery in a skillfully converted historic log cabin with a fireplace and lake view.

Reed and Boggs Book Merchants
downtown at 760 N. Lake Blvd. *583-9461*
This contemporary little shop has a well-chosen selection of books on many topics.

The Roundhouse
downtown next to the Boatworks
A refurbished turn-of-the-century roundhouse by the lake is now an enclosed shopping mall with specialty shops and restaurants.

The Store
downtown at 850 N. Lake Blvd. *583-6511*
Many current magazines and selected books of regional interest are among the features in a contemporary version of a general store.

NIGHTLIFE

Entertainment in Tahoe City is sedate when compared to the non-stop gambling and fast-paced entertainment in glitzy casinos just beyond the nearby state line. Several of the best places in town for a quiet drink or live entertainment also feature spellbinding views of Lake Tahoe.

★ **The Chart House**
downtown at 700 N. Lake Blvd. *583-0233*
A large contemporary wood-toned lounge is beautifully accented by a huge, see-through river-rock fireplace, several seating areas with plush leather and fabric sofas, luxuriant greenery, and a picture window view of the marina, lake, and mountains.

Crystal Bay Club
11 mi. NE on CA 28 - Crystal Bay *(702)831-0512*
A variety of live entertainment is offered nightly in the corner lounge of this modern casino.

★ **Gatsby's**
downtown at 850 N. Lake Blvd. *583-5131*
A sleek newer lounge in the Lighthouse Center offers live entertainment on weekends and a view of the lake. The room is comfortably outfitted with sofas and armchairs and a dramatic fireplace. Light meals are also served.

Honkers
downtown at 640 N. Lake Blvd. *583-5700*
The live music featured nightly might be rock, bluegrass, or whatever is current. It's showcased in a cozy, polished wood/brass/greenery bar next to a popular dining room.

★ **Hyatt Lake Tahoe**
15 mi. NE via CA 29 - Incline Village *(702)831-1111*
The north shore's largest hotel and classiest casino also features live entertainment nightly in a comfortable, contemporary lounge.

★ **Jake's on the Lake**
downtown at 780 N. Lake Blvd. *583-0188*
Great lake views both inside and out on the deck are the main attraction of this artistically wood-trimmed bar/restaurant. It's a popular place to relax over a drink and watch the boats come and go at the docks below.

Nevada Lodge
11 mi. NE on CA 29 - Crystal Bay *(702)831-0660*
The large casino and nightly live entertainment in the theater/restaurant attract crowds. This plain, 1950s-style facility also includes a motor hotel.

★ **Pete 'n Peter's**
downtown at 395 N. Lake Blvd. *583-2400*
Pool tables, shuffleboard, and a darts room fit comfortably into a handsome wood-toned barroom with lots of plants and stained glass. Tahoe City's oldest saloon, tucked away off the main street, has been popular with natives and tourists alike for more than a quarter-century.

Sunnyside Resort
2.5 mi. S on CA 89 at 1850 W. Lake Blvd. *583-4226*
Live entertainment and dancing are offered every weekend in a casual Tahoe-style wood-trimmed lounge with a big rock fireplace and a panoramic view of the lake. Wines by the glass, etc. can be enjoyed in the lounge or on a lakeside deck. The view is shared by an adjoining dining room.

Tahoe House Lounge
.8 mi. S on CA 89 at 625 W. Lake Blvd. *583-1377*
An iron fireplace and an unusual tree trunk view are part of the decor in a cozy lounge well-outfitted with sofas and armchairs.

Victoria Station
downtown at 425 N. Lake Blvd. *583-6939*
Live entertainment and dancing are offered most weekends in a big casual bar. One area has plush sofas, while an enclosed porch offers views of the lake across the highway. A large contemporary railroad-theme restaurant adjoins.

RESTAURANTS

In recent years, Tahoe City has become the center of a major concentration of fine restaurants. Several feature both gourmet cuisine and wonderful views of the lake and mountains. Rustic Tahoe-style natural wood decor predominates, but formally elegant dining is also available.

Bacchi's Inn
2 mi. NE at 2905 Lake Forest Rd. *583-3324*
D only. *Moderate*
Italian family-style dinners, including appetizers, soup, salad, entrees, and pasta have been served in this big old-fashioned restaurant for more than fifty years.

The Bridge Tender
downtown on CA 89 at 30 W. Lake Blvd. *583-3342*
L-D. *Moderate*
The fare is casual and the decor is quintessential Tahoe City—rough beams, wood floors, a rock wall, two iron fireplaces, two handcrafted bars, and lots of plants, including pine trees growing through dining areas. An adjoining patio has a delightful view of the Truckee River and Fanny Bridge.

Cafe Cobblestone
downtown at 475 N. Lake Blvd. *583-2111*
B-L. *Moderate*
An American cafe menu is offered in a contemporary restaurant where both the dining room and an inviting outdoor patio have lake views across the highway.

★ **Cafe Lilli**
15 mi. NE at 333 Village Blvd. - Incline Village *831-5057*
D only. Closed Tues.-Wed., Mon. in winter. *Very Expensive*
New California cuisine highlights a short, imaginative menu that changes weekly to reflect seasonally fresh produce. Crisp linen and a fireplace lend appeal to two cozy dining areas.

★ **Captain Jon's**
8.2 mi. NE on CA 28 at 7220 N. Lake Blvd. *546-4819*
L-D. Closed Mon. No L fall-spring. *Expensive*
Unusual seafood dishes are the highlight served in intimate, plush dining areas. A spectacular view lounge extends out over the lake.

Carnelian House
5.2 mi. NE on CA 28 at 5000 N. Lake Blvd. *546-5954*
D only. Closed Mon. *Expensive*
Continental dishes are accompanied by lake views from every table in a large, dark-toned dinner house. A grand piano, fireplace, and lakeside views distinguish the adjoining lounge.

Chart House
downtown at 700 N. Lake Blvd. *583-0233*
D only. *Expensive*
Steaks and prime rib are specialties in a large, attractively furnished dining room with a fine shoreline view of the marina, lake, and mountains. A big, comfortable lounge shares the skillfully converted space in a historic roundhouse.

★ **The Christy Hill Inn**
8 mi. NW via CA 89 at 1650 Squaw Valley Rd. *583-8551*
D only. Sat. & Sun. brunch, plus B-L in winter only. *Very Expensive*
Exciting New California cuisine skillfully prepared with the freshest available ingredients is the highlight of an informally elegant firelit dining room overlooking Squaw Valley.

Colonel Clair's
7.8 mi. NE via CA 28 at 6873 N. Lake Blvd. — *546-7358*
D only. — *Expensive*
Creole/Cajun specialties are worth trying in this new restaurant. The cozy dining room is attractively furnished.

Fast Eddie's Texas Bar-B-Que
downtown at 690 N. Lake Blvd. — *583-0950*
L-D. — *Low*
Texas-style oakwood barbecue was recently introduced to the north shore in this down-home, casual Q parlor.

★ **Fire Sign Cafe**
2.3 mi. S at 1785 W. Lake Blvd. — *583-0871*
B-L. Closed Wed. — *Moderate*
Delicious fresh baked breads, pastries, and desserts complement light, homestyle meals served amidst antique furnishings in a fireside atmosphere.

Hacienda del Lago
downtown at 760 N. Lake Blvd. — *583-0358*
D only. — *Low*
A good assortment of California-style Mexican specialties, wood-and-tile decor, and a choice of cushioned booths or tables on an outdoor deck accompany a stunning Lake Tahoe waterfront scene.

Honkers Bar & Grill
downtown at 640 N. Lake Blvd. — *583-5700*
L-D. Sat. & Sun. brunch. — *Moderate*
Marinated rabbit, roast duckling with blueberry sauce, and charbroiled quail are among distinctive dishes prepared in the style of New California cuisine. Crisp linens and wood armchairs enhance the cheerful, contemporary dining room. Lake Tahoe can be viewed through the trees from the dining room, bar, or deck. Horseshoe pits and darts are available in an adjacent garden.

★ **Hyatt Lake Tahoe**
15 mi. NE via CA 28 at Lake Shore & Country Club Dr. — *831-1111*
D only. — *Expensive*
Hugo's Rotisserie, the hotel's finest restaurant, offers contemporary Continental dishes complemented by an outstanding salad, pasta, and dessert bar. The elegant lakefront dining room, and a comfortable little adjoining lounge, share a spectacular view of Lake Tahoe.

Jake's on the Lake
downtown at 780 N. Lake Blvd. — *583-0188*
L (summer only) - D. — *Moderate*
American dishes accompany a splendid lakefront view from contemporary wood-toned dining rooms. The stylish bar also has a terrific view, plus a seafood appetizer bar menu.

Lake House Omelette Co.
downtown at 120 Grove St. *583-2225*
B-L. *Moderate*
All kinds of omelets are offered in a casual little upstairs dining room. A rustic bar has a lakefront view. Downstairs, the pizza parlor has a popular outdoor view deck, a view bar, and a fireplace in the dining room.

★ **La Cheminee**
9.2 mi. NE via CA 28 at 8504 N. Lake Blvd. *546-4322*
D only. Closed Tues.-Wed. *Very Expensive*
French nouvelle cuisine is beautifully presented in an intimate, elegant cottage.

La Playa
8 mi. NE on CA 28 at 7046 N. Lake Blvd. *546-5903*
D only. *Expensive*
The new management of a historic lakeside building offers casually prepared seafood dishes amidst informally elegant decor. But, the real attraction is the panoramic picture window view of Lake Tahoe.

La Vieille Maison
16 mi. N on CA 267 at E. River - Truckee *587-2421*
D only. Closed Mon.-Tues. *Very Expensive*
Robust French cuisine with a garlic accent is presented fixe prix amidst charming, intimate atmosphere.

★ **Le Petit Pier**
8.2 mi. NE on CA 28 at 7252 N. Lake Blvd. *546-4464*
D only. Closed Tues. *Very Expensive*
French specialties are served amid congested elegance in a French provincial-style dinner house. Window tables in tiny indoor rooms or on a heated deck have splendid lakefront views. The larger room also has a wood-burning fireplace.

Olympic Village Inn
9 mi. NW via CA 89 at 1900 Squaw Valley Rd. *583-1501*
D only. *Expensive*
In the hotel's restaurant, The Creekside, updated American fare is casually prepared and served in a well-spaced, informally elegant dining room, with an expansive view of the ski mountain and resort.

Pfeifer House
.8 mi. W on CA 89 at 760 River Rd. *583-3102*
D only. Closed Tues. *Moderate*
Middle European specialties are the feature of this inviting alpine-style dinner house.

Ric's Restaurant
downtown at 395 N. Lake Blvd. *583-1835*
L-D. Closed Sun. *Moderate*
An eclectic menu of seafoods, pastas, steaks, and other dishes is served in a tiny, tucked-away dining room with informal modern decor.

River Ranch
4 mi. NW on CA 89 at Alpine Meadows Rd. *583-4264*
D only. L on patio in summer. *Moderate*
A good selection of American entrees is served in several small, well-furnished dining rooms with a two-sided fireplace and river and forest views. The pine-shaded terrace overlooking rapids of the Truckee River is used for luncheon barbecues. A circular lounge has live entertainment most nights, and great river views.

★ **Rosie's Cafe**
downtown at 571 N. Lake Blvd. *583-8504*
B-L-D. *Moderate*
Delicious breakfasts are served with freshly made bagels or sopaipillas. Attention to details, skillful cooking, and innovative dishes make lunch or dinner special, too. The dining room/bar is a study in casual "old Tahoe" decor, with well-worn wooden floorboards, a big, brick see-through fireplace, many hanging plants, some etchings over the bar, and honey and blackberry jam dishes gracing simple table settings accented by fresh flowers. Several tables are also used on the lakeview porch when weather permits.

★ **Steven**
15 mi. NE via CA 28 at 341 Ski Way - Incline Village *(702)832-0222*
L-D. Sun. brunch. *Expensive*
New California cuisine with Santa Fe-style accents is skillfully prepared in a stylish newer restaurant perched on a ridge high above the lake. The comfortably elegant dining room offers panoramic picture window views of the lake and mountains. Scenery beyond an adjoining dining terrace is similarly breathtaking. The lounge features a massive stone fireplace and a grand piano, plus a sleek moderne bar featuring wines by the glass.

★ **Swiss Lakewood Lodge**
6.4 mi. S on CA 89 at 5055 W. Lake Blvd. *525-5211*
D only. Closed Mon. *Expensive*
Continental and Swiss specialties receive disciplined gourmet treatment. Full linen, fresh flowers, and Swiss background music enhance the long-established restaurant's decor.

Tahoe House
.9 mi. S at 625 W. Lake Blvd. *583-1377*
D only. Closed Mon. *Moderate*
Swiss and Continental specialties are featured. A natural stone fireplace and stained glass lend distinction to comfortably furnished dining rooms. An intimate fireside lounge adjoins.

★ **Water Wheel**
downtown at 115 W. Lake Blvd. *583-4404*
D only. Closed Mon. *Moderate*
Carefully prepared Szechwan dishes are presented at tables set with

crisp linens in an intimate firelit dining room that incorporates both Oriental and Western touches. A picturesque riverside deck is also used when weather permits.

★ **Wolfdale's**

6.8 mi. S on CA 89 at 5335 W. Lake Blvd. *525-7833*
D only. Closed Mon.-Tues. *Expensive*

Innovative gourmet cuisine is skillfully prepared from scratch—seasonally fresh ingredients are emphasized, and all breads and pastries are homemade. The eclectic elegance of the sophisticated little dining room is just right for one of the region's finest culinary experiences. (During July and August, the chef also prepares notable luncheons for diners served in the garden of a nursery just south of town.)

LODGING

There aren't a lot of accommodations in town, but they are distinctive. A small cluster of hotel/casinos are on the Nevada side of the state line starting twelve miles northeast. Numerous motels are concentrated along CA 28 in Tahoe Vista and Kings Beach between seven and twelve miles northeast of town. Bargains and vacancies are scarce during summer, but rates are usually at least 20% less in spring and fall. Toll-free numbers for making reservations in many of the named facilities are: in California (800)822-5959, and (800)824-8557 outside of California.

★ **Fantasy Inn III**

downtown at 790 N. Lake Blvd. (Box 634) *583-8578*

The indulgent decor of this modern motel is remarkably popular with adult visitors interested in something truly different than they have back home. Rooms in bold red, brown, or blue decor are outfitted with closed-circuit TV and X-rated movies, phones, stereo radios, and carpet and mirrors everywhere—even on the walls and ceiling.

#32 "Blue Suite"—in-room heart-shaped whirlpool, heart-shaped K waterbed...$115
deluxe room—in-room raised whirlpool, K waterbed...$95
regular room— K waterbed...$80

Lake Pines Motel

1.8 mi. NE via CA 89 at 2815 Lake Forest Rd. (Box 43) *583-3209*

Bargain cottages are available in a quiet forested setting two blocks from a Lake Tahoe beach. Each of the modest, nicely maintained little units has cable color TV.

studio—kitchen, 2 T or D bed...$35
regular room—cottage, 2 T or D bed...$25

Lakeside House

2.3 mi. S via CA 89 at 1745 Sequoia Av. (Box 7108) *583-8796*

A large older home near the lake has been carefully transformed into a bed-and-breakfast inn. Attractively furnished rooms share baths. A full breakfast and afternoon refreshments are complimentary. Guests have free use of a private beach and bicycles. Self-contained cottages are also available.

"Steamer Tahoe"—private half bath, antique brass Q bed...$70
cabin—kitchen, private bath, Q bed...$70
regular room—shared bath, Q bed...$60

Mayfield House
downtown at 236 Grove St. (Box 5999) *583-1001*
A charming older home has been attractively converted into a bed-and-breakfast inn a block from the downtown beach. Each room is beautifully furnished and shares a bath. Homemade pastries and fresh fruit for breakfast, and afternoon wine, are complimentary.

"Mayfield"—spacious, K bed...$75
"Julia"—spacious, K bed...$65
regular room— Q bed...$55

★ **Olympic Village Inn**
9 mi. NW via CA 89 at Squaw Valley (Box 2648) *583-1501*
A large new resort hotel was recently completed as the first phase for a whole new alpine village at the base of the ski lifts. Amenities in the spectacular showplace include an unusual "water garden" with hot tubs nestled amidst wildflowers by a meandering stream. A waterfall tumbles from fanciful boulders into a large outdoor pool. Horseback riding and tennis are offered (for a fee). Inside, an enormous lobby is distinguished by contemporary Western decor. The lounge and the toney dining room are well-suited to a luxurious mountain resort. Each beautifully furnished one-bedroom suite has a phone, cable color TV, kitchenette with a microwave oven, and a private garden/mountain view balcony. Winter rates are approximately twice the quoted summer rates. For toll-free reservations in California, call: (800)845-5243.

regular room—1 BR suite, Q bed...$95

★ **Peppertree Inn**
downtown at 645 N. Lake Blvd. (Box 29) *583-3711*
This modern seven-floor motel offers good lake views from upper floors. The public beach is across the highway. There is an outdoor pool (covered in winter) and a whirlpool, plus covered parking. Each spacious room has a phone and color TV.

#601—lake view beyond public walkway, K bed...$52
#701,#704,#705—lake view beyond public walkway, Q bed...$47
regular room— Q bed...$47

River Ranch
4 mi. NW on CA 89 at Alpine Meadows Rd. (Box 197) *583-4264*
A scenic restaurant, lounge, and dining terrace by the Truckee River are features of this refurbished lodge. Each room is nicely furnished with some antiques, a phone, and cable color TV with movies.

#26—spacious, corner, river view, 2 pvt. balconies, K bed...$60
#23—spacious, corner, river view windows, 2 pvt. decks, Q bed...$60
#1,#2—next to river rapids, Q bed...$60
regular room— Q bed...$60

Tahoe City Travelodge
downtown at 455 N. Lake Blvd. (Box 84) *583-3766*
Only steps away from the beach and golf course in the center of town is a modern motel with a heated pool. A whirlpool is on a deck overlooking the lake. Each spacious room has a cable color TV and phone.
#224,#217—private view of golf course, Q bed...$58
regular room— Q bed...$58

★ **Tahoe Marina Lodge**
downtown at 270 N. Lake Blvd. (Box 92) *583-2365*
This contemporary Western-style condominium motel is perfectly sited by Lake Tahoe and the Truckee River outlet. Well-landscaped grounds include a peaceful private sandy beach, a pier, tennis courts, and a large scenic outdoor pool. Each well-furnished unit has a cable color TV, phone, kitchen, private deck and/or patio, and a native-stone fireplace.
#37 thru #40—2 BR, pvt. beachfront view, 2 T beds in loft, Q bed...$130
#1—1 BR, fine lake view, Q bed...$95
regular room—1 BR, garden view, Q bed...$95

★ **Tahoe Vintage Inn**
4 mi. NE via CA 28 at 4170 Ferguson Av. (Box 7191-G) *583-6091*
A large lakefront home has been converted into a spectacular bed-and-breakfast inn. Guests can enjoy lake views while playing billiards in a living room with a big stone fireplace and enormous picture windows. Terraced flower gardens lead to a private pier. Generous breakfasts, and wine in the afternoon, are complimentary. Each attractively furnished room has a private bath.
"Captain's Suite"—wood-burning stove in sitting room, wet bar, deck, lakeview tub, Q bed...$100
"Lake View Suite"—sitting room, pvt. entrance and deck, Q bed...$80
regular room— Q bed...$70

Tamarack Lodge Motel
1.2 mi. NE on CA 28 at 2311 N. Lake Blvd. (Box 859) *583-3350*
Off the highway in the pines a stroll from the beach is an older one-level **bargain** motel with a newer two-story addition. Each unit has a knotty-pine interior and cable B/W TV.
#32—spacious, kitchen, partial lake view, K bed...$34
regular room—older motel room, Q bed...$24

CAMPGROUNDS

One picturesque campground by Lake Tahoe is a stroll from downtown. Two other lakeside campgrounds are only a few miles from town.

★ **Lake Forest Campground**
2 mi. NE via CA 28 on Edgewater Dr. *583-5544*
This small campground has a pine-shaded site near Lake Tahoe. Swimming, sunbathing, boating, fishing, hiking, and bicycling are popular activities. Flush toilets, showers, and hookups are available. Each site has a picnic table and a fire area. base rate...$5

★ **Sugar Pine Point State Park**
10 mi. S on CA 89 *525-7982*
The State of California operates this large campground in a spectacularly scenic, pine-forested location by Lake Tahoe. A sandy beach for swimming and sunbathing, boat dock, hiking trails, tennis courts, and the Ehrman Mansion Visitor Center are features. Flush toilets, hot showers, and hookups are available. Each pine-shaded site has a picnic table and fire area. base rate...$7

★ **Tahoe State Recreation Area**
.3 mi. NE on CA 28 *583-3074*
This state-operated campground has an ideal location by the lake on the north side of town. Swimming, boating, pier fishing, and bicycling on nearby paths are popular activities. Flush toilets and hot showers are available, but there are no hookups. Each pine-shaded site has a picnic table, fire ring, raised grill, and a storage cabinet. Some sites also have a view of the lake. base rate...$7

SPECIAL EVENTS

Oktoberfest *downtown* *fourth weekend in October*
Fall colors coincide with a fun-filled Oktoberfest—complete with a "battle of the bands" music festival, dancing, dining, and beer drinking.
Snowfest *in and around town* *starts first Friday of March*
Beginning with a torchlight parade at Squaw Valley, this nine-day winter carnival boasts nearly one hundred events for all ages and interests. Snow sculpture, street dances, live entertainment, fireworks, and races (including the largest cross-country ski race in California, and a race featuring inflatable rafts on snow) are all part of the fun to be shared in Tahoe City, Truckee, and points in between.

OTHER INFORMATION

Area Code: *916*

Zip Code: *95730*

California State Parks Department *831-0494*
North Lake Tahoe Chamber of Commerce
downtown at 950 N. Lake Blvd. *583-2371*
North Lake Tahoe Lodging Information *Box 5578* *583-3494*
U.S. Forest Service
2 mi. S on CA 89 at William Kent Campground *583-3642*

INDEX

About the Author

David Vokac was born in Chicago. But, growing up on a ranch near Cody, Wyoming was the basis for his lifelong affinity with the West. From the beginning, he opted to live and work exclusively in locations throughout that region. During summers while an undergraduate, he served as an airborne fire-spotter for the Shoshone National Forest in Wyoming. He taught courses in land economics while completing a Master's degree in geography at the University of Arizona in Tucson. In Denver, Colorado, Vokac was in charge of economic base analysis for the city's first community renewal program, and later became Chief of Neighborhood Planning. He moved to the West Coast during the mid-1970s to prepare San Diego County's first local parks plan, and stayed to act as Park Development Director.

Mr. Vokac is now a full-time writer, and founder of a Western travel and leisure advisory service. During the past year, he logged almost forty thousand miles in a silver Audi criss-crossing the Golden State while thoroughly investigating, updating, and adding new material about all of the great towns of California. When not researching, speaking, or consulting, he can be found traveling for the sheer joy of it somewhere in the West.

If you enjoyed *The Great Towns of California* you will also like:

ORDER FORM

Here are two travel guides with the detailed information you need to get the most out of your leisure time in the West.

THE GREAT TOWNS OF CALIFORNIA, by David Vokac $8.95
New in 1986, this guide has more complete and current information than any other to help you plan and enjoy your visits to exceptional out-of-the-way places throughout the Golden State. The handy, 304-page book includes 50 illustrations and photos.

THE GREAT TOWNS OF THE WEST, by David Vokac $14.95
The first comprehensive travel guidebook about fifty special towns in spectacularly remote locales from the California coast to the Canadian Rockies was published in 1985. The convenient, 464-page book includes more than 100 illustrations and photos.

As a way of saying "thanks," West Press will pay postage and handling (California residents please add 6% sales tax), and the author will personally autograph all mail order copies upon request.

To order, send your check or money order to:
WEST PRESS
P.O. Box 99717
San Diego, CA 92109